T0351902

CO-MANAGEMENT OF NATURAL RESOURCES IN ASIA

NORDIC INSTITUTE OF ASIAN STUDIES

Man & Nature in Asia
Series Editor: Arne Kalland
Professor of Social Anthropology, University of Oslo

೫

The implication that environmental degradation has only occurred in Asia as a product of Westernization ignores Asia's long history of environmental degradation and disaster. The principle aim of this series, then, is to encourage critical research into the human–nature relationship in Asia. The series' multidisciplinary approach invites studies in a number of topics: how people make a living from nature; their knowledge and perception of their natural environment and how this is reflected in their praxis; indigenous systems of resource management; environmental problems, movements and campaigns; and many more. The series will be of particular interest to anthropologists, geographers, historians, political scientists and sociologists as well as to policy makers and those interested in development and environmental issues in Asia.

RECENT AND FORTHCOMING TITLES

CO-MANAGEMENT
OF NATURAL RESOURCES
IN ASIA
A Comparative Perspective

edited by
Gerard A. Persoon,
Diny M.E. van Est and Percy E. Sajise

NIAS
Press

Nordic Institute of Asian Studies
Man & Nature in Asia series, no. 7

First published in 2003 by NIAS Press
Nordic Institute of Asian Studies
Leifsgade 33, DK–2300 Copenhagen S, Denmark
tel: (+45) 3532 9501 • fax: (+45) 3532 9549
E–mail: books@nias.ku.dk • Website: www.niaspress.dk

Typesetting by NIAS Press
Produced by Bookchase
and printed in Great Britain

British Library Cataloguing in Publication Data
Co-management of natural resources in Asia : a comparative
  perspective - (Man & nature in Asia ; 7)
  1.Natural resources Asia - Management
  I.Persoon, Gerard II.Est, Diny M.E. van III. Sajise, Percy
  333.7'095

ISBN 0-7007-1485-5 (RoutledgeCurzon edition)
ISBN 87-91114-13-6 (NIAS edition)

Contents

List of Figures

List of Tables

Preface

*T*his book originated from an international workshop of the same name that took place in Cabagan, Isabela Province, the Philippines in September 1998. The workshop was a joint initiative of the SEAMEO Regional Centre for Graduate Study and Research in Agriculture (SEARCA) and the Cagayan Valley Programme on Environment and Development (CVPED) with financial support from the Nordic Institute of Asian Studies (NIAS) in Copenhagen and the International Institute of Asian Studies (IIAS) in Leiden. During the workshop some 24 papers were presented and discussed by a group of predominantly social scientists, but there were also a number of natural scientists and project planners of protected areas. With regard to the international aspect of the workshop it is worth noting that there were participants from various European countries (Norway, the United Kingdom, the Netherlands, France), representatives of Asia and the Pacific (India, Indonesia, Papua New Guinea, China, Thailand, Vietnam, the Philippines) and from the United States.

After the workshop a number of papers were selected for publication. Most of them were substantially revised, based on the discussions and issues raised during the workshop. Two new papers, which were submitted to the editors after the workshop, are included in the present book because they fit nicely in the general theme. The epilogue, which was presented orally in an abridged form at the workshop, is also included in an extended form.

The workshop was one in a series of meetings of a loosely organized network called East West Environmental Linkages (EWEL) consisting of mainly social scientists from Europe, Asia and the United States. Earlier workshops were organized on 'Environmental Movements in Asia' (Leiden 1994), 'Nature Protection and Human Rights' (Oslo 1995), 'Environmental Discourse' (Honolulu 1996), and 'Indigenous Environmental Knowledge and Its Transformations' (Canterbury 1997). Future meetings may be organized by this network on other related topics.

The editors would like to thank first of all Professor Dr Wim Stokhof and Drs Sabine Kuipers, director and deputy director of IIAS, and Professor Dr Robert Cribb, at that time director of NIAS, for financial support of the workshop. SEARCA had also kindly offered its facilities at the campus of the University of the Philippines at Los Baños to host the participants before leaving for Isabela in Northeast Luzon. In particular we would like to thank Dr Gil Saguiguit and Alice Perez for all their kind and efficient support. CVPED and its home institutions (Centre of Environmental Science of Leiden University and Isabela State University) are gratefully acknowledged for their general support in hosting this meeting. In particular we would like to thank Dr Denyse Snelder and Dr Andy Masipiqueña for all the work they put into this meeting, including the organization of some very interesting fieldtrips along the way from Manila to Cabagan. Annelies Oskam of the Centre of Environmental Science has been of great help in the editing of the contributions. We are also grateful to NIAS Press for their assistance and encouragement during the process of bringing this manuscript through to publication.

List of Contributors

DANTE M. AQUINO is researcher and teacher at the College of Forestry and Environmental Management of Isabela State University in the Philippines. He was trained as forester at the University of the Philippines at Los Baños. At present he is preparing his dissertation on natural resource management of the Bugkalot, to be defended at Leiden University.

CRISTINA EGHENTER took her PhD from Rutgers University, NJ, USA. She has specialised in economic and environmental anthropology and the ethnohistory of Borneo. She has worked as a research fellow at the University of Hull and is currently involved in a WWF-funded project in East Kalimantan.

ROY F. ELLEN is professor of anthropology and human ecology at the University of Kent at Canterbury, United Kingkom. His current research interests are in ethnobiology, environmental anthropology and the social organisation of inter-island trade. He has done extensive fieldwork in Indonesia, particularly in the Moluccas.

DINY M.E. VAN EST took her PhD at Leiden University on research on inland fisheries in the Northern part of Cameroon, after which she worked as a post-doc researcher at the Centre of Environmental Science at the same university. At present she is working as researcher at the Netherlands Court of Audit in the Hague.

FRANCISCO P. FELLIZER, JR (PhD) has written on community-based natural resource management in the Philippines. His interests and expertise are also on policy and local governance as it relates to sustainable development. A former Undersecretary of the Philippine Department of Science and Technology and

Deputy Director of SEARCA, he is now a visiting professor on environment at the Ritsumeikan University Asia Pacific University, Kyoto, Japan.

INGVILD HARKES is a cultural anthropologist who has been working in the field of Environment and Development since 1995. Areas of special interest are co-management, CBRM, gender and participatory research methods. She has worked four years in the ICLARM/IFM Fisheries Co-management Project doing field research in Southeast Asia and Africa. At the moment she is a freelance consultant.

MARIEKE HOBBES is a junior researcher at the Centre of Environmental Science at Leiden University, the Netherlands. She has done fieldwork in the Philippines and Vietnam. At present she is preparing her dissertation on comparing various methodological frameworks for the study of transition processes of rural communities in the Philippines.

ARNE KALLAND is professor of social anthropology at the University of Oslo, Norway. His research interests are in environmental anthropology, particularly marine resource management and the anti-whaling movement. He has done extensive fieldwork in fishing villages in Fukuoka, Japan.

BRENDA KATON is a marine scientist with extensive work experience at ICLARM, the Fish Centre in Manila. She was one of the leading scientists in the co-management project in Southeast Asia. At present she is working at the Asian Development Bank.

IRENE NOVACZEK (PhD) serves as a research associate with the Institute of Island Studies, University of Prince Edward Island, Canada. She is currently co-ordinating a project in the South Pacific through which indigenous researchers will develop gender sensitive case studies dealing with small-scale and subsistence fisheries in eight Pacific Island nations.

MANON OSSEWEIJER is a post-doc research fellow at the Royal Netherlands' Institute of Southeast Asian and Caribbean Studies (KITLV) in Leiden, the Netherlands. Her research interests are in the anthropology of fisheries and she has done extensive fieldwork in Eastern and Western Indonesia. Her dissertation (2001) was based on research on marine resources in the Aru Archipelago.

PAULO PASICOLAN is a teacher and researcher at the College of Forestry and Environmental Management at Isabela State University in the Philippines. He took his PhD at Leiden University (the Netherlands) on a research project that compared various reforestation projects in the Cagayan Valley (Northeast Luzon). He has also worked on grassland rehabilitation projects.

ROBERT (BOB) POMEROY (PhD) is currently an associate professor-in-residence at the Department of Agricultural and Resource Economics as well as Sea Grant College Fisheries Extension Specialist at the University of Connecticut. He worked at the World Resources Institute in Washington D.C. and at the International Center for Living Aquatic Resources Management (ICLARM) in Manila from 1991 to 1999. His areas of professional interest are marine resource economics and policy.

GERT POLET is a social geographer from Utrecht University (the Netherlands) with previous work experience in the Philippines and Nigeria. At present is the project leader of the WWF funded project for the management of the Cat Tien National Park in Southern Vietnam, in charge of rersource inventories, awareness campaigns and management implementation.

GERARD A. PERSOON (PhD) is an environmental anthropologist and head of the Programme for Environment and Development of the Centre of Environmental Science (CML) of Leiden University, the Netherlands. His research interests include the position of indigenous peoples and natural resource management with a focus on Southeast Asia.

GIL C. SAGUIGUIT JR. (PhD) is an agricultural economist with extensive experience in managing and implementing rural development programmes in the Philippines and Southeast Asia. Most of his recent work has been on piloting and promoting soil and water conversation practices at the village and community levels. He is currently the deputy director for professional services and administration of SEARCA, Los Baños.

PERCY E. SAJISE is a plant ecologist, and environmentalist from the Philippines. Former Director of the Los Baños-based SEAMEO Regional Center for Graduate Study and Research in Agriculture (SEARCA), he has written extensively on natural resource conservation and management. He is currently the Regional Director for Asia, the Pacific and Oceania, of the International Plant Genetic Resources Institute (IPGRI), based in Serdang, Malaysia.

WEI HU is a PhD fellow at the University of Cambridge, England. His present research interests are in the transition of management of natural resources in China.

GAUTAM N. YADAMA, Ph.D., is associate professor and Director of International Programs at the George Warren Brown School of Social Work, Washington University in St. Louis. He is interested in understanding how institutional arrangements affect governance at the local level. Most recently, he was a Fulbright Professor in Nepal.

CHAPTER ONE

Co-management of Natural Resources: The Concept and Aspects of Implementation

GERARD A. PERSOON AND DINY M.E. VAN EST

INTRODUCTION

C o-management of natural resources, whereby responsibilities for management (including exploitation and conservation) are shared among government and individual or collective users, is becoming increasingly common in Asia and elsewhere. This has come about as a result of the limited success of top-down conservation projects and the continuing deterioration of environmental conditions in many countries in the region. The trend is also inspired by feelings that local people were unjustly treated in the past, however. In many of the countries currently undergoing decentralization, granting rights to local communities and indigenous peoples is part of social reform and political agendas. Local NGOs have become more vociferous on this issue and have been successful in gaining political support for their struggles. In part they draw their inspiration from several widely publicized resistance campaigns like the Chipko movement in India, the Punan struggle against logging in Sarawak and the Kalinga fight against the damming of the Chico river in the Philippines. Big international donor organizations like the World Bank and the Asian Development Bank are now also playing a key role in this trend towards new forms of management along with environmental NGOs like the World Wildlife Fund (WWF) and International Union for the Conservation of Nature (IUCN). In fact this process was initiated by the IUCN's World Conservation Strategy (1980).

Various forms of co-management can be distinguished, depending on the natural resources involved as well as the type of community and the organization and strength of the government in question. This chapter discusses the concept of co-management and some of its implementation aspects, thereby examining some of the common problems occurring in the field, where co-

1

management ideas and ideals are put into practice. Some of these issues are raised by people who themselves are not actors in co-management operations and who adopt a more reflective position. The aim of this chapter is to introduce some of the themes relevant to co-management.

NATURAL RESOURCE MANAGEMENT IN ASIA

In the Asian context, as elsewhere, most natural resources were formerly either locally owned and exploited, or they enjoyed some form of open access regime with no clear form of ownership or management. Some of the practices now classed under the heading 'management' were chiefly inspired by a religion or a world view. Indeed, some 'management practices' may not have had an explicit ecological purpose at all. In other words, any environmental effects may have been unintended results of actual behaviour (Vayda 1996). In many places wild natural resources were not merely harvested but were also gradually domesticated and made more productive. In the process, certain wild and 'useless' resources were lost (Wiersum 1996). Communal fishing grounds and forest lands were managed by clearly defined communities. In addition, individuals might own resources as private property, sometimes on a temporary basis.

Over time, these natural resources were appropriated from local communities by colonial governments. Some, like timber and minerals, were taken for immediate use, with concessions being granted to private or parastatal organizations. In other cases the status of the resource was simply redefined. Areas of primary rainforest were often declared 'empty land', for example, ready for more productive purposes than mere standing forest. Large tracts of land were thus transformed into plantations for industrial crops or into agricultural land, either by national governments or European or American entrepreneurs.

In general, colonial states claimed jurisdiction over all uncultivated lands, as well as the sea shores and the open seas. They did so far in excess of what their administrative staff could manage and in practice many of these resources consequently became open access resources at the frontiers of colonial society. Some areas were declared protected, either for nature conservation or as forest reserves for hydrological or other purposes. Rights of local communities were limited to land showing clear signs of human cultivation (Lynch and Talbott 1995; Ghee and Valencia 1990).

Following independence, most national governments did not change this system of state-owned resources. Indeed, they reinforced it with new legislation, often based on the colonial legal system. In most cases they also incorporated the national park ideology, as developed in the United States towards the end of the nineteenth century. An interesting exception is Papua New Guinea, where 90–97 per cent of the land is still owned by tribal communities (Lynch and Talbott 1995: 100).

The practical implications of this state ownership of generally poorly managed resources increased tremendously as a result of unexpected techno-logical innovations in the 1960s and 1970s. As new, more powerful equipment became available, the frontiers of resource exploitation could be pushed ever further. Chain saws, bulldozers and trucks made large-scale logging and land conversion much easier and allowed them to progress at a far greater pace. In fisheries, powerful engines, bigger nets and electronic equipment have allowed fishing boats to locate and take huge catches at ever greater distances. Scuba diving replaced skin diving and allowed divers harvesting marine products to go much deeper and stay under water far longer.

The poor management of many of these resources can be attributed to such causes as inadequate government staffing with inadequate equipment, poor legislation and law enforcement, and the close ties between policy-makers and private companies. As new technologies made inroads, these deficiencies led to further erosion and breakdown of local systems of management. Local com-munities lost the resources they had managed over long periods of time. More-over, waves of encroaching farmers and fishermen, often equipped with more powerful equipment and political backing, pushed many of these traditional communities into the margins of their traditional homelands.

Following several decades of state and centralized forms of management, the condition of the environment in many countries is alarming. Forests have been depleted, fishing grounds overexploited or even destroyed, as in the case of coral reefs being bombed, and much biodiversity has been lost in this process, in terms of both quality and quantity. There is a widespread feeling, moreover, that centralized forms of management have also done major injustices to local communities who have been deprived of their basic resources. In some cases local populations have been physically ousted or cut off from their subsistence base because their homelands were declared a protected area, which by definition should exclude any human habitation. This ideology was certainly alien to Asian culture, where the cultural and natural landscape are closely aligned and not defined as separate entities (Asquith and Kalland 1997).

CO-MANAGEMENT

In recent years there has emerged a loosely knit transnational movement, con-sisting of environmental organizations and non-governmental organizations working together with local groups, national governments and transnational donor agencies to build and extend new forms of environmental management. One of the most significant developments has been the broad promotion of co-management programmes, policies and projects. (Other terms used in the literature are 'joint management', 'adaptive management' and 'collaborative management'.) Loosely defined (there is no generally accepted definition), co-management means 'the sharing of power, responsibilities and benefits with respect to the management of natural resources (including their exploitation and conservation) among government and individual or collective users'. Financially, these world-wide initiatives receive substantial support from international financial institutions.

In Asia co-management has become far more than an abstract idea. Community boundaries are being mapped (Osseweijer, Chapter 9 in this volume) and across the continent many experiments in local resource management are in progress. India has reformulated its forest policies in terms of joint forest management and the Philippines is embarking on a completely new era of resource management under the National Integrated Protected Areas System (NIPAS) law (1992) and the Indigenous Peoples' Rights Act adopted at the end of 1997. Even Indonesia is reconsidering its forest policies, thereby giving more scope to social forestry and recognition of local community rights. This re-orientation of management styles relates to various kinds of resource, including production forests, non-timber forest products, irrigation water and fishing grounds, as well as to the management of protected areas and surrounding buffer zones.

This renewal of management styles has come about largely through an interplay of factors; here we mention the most important (see also Pomeroy 1996).

1) Failure (or limited success) of the centralized, 'blueprint' approach to natural resource management by the state, which has frequently proved incapable of actually managing the resources according to its own regulations. This basic weakness was exacerbated by the frontier character of many exploitation zones. Although it took a long time for the failure of state-dominated management to be admitted, there are few states today that refuse to discuss greater involvement of local people.

2) Processes of democratization in many countries, whereby greater prominence was given to local interests. In many countries these processes have gained enormously in importance since the fall of repressive governments and their replacement by democratic successors. The Philippines is a particularly good example: since the EDSA revolution in 1986 and the fall

of Marcos, local people and local government have become ever more empowered. Similar processes are taking place in other countries, of which Indonesia is the most dramatic example at the moment. Rapid 'reformasi' processes lead first of all to dissolving state responsibilities without other institutions taking over.

3) Environmental NGOs, many with strong financial backing from abroad, have become more powerful and vocal in advocating local people's interests, in tandem with more sustainable use of resources at the expense of state power.

4) 'The spirit of the time', as promoted by the big donor agencies, with increased emphasis on the participation of local populations, women and indigenous peoples (see, for example, WWF 1996). These notions have now trickled down from the global centres to the regions. To give just one example: almost all the major agencies have by now adopted guidelines on the rights of local or indigenous peoples (the World Bank, EU, ADB and many individual donor countries). They have also issued guidelines on procedures for designing and implementing projects in close co-operation with the local people.

5) Romanticization of the past as part of an increased ethnic awareness and identity, providing a basis for 'revitalization' of traditional management structures adjusted to present-day circumstances. In many cases the past is 're-discovered' or even invented, with contemporary rhetoric from diverse environmental discourses sometimes being 'read into' the traditions. (On this point, see, for example, Bennagen and Lucas-Fernan 1996) To some extent this romanticization is paying off, for it is in part on the basis of these images that support for the struggle of local groups or indigenous peoples is generated, even in diplomatic circles.

6) Aspects of distributive justice are being incorporated in natural resource management in tandem with the alleviation of poverty. More attention is thus being paid to the effects of such processes.

7) Food and environmental security are now higher on the political agenda, and there is acknowledgement that local potential for self-sufficiency might be strengthened by new management arrangements.

Driven by these factors, new management styles are being developed in many Asian countries. There is considerable variation, of course, and the same holds for the labels they bear, but they refer to the same basic notion. As mentioned, terms employed in this context besides co-management include 'collaborative management', 'joint management', 'adaptive management', 'community-based or local management' or 'indigenous management' (Western *et al.* 1994; Kothari *et al.*. 1996; IUCN 1996, IUCN 1998).

Co-management is usually defined as the sharing of responsibilities for managing a specified natural resource between the local community and the state, as represented by a particular institution. Proceeding from this general idea, a wide variety of arrangements are feasible between the extremes of management by a centralized government on the one hand and strict local management on the other (see Figure 1.1 and Pomeroy 1996).

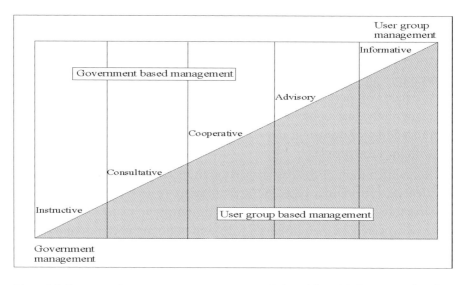

Figure 1.1: Spectrum of co-management arrangements (adapted from McCay 1993 and Berkes 1994 as cited in Sen and Raakjaer Nielsen 1996).

The actual form arrangements take will depend on the structure of the government, the willingness by the state to hand over authority and the nature of the community involved (size, internal cohesion, type of leadership, ethnic or economic differentiation). There should, moreover, be a suitable match between the nature of the resource and the management regime. Obviously, managing mobile stocks of fish requires a different kind of arrangement from managing agricultural land, irrigation water or non-timber forest products.

It is important to introduce a few terms from the legal lexicon, as these constitute the basis for the various arrangements. In relation to the management of resources four kinds of property regime are usually differentiated:

1) *open access*, which is in fact not a management regime at all (property rights are non-existent and access is free and open to all);

2) *private property*, whereby the claim rests with an individual (or with a collective actor like a company);

3) *state property*, whereby the claim and sole jurisdiction lie with the government in its role as representing the interests of present-day and future citizens as well as other interests;

4) *communal or common property*, whereby the resource is controlled by a 'clearly defined community of users (Berkes 1994).

Co-management arrangements can be applied to all these categories. The crucial element here is the sharing of responsibilities for resource management by the government and the user or user group. Introduction of co-management arrangements redefines the rights and obligations of the parties involved. It is not always necessary for common property institutions to pre-date co-management arrangements. In some cases, new management institutions may be created. The rights and duties associated with the various property regimes are crucially important, because subsequently it is the upholding of these rights and duties that determines the outcome of the arrangements (see Table 1.1).

These property regimes can be related to three other important concepts that relate to the actual rights to be enjoyed under various property regimes:

1) *Unrestricted property*, i.e. property over which the owner enjoys total freedom with respect to usage.

2) *Restricted property*, i.e. property that is perceived as normal and secure, although bounded in the ways or degrees the property rights may be exercised, usually by restrictions or obligations set by the state. The owner of a wet-

Table 1.1: Types of property rights regimes, with owners, rights and duties

Regime	Owner	Owner rights	Owner duties
Private property	Individual	Socially acceptable uses; control of access	Avoidance of socially unacceptable uses
Common property	Collective	Exclusion of non-owners	Maintenance; constrain rates of use
State property	Citizens	Determine rules	Maintain social objectives
Open access (non-property)	None	Capture	None

Source: Hanna *et al.* (1996)

land may not be allowed to drain it, for instance, the owner of a forest may be obliged to maintain a certain tree cover, or the owner of a house may be obliged to maintain it. All the while they remain owners, however.

3) *Quasi-property*, i.e. property, irrespective of the possible restrictions, of which the ownership is unclear or may be repealed outside the eminent domain, usually by the state that has allocated the property rights. The holder of a quasi-property may state that he/she 'has' this quotum, this permit, this land or whatever, but there is no perception of actually owning it.

In most countries the notion of unrestricted 'property' in relation to natural resources is almost unknown. Numerous restrictions apply as to how owners are permitted to behave in relation to their land and water resources as well as to their flora and fauna. The notions of restricted property and quasi-property are far more common and it is these that are encountered in many co-management arrangements. To mention just a few examples:

1) Stewardship contracts under which people are allowed to use land or forests on specific terms. The land remains state property, however, and the people only enjoy the right of usufruct. This is a form of 'quasi-property'. This has been the dominant policy for instance of Integrated Social Forestry (ISF) projects in the Philippines.

2) Extractive reserves, most common in relation to the harvesting of non-timber forest products, in which specified products may be harvested in a clearly demarcated area by a clearly defined community up to a pre-set maximum. Extractive reserves were first established in Latin America (rubber tappers) but later spread to other countries (e.g. the Batak in Palawan, Philippines).

3) Lease contracts, by which the true owner leases the resource to a second party. An interesting example is provided by certain Aboriginal groups in Australia who are the legal owners of the land but who lease it to the national government on pre-defined terms (including compensation to the Aboriginals). In this case the Australian government has quasi-ownership of the resource. This is also being proposed for a number of forest areas in order to provide the owner (often a 'poor' state) with income more or less equal to the income to be earned from logging.

In most cases co-management arrangements are laid down in the form of contracts between a government institution and a user group. Introduction of contracts as a basis for the exploitation and protection of resources involves a number of interesting aspects and assumptions. First of all, a contract pre-supposes some kind of equality between the contract partners, as if negotiations about terms and conditions take place in a 'free market' situation in which partners enjoy substantial freedom as to whether or not to come to agreement. This is rarely the case. Co-management contracts are usually drawn up in a legal-istic fashion, stipulating at great length the rights and obligations of the respective partners. Although it may be common practice for government institutions to live by carefully formulated and officially authorized, written documents, this is rarely the case for local fishermen or groups of farmers at the forest fringe in their daily struggle for survival. A contract between two parties should also include provisions on how to deal with violations of the norms laid down in the contract. In the case of inadequate compliance with contract obligations, proceed-ings against government institutions or individual civil servants are not readily instituted; and if they are, governments generally claim a lack of staff or infra-structure for monitoring and control.

Co-management arrangements are pre-dominantly future- and outcome-oriented with respect to the aims of the government. The contract is an instru-ment to achieve a particular end: the protection of animals and plants. For local groups it is a licence to do something, to harvest, to exploit, to take. This difference in emphasis is crucial. Contracts are usually signed between well-defined parties. This leads to the exclusion of so-called 'outsiders'. Although this form works perfectly in a free market, it may create feelings of injustice among those excluded from the arrangements, particularly if they are living amongst or near the resources now covered by the contract.

POTENTIALS AND PROBLEMS OF CO-MANAGEMENT

A number of collections of case studies have been published recently on projects with a wide variety of co-management arrangements, some successful, others not (see, for example, West and Brechin 1991; Kemf 1993; Lynch and Talbott 1995, Western *et al.* 1994, Kothari *et al.* 1996, Stevens 1997). Some of these case studies, like the CAMPFIRE project in Zimbabwe and the extractive reserves in Latin America, are posited as almost ideal models for co-management arrange-ments. These and other cases tell stories of local people, non-governmental organizations and field officials from government institutions trying creatively to overcome situations of growing environmental degradation and poverty. Their successes and failures, however measured, provide interesting material for those who wish to learn from past failures in order to come up with better alternatives.

By design and by discovery, and through the inspiration of example, a concerted effort is made to overcome situations in which people might logically be expected to exhibit short-term and individualistic, or 'rational' behaviour. In contrast, the new projects endeavour to create new circumstances and longer-term perspectives. They provide additional knowledge and tell different stories of value prioritization that may make people reconsider their immediate, in-tuitive response. In other words there is a desire to provide a new perspective on rationality, based on collective action in relation to the management of nature. All the publications cited end, in inductive fashion, with 'lessons learned' or 'conditions for common resource management', which provide further inspiration to those involved in designing or implementing other projects or policies (Ostrom 1990, Pomeroy 1994 and Pomeroy *et al.*, Chapter 13 in this volume).

On the other hand, co-management arrangements, however well designed and implemented by committed people, can never solve all environmental problems. Different management structures will still be necessary for some resources, user groups and circumstances. In general, though, co-management arrangements have proven to be a helpful instrument in overcoming a variety of problems formerly associated with state and centralized styles of manage-ment. This does not imply that co-management projects are always successful, nor that implementation of these new management regimes is unproblematic (see Pimbert and Pretty 1995, Western *et al.* 1994, Leach *et al.* 1997). In fact, we are still in a learning stage.

Based on some experience in Asia, in this context we would like to examine the following issues:

- differences in time perspectives
- 'community' and 'management' in 'community-based management'
- dissolving state responsibilities and non-local interests
- third parties in co-management arrangements
- failure and success in co-management: a comparative perspective
- the ecological basis of natural resources under co-management arrange-ments.

We want to discuss these issues, in particular the first two, in greater detail.

Differences in time perspectives
Images of time, by which we mean views about the past, present and future, play an important role in the management of natural resources. For some the past is taken as a basis for claiming and recognizing rights to natural resources, while for others events in the past provide a basis for urgent action in an effort to redirect the present course of events.

Although the global sustainability debate emphasizes 'the future' and 'future generations', it is our assertion that scarcely any attention has been explicitly paid to the dimension of time and the future, either in this debate in general (Boersema 2000) or in the co-management debate in particular (Persoon and Van Est 2000). Multiple time perspectives do co-exist within the 'real' world of nature conservation and co-management arrangements. They are used by a variety of people – nature conservationists, donor agencies and development bureau-cracies, economists, anthropologists and local people and their advocates – representing different institutions from various spatial contexts. They operate from diverse, often implicit, normative viewpoints and different time-order or time-value systems. To understand the way these views coalesce in the real world of co-management, it is necessary to consider these differing timescapes (Adam 1998) and render them more explicit.

Nature conservationists' time perspective can be summarized as 'acting now for tomorrow's world' and 'extinction is for ever'. Certainly, that is the conception that informed attempts to set up biosphere reserves and national parks in the (recent) past. Conservation-minded ecologists are by definition very much future-oriented. They want to conserve species, plants and animals or even entire ecosystems and landscapes. They base their plans of action on lessons learned from the past. In their writings, two very different images of the future prevail. Trends over the past few decades indicate that the areas covered with natural habitats are in rapid decline, that the number of species sliding into extinction is on the rise and that factors contributing to environmental degradation (population growth and growing volumes of consumption) are increasing. These trends lead to pessimistic, calamitous or even apocalyptic projections for the future (see, for example, Western 1994, McNeely 1996). These images, often supported by powerful symbols or metaphors, serve as negative points of reference, to be avoided at all costs. Plans of action are based on an alternative vision for the future, a world in which things can change for the better. This vision of a better world is seen in terms of the maintenance of biodiversity and protected areas and the sustainable use of available natural resources. The benefits are intended for unspecified 'future generations' (Boersema 2000). In order to generate sufficient support for these alternative visions, a variety of policy instruments (varying from economic incentives to environmental master plans) are being developed to turn these alternatives into reality.

Although conservation explicitly addresses the long-term future, project-type activities are generally narrowly instrumental and planned in short-term episodes governed by the project rhythm of donor agencies. There is consequently a need to 'unpack' the time perspective of development bureau-cracies, both national and international, both in general and in the specific case of Asia. These bureaucracies, with their multiple aims and internal contra-dictions, have time perspectives that are organized predominantly around the 'timing of project cycles'. These project formats of two to five years are repeated again and again, each time reflecting changes in development discourse. The time perspectives of development bureaucracies are linked closely and in multiple ways to the rise and fall of politicians or political parties. This is also the case for bureaucratic institutions engaged in nature conservation, which have generally adopted the style of development agencies.

Economists can also be said to have a dominant way of perceiving time and the future: 'the timing of money'. The most important conceptual instrument at their disposal for expressing the present and future value of goods, including natural resources and services, is that of 'discount rates'. Present-day satis-faction of needs is thereby ascribed a higher value than the satisfaction of future needs. Natural resources are generally assigned a market value, broadly equivalent to the present market value. This raises problems of market imperfections and difficulties in the pricing of ecological functions. One result is that the future in all its dimensions (satisfaction of needs, rights of future generations, future value of biodiversity) is accorded a lower priority than the present. As a consequence of this powerful discounting logic, investments in the long-term productivity of forests or the conservation of nature as an 'heroic sacrifice' (Passmore 1980) are automatically deemed uneconomic, irrational ventures. This may be partly solved by introducing appropriate pricing mechanisms for the environmental functions of natural resources, but this is not yet the case. The horizon of economists in relation to the exploitation of natural resources is not generally a long-term one: the further removed in time the benefits and problems are, the less they will be taken into account. The economic per-spective leads to a kind of 'free-market environmentalism', to use Eckersley's term, characterized by an attitude of scepticism towards limits to growth and non-economic uses and an emphasis on quantifiable material values and a maximized economic output.

Generally speaking, the future is remarkably absent as a topic of research in the anthropological literature (Wallman 1992, van Dijk 1997). While in the field, anthropologists are more interested in the present and its genesis. In other words they stand with their back to the future. Even in some studies dealing explicitly with the anthropology of time, the future is considered to be of only minor importance (e.g. Gell 1996: 314).

It is only once anthropologists have returned from the field that they start to reflect on the 'future'. They feel the need to finish their monograph on a particular people with a chapter that includes the future in its title. The chapter is generally a reflection on what might happen to the people in the future. Usually this reflection is not based on field research and does not therefore reflect how local people apprehend the future. It is based, rather, on projections of what the anthropologist thinks might happen, and not infrequently these projections prove a long mark from reality (see, for example, Boissevain 1992). In other words, it is not the local community's perspective on the future that counts, but the anthropologist looking ahead, thereby introducing all manner of external factors and projections. The future, it would seem, was not deemed an issue worthy of investigation during fieldwork. Research handbooks pay little substantive attention to this topic, and numerous monographs could be listed in which the future is dealt with in this way. An exception, of course, is formed by those studies examining messianistic movements or with revitalization movements, originating mainly within the Melanesian region.

We are convinced that people in general, in their daily subsistence activities, are far more occupied with the future than with the past. There are also other kinds of future, however, that imply alternative options not only in the field of natural resource exploitation but also in social domains, in relation to kin as well as to those in power. People may also plan for a more distant future, for themselves or for their offspring. They decide on the resources needed to make particular social or economic investments. They may do so individually or collectively.

Particularly in rapidly changing circumstances, the past and even the present cannot teach us all we need to know about the future. Even the present can only be understood once we understand the image or perception of the future that is held by the people involved. People may opt for radically different alternatives.

By focusing too much on the present and the past, researchers overlook options and opportunities for change and innovation. An outstanding example in this context is agricultural transition. Through altering circumstances, people initiate changes, become able to reorganize their lives, value familiar ways of behaviour in a new perspective and set out in new directions. What for some may have seemed an unrealistic, distant future can become radically more accessible by the actions and discourse of innovative, risk-taking individuals (see, for example, Conelly 1992).

'Community' and 'management' in community-based management
Although the concepts of community and management are crucially important to a proper understanding of co-management, these terms are often used

extremely loosely and their actual meaning in the field it is not always entirely clear. What kind of phenomena does 'community-based management' cover, then, and what is the meaning of the term with respect to the actions of real men and women dealing with particular resources in particular places?

It may be asked how this emphasis on 'the community' originated in relation to resource management. It is assumed that the support and commitment of rural people emerged as being indispensable for halting resource degradation (Cernea 1985). Because of their knowledge and skills, local and indigenous communities were regarded as victims of degradation as well as the possible 'savers' of the environment (WWF 1996, IUCN 1997). In a sense, nature conservation and lifestyles in indigenous communities were considered more or less synonymous. Indigenous or tribal people and nature conservationists were often thought of as natural allies. The success stories of particular instances of local management from across the world spread rapidly, furthermore, prompting a certain shift in environmental policies. Projects and donors began to focus on local communities on the assumption that they would induce their members to plant trees, mobilise labour and protect 'their' natural resources. It was further assumed that communities could ensure the distribution of benefits among the inhabitants (Cernea 1985:280). Often communities were equated with villages as social units.

The word 'community' is always, as Williams put it, warmly persuasive. Unlike all the other terms of social organization (state, nation, society) it seems never to be used unfavourably (Williams 1983:76). This 'cosy' term also tends to imply something synonymous with internal solidarity and mutual care. In a certain sense, then, as Crehan puts it, 'a community can be treated as a single entity with a single set of interests' (Crehan 1997: 227). Reality is far more complex, however. For example, von Benda-Beckmann *et al.* (1992) consider this conception of community highly problematic, stating that there is no such thing as 'the community as a whole' (see also Vayda 1996).[1]

One must always make due allowance for specific local realities such as power dynamics and differences in access to resources among men and women, ethnic groups, age groups and individuals. This idea of fractured communities is elaborated by Kate Crehan (1997). She makes clear that it is necessary to distinguish between the ideal definition of what constitutes a community and communities as substantive realities, i.e. what actually happens in them. The fact that ideals differ from reality when it comes to 'communities' has important practical implications for resource management. This is also evident from those events that occur in relation to resource allocation to indigenous peoples. In many cases they do not form socially integrated units that can handle the allocated resources in an effective manner because of their lack of international checks and balances. Group formation based on other criteria (in addition to being 'indigenous') proves necessary. Communities may, as Murray-Li (1993:3) states, 'have culturally-based practices relating to resource use and management, but this does not imply that all individuals and groups within the community have equal access'. This criticism vis-à-vis the community concept in relation to community-based management should not close our eyes to the fact that in some cases and under certain conditions, people do unite and collaborate in order to achieve a common good. Marieke Hobbes (Chapter 3 in this volume) and numerous other examples show that people can manage their resources on a collective basis. What is important here is to determine under what conditions and for what kind of purpose people start organizing themselves. Gautam Yadama (Chapter 11 in this volume) emphasizes the importance of trust.

It is obvious that communities cannot be pre-defined: boundaries, internal cohesion and collective action should be topics for research and not for postulation. This means that we need to place 'community' in an analytical context and look beyond it.

This takes us to the second term in 'community-based management' – *management* – which we will distinguish here, for the sake of clarity, from the term 'sustainable management'. To start with the latter, we learn from the literature that many different definitions are used, ranging from rather broad (Brundtland) to narrower descriptions (IUCN, WWF). The broad definition is globally agreed upon and, generally speaking, regarded as a useful concept in efforts to halt environmental degradation. It also raises problems, however, because it is so general and open. For a significant 'global' community of development experts (from the south as well as the north) and environmentalists backed by strong environmental NGOs, sustainable management relates very much to the global concern for maintaining biodiversity, i.e. the existing species richness of the Earth, perceived in terms of a common heritage of mankind. These global NGOs are hugely influential in the field of environmental management, because it is at this level that policies are formulated, values of nature and wildlife assessed and decisions made as to what, where[2] and how sustainable management efforts should be implemented.

This environmental discourse has trickled down from the international arena to the national and local levels. Before discussing the influence of these supra-local values on the various other levels, however, let us examine the notion of local management more closely. Researchers differentiate between the use and the management of a resource, the latter implying that 'measures are taken to increase and sustain the resource and its yield' (van den Hombergh 1993:74). We would add that there are also forms of resource use that do sustain resources, though not as a result of clear, explicit measures. They are the outcome of cultural restrictions (often related to gender, age and clans) or local power relations. These regulations might restrain resource use, but should not misconstrued in terms of local people aiming to conserve nature as a purpose in itself, as if it were based on a traditional conservation ethic (Polunin 1991). One often encounters this type of misunderstanding among romanticizing environmental activists. Wiersum (1996) argues that the term (forest) 'management' is a concept used to refer to a variety of empirical situations ranging from controlled utilization, protection and maintenance to purposeful regeneration. It also includes transitions from one type of management to another.

The influence of the aforementioned, supra-local values on the various other levels is dominant but not without complexities. We have seen that the meaning of the term 'sustainable management' differs from one interest group to another. Interest groups may range from international through national to local levels. Supra-local resource interests relate to the conservation of bio-diversity, while for local people resource use relates to daily needs (material and cultural), which are not sustainable *per se*. The state has the highly complex task of combining economic growth and environmental health, which in the south may lead to a range of contradictions, as natural resources often serve as the countries' 'green gold'. However, the international community dominates the management debate at the various levels, including the local and regional, and in this configuration several problems arise in matching supra-local values with specific local understandings and forms of management. This is specifically the case for the conservation of protected areas,[3] which include tropical forests, national parks and wildlife sanctuaries. Here, the object of management is state property and the propagated management form is known as 'co-management'.

Although supporters of conservation claim that there various benefits may accrue to those living around protected areas, for several reasons this match is usually very complex. There are evident differences between professional nature conservation organizations and local people in terms of objectives, views and practices. The former wish to protect 'ecosystems' (forests, wetlands, savannah) as a whole, while local people are more interested in specific resources relevant for fulfilling human needs (Wiersum 1996). Richards points to the large cognitive gap that exists between the 'global credo' of environmentalists, who consider themselves as 'savers of the forest' and local people's perceptions of forest and forest resources (Richards 1992:153). Kessy (1998) shows that the integration of various formal and informal local forms of management (with apparent potential use in conservation initiatives) in conservation activities is very difficult. Local forms of management have proven to be less simple, obvious and direct than expected, as the ecological aspect of local management (presently over-emphasized) is just one aspect among of many (religious, political, economic), forming an integrated part of local livelihood strategies and power relations.

Because of the heterogeneity of communities, the presumed 'whole community' might not always be the most appropriate unit for resource management for two reasons. First, issues of access to and control over natural resources almost always signal arenas of competition and potential conflict in which some groups are likely to gain or lose more than others. In both cases, interventions may make life more problematic for those concerned, especially when interventions are related to increased income, access and power. Second, in actual practice there is always a need to define who, or which categories of people, are the legitimate representatives of the local population. To answer this question requires a thorough understanding of community dynamics, the role of traditional councils leaders and elite, and a willingness to demystify the ideal image of the community. Any policy which excludes these components will frustrate the goal of resource management.

Failure and success in co-management: a comparative perspective
Indicators and perceptions of the success or failure of co-management projects differ widely. The parties involved in such projects – fishermen or forest dwellers, project staff, donor agencies or ecologists – evaluate them with different terms of reference in mind. In particular, the spatial and temporal contexts in which the projects are evaluated may also differ. Because projects directed towards resource management do not materialize in 'empty' time or space, they are evaluated by local people on their own terms. Projects may be perceived as resources in their own right, because they bring direct gains in terms of material benefits, paid labour, increased access to resources and new opportunities. In some cases these benefits, intended as incentives in relation to overall project aims, are valued in themselves, irrespective of the purpose they are supposed to serve. Project evaluators usually seek sustainability of project organizations and devote less attention to the trickle-down effects and internal changes occurring within communities. Ideally, there should be better clarification of the evaluation criteria for these projects (Harkes 1998). For the time being, more comparative studies should be addressed to comparing the outcomes of different management regimes (see, for example, Gilbert and Janssen 1998).

One general problem with project evaluation is the tendency to adopt a rather isolated perspective on the project thereby forgetting its wider context, which may be of crucial relevance for understanding the results and achievements. A recent study of reforestation projects in the Philippines clearly indicates that apart from a number of intrinsic characteristics of the projects, contextual factors outside the scope of the project had a major effect in determining the results (Pasicolan 1996). In other words, co-management projects, just like other types of project, to a certain extent follow the flow of life in their specific setting. Factors external to the projects are of crucial importance and are at the same time more difficult to evaluate.

Third parties in co-management arrangements

In principle co-management arrangements are between individual or collective users of resources and governmental institutions. However in many cases third parties play a crucial role in the creation and facilitating of these arrangements. The organizations claim to be instrumental in the implementation of such arrangements. By their presence and actions they become an important actor in the social and political context. International organizations like the IUCN, WWF and Conservation International, but also the national non-governmental organizations, often assume such an intermediate role. They do so on the basis of their own programme of action and they seek opportunities to take up this position. In many cases they assume such a role because of the relatively weak governmental representation in the area and because they believe they can play a constructive role in bringing about positive changes either in the field of nature conservation or the protection of rights and interests of local people (see, for example, Chapters 2, 6, 9 and 10 in this volume).

This intermediate role brings about a delicate position because of the complex interests at stake. In the first place the organization is tied to the regulations of the government and the available legal instruments. In the second place it is necessary for the organization to ensure the confidence of the local population in order to perform well. And in the third place it is necessary to satisfy the constituency of the organization, i.e. the donor agency or supporters of the organization. This third aspect might conflict with the required instrumental nature of the performance of the organizations as the constituency of the organization might require clear visibility in the local context and successes within relatively short periods of time in order to ensure continued support for the activities. The organizations might be tempted to assume a stronger role if governmental performance is weak. But this situation might lead to a susceptibility to criticism and tensions from both sides: the local population might identify the organization with the governmental institutions and thus question its reliability, while on the other hand criticism might also come from the government if employees of the organization take on governmental roles or identify too strongly with local interests. Finally there is a certain time constraint connected to the presence of the organization: duration of their projects can rarely go beyond a limited number of years. Success stories and new challenges or new battles to fight in other places are necessary to retain the interest of the constituencies and their willingness to continue their support (Kalland and Persoon 1998). The departure of the organization from the local scene might lead to flaws in the implementation of the activities as a smooth and complete transfer of responsibilities is rarely ensured.

Dissolving state responsibilities and non-local interests
In many discussions about the failure of state-controlled management of natural resources, local, or community-based management is proposed as a more viable alternative. In many case studies the state and its local institutions are seen as the embodiment of an evil force, misappropriating what is considered to be intrinsically local. In many Asian countries processes of decentralization have come about as a result of an awareness of the inadequacy of centralized forms of government. Local people, frequently supported by dissident politicians, the media, NGOs and scientists, have been successful in acquiring greater political power. In recent years international donors have adopted a similar position, now preferring to work directly with local organizations. In their implementation of programmes and projects, government institutions have shown themselves prone to corruption, inefficient bureaucracy and other problems.

This movement towards decentralization has a number of important potential implications. Can supra-local or non-local interests, like those of downstream farmers and fishermen, of urban people, or even the global community now and in the future, and like taking care of nature for its own sake, be entrusted to the care of local communities, who are not generally in a position to deal adequately with such interests. The emphasis on stakeholder involvement is certainly problematic if the process is dominated by aversion to the state, the collective representative of all those interests that cannot be heard at the local level. Somehow, checks and balances must be built into the process to avoid the denial of interests beyond the merely local (van den Top and Persoon 2000).

The ecological basis of natural resources under co-management arrangements
An important issue in relation to resource management that often draws little explicit attention is the ecological nature of the resource in question and the managerial consequences that follow. Natural resources are of themselves very

heterogeneous. Co-management of harvested resources such as timber and fish differs fundamentally from community conservation of biodiversity. The former is management of directly utilized resources yielding immediate value to those extracting them from nature, while the latter provides only indirect, delayed or cultural value (Uphoff 1998:3). On the other hand, highly mobile stocks of fish or marine mammals with territories far beyond the jurisdiction of particular communities cannot be managed along similar lines to localized non-timber forest products or animals that are much more territorially bound. Effective management of water resources requires clear and rapid procedures in times of both scarcity and abundance. Conflicts over scarce irrigation water, for instance, cannot linger on, for otherwise the resource loses its value to the dis-advantaged party. Similarly rapid procedures are necessary when flooding threatens. Conflicts over access to land and other immobile resources, in contrast, require less urgent action.

Resources also require specific knowledge and are subject to specific manage-ment aims, and because of differences in regenerative capacity they also require different time perspectives if they are to be adequately managed. In successful management projects, ecological realities are matched with the social and cultural facts of life. Uphoff suggests that we ask ourselves whether or not a resource is 'bounded' (known and predictable) and if the resource users are a 'bounded' set: identifiable and coherent or lacking group identity and structure (1998:13). Management of protected areas is a situation in which the resource is delimited, as in the case of Cat Tien in Vietnam, as described by Polet (Chapter 2 in this volume). Most users, on the other hand, have little in com-mon except for being close to the park.

In general, however, we feel that in discussions on resource management there is too much emphasis is on social and political issues and context, and too little on the ecological dimension of the resources to be managed. This is to be attributed partly to the ecological 'naiveté' of those engaged in relevant discussions and partly to the fact that natural scientists have not been able to bring forward with sufficient clarity the ecological characteristics of particular resources. This underscores the importance of the biophysical perspective for co-management. Proposed co-management arrangements should correlate with the quality and extent of the natural resources. While state-controlled manage-ment and protection of nature used to be dominated by biologists and ecologists, under the new management arrangements the role of these disciplines has been greatly diminished. In our opinion, greater importance should be attached to the role of other disciplines and the contribution of interdisciplinary research in the debate on co-management and in the design and implementation of co-management projects (see, for example, Gilbert and Janssen 1998).

CONTENT AND ORGANIZATION OF THE BOOK

This book seeks to describe, analyse and compare a variety of co-management regimes, as implemented in six different countries in Asia. They are selected so as to reflect contemporary practice in the field of co-management in the region. In general the book starts with concrete descriptions of co-management practices. The case studies by Polet, Hobbes, Harkes and Novaczek, Pasicolan, Aquino and Wei Hu are focused on descriptions of co-management efforts in national parks, community forests and coastal zones. Though we tend to think of co-management as a rather new fashion in the world of nature conservation and resource management, Kalland provides a case from the Japanese past in which he analyses arrangements that would nowadays be called 'co-management'. The chapters by Osseweijer, Eghenter and Yadama take a more distant view on various aspects of co-management. Osseweijer describes the use of mapping as an instrument in co-management. Eghenter compares historical practices with their present-day images and Yadama brings in some theoretical notions in the general way of thinking of management arrangements.

The following two chapters are of a more comparative nature. In Chapter 12, Sajise, Fellizar and Saguiguit describe the history and pitfalls of the community based resource management experiences in the Philippines, both in forestry, irrigation and fisheries. The following chapter by Pomeroy, Katon and Harkes expands the comparison to a number of Asian countries but focuses exclusively on the fishery sector.

In the epilogue, Ellen comments on the volume as a whole and on the issues raised, identifying some of those that are crucial when analysing or trying to implement co-management arrangements in a particular area. His synthesis brings the variety of cases and experiences back to the central issues in co-management in Asia.

NOTES

1   Murray-Li comments that it is not only outsiders that like to idealize communities. For their part, 'communities' (represented by the village council) are also often keen to convey images of solidarity and co-operation to outsiders (1993: 3).

2   This results in a far greater focus on tropical rainforests than on semi-arid regions, for example.

3   Ghimire and Pimbert (1997: 1) have grouped many types of conservation measures into two broad categories: improvement of environmental resources to ameliorate

living conditions (through reforestation, soil and water conservation, for example); and conservation of protected areas.

REFERENCES

Adam, B. (1998) *Timescapes of Modernity. The Environment and Invisible Hazards.* London: Routledge

Asquith, P. and A. Kalland (eds) (1997). *Japanese Images of Nature. Cultural Perspectives.* Richmond: Curzon Press.

Benda-Beckmann, F.K. von and A. Brouwer (1992). '*Changing Indigenous Environmental Law in the Central Moluccas: Communal relations and Privatization of Sasi*'. Paper presented to the Congress of the Commission on Folk Law and Legal Pluralism, Victoria University, Wellington.

Bennagen, P.L. and M.L. Lucas-Fernan (eds)(1996). *Consulting the Spirits, Working with Nature, Sharing with Other. Indigenous Resource Use in the Philippines.* Quezon City, Sentro Para sa Ganap na Pamayanan.

Berkes, F. (1994) 'Property rights and coastal fisheries'. In R.S. Pomeroy (ed.), *Community Management and Common Property of Coastal Fisheries in Asia and the Pacific: Concepts, Methods and Experiences*, Manila, ICLARM, pp. 51–62.

Boersema J. (2000) 'Only the present counts when the future is at stake'. In G. Persoon, D. van Est and W. van Beek (eds), *The Study of the Future in Anthropology. Focaal* 35, pp. 89–112.

Boissevain, J. (1992) 'On predicting the future: parish rituals and patronage in Malta'. In S. Walmann (ed.) *Contemporary Futures. Perspectives from Social Anthropology.* IASA Monograph 30. London: Routledge.

Cernea, M. (1985) 'Alternative Units of Social Organization Sustaining Afforestation Strategies'. In M. Cernea (ed.), *Putting People First: Sociological Variables in Rural Development.* Washington, DC: World Bank and Oxford University Press, pp. 267–293.

Conelly, W.T. (1992) 'Agricultural intensification in a Philippine frontier community: impact on labour efficiency and farm diversity'. *Human Ecology* 20(2): 203–221.

Crehan, K. (1997) *The Fractured Community. Landscapes of Power and Gender in Rural Zambia.* Berkeley: University of California Press.

Dijk, R. van (1997) *Fundamentalism, Cultural Memory and the State: Contested Representations of Time in Post-Colonial Malawi.* Working Paper 2. The Hague: WOTRO.

Gell, A. (1996) *The Anthropology of Time: Cultural Constructions of Temporal Maps and Images.* Oxford: Berg.

Ghee, L.T. and M.J. Valencia (eds)(1990) *Conflict over Natural Resources in South-East Asia and the Pacific.* Manila: Ateneo de Manila University Press.

Ghimire, K. and M. Pimpert (1997) *Social Change and Conservation. Environmental Politics and Impacts of National Parks and Protected Areas.* London: Earthscan Publications Ltd.

Gilbert, A.J. and R. Janssen (1998) 'Use of environmental functions to communicate the values of a mangrove ecosystem under different management regimes'. In *Ecological Economics* 25: 323–346.

Hanna, S., C. Folke and K.G. Mäler (eds) (1996) *Rights to Nature. Ecological, Economic, Cultural and Political Principles of Institutions for the Environment.* Washington, DC: Island Press.

Harkes, I. (1997) '*Measuring success of co-management and CBRM*'. Paper presented at the Fisheries Co-management Project Asian Workshop, Phuket, Thailand, 21–23 October 1997.

Hombergh, H. van den (1993) *Gender, Environment and Development: a Guide to the Literature.* Utrecht: International Books.

IUCN (1996) *Collaborative Management of Protected Areas: Tailoring the Approach to the Context.* Gland: IUCN.

—— (1997) *Indigenous Peoples and Sustainability. Cases and Actions.* Utrecht: International Books.

—— (1998) *Enhancing Sustainability. Resources for Our Future.* SUI Technical Series, Vol. I., Gland: IUCN

Kalland, A. and G.A. Persoon (eds) (1998) *Environmental Movements in Asia.* Richmond: Curzon Press.

Kemf, E. (ed.) (1993) *The Law of the Mother. Protecting Indigenous Peoples in Protected Areas.* San Francisco: Sierra Club.

Kessy, J. (1998) *Conservation and Utilization of Natural Resources in the East Usambara Forest Reserves: Conventional Views and Local Perspectives.* Tropical Resource Management Papers No.18, Wageningen.

Kothari, A., N. Singh and S. Suri (eds) (1996) *People and Protected Areas. Towards Participatory Conservation in India.* New Delhi: Sage Publications India.

Leach, M. R.Mearns and I. Scoones (1997) *Environmental Entitlements: a Framework for Understanding the Institutional Dynamics of Environmental Change.* IDS discussion paper 359.

Lynch, O. and K. Talbott (1995) *Balancing Acts: Community Based Forest Management and National Law in Asia and the Pacific.* Washington, DC: World Resource Institute.

McNeely, J.A. (1996) *Conservation and Future: Trends and Options toward the Year 2025. A Discussion Paper.* Gland: IUCN.

Murray-Li, T. (1993) *Gender Issues in Community-Based Resource Management.* Manila: CERMP.

Ostrom, E. (1990). *Governing the Commons. The Evolution of Institutions for Collective Action.* Cambridge: Cambridge University Press.

Pasicolan, P. (1996) '*Tree growing in different grounds: an analysis of local participation in contract reforestation in the Philippines*'. PhD thesis, Leiden: Leiden University.

Passmore, J. (1980) *Man's Responsibility for Nature.* London: Duckworth.

Persoon, G.A. and D.M.E van Est (2000) 'The study of the future in anthropology in relation to the sustainability debate'. *Focaal* 35, pp. 7–28.

Pimpert, M. and J. Pretty, (1995) *Parks, People and Professionals: Pputting Participation into Protected area Management.* UNRISD Discussion Paper No 57.

Polunin, N.V.C. (1991) 'Delimiting nature: regulated area management in the coastal zone of Malaysia'. In P.C. West and S.R. Brechin (eds), *Resident Peoples and National Parks*. Tuscon: University of Arizona Press.

Pomeroy, R.S. (ed.) (1994) *Community Management and Common Property of Coastal Fisheries in Asia and the Pacific: Concepts, Methods and Experiences*. Manila: ICLARM.

Pomeroy, R. (1996) Community-based and co-management institutions for sustainable coastal fisheries management in Southeast Asia. *Ocean and Coastal Management, 27(3): pp. 143–162.*

Richards, P. (1992) 'Saving the rainforest? Contested futures in conservation'. In. S. Wallman (ed.), *Contemporary Futures. Perspectives from Social Anthropology*. IASA Monographs 30. London: Routledge, pp. 138–153

Sen, S. and J. Raakjaer Nielsen (1996) 'Fisheries co-management: a comparative analysis'. In *Marine Policy* 20(5): 405–418.

Stevens, S. (ed.) (1997) *Conservation through Cultural Survival. Indigenous Peoples and Protected Areas*. Washington: Island Press.

Uphoff, N. (1998) 'Community-based Natural Resource Management: Connecting Micro and Macro Processes, and People with Their Environments'. Paper presemted at the International Workshop on Community-based natural resource management, Washington DC, May 10–14.

van den Top, G.M. and G.A. Persoon (2000) 'Dissolving State Responsibilities for Forests in Northeast Luzon'. In Ch. J-H. Macdonald and G.M. Pesigan (eds), *Old Ties and New Solidarities*. Studies on Philippine Communities. Manila: Ateneo de Manila University Press, pp. 158–176.

Vayda, A.P. (1996) *Methods and Explanations in the Study of Human Actions and Their Environmental Effects*. Bogor: CIFOR/WWF.

Wallman, S. (ed.) (1992). *Contemporary Futures. Perspectives from Social Anthropology*. IASA Monographs 30. London: Routledge.

West, P.C. and S.R. Brechin (eds.) (1991) *Resident Peoples and National Parks*. Tuscon: University of Arizona Press.

Western, D. and R. Wright(1994) 'Vision of the future. The new focus of conservation'. In: D. Western, R. Wright and S. Strum (eds) *Natural Connections. Perspectives in Community-Based Management*, pp. 548–556. Washington: Island Press.

Wiersum, F. (1996) Indigenous exploitation and management of tropical forest resources: an evolutionary continuum in forest-people interaction. In *Agriculture Ecosystems & Environment 63, pp.1-16.*

Williams, R. (1983) *Keywords*. London, Fontana.

WWF (1996) *Indigenous Peoples and Conservation. WWF Statements and Principles*. Gland: World Wide Fund for Nature (WWF).

CHAPTER TWO

Co-management in Protected Areas: The Case of Cat Tien National Park, Southern Vietnam

GERT POLET

INTRODUCTION

M any aspects of protected area management in relation to local human communities have been described in literature. Primack (1993) gives a general overview of the various aspects involved. It is clear that protected area management in less-developed areas is a complex matter because, being driven by poverty, local human populations often rely primarily on natural resources that are found in protected areas but which are also exploited by outside actors capitalizing on skewed economic and political powers. However, this is not just a matter of poor socio-economic conditions or unequal political powers; more and more it is understood that virtually no place on earth has not been part of a human utilization system (Lewis 1996). Hence protected areas are situated most often on land that has been traditionally used for many generations by local communities. Thus a large number of cases exist which describe the pressures protected areas are facing from 'encroaching' local populations being driven by poverty.

The general aim of Protected Area Systems has been and is to maintain biodiversity and natural wilderness for future generations. Traditionally this aim has often been operationalized in a management style that severely restricts, if not forbids, human utilization of biological resources situated within the protected area. This management style may be appropriate for areas with unique ecological features that cannot tolerate any (further) human disturbance. It has successfully conserved important biological values in many parts of the world, values which otherwise would likely to have been lost to increasing human populations and expanding socio-economic systems.

The management style that puts all responsibility in the hands of the agency in charge and does not tolerate interference from local communities has, however, come under a great deal of criticism. It is said that it ignores the fact that virtually all land on Earth is and has been part of human utilization systems. Therefore many protected areas face claims on the resources situated within their boundaries on the basis of traditional and ancestral rights. In other cases, poor socio-economic conditions force local communities to utilize the resources located in protected area regardless of whether that is allowed or not. In this context it has been said that protected areas are based on 'a charming myth, but still a myth: that nature is separate from people, and that nature is diminished whenever people try to live among it' (McNeely in Lewis 1996).

That protected area–local community relations are often conflicting has been well recognized in literature (e.g. Lewis 1996; Borrini-Feyerabend 1997). Recognizing these realities, modern protected area management includes strategies often referred to as 'co-management'. These strategies build on the growing recognition that some local communities have long-standing traditional rights to the resources located in protected areas and that in several cases local communities indeed have managed those resources in a manner that has apparently been sustainable. These co-management strategies are also based on the conviction that, among others, 'social acceptance is crucial for conservation to be sustainable' and that 'the costs of top-down approaches are staggering' (Borrini-Feyerabend 1997).

Borrini-Feyerabend (1997: 21) gives a continuum of 'participation in conservation initiatives' that runs from full control by agencies in charge and no interference or contribution from stakeholders to 'full control by stakeholders and no interference or contribution from agency in charge'. Concrete management styles thus range from 'actively consulting, seeking consensus, negotiating, sharing authority to transferring authority and responsibility' to local communities.

Modern protected areas consist of a core zone and a surrounding buffer zone. An accepted definition of a buffer zone is: 'A zone, peripheral to a national park or equivalent reserve, where restrictions are placed upon resource use or special developments measures are undertaken to enhance the conservation value of the area' (Sayer 1991: 2).

Gilmour (1998) identifies an alternative livelihood approach, an economic development approach and a participatory planning approach in so called integrated conservation-development projects (ICDPs) which became the answers in conservation action to top-down, strict conservation activities of earlier decades. The alternative livelihood approach aims at developing alternative sources that meet the local communities' development needs but which are less harmful for the environment. The economic development approach reasons that, if standards of living rise, interest in conservation will be enhanced and that it is unrealistic to expect a conservation interest from impoverished communities. The participatory planning approach argues that the more local communities are involved in planning, management and sharing of conservation activities and benefits, the more likely they are to agree to conservation initiatives (Gilmour 1998).

Recent publications in *Oryx* (Vol. 33 [1]; Vol. 33 [4]; e.g. Spinage 1998) argue that modern co-management approaches (such as ICDP's) have proven to be detrimental for ecological values in protected areas. Implementing co-management arrangements requires tremendous efforts to control the arrangements and it is doubted whether present capacities can deal with such complex management structures. Furthermore it is pointed out that biodiversity values have been lost and that the goal of wildlife conservation has not been served by co-management arrangements. Roe *et al.* point out that:

> The old is not yet invalid and the new has not yet been coherently argued, much less proven. Just as the old ways of fortress conservation are failing because the instruments used were too blunt, lacking ideological refinement, CMW (Community-based Wildlife Management) in many cases is still quintessential idealism, lacking the robustness and application required for use as a development tool. (Roe *et al.* 2000: 4)

This case study describes the situation of a national park in southern Vietnam in terms of biological values and the socio-economic, political and cultural context it is operating in. An assessment is made of how the current management style of restriction-in-the-core-zone and dialogue-in-the-buffer-zone has worked out in ecological and socio-economic terms and whether alternative approaches are desirable and realistically workable.

CAT TIEN NATIONAL PARK

One of the biggest protected areas in Vietnam is Cat Tien National Park, located 150 km north-east of Ho Chi Minh City. The park (73,878 ha) consists of three sectors: Nam Cat Tien (38,202 ha) in Dong Nai Province, Tay Cat Tien (5,382 ha) in Binh Phuoc Province and Cat Loc (30,635 ha) in Lam Dong Province (Cox *et al.* 1995). Cat Loc is separated geographically from the Nam Cat Tien and Tay Cat Tien sectors (see Figure 2.1). Nam Cat Tien received protected status in 1978 and became a national park in 1992. Cat Loc was declared a Rhino sanctuary in 1992. The three sectors were managed separately by the three provinces until 1998, when the three areas were administratively integrated into what is now known as Cat Tien National Park.

Table 2.1: Vegetation cover of Cat Tien National Park

Vegetation Types	Sector totals (hectares)			Park totals	
	Nam Cat Tien	Tay Cat Tien	Cat Loc	Area	% of area
Evergreen forest	7,844	147	9,828	17,819	24.0
• primary	662	25	–	687	0.9
• logged	7,182	122	9,828	17,132	23.1
Semi-evergreen forest	5,097	–	–	5,097	7.0
Bamboo forest	10,519	2,692	16,594	29,805	40.1
Mixed forest	11,760	529	2,072	14,361	19.3
Plantation	–	62	–	62	0.1
Bush/scrub forest	487	–	–	487	0.6
Grasslands	1,109	577	702	2,388	3.2
Cultivation/settlement area	69	1,001	1,439	2,509	3.4
Wetlands and lakes	1,287	343	–	1,603	2.2
Other	30	31	–	61	0.1
Total natural area	38,202	5,382	30,635	74,219	100.0

Source: Cox *et al.*, 1995.

The topography of the park is characterized by areas with steep hills and largely flat areas. Cat Loc, being the southern edge of Vietnam's central plateau, is rather hilly (Cox *et al.* 1995). Although altitudes range only from 200 to 600 metres above sea level, slopes are relatively steep. Cat Tien National Park is located in the monsoon tropical region. Average rainfall is approximately 2,300 mm. Average temperatures are approximately 15–35ºc (JICA / MARD 1996).

ECOLOGICAL HIGHLIGHTS

Flora

Table 2.1 provides an overview of the vegetation cover in classes in Cat Tien National Park. Only a minute area can be regarded as pristine. Roughly half of the area's forest has been replaced by bamboo while the remainder of the area consists mainly of logged semi-evergreen forest and mixed forest. Especially the Cat Loc and Tay Cat Tien sectors of the park have been severely denuded by warfare, logging and conversion of forestland into agricultural land.

Nevertheless, Cat Tien National Park harbours the largest lowland tropical forest of southern Vietnam that is still in reasonable condition; it does, moreover, show signs of recovery. It is therefore not surprising that the area is regarded by

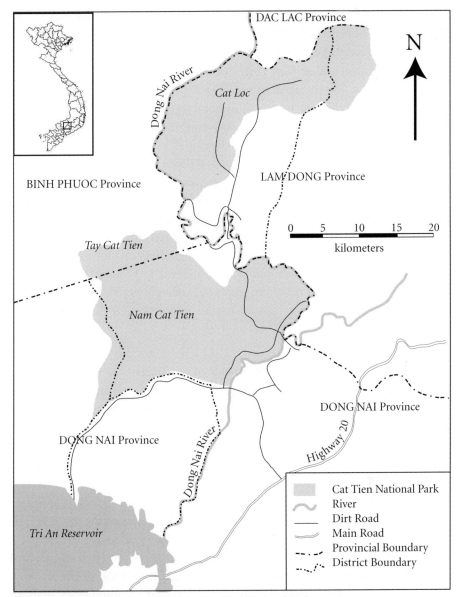

Figure 2.1: The three sectors comprising Cat Tien National Park

both scientists and policy-makers as an irreplaceable ecosystem which deserves to be conserved as an example of Vietnam's original lowland rainforest ecosystem.

Considerable parts of the park suffered from heavy spraying of defoliants during the American war. After the war Vietnam experienced a rapid deforestation (in 1943, 45 per cent of Vietnam was covered by forest; that figure had dropped to 10–12 per cent by 1989). Principal general factors contributing to this trend are expansion of agriculture into forest areas, commercial logging, fuelwood consumption and shifting cultivation damage (ANZDEC 1996).

The evergreen forests are dominated by *Dipterocarpaceae spp.* and various *Leguminosae.* The regrowth forests show good signs of recovery and have a well established four-layer structure. The semi-evergreen forests are dominated by *Lagerstroemia spp.* Bamboo forests have developed in areas that were burned for cultivation. Dominant species are *Bambusa balcooa* and *Diospyros mun.* Mixed forests have a mixture of bamboo and tree species. The dominant tree species here are *Lagerstroemia spp.*, and *Bambusa balcooa* and *Diospyros mun.* The wetland areas are dominated by *Hydnocarpus anthelmintica* mixed with *Ficus benjamica* (in flood forests) and the seasonally flooded grasslands contain *Saccharum spontaneum, S. arundinaceum* and *Neyraudia arundinacea.* One per cent of the species found in Cat Tien National Park is endemic to Vietnam. Rare and endangered plant species found in the park are *Dalbergia bariensis, D. mammosa, D. cochinchinensis, Aquilaria crassna, Afzelia xylocarpa* and *Calamus poilanei* (Cox *et al.* 1995).

Fauna

For most fauna inventories have been made of the diversity present in Cat Tien National Park. However, most of these inventories are incomplete while fish, bats, rodents and reptiles have not yet been studied comprehensively. Table 2.2 provides an overview of the number of species occurring in the park and an overview of those IUCN Red List species found there. The park hosts at least 82 mammal, 318 bird, 58 reptile, 28 amphibian and 130 fish species. In total at least 48 IUCN Red Listed species occur in the park, three of which are critically endangered (the Javan rhinoceros, orange-necked partridge and Siamese crocodile).

Of special significance is the existence of a sub-species of the Javan rhinoceros (*Rhinoceros sondaicus annamiticus*) in the Cat Loc sector of the park. Recent studies and pictures from automatic photo-traps (Polet, Tran Van Mui *et al.* 1999) confirmed the existence of a very small population of five to seven individuals. Based on the analysis of footprint sizes and on-going DNA analysis, it is clear that these rhinos represent a completely different gene pool from that of the Javan rhinoceros in Ujung Kulon (*Rhinoceros sondaicus sondaicus*) in Java, Indonesia. Should the Cat Tien National Park rhinos become extinct, the world will lose a unique sub-species of large mammal.

Another critically endangered species endemic to Cat Tien National Park is the orange-necked partridge (*Arborophila davidi*). Recent studies confirmed its

Table 2.2: Overview of number of species and IUCN Red Listed species found in Cat Tien National Park

	Mammals	Birds	Reptiles	Amphibians	Fish
Total no. of species	82 (21)	318 (20)	58 (7)	28 (0)	130 (1)
IUCN Red List 'Critical'	Rhinoceros sondaicus annamiticus	Arborophila davidi	Crocodylus siamensis		
IUCN Red List 'Endangered'	Pygathrix nigripes Panthera tigris corbetti Elephas maximus	Cairina scutulata Pseudibis davisoni			Scleropages formosus
IUCN Red List 'Vulnerable'	Nycticebus pygmaeus Macaca arctoides Macaca leonina Cuon alpinus Neofelis nebulosa Bos gaurus Hystrix brachyura	Gallus gallus Lophura diardi Polyplectron germaini Leptoptilos javanicus	Hieremys annandalii Indotestudo elongata Amyda cartilaginea		
IUCN Red List 'Near threatened'	Manis javanica Macaca fascicularis Macaca mulatta Trachypithecus cristatus Aonyx cinerea Prionailurus viverrinus Catopuma temminckii Myotis rosseti	Bubo nipalensis Ketupa zeylonensis Grus antigone; Vanellus cinereus Aviceda jerdoni Ichthyophaga ichthyaetus Anhinga melanogaster Mycteria leucocephala Pitta soror; Pitta elliotii Cissa hypoleuca Macronous kelleyi Ploceus hypoxanthus	Python molurus Cuota amboinensis Heosemys grandis		
IUCN Red List 'Data deficient'	Hylobates gabriellae Helarctos malayanus				

Note: Number of IUCN Red Listed species shown in parentheses.
Sources: Polet and Khanh (1999); Polet (2000); Polet and Khanh (2000).

occurrence in the park and highlighted the deteriorating situation these birds find themselves in (Atkins and Tentij 1998; Vy *et al.* 2000). The natural habitat of both the rhinoceros and the partridge has been severely affected by human activities such as defoliation during the American war, logging, conversion of forest into agricultural land, and hunting.

The fate of the Siamese Crocodile (*Crocodylus siamensis*) in Cat Tien National Park has been even worse. Resent surveys indicate that this critically endangered species has most likely become extinct in the park due to hunting for skins and taking of stock for crocodile farms (Bembrick and Cannon 1999). Unlike the other two critically endangered species, the Siamese crocodile is not endemic to the park and other populations are known to occur in Cambodia, Thailand and in crocodile farms. At the moment, Cat Tien National Park is collaborating with the WWF, Saigon Zoo, Queensland University and a private crocodile farmer in Ho Chi Minh City to re-introduce the crocodile in the park (Polet, Ton That *et al* 1999).

Compared to other national parks in Vietnam (Table 2.4), Cat Tien National Park stands out as the richest in faunal biodiversity, although the high numbers of different taxa may also be attributed to more intensive studies having been conducted in Cat Tien National Park than in other national parks in Vietnam.

More important than having high numbers of different species, Cat Tien National Park's ecosystem has been widely recognized of being of significant importance for birds (Robson *et al.* 1993a and 1993b; Polet and Khanh 1999), ungulates (Ling 2000) and primates (Geismann *et al.* 2000; Nadler *et al.* in press).

From the above it is clear that Cat Tien National Park is of international importance in terms of biodiversity. The Biodiversity Action Plan for Vietnam (GSRV/GEF 1994) regards the area also as a prime example of a lowland forest ecosystem in Vietnam. The rather high number of IUCN Red Listed species and the occurrence of a number of endemic species makes Cat Tien National Park a biodiversity hotspot but also highlights the extremely difficult situation in which nature in general and wildlife in particular finds itself in Vietnam.

HUMAN CONTEXT

Population history and patterns

The area of Dong Nai, Lam Dong and Binh Phuoc provinces in which Cat Tien National Park is located was originally sparsely populated. For generations, tndigenous ethnic groups residing in the area, i.e. the S'Tieng and Chau Ma, have engaged in shifting cultivation and hunting-gathering.

After the American war development of the Vietnamese economy was feeble. In an attempt to provide better opportunities for the inhabitants of the over-populated Red River and Mekong River deltas, the government initiated the New Economic Zones policy in the mid-1980s. Under this policy large numbers of people (notably Kinh Vietnamese from the lowlands but also ethnic minorities from central and northern Vietnam) were relocated to less crowded areas. Hence, a number of New Economic Zones were established in what is now Cat Tien National Park and its vicinity. Poor co-ordination between different government bodies resulted in the creation of Cat Loc Rhino Sanctuary in 1992 while simultaneously large parts of the sanctuary were designated as a New Economic Zone.

Natural population growth, relocation of people and the following spontaneous in-migration led to a massive influx of people which in turn resulted in a rapid transformation of the area's natural vegetation into lowland rice fields and sloping agricultural lands. Since most immigrants had little experience with sloping land agriculture and with a quickly increasing pressure on the land, most hills became denuded. Erosion is a serious problem nowadays.

Table 2.3 provides an overview of the present-day human habitation of Cat Tien National Park. An estimated 9,484 people live within the park, especially within the Cat Loc and Tay Cat Tien sectors, with a concentrated presence in Talai Commune in the Nam Cat Tien sector. About a quarter of the human population (2,798 people) are indigenous minorities who have been living in the area for generations. Most people living within the park are non-indigenous people, being settled there under New Economic Zone programmes or arriving spontaneously.

Table 2.3: Number of people inside Cat Tien National Park, 2000

Location	Indigenous minorities	Non-indigenous	Total
Dak Lua Commune	0	245	245
Ta Lai Commune	1,341	0	1,341
Nam Cat Tien sector sub-total	1,341	245	1,586
Dang Ha Commune	0	2,008	2,008
Tay Cat Tien sector sub-total	0	2,008	2,008
Tien Hoang Commune	1,178	0	1,178
Gia Vien Commune	70	2,113	2,183
Phuoc Cat II Commune	209	2,320	2,320
Cat Loc sector sub-total	1,457	4,433	5,681
Total	2,798	6,686	9,484

Source: San, 2000.

In terms of land titles, many different situations exist. Most among the indigenous ethnic minority have no official land titles. This seems to be because they have never felt a strong need to register their property but also because many indigenous people live on land which is officially designated as forestland. Under Vietnamese law, no land titles can be issued on land which is designated forestland (only on land designated as agricultural). Within Cat Tien National Park, most land is designated as forestland. Even so, quite large areas are designated as agricultural land, these being managed by the regular government administration (commune, district, province). In the Cat Loc sector alone, out of a total of 30,635 ha, about 4,950 ha (16 per cent) is officially designated agricultural land while additional areas are covered with illegal plantations. Even though these areas are situated within the protected area, Cat Tien National Park management does not have authority over any area designated as agricultural land.

Most people who arrived in the region under the New Economic Zone programme received land titles, but not all of them. Because provincial boundaries were not demarcated in the field, the situation could develop that people in one village have land titles from Binh Phuoc Province (which at the time of issue was not a protected area) but have actually been living in Dong Nai Province within the protected area. Hence there are people living legally within the protected area (with land title and on designated agricultural land); others live there illegally (no land title and on designated forestland); and others semi-legally (with land titles but on designated forestland). The above illustrates the legal complexities in which the authorities of Cat Tien National Park have to operate when trying to fulfil their primary mandate: conservation of the ecosystems in the protected area.

Human utilization patterns
The non-indigenous people live mainly along the edges of the park, in the fertile floodplains of the Dong Nai River and valleys of streams penetrating further into the park. The main livelihood is rice cultivation and farming a variety of crops such as black pepper, beans and maize in the lowlands. Most families have upland farms further inside the park where cashew is grown.

Most indigenous people live further inside Cat Tien National Park, depending on cashew and coffee as cash crops and a range of subsistence crops including rice. Shifting cultivation has been the traditional basis of livelihood of the ethnic minorities residing the area. The Chau Ma and S'Tieng people still practise this farming system but, instead of leaving the land fallow to regenerate the natural vegetation cover, cashew is planted. This process combined with the cashew enterprises of newcomers has resulted in large areas of forest being converted into plantations.

Hunting and gathering is part of the traditional lifestyle of the S'Tieng and Chau Ma people. The primary aim of hunting and gathering has always been to obtain food for home consumption, but surpluses have always been bartered and traded as well. The American war brought sophisticated and powerful weapons to the area and wildlife numbers seem to have declined sharply ever after. People from outside the area became active in the hunting industry and soon all but a few tigers, elephants and rhinos were wiped out from what is now Cat Tien National Park. A leader of the S'Tieng community in Cat Tien National Park explained that the rule was to 'kill only one rhino, because otherwise rhinos die out' and 'everybody in the village had to be invited to enjoy the meat – skin, bones and horn were discarded' (K'Mot personal comment, 4 May 2000). From his own memory he could list 20 rhinos killed between 1962 and 1988, including males, females and juveniles. Most of these rhinos were killed by local people. Subsistence snaring of different *Phasianidae* (including orange-necked partridge and Siamese fireback, both IUCN Red List species) is still commonly practised (Vy 2000).

It seems that during the 1970s and '80s, rhinos were also hunted for their horn and skin as Mr. K'Mot wondered at the time 'why people [Kinh Vietnamese] wanted to buy the skin of rhinos'. But since 1988 no rhinos have been lost to poachers (Polet *et al.* 1999). Wildlife traders from large towns, however, do still place orders with local communities who infiltrate the park. Quarry species are mainly birds and monkeys for the pet market (ICBP 1991). Common wild pig, lesser chevrotain, Sambar deer and common barking deer are hunted for consumption. Extreme pressure on Vietnam's wildlife has been well documented (Duckworth and Hedges 1998). Export to China and domestic use for traditional medicines have been recognized as the main factors in the decline of Vietnam's key wildlife species (Compton 1998).

Apart from converting forests into agricultural land and hunting, logging is of concern in Cat Tien National Park. The whole of present-day Cat Tien National Park has been logged commercially. Only a small percentage of primary forest remains intact (see Table 2.1). Commercial logging ceased to exist when the area received protected status. Illegal logging still does occur in the park, notably in the Tay Cat Tien and Cat Loc sectors, although tree-poaching incidents have diminished over the last few years. Both people who live inside the park as well as people who come from outside are involved in these operations.

Since large-rattan processing units are available at close range (both within the immediate vicinity of the park as well as in Ho Chi Minh City), rattan harvesting in the park is a popular business, especially during the period of low agricultural activity. Rattan harvesting is done by the people living within the park as well as by people commuting from outside.

Resin tapping has been an important activity in Cat Tien National Park (ICBP 1991). Holes are cut in *Dipterocarpaceae* trunks to tap the resin which is used to waterproof boats. Indigenous ethnic minorities are involved in this form of gathering forest products. Over the last few years, the practice has largely diminished but because only large adult trees are targeted, resin tapping still poses a serious threat to the park's ecosystem. There are not many large trees left in the park and the cutting holes in the trunk for resin tapping will eventually kill the tree.

Park management
Being a legally protected area under Vietnam Forest Law, Cat Tien National Park is classified as a Special Use Forest. Under this classification the prime objective of maintaining the area is to maintain biodiversity values. Secondary activities permitted are scientific research and tourism. An other objective is to conserve the natural state of the vegetation in order to maintain the watershed function of the park as to avoid siltation of the downstream Tri An Reservoir which is a key site for electric power generation for southern Vietnam. Legally no other activities than the aforementioned are permitted in the park.

Current management practice of the park is very much geared towards law enforcement within the core zone. In total the park has 16 guard stations and two mobile patrol teams. People violating park rules receive a warning note. Those found violating the park rules repeatedly can be fined or ultimately be prosecuted in court.

For the Nam Cat Tien sector alone, 560 violations were recorded in 1998 (Wells 1999). Roughly 80 per cent of the violations involved people who live within the national park or just outside its borders. The others come from farther afield. About 22 per cent of the violations involved 'illegal entries', about 23 per cent fishing and about 22 per cent bamboo cutting. The other 32 per cent involved more serious offences such as hunting, logging, rattan and resin collecting and encroachment on the park (Wells 1999).

Land classification policies are not in line with land use policies in Vietnam. Large areas within Cat Tien National Park are classified as agricultural land. The management responsibility for these areas lies with line agencies of the government of Vietnam (i.e. communes and districts). Although these areas are situated within Cat Tien National Park, the park management has no management responsibility in these areas and cannot enforce its conservation objectives there. As mentioned above, 16 per cent of the Cat Loc area is thus beyond the control of the national park authorities.

Buffer zones are officially defined as a 1-km-wide strip around the park where it is bordered by logging concessions and includes the entire neighbouring commune where it is bordered by inhabited areas. The buffer zone is not demarcated in the field. Land and human activities in the buffer zone are managed either by logging concessionaires or by the Vietnam government line agencies (commune and district administration). Park officials have no legal authority in the buffer zone. As economic development has a higher priority than conservation in most districts, the so-called buffer zones tend to be entirely under cultivation. They bear little resemblance to actual buffer zones that maintain biodiversity values by restricting certain human activities in order to buffer further human impact on the core protected area.

The Cat Tien National Park authorities have been continuously seeking dialogue with different administrative levels in the buffer zones. Park management has been very active in maintaining face-to-face contacts with commune, district, provincial and central government administrators and different line agencies. Regularly, formal and less formal meetings are held in which protection and development issues are discussed with different government agencies. This approach has been followed in the Nam Cat Tien sector for a longer period of time than in the other two sectors which only became part of Cat Tien National Park in the end of 1998.

DISCUSSION

Table 2.4 shows that in terms of numbers of different mammal, bird, reptile and amphibian species, Cat Tien National Park is the richest of all Vietnam's national parks. A quarter of its mammal species, 6 per cent of its bird species and 12 per cent of its reptile species are IUCN Red Listed (see Table 2.2). Of global importance is the occurrence of three 'Critically Endangered' species. Cat Tien National Park's biodiversity should therefore be evaluated as being of national importance to Vietnam and in certain aspects (e.g. the Javan rhinoceros and orange-necked partridge) of global importance, signifying the need to be conserved. This is even more evident if one takes into account that there is not much room for optimism concerning Vietnam's general conservation status (Duckworth and Hedges 1998; Compton 1998).

The size of Cat Tien National Park may be rather large by Vietnamese standards but, in comparison with protected areas in countries such as Laos, Cambodia and Indonesia, it is rather small. Moreover, Cat Tien National Park's 75,000 ha is effectively split into two even smaller parts, separated by a stretch of cultivated land. Just by virtue of its size, Cat Tien National Park is not thought

Table 2.4: Comparison of faunal biodiversity in Vietnam's national parks

National park	Mammal species	Bird species	Reptile species	Amphibian species	No. of faunal species (rank)
Cat Tien	82	318	58	28	486 (1)
Cuc Phuong	64	137	36	17	254 (2)
Yok Don	62	196	-	13	271 (3)
Ba Vi	38	113	41	27	219 (4)
Bach Ma	55	158	-	-	429 (5)
Ba Be	38	111	18	6	173 (6)
Ben En	41	82	3	27	153 (7)
Con Dao	18	62	19	6	105 (8)
Cat Ba	28	37	20	-	85 (9)

Source: Trai *et al.*, 1999 (except for Cat Tien data, from this study).

to be able to maintain viable, large carnivore populations without connecting corridors between the two parts of the park as well as maintenance of other natural areas. (Ling 2000).

Furthermore, almost 9,500 people live within the national park and large stretches of its area are dedicated agricultural land over which the park management has no authority. Although Cat Tien National Park management is quite active in law enforcement activities, it can not avoid continued violations. It is obvious that the pressure on the resources occurring in Cat Tien National Park is high and only diminishing slowly.

These violations mainly involve people living within or right at the border of the park. A large number of these cases concern minor violations such as collecting bamboo, also indicating that people depend on the park for even relatively simple resources to meet their daily needs.

As pointed out above, management responsibilities within the national park are shared between the national park (i.e. within areas designated as forestland) and commune and district authorities (i.e. within areas designated agricultural land). Within the national park's buffer zones, the national park authorities have no management authority at all. Buffer zones are therefore not managed to buffer development activities which impact on the core zone's biodiversity values but rather for a one-sided economic development objective.

Gilmour and San (1999) concluded that in Vietnam:

> The biodiversity values of the buffer zones have declined dramatically in recent decades due to conversion of forest to agricultural land and to heavy (unsustainable) exploitation of forest products. It is doubtful if the buffer zones make any significant contribution to the conservation value of the national parks … [and that] [f]ew activities in the buffer zones are designed to link conservation objectives with socio-economic development.

Part of the problems seems to stem from the fact that '[t]he overlapping and sometimes conflicting lines of authority and responsibility for activities in buffer zones leads to confusion, uncertainty and frustration among the various actors'. Although Cat Tien National Park management is making a considerable effort to seek co-operation with communities in the buffer zone, the above general conclusions seem to apply here as well. In general, Vietnam's experience with buffer zone management leaves not much hope for an effective co-management approach to be applied within its national parks without compromising their biodiversity values.

CONCLUSIONS

Cat Tien National Park's biodiversity values are internationally important and deserve to be conserved. Due to rapid deforestation taking place in Vietnam and the severe hunting pressure on wildlife, it is clear that currently conservation in Vietnam is at a crossroad. Drastic measures are required to maintain what is left of Vietnam's unique biodiversity or soon it will be gone for ever. The critical state of Cat Tien National Park's biodiversity is just an example of a general trend in Vietnam.

Park management has put much effort into restricting human interference in accordance with Vietnamese law. Management responsibility within the national park is shared between the agency responsible for conserving biodiversity values (i.e. the national park) and agencies responsible for economic development (i.e. commune and district). This arrangement is an example of co-management in which authority is shared, on a basis embedded in law, between the responsible conservation authority and local communities. The agenda for management of the agricultural lands within the national park is geared towards economic development and the national park authorities have no say in this. On the ground, realities are therefore that within the national park there are areas in which conversion of forest into agricultural land is encouraged, access roads to these areas built, power lines erected and wildlife preying on crops eradicated while the national park authorities cannot intervene and are not even consulted. The realities of this co-management arrangement are that slowly forests are further degraded, human populations continue to grow within the national park and poaching cannot be controlled effectively. Experiencing the practical effect of this co-management arrangement does not leave much hope for the future of critically endangered biodiversity values in the national park.

Within the park's buffer zones the national park authorities have no management responsibility at all, and experience with buffer zone management in Vietnam shows that biodiversity values are ill protected in these zones (Gilmour and San 1999). Buffer zone management in this case is an illustration of a situation in which management objectives and responsibilities should be shared between those responsible for conservation and development, but in fact they are not; all management responsibility lies in the hands of communities whose only pursuit is economic development.

Regulations that apply to the national park's areas designated as forestland are clear, straightforward (i.e. resources from the national park cannot be removed), and are known to everybody in and around the park. But, as there are agricultural lands within the national park to which these regulations do not apply, it is extremely difficult to ensure that these are enforced. Forest guards encounter people with logs but cannot be sure whether those logs are taken illegally from the area designated as forestland or legally from the area designated as agricultural land. Forest guards cannot take measures against people who chase away and exterminate wildlife raiding their crops located in the national park on land designated as agricultural. In short, it is almost impossible to implement such a co-management arrangement without losing biodiversity values because controlling and checking complex co-management arrangements is understandably beyond the capacity of the park authorities.

The case of Cat Tien National Park and its buffer zones illustrates that co-management arrangements within the protected area leads to loss of biodiversity values and that there is no co-management arrangement in its buffer zones, again resulting in the loss of biodiversity values. Observing the critical state of the country's conservation achievements and the rapid growth of its human population, the way forward is to ensure that authority of the national park management within the protected area is strengthened and that civil administration in the buffer zones is shared with national park authorities. The issue here is that national park authorities should obtain a stake in the management of its buffer zones and a transfer of some responsibility has to be arranged from the civil administration (communes and districts) to the national park management. Maybe then buffer zones can make a significant contribution to the conservation of biological values of the national park.

AUTHOR'S NOTE

The views and opinions presented here are the author's personal ones and do not necessarily reflect the views and opinions of the WWF, the Cat Tien National Park Conservation Project or those of Cat Tien National Park.

REFERENCES

ANZDEC (1996) *Vietnam Biodiversity Conservation and Rural Development Project.* Project Proposal to the World Bank. Hanoi.

Atkins, R.A. and M. Tentij (1998) *The Orange-necked Partridge Arborophila davidi and five other galliforms in two protected areas in southern Vietnam.* Institute of Systematics and Population Biology, University of Amsterdam.

Bembrick, J. and Z. Cannon (1999) 'A Report on the Siamese Crocodile, *Crocodylus siamensis*, in Cat Tien National Park'. Unpublished Technical Report No. 1 to WWF. Cat Tien National Park Conservation Project.

Borrini-Feyerabend, G. (ed.) (1997) *Beyond Fences: Seeking Social Sustainability in Conservation.* Gland: IUCN.

Compton, J. (1998) *Borderline, A Report on Wildlife Trade in Vietnam.* Hanoi: WWF Indochina Programme.

Cox, R., J.W.F. Cools and A. Ebregt (1995) *Cat Tien National Park Conservation Project, Project Proposal.* FIPI, MoF, WWF. Hanoi.

Duckworth, J.W. and S. Hedges (1998) *Tracking Tigers, A Review of the Status of Tiger, Asian Elephant, Gaur and Banteng in Vietnam, Lao, Cambodia and Yunnan (China), with Recommendations for Future Conservation Action.* Hanoi: WWF Indochina Programme.

Geismann T., Nguyen Xuan Dang, N. Lormee and F. Momberg (2000) *Primate Conservation Status Review, Vietnam 2000. Part I Gibbons.* Hanoi: Fauna and Flora International, Indochina Programme.

Gilmour, D.A. (1998) 'Forest Management in a Changing World'. In J. Blaser, J. Carter and D. Gilmour (eds) *Biodiversity and Sustainable Use of Kyrgyzstan's Walnut Forest.* Gland: IUCN.

Gilmour, D.A. and Nguyen Van San (1999) *Buffer Zone Management in Vietnam.* Hanoi: IUCN.

Government of the Socialist Republic of Vietnam and Global Environment Facility Project VIE/91/G31 (1994) *Biodiversity Action Plan for Vietnam.* Hanoi.

International Council for Bird Preservation (1991) *Forest Bird Surveys in Vietnam 1991.* Study Report 51. Hanoi.

JICA/MARD (1996) *The Master Plan Study on Dong Nai River and Surrounding Basins.* Tokyo: Water Resources Development.

Lewis, C. (1996) *Managing Conflicts in Protected Areas.* Gland: IUCN.

Ling, S. (2000) 'A Survey of Wild Cattle and Other Mammals, Cat Tien National Park – Vietnam'. Unpublished Technical Report No. 14 to WWF. Cat Tien National Park Conservation Project.

Nadler, T., N. Lormee and F. Momberg (in press) *Primate Conservation Status Review Vietnam 2000. Part II Leaf Monkeys.* Hanoi: FFI Indochina Programme.

Oryx: the international journal of conservation (1999). 'Opinion' in Vol. 33 (1) January and Vol. 33 (4) October.

Polet, G. (2000) 'List of Reptiles and Amphibians in Cat Tien National Park'. Mimeo, WWF. Cat Tien National Park Conservation Project.

Polet, G. and Pham Huu Khanh (1999) *List of Birds of Cat Tien National Park*. Ho Chi Minh City Publishing House.

—— (2000) 'List of Mammals in Cat Tien National Park'. Mimeo, WWF. Cat Tien National Park Conservation Project.

Polet, G., Ton That Hung and Nguyen Quoc Thang (1999) 'Outline Plan for the Re-Introduction of Siamese Crocodile (*Crocodylus siamensis*) in Cat Tien National Park'. Mimeo, WWF. Cat Tien National Park Conservation Project.

Polet, G., Tran Van Mui, Nguyen Xuan Dang, Bui Huu Manh and Mike Baltzer (1999) 'The Javan Rhinoceros, *Rhinoceros sondaicus annamiticus*, of Cat Tien National Park, Vietnam: Current Status and Management Implications'. *Pachyderm* 27: 34–48.

Primack, R.B. (1993) *Essentials of Conservation Biology*. Sinderland, MA: Sinauer Associates Inc.

Robson, C.R., J.C. Eames, Nguyen Cu and Truong Van La (1993a) 'Further Recent Records of Birds from Viet Nam'. *Forktail* 8: 25–52.

—— (1993b) 'Birds recorded during the third BirdLife/Forest Birds Working Group expedition in Vietnam'. *Forktail* 9: 89–119.

Roe, D., J. Mayers, M. Grieg-Gran, A. Kothari and C. Fabricius (2000) *Evaluating Eden: Exploring the Myths and Realities of Community-Based Wildlife Management*. Evaluating Eden Series No. 8. London: IIED.

San, N.V. (2000) *Nhung Khia Canh Kinh Te – Xa Hoi Cua Cac Cong Dong Nai Cu Song Ttrong Vuon Quoc Gia Cat Tien (ban thao thu nhat)* [Socio-economic aspects of the communes in Cat Tien National Park (first draft)]. Technical Report to WWF. Cat Tien National Park Conservation Project.

Sayer, J. (1991) *Rainforest Buffer Zones: Guidelines for Protected Area Managers*. Gland: IUCN.

Spinage, C. (1998) 'Social Change and Conservation Misrepresentation in Africa'. In *Oryx* 32 (4): 265–276.

Trai, L.T., W.J. Richardson, Bui Dac Tuyen, Le Van Cham, Nguyen Huy Dung, Ha Van Hoach, A.L. Monastirskii and J.C. Eames (1999) *An Investment Plan for Ngoc Linh Nature Reserve, Kon Tum Province, Vietnam: A Contribution to the Management Plan*. Hanoi: BirdLife International Vietnam Programme.

Vy, N.T., Nguyen Hoang Hao, Le Van Tinh and Tran Dinh Hung (2000) *Su Phan Bo Cua 7 Loai Chim Tri O Vuon Quoc Gia Cat Tien – Viet Nam* [Distribution of seven species of *Phasianidae* in Cat Tien National Park, Vietnam]. Technical Report No. 20 to WWF. Cat Tien National Park Conservation Project.

Wells, P. (1999) 'Rapid Assessment of Law Enforcement and park Protection in the Cat Tien National Park – Vietnam'. Unpublished Technical Report No. 9 to WWF. Cat Tien National Park Conservation Project.

CHAPTER THREE

Pala'wan Managing Their Forest
(Palawan Island, the Philippines)

MARIEKE HOBBES

It is raining cats and dogs in the tropical rainforest in south Palawan, the Philippines. About 30 men and women are soaked to the skin and all the children are shivering with cold. To kill time, waiting for the new cargo of rattan seedlings to arrive, some guys are swinging on lianas. I am the only non-Pala'wan around and moreover crawling on all fours attempting to plant: first select a place between the old trees, then dig a hole with a knife and plant a seedling spacing plants a meter apart as taught. Or more efficiently, one person digs the holes while another follows with the seedlings. It will probably take the whole day before one of the leaders, Bernas Likos, will have transferred all the 3,000 rattan seedlings from the community nursery to the planting site with help from his carabao and before the others will have planted them on the very steep degraded slopes along the river bank of the Agas creek in sitio *Saray.*

W hy are these people making such a great effort to plant trees? They are not forced to plant trees, nor will they receive money for it. Taking a closer look at the tree-planting endeavour, it appears that the people are stimulated by a project. The project also aims to establish co-management between these Pala'wan indigenous people and the local government. In the context of the discussion about co-management, this chapter will explore the rationale behind the process of change towards forest management and conservation of this Pala'wan community in the uplands on southern Palawan Island in the Philippines. The outcomes of the case study will be analysed and linked with Ostrom's (1990) eight design principles for successful common property management, supplemented with some key issues that Pomeroy *et al.* (Chapter 13) identify for successful co-management, and with a behavioural approach to the rational choice theory of collective action (Ostrom 1998).

INTRODUCTION ON CO-MANAGEMENT

Based on the insight that both local people and the global community have justifiable interests in and visions about the future of the rainforests, co-management of the rainforests is considered world-wide as the solution for socio-economic development and sustainable resource management. The concept of co-management, the sharing of responsibilities and benefits of the management of natural resources between the government and individual or collective users, may be regarded as the result of the application of the participatory development approach in the field of local use and management of resources.

For decades, environmental policy has been dominated by a centrally determined, top-down approach in favour of commercial logging in the Philippines (Kummer 1992; Broad and Cavanagh 1993). Local communities were merely blamed for forest destruction by practising slash and burn farming and illegal logging (ibid.). However, nowadays the Philippines have comparably progressive environmental policies, as is reflected in the development of the Philippines' Agenda 21 in response to the Rio Conference, and the National Integrated Protected Areas System law of 1992 funded by the European Union. Both laws have the twin objective of biodiversity conservation and socio-economic development. Devolution of decision-making power of forestry projects to local government units (provinces, cities, municipalities and *barangays*) is embodied in the Local Government Code of 1991 (Republic Act 7160), and various land allocation approaches are being adapted. The rationale is that decision-making power and responsibilities recognizing political and administrative realities should be entrusted to the local population. In addition, the people should have an important share in the benefits of their efforts. In line with this, the local forms of organization and management should be used to maintain and develop natural resources and effectively control the practice of desirable behavioural changes. Futhermore, the Indigenous Peoples' Rights Act was enacted in 1997 its primary objective being to recognize, protect, and promote the rights of indigenous cultural communities and to put an end to their dispossession and displacement.

PALAWAN ISLAND

Palawan's people and natural resources
Of the 7,100 islands comprising the Philippine archipelago, about 1,768 are part of the administrative region of Palawan (Figure 3.1). Mainland Palawan is long and narrow, extending 425 km from north-east to south-west. It varies in width from over 40 km at its widest point to 8.5 km at its narrowest. A mountainous

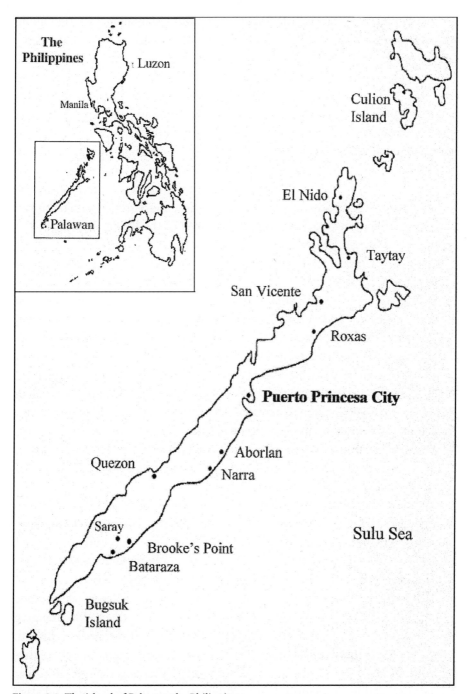

Figure 3.1: The island of Palawan, the Philippines

spine, reaching 2,086 m at the highest point of Mount Mantalingahan, runs along almost the whole length of the island. Because of the narrowness of the island, the slopes of the mountain range are generally steep and river courses short.

Palawan is often called the Philippines' last ecological frontier (Broad and Cavanagh 1993; Dumagat 1996; Eder and Fernandez 1996; Sandalo 1996). This is also recognized by the international community, Palawan being part of Unesco's international network of Biosphere Reserves since 1990 (for example Sandalo 1996). Many of Palawan's rich natural resources are still relatively intact. Forty per cent of the country's coral reefs are found in Palawan and the in-shore coastal marine waters are considered the richest fishing grounds of the Philippines. Additionally, the province still possesses the largest intact area of mangrove and the largest continuous tract of tropical rainforest of the Philippines (Eder and Fernandez 1996; Sandalo 1996).

At the beginning of the twentieth century, more than 90 per cent of the total land area was forested, but current estimates show a reduction to about 50 to 60 per cent (Eder and Fernandez 1996). Although many of the forests on the steeper slopes and at high altitudes remain intact, migrant lowlanders have cleared many of those in the plains and lower hills for logging, agriculture and mining. The immigration of these mostly landless farmers from all parts of the country induced an exceptional population growth. The population of Palawan exceeded 600,000 persons in 1994 while estimates show 35,369 in 1903, 106,269 in 1948 and 162,669 in 1960 (National Statistics Office 1990; Eder and Fernandez 1996). The immigrants encroached on indigenous lands, a process which intensified in the 1970s with the arrival of large logging and mining corporations (Ocampo 1996). The population ratio of indigenous cultural communities *vis-à-vis* other groups of Palawan has deteriorated from roughly 20 per cent in 1948 to 10 per cent in 1990 (Dumagat 1996). The indigenous population can be divided into three principal ethnic groups: the Pala'wan,[1] inhabiting the southern mountains, the Batak in the northern central part of the island; and the Tagbanua, who live along the riverbanks and valleys of the central mountains (Eder and Fernandez 1996). In 1990, the Pala'wan population was 39,421, the Tagbanua 7,106 and the Batak 269 (National Statistics Office, 1990). They all have a heterogeneous mode of livelihood, mainly centred on swidden cultivation that, due to the changing social, economic and natural environment, has become unsustainable (Brown, 1996). As a result, the principal causes of forest destruction in Palawan are extensive commercial and illegal logging, combined with an increasing population that extends demand for agricultural and residential lands on the forests, and slash and burn farming (Dumagat 1996; Eder and Fernandez 1996; Sandalo 1996).

Forest clearance combined with fierce rainfall, short river courses and run-off slopes with steep gradients lead to an increase in topsoil run-off. Soil removal and gullied relief destroy the upland forest-bearing capacity and agricultural potential. Flash floods have devastated hundreds of hectares of agricultural land in the southern part of Palawan. The rapid run-off makes irrigation for lowland farmers impossible and it also threatens drinking water systems. Silt from the denuded mountains is flowing down rivers into the sea, smothering coral reefs and thus depleting fish resources. Dynamite and cyanide fishing methods, over-fishing and clearance of large areas of mangrove forests to various ends, such as fish industry expansion and settlement, have likewise contributed to the depletion and destruction of the coastal and marine areas (Broad and Cavanagh 1993; Sandalo 1996). Competition to control and exploit or, more recently, to preserve resources has increased and currently dominates government development planning and the everyday lives of the island's inhabitants (Eder and Fernandez 1996).

Palawan's environmental policies
To guard its title as the country's last ecological frontier, the province of Palawan has obtained a prototype status in environmental policies within the Philippines. The provincial policies to attain the twin objectives of environmental protection and socio-economic development have been developed step by step, starting in 1979 with the initiation of the Palawan Integrated Area Development Programme. The Asian Development Bank supported it and the European Union provided assistance for the environment component. Taking into account the positive and negative experiences of this programme, the Strategic Environmental Plan for Palawan Act (Republic Act 7611) was enacted in 1992. Although of provincial application, the law is parallel to the National Integrated Protected Areas System law of 1992 that covers eight protected areas, three of which are found in Palawan. Although slash and burn farming has been prohibited nation-wide since 1904, in 1994, the city government of Puerto Princesa City (the capital of Palawan province) actually enforced this ban, together with the ban on logging.

The Strategic Environmental Plan for Palawan Act is a pioneering piece of legislation, declaring that it is national policy to safeguard, develop and conserve the country's natural resources by supporting the implementation of environmental plans, programmes and projects. It provides a framework for sustainable development of Palawan by adopting the Environmentally Critical Areas Network strategy that provides zoning of the province with different levels of protection, i.e. allowable human activities, and management schemes. The Palawan Council for Sustainable Development was established to implement the law. In turn, the

Palawan Tropical Forestry Protection Programme was brought into existence as a special programme of the Palawan Council for Sustainable Development to facilitate the implementation of the law, again co-financed by the European Union for seven years (until December 2002). This programme has two main objectives: it aims to establish genuine co-management between the local communities and local government units, and it intends to initiate internalization and self-mobilization for resource management at the local community' level. The programme has a top-down character, aiming to implement the Strategic Environmental Plan with the prescribed rules and regulations of the Environmentally Critical Areas Network strategy. It also works with fixed priorities and includes domains such as relief, women, literacy and environmental conservation in a programme funded by the European Union. At the local level the programme adopts a people-orientated approach with a community-based participatory rhetoric, by which the general rules and regulations prescribed at a higher level are adapted to the social and environmental reality.

IMPLEMENTATION OF CO-MANAGEMENT IN SOUTHERN PALAWAN

Initiating co-management with the local government

In southern Palawan, the Palawan Tropical Forestry Protection Programme lobbied and assisted the local government units of the five municipalities to agree upon the establishment of the Mount Mantalingahan Protected Area. Bataraza is one of the five municipalities where the programme and the local government have agreed to establish catchment management zones and plans and selected Inogbong as the priority catchment area. The case study concerns the indigenous Pala'wan community of Saray on the east side of Mount Mantalingahan in *barangay* Inogbong in the Bataraza municipality. Out of the municipality's population of 29,242 in 1990, about 25 per cent consists of indigenous Pala'wan, while the rest are Christian and Muslim immigrants (both about the same percentage) (National Statistics Office, 1990).

The municipal government has hardly visited the upper Inogbong catchment area. The Palawan Tropical Forestry Protection Programme has taken up the role as advocate for and representative of the indigenous people to the local government. Thus the programme acts as facilitator of communications between the Pala'wan and local government staff. The programme explains to the local Pala'wan leaders what their legal rights are and tries to press government staff to assist and co-operate with the local communities. In addition, the programme gives impetus to negotiations and tries to put the Pala'wan in a positive light by organizing and financing festivities for the local communities. However, the invited local government representatives rarely show up. Whereas the indigenous people of Inogbong are positively approached at *barangay* level, they are not viewed as equal partners with the municipality's government. On the contrary, they are rather stigmatized as simple upland dwellers and blamed for destroying the forest but becoming a little bit more knowledgeable through education these days. One government official stated while others endorsed: 'The tribal people are the only cause of deforestation, but, thanks to the programme, they have learned and are aware now that they should protect the forest instead of burning it.' The municipality's government also regards the programme as a pedantic organization wasting huge amounts of money. It accuses the programme of imposing its ideas and plans while not keeping its promises. After substantial arguments arose, the municipal government submitted a resolution to withdraw all commitments to the programme. However, according to one government official the municipality has no environmental budget to take responsibility for the development and the implementation of environmental programmes as ordered in the Local Government Code of 1991 and the Strategic Environmental Plan because of 'politics' (money and votes). This argument is underlined by members of the programme and the Palawan Council of Sustainable Development in Bataraza. Without co-operation from the municipality's government, the programme has started to implement the law together with the upland indigenous communities and has initiated community-based resource management in the Inogbong catchment.

Initiating community-based resource management with the Pala'wan

The Palawan Tropical Forestry Protection Programme in Bataraza started in the Pala'wan community of Saray in the Inogbong catchment, because it is relatively easily accessible and the biggest of the ten upland communities. Successful projects from Saray were later replicated and adapted in the other nine communities. To reach Saray, located at 200–300 m elevation, one has to hike along a trail for 3–4 km from the highway in *barangay* Inogbong. After about half an hour's walk through the lowlands, mainly consisting of shrubs and grasses, the trail starts to rise entering the hilly plains of the mountains. The area is highly degraded and nearly devoid of primary forest. The landscape is characterized by some second-growth forests, grasslands and shrublands. Saray consists of 52 households divided over nine hamlets, of which the furthest is about a two-hour hike from the centre. The hamlets are on different hills of Mount Mantaling-ahan with slopes ranging from 8 per cent to more than 40 per cent.

The province's Environmentally Critical Areas Network strategy has divided the area of Saray into two zones, a restricted use zone and a traditional use zone. Both are part of a buffer zone. The management schemes for these zones prescribe that 'limited and non-consumptive activities may be allowed' in the restricted use area, and 'where traditional landuse is already stabilized or is being stabilized' in the traditional use zone (Republic Act 7611). Stabilization of traditional landuse actually seems to imply the introduction of a sedentary way of farming: now the people are not allowed to open new agricultural fields in the forests anymore. To protect the forest, the Pala'wan have to change their normal behaviour of slash and burn farming and stop changing fields as they used to do. Instead, an agricultural transition is required, because the Pala'wan have to stay at a place, which requires different farming techniques. They are also encouraged to limit or refrain from other subsistence activities, because the law prohibits the felling of (big) trees and protects some bird and wildlife species as well.

To assist the community in implementing the law, the Palawan Tropical Forestry Protection Programme took the only possible entry point any organization could have taken to have a chance of becoming acquainted with the Pala'wan of Saray, namely via *panglima* Purekto Sugaan. He is the elected local leader, who enjoys respect within the community. He resides in the village centre, in the biggest of the nine hamlets. Pala'wan society is characterized by a high level of group cohesion, shared norms of behaviour and the absence of hierarchy. The *panglima* is an expert in customary law and mediates in local conflicts. In order to maintain the balance of the society the people follow a moral code built on sharing and mutual help. There are respectful, polite relationships between youngsters and elders and physical and verbal violence is avoided. The people seem to know what they can expect from each other, trust each other and meet regularly.[2] Some people were afraid that they would not be allowed to harvest the trees they were to plant outside their fields. They did not fear that their fellow Pala'wan would harvest the trees, but that the programme or other outsiders would. Indeed, the Pala'wan have their own ways of governing access to resources.[3] The private fields, for example, or the Almaciga trees (*Agathis dammara*) that grow in virgin forest of more than 800 m elevation and are used for tapping resin, are in 'possession' of the man who looks after them. Residence and land use show a complicated picture, because the Pala'wan household composition is based on a matrilocal residence pattern. Inheritance of land is paternal and borrowing land from kin is common. Although some

Pala'wan of Saray possess an official stewardship contract,[4] official tenure arrangements seem to be of no use. Everyone knows which field belongs to whom, whether officially or unofficially, and respects the owner's rights.

However, the Pala'wan of Saray hardly ever trust outsiders and regard them as intruders. Though Pala'wan are not likely to show this openly, they have an aversion to people imposing ideas and interfering with their life. No patronizing, but respectful treatment, keeping one's word and showing consideration for other peoples' way of living is what they want. As long as the Pala'wan can remember they have been in contact with non-Pala'wan, have worked for the lowlanders and have traded products, but they always go back to their own community in the mountains. However, the Pala'wan of Inogbong upper catchment have had hardly any confrontation with other organizations or projects before that could have caused negative experiences and, in turn, possible repercussions that could have an impact on subsequent organizations.

The programme focused on the development of a core group of leaders in the uplands of Inogbong. These were *panglima* Purekto Sugaan, three other people from Saray who have always been active members in the community and two *panglimas* from other upland communities. The leaders have attended many leadership courses and cross-field visits. The courses focused on the establishment of a continuous dialogue between the leaders and the programme to identify problems and, subsequently, find solutions. It was *panglima* Purekto Sugaan of Saray (and later on the other *panglimas* of Inogbong upper catchment) who agreed to the programme implementing a controlled burning bonus scheme and the establishment of a protected area, at first using material incentives. The programme offered some micro projects and stimulated the people to participate in community tree-planting activities with the 'plant a tree, own a radio' project. In addition, according to the Pala'wan, their area was protected from lowlanders when a *barangay* ordinance was enacted with help from the programme. The lowlanders used to practise illegal logging and to burn the forests to hunt in the uplands. The upland development leaders mobilized and motivated others to take action, by setting an example to follow, and they played an active and substantial role in the implementation and monitoring of projects. The leaders have the legal competence to go to the *barangay* captain to report violators of the new rules, but it seems like they would not dream of betraying their fellow Pala'wan. However, everyone obeys the new rules because they are prescribed by *panglima* Purekto Sugaan in deliberation with the other leaders. This way, the leaders have obtained more power in the community.

THE PERFORMANCE OF PALA'WAN IN NATURAL RESOURCE MANAGEMENT

Although they live close to the margin of survival, the people are proud to be Pala'wan upland subsistence farmers and are always busy with their work. They would like to have a better livelihood that is dependent on their immediate surroundings. Nobody would even dream about leaving the uplands, not even if the possibility presented itself to become rich in the lowlands.[5] Some would like to make and sell more handicrafts and agricultural products as an additional income, but none wants to be totally dependent on a money income. Living in the uplands together with their fellow Pala'wan is what people favour. The ideal for the Pala'wan is to live like the older people used to live, in such a way that the (rice) yields are sufficient and that the forests will provide enough products and game. Stories are told about a mythical past when the natural world was so fruitful that the animals presented themselves voluntarily and that people were buried in the abundance of rice in a *lagkau* (a solid granary), currently empty most of the time.

Nonetheless, these days most people of Saray do not stand around and wait for Ampo, the deity in Pala'wan religion, to help. Instead, a more active attitude and innovative behaviour towards environmental management of the forests and of the private fields is shown to achieve these objectives. Indeed, the field team of the Palawan Tropical Forestry Protection Programme has spent much time with the Pala'wan of Inogbong catchment, especially in Saray. In doing so, both parties have become acquainted with one another and for the Pala'wan the ideas and approaches of the programme have become evident. The regular contacts, seminars, personal visits in the field and living with the Pala'wan must have removed considerable distrust. It appears that the Pala'wan and members of the programme's field team have co-operated intensively with each other and almost all of the Pala'wan I spoke with were very enthusiastic about the programme. However, a social division has appeared, because about a third of the households living in clusters further away from the centre of Saray, and thus closer to the restricted use area of the Environmentally Critical Areas Network strategy, do not want to participate. They regard the people of the programme as intruders who will take away their land. Gossip says that the participating Pala'wan have already converted from their own religion to Christianity by wearing Christian clothes, working with the programme and listening to the Christian radio. The leaders say that the resisting group refuses to believe in what the leaders or the programme tell them about the environment. The leaders would like to see all the Pala'wan as winners, but in line with the Pala'wan mode of conduct both parties just leave each other to themselves. This way, a small group broke with the rest of the Pala'wan society of Saray, meaning that further disagreements are avoided. The resisting group does obey the new rules out of fear for punishment, but has more difficulty in meeting their needs than the actively participating group. To interpret the Pala'wan perception of the environment, it is helpful to understand the way the Pala'wan use and approach their different resources, the forests and the personal fields.

Private fields

The swidden fields are in private ownership and cover between 2 and 3 hectares but do not bring enough yields for subsistence. The Pala'wan traditionally utilized the forests for low-intensity slash and burn farming, meaning that rainforest fields used to be cleared with fire to produce ash to serve as fertilizer. The fields were cultivated for a short period, succeeded by a fallow period lasting up to a generation. By giving the natural vegetation a chance to regenerate, it is possible for the soil to gain its fertility. However, opening new lands in the forests is strictly forbidden by law and not practised anymore these days. Instead, the Pala'wan only clear the bushlands or cogon grasslands that have grown during the fallow period. The heavy sod of the bush and grasslands and the poor, stony soils make it difficult to practise agriculture. Normally, the fields are cleared (by example cutting bushes, felling trees) in January and February to be burned in March and prepared and planted in April. Half a hectare is usually planted with traditional upland rice intercropped with cassava and/or (native yellow) corn. Until the regrowth of grasses and other vegetation makes it necessary to open up a new field, the old field is left fallow for three to five years, which is actually not enough to restore the soil fertility. However, from 1997 to 1999, the El Niño and La Niña climatic phenomena resulted in unpredictably long dry summers and short wet seasons that have played a significant role in the harvests according to the Pala'wan.

Another reason for the low harvests is that pests, like rats and birds, attack the rice and affect the roots. As a cure, the Pala'wan employ traditional medicines and some religious rituals to their fields. They have learned these practices from their grandfathers, but everyone told me that nowadays these methods are not very successful. In line with this, the Pala'wan also referred to Ampo in the hope for a better rice harvest next year. During the yearly rice harvest ceremony, the *panglima* communicates with the deity Ampo and a share of the harvest is steamed in bamboo sticks. This is then divided among relatives. The ritual aims at maintaining a reciprocity relation with Ampo and between the Pala'wan themselves. Rice is supposed to be the staple crop to be eaten three times a day.

This year, the single rice harvest provided none of the households with enough for subsistence.

The people who actively participate in the programme said that they have been planting more trees and since the Palawan Tropical Forestry Protection Programme began, although everyone already had some fruit trees. The leaders attended cross-field visits showing them new techniques and species, applied them themselves and extended the information to the rest of the community. The programme provided several kinds of seedlings and taught how to take better care of the trees. In addition, community nurseries have been established to provide a continuous source of seedlings. Apart from planting more trees, the participants have applied other agricultural innovations to their own fields. Some are endeavouring new crops provided by the programme or receive seeds from other Pala'wan. They are enthusiastic about the knowledge they have acquired from the programme to take better care of their fields: i.e. new clearing, planting and harvesting techniques; the use of organic fertilizers and planting more diverse crops. Because of this, they achieve better subsistence farming outcomes and more independence from the lowlanders for their income.

The forests
Next to agricultural activities, people of Saray use the forest for extra food, medicines and non-timber forest products to sell at the markets in the lowlands. These days, there is not much forest left and the animals have disappeared as well. Only some men, who have handmade airguns, still hunt for wild chickens or wild cats. A blowgun (*sopok*) is used to shoot birds by piercing. The people hardly hunt for wild pigs anymore; instead the forest is full of pig-traps. While hunting has lately not been a prosperous activity anyway, the law also forbids the hunting of certain protected species. Other seasonal forest products like snails, mushrooms, honey, various fruits and vegetables are gathered for consumption. Some forest products are collected to sell at the market such as rattan, orchids, bamboo and a resin from Almaciga trees. The men also haul small timber products from the forest for house building materials and handicrafts.

In addition to their practical use, the forests are perceived as a spiritual world. The forests are owned by Ampo and home to uncountable invisible beings who can be do-gooders, but who can also be harmful to humans. Only some Pala'wan can see these beings and communicate with them. Many rituals and religious rules exist concerning the use of the forest and its products, with the aim of making the spirits more kindly disposed toward the people. For instance, newly built houses are 'de-ghosted' with offers and prayers because bad sprits can still be residing in the wood of the house. Also traditional medicine consists of offerings and prayers by specialists to make the spirits well disposed. If the rules are disregarded, the spirits cause sickness and doom.

These practices demonstrate that the Pala'wan do not perceive the forest as an entity on its own with its own intrinsic rights, as it is actually acclaimed by the national and provincial laws.[6] In line with this, the term sustainability, if present at all, must have a different meaning for the Pala'wan than for the Palawan Tropical Forestry Protection Programme. Although the ideological conceptions of nature may differ, the time perspective of the Pala'wan results in almost the same perspective towards the overall policy that explicitly addresses the conservation of nature for the present and the unspecified future generations of Palawan Province. Whereas the Pala'wan are inclined to invest in their own fields, it appeared that the harvesting rights for trees that people plant outside personal fields are not clear to the people who do not co-operate with the programme. There is no fear that their fellow Pala'wan would harvest the trees, but some people think that the trees will still be owned by the programme. However, everyone says that they are willing to protect the remaining forests and to participate in community tree-planting activities for the Pala'wan community. Yet, only the people who co-operate with the programme actually participate in the planting activities arranged by the leaders. Observance of the results of their management activities and environmental awareness programmes have made people aware of other environmental benefits, namely prevention of local climatic changes, landslides, erosion and soil fertility, which all affect their agricultural practices as well. In addition, along with conserving the remaining forests, the Pala'wan are protecting the world of their ancestors. Although the poor economic circumstances make it hard for the Pala'wan to meet their basic needs and difficult to invest in long-term objectives for the community as a whole, several community tree-planting activities have taken place, at selected places along the riverbank and close to the forest frontier. The people look after the trees they planted and they are planning to plant more. The Pala'wan ideal is that the forest including all its animals will come back, by which means they will become rich again.

ISSUES REGARDING THE SUCCESS IN ENVIRONMENTAL MANAGEMENT AMONG THE PALA'WAN

The community tree-planting activity has indeed heralded a process of change towards forest management and conservation in an indigenous Pala'wan community in the uplands on southern Palawan island. The question arises as to which requirements appear to be necessary for co-management to function of among the Pala'wan of Saray. The point of departure for investigation will be Ostrom's (1990) eight design principles for so-called robust, long lasting common pool resources at the local level, supplemented with a behavioural approach to the rational choice theory of collective action (Ostrom 1998). Whereas the first six design principles are local requirements, the last two refer to external institutional conditions (see Table 3.1).

Table 3.1: Design principles identified by Ostrom (1990) for long-lasting common pool resource institutions

---
1. Clearly defined boundaries and membership

2. Congruence between appropriation and provision rules and local conditions

3. Collective-choice arrangements

4. Monitoring

5. Graduated sanctions

6. Conflict resolution mechanisms

7. Minimal recognition of rights to organize

8. Nested enterprises

Nevertheless, in this case study, the outside world plays a significant role, as it is concerned with a form of co-management. Two parties other than the local people are actively involved: the local government and a provincial environmental programme. Therefore, several of Pomeroy and others (see this volume Chapter 13) 28 general key issues for successful co-management will be addressed as well. The difficulty with these issues is that 'none of these conditions exist in isolation, but each supports and links to another to make a complex process and arrangements for co-management to work' (Pomeroy *et al.* Chapter 13 this book). Indeed, the complexity of the interrelation and overlap between the key issues at different levels, the relevance of the specific national and local contexts and even contra-dicting principles actually lead to an unclear overview of key issues. For example, the first principle concerns individual incentive structure, inducing various individuals to participate, which actually covers all other aspects for successful co-management. Nonetheless, I will address some issues that appear to be significant for the co-management process in this specific case study.

Internal requirements

This case study shows that Ostrom's (1990) first requirement of clearly defined boundaries and membership (see Table 3.1) forms an important incentive for people to invest in resource management activities. The Pala'wan are much inclined to invest in private fields whether they are in possession of official tenure rights or not. There, the Pala'wan have planted fruit trees and have experimented with agricultural innovations, because they assume that they, their children, or other relatives will harvest the fruit as economic and nutritional benefits. Indeed, the Pala'wan have a notion of land ownership concerning private fields, but have their own ways of governing access to private as well as common land and resources. The Pala'wan show less willingness to invest in areas outside their own field, although they participate in community planting activities for the future of the community. Here, an ordinance has resulted in the creation of tenure security by excluding the claims of lowlanders on the forests for logging and hunting. This can be considered as an investment security for the Pala'wan. However, general preconditions of acknowledgement of the legitimacy of private or community land tenure as an incentive for environmental management turn out to be of no effect in this case study. Rather, they show, in line with Malayang's (1991) claim, that tenure security is an important incentive that may be created by exclusion without official tenure rights.

In spite of the investment security, the economic resources of the Pala'wan of Saray are almost zero, which means that they do not have much scope for investments. The Palawan Tropical Forestry Protection Programme seeks to motivate the people towards environmentally friendly activities that at the same time increase their economic resources, in terms of money or food earned from trade of agricultural products and handicrafts. In first instance, the programme provided direct material incentives for participating that can be regarded as a welcome introduction. The rules concerning the forest, resulting from the zoning management scheme, are prescribed by the law, and thus not developed within the local community. Further, the controlled burning rules have been imposed by the people's leader in consultation with the programme and the community and are enforced at *barangay* level. Consequently, the imposed rules that limit or forbid the use of the forest do not show much congruence with local conditions (principle 2 in Table 3.1). The rules relating to fire and the voluntary tree-planting activities show a higher degree of congruence, but the people cannot participate in modifying any of the rules (principle 3).

However, everyone intends to maintain the management rules. All the Pala'wan of Saray have noticed a decline in the forest cover, including its availability of products, and want the forest to return. Next to the economic benefits, people have observed positive environmental effects resulting from compliance with the rules and community tree-planting activities. This stimulates them to continue without requiring material incentives, but they also fear the severe punishment that may follow when one of the upland development leaders, who can officially report violators, sees them breaking the rules. Still, it is not likely that the leaders will betray their fellow Pala'wan. Instead, this example shows that this condition helps to make people wary, but that the internal organization of the community provides a more decisive incentive for compliance. Compliance with the rules is also a matter of social control among the Pala'wan. Thus, Ostrom's principle of monitoring of people's compliance with the management rules is addressed (principle 4), but since sanctioning has not yet been applied, there can be no exact information about graduated sanctions (principle 5). Nevertheless, conflict resolution mechanisms (principle 6) have traditionally been arranged very well.

Indeed, the local organization seems to provide convincing impetus for participating in collective action. Ostrom's (1998) behavioural theory of boundedly rational and moral behaviour addresses this issue. The basic idea is that people act 'better than rational' as a result of the expectations individuals have about others' behaviour (trust), the norms that individuals learn from socialization and life experiences (reciprocity), and the identities that individuals create, projecting their intentions and norms (reputation). Levels of trust, reciprocity and reputation are positively reinforcing (Ostrom 1998). This case study shows several resources embedded in social relations that seem to affect these core relationships. As has been described, the community of Saray is characterized by socio-economic and cultural homogeneity, marked by shared norms of behaviour, shared interests concerning the environment (forest), agricultural and economic activities, and maintenance of regular communications. The decision-making structure of the society has always relied on the elected local leader and kin-group decision-making. Nevertheless, substantial disagreements have arisen between members of the community, by which a third of the households in hamlets at higher elevation keep aloof from the rest and do not participate in community planting activities or adopt agricultural innovations, although they comply with the imposed rules.

External requirements
Prosperous co-management not only requires trust among the participants of collective action at local level but also among the different parties (see Pomeroy *et al.* this volume Chapter 13). Whereas trust is prevalent among the Pala'wan themselves, they have a low level of trust with regards to outsiders. For the development of partnership and trust between the Palawan Tropical Forestry Protection Programme and the Pala'wan in Bataraza, meeting mutually agreed

objectives and methods of communication, co-ordination and consultation would seem to be imperative.

To attain the goal of forest protection the programme requires self-mobilization and self-reliance from the Pala'wan communities in Inogbong catchment, starting in Saray. It sought to connect with the existing social and cultural institutions and structures in Pala'wan society via the *panglima*, who is respected by his community. Although the whole community has been involved, the programme has specifically focused on the *panglimas* and the development of a core group of leaders so that no dependence is created on one single person or the programme's leaders. The leadership training aimed at developing responsibility among a variety of individuals for environmental management processes by providing an example and setting out courses of action for others to follow. This endorses Pomeroy and others. (in press) view of the need for appropriate local leadership for success in co-management. The programme itself has played a catalytic role in the development process as an external agent having a only temporary relationship with the co-management process.

The Palawan Tropical Forestry Programme cannot be regarded as objective; it is a special programme of the government to assist the implementation of the Local Government Code of 1991 and specifically the Strategic Plan for Palawan Act that adopts management schemes and zoning of the province. Nevertheless, the enabling policies and legislation have created a supportive environment for co-management to prosper that, returning to Ostrom's (1990) eight design principles, meets principle 7: recognition of rights to organize. Yet, in this particular case study struggles have arisen between the programme and the local government. The programme seems to have assumed the role of advocate for the indigenous people in relation to the local government (and vice versa) to implement the law. The Pala'wan have thus already implemented new rules that have not yet been officially enforced. This implies that this case does not meet Ostrom's principle 8 that states that management institutions are organized in multiple layers of nested enterprises, since the local government has not taken up its prescribed active role and responsibility in the development and the implementation of environmental programmes. However, this case shows that this does not seem to be necessary for effective implementation of regulations and the initiation of community-based resource management processes. Indeed, several other key issues internal to the Pala'wan community and between the community and the programme have been identified in the process of change towards forest management and conservation.

CONCLUSION

In the context of the effects of co-management policies on local conditions, this chapter has examined the rationale behind the process of change towards forest management and conservation among a Pala'wan community. What lessons are to be learned from the aforementioned issues regarding general internal and external requirements for the successes made so far in environmental management among the Pala'wan? A general point is that the enabling policies and legislation in the Philippines and in Palawan specifically have created a supportive environment for co-management to prosper but the government's only role in this case has been to officially exclude the area to non-Pala'wan. In this way, the homogeneity of the society is confirmed and customary law is allowed to address the system of rights to resources among the Pala'wan. This case demonstrates that a party other than the government has been the driving force behind the initiation of a process towards local resource management in which the notion of the importance of trust between the different parties involved for successful co-management is supported. This leads to the main conclusion one can draw from this case study, namely that it supports Ostrom's (1990) institutional approach for sustainable and durable management of common property resources as well as Ostrom's (1998) behavioural theory of boundedly rational and moral behaviour. Although all the Pala'wan of Saray have roughly corresponding interests, a small group broke with the main group but the main group is an almost perfect example of a cohesive organization forming a permissive institutional environment for collective action to prosper.

NOTES

1   The Ken-ey and the Tau't Batu are included, although some people say that they represent distinct ethnolinguistic groups, while according to others they represent a cultural variation among the Pala'wan (Eder and Fernandez 1996).

2   Roquia (1998), based on Fer (1985), explicates these unique characteristics of social and political organization among Pala'wan society in general and states, for example, that the Pala'wan cannot defend themselves against outsiders for they have no institutional means of organizing violence but only know how to avoid it, at which they are exemplary, but remain extremely vulnerable. Brown (1996) notes that Pala'wan relations with early settlers were mostly amicable but that the Pala'wan shied away from them. She also states that in the course of social, economic and political displacement, the Pala'wan have demonstrated remarkable cultural resilience; they still grant importance to the headman of each hamlet, to elders and shamans for intra-Pala'wan dispute settlement and to ceremonies and kin-group decision-making (Brown 1996).

3   Especially reference to outside areas, Novellino's claim about the cultural notion of landownership seems to be at stake (1998b). He states that the Western notion of land tenure implies utilitarian criteria of human action and thus might not represent epistemologically valid concepts for indigenous societies as he concluded regarding the Batak of Palawan that have their own ways of governing access to land and resources (Novellino 1998b).

4   The former mayor of Bataraza arranged these privately granted, renewable, 25-year Certificate of Stewardship Contracts that date back to the 1980s. In line with the current community-based forestry programmes, the Pala'wan can obtain a Certified Ancestral Domain Claim, by which the rights of the indigenous communities to their ancestral domains are recognized, protected and promoted.

5   Brown (1996) also notes that most Pala'wan she spoke with were very articulate about their pride in being Pala'wan and in wanting to find ways to make Pala'wan lifestyles economically and socially feasible in today's world.

6   Brown (1996) notes that the Pala'wan respected the domains of their ancestral spirits that are not viewed as forests reserves in the Western sense. This Pala'wan view seems to correspond to others among indigenous peoples groups in Southeast Asia. Dove (1998), for example, distinguishes spatial and temporal dimensions of sustainability. The indigenous environmental representation of the Kantu' of West Kalimantan emphasizes the nature of the relationship between society and environment, i.e. it is not based on the separation but on the unity of culture and nature. The same argument is stressed by Novellino with reference to the Batak of Palawan (1998a and 1998b). According to him, the Batak do not regard the physical reduction of resources as important as the deterioration of their 'social' relationship with the environment as a whole, including reference to themselves, to their ancestors, to the 'Masters of game animals' and to their historical mythological past (Novellino 1998b). In line with this, Schefold concluded for local people on the island of Siberut (West Sumatra, Indonesia) that the environment is not a wilderness full of endemic species, but a 'world beyond' – the domain of the ancestors, who require certain modes of conduct (cited in Persoon and Van Est 2000).

REFERENCES

Broad, R. and J. Cavanagh (1993) *Plundering Paradise. The struggle for the environment in the Philippines*. Berkeley and Los Angeles: University of California Press.

Brown, E.C. (1996) 'Tribal displacement, deculturation and impoverishment'. In J.F. Eder and J.O. Fernandez (eds), *Palawan at the Crossroads. Development and the Environment on a Philippine Frontier*. Manila: Ateneo de Manila University Press, pp 97–110.

Dove, M.R. (1998) 'Living rubber, dead land, and persisting systems in Borneo; indigenous representations of sustainability', *Bijdragen tot de Taal, Land- en Volkenkunde*, vol. 154, pp. 20–54.

Dumagat, F.L. (1996) 'Palawan's indigenous peoples and their ancestral domain'. In *Indigenous Peoples of the Philippines. Knowledge, power and struggles*. Proceedings of the Ugnayang Pang-Aghamn Tao (UGAT) 18th National Conference. Manila, pp. 122–136.

Eder, J.F. and J.O. Fernandez (1996) 'Palawan, a last frontier'. In J.F. Eder and J.O. Fernandez (eds), *Palawan at the Crossroads. Development and the Environment on a Philippine Frontier*. Manila: Ateneo de Manila University Press, pp. 1–22.

Kummer, D.M. (1992) *Deforestation in the Postwar Philippines*. Manila: Ateneo de Manila University Press.

Malayang III, B.S. (1991) 'Tenure rights and exclusion in the Philippines', *Nature and Resources*, vol. 27, pp. 18–23.

National Statistics Office (1990) *Provincial Profile: Palawan*. Manila: National Statistics Office.

Novellino, D. (1998a) 'Sacrificing peoples for the trees: the cultural costs of forest conservation on Palawan island (Philippines)'. In *Indigenous Affairs*, vol. 4, pp. 5–14.

—— (1998b) 'The ominous switch: from indigenous forest management to conservation. The case of the Batak on Palawan island, the Philippines'. In M. Colchester and C. Erni (eds), *Indigenous Peoples and Protected Areas in South and South-East Asia*. Copenhagen: IWGIA, pp 250–297.

Ocampo, N.S. (1996) 'A history of Palawan'. In J.F. Eder and J.O. Fernandez (eds), *Palawan at the Crossroads. Development and the Environment on a Philippine Frontier*. Manila: Ateneo de Manila University Press, pp. 23–37.

Ostrom, E. (1990) *Governing the Commons. The Evolution of Institutions for Collective Action*. New York: Cambridge University Press.

—— (1998) 'A behavioral approach to the rational choice theory of collective action', *American Political Science Review*, vol. 92, pp.1–22.

Persoon, G.A. and D.M.E. van Est (2000) 'The study of the future in anthropology in relation to the sustainability debate', *Focaal 35*, pp.7–28.

Roquia, F.H. (1998) 'The socio-cultural environment of the Pala'wans'. In SEARCA, Purdue University (US) and University of the Philippines Los Baños, *Living on the Edge. Economic and Environmental Impacts of Lowland Agricultural Development on Upland Communities in Palawan*. Final report submitted to the Ford Foundation. Los Baños, Phillipines, pp. 70–76.

Republic Act 7160 (1991) 'The Local Government Code of the Philippines'. Manila.

—— 7611 (1992) 'An act adopting the Strategic Environmental Plan for Palawan, creating the administrative machinery to its implementation, covering the Palawan Integrated Area Development Project Office to its support staff, providing funds therefore, and for other purposes'. Puerto Princesa City, Palawan: PCSDS.

Sandalo, R.M. (1996) 'Sustainable development and the environmental plan for Palawan'. In J.F. Eder and J.O. Fernandez (eds), *Palawan at the Crossroads. Development and the Environment on a Philippine Frontier*. Manila: Ateneo de Manila University Press, pp. 127–135.

CHAPTER FOUR

Institutional Resilience of Marine Sasi, a Traditional Fisheries Management System in Central Maluku, Indonesia

INGVILD HARKES AND IRENE NOVACZEK

INTRODUCTION

*I*n Maluku province (Figure 4.1), certain marine tenure rights and management responsibilities are a part of a culturally embedded institution known as *sasi* (Riedel 1886; Holleman 1923; Volker 1925; Cooley 1962; Zerner 1994; von Benda-Beckmann *et al.* 1995; Nikijuluw 1995). *Sasi* encompasses spatial and temporal prohibitions on harvesting crops, cutting wood or gathering other products from the forest, tidal zone or marine territory of a village. It also regulates social interactions (Thorburn 2000). Marine *sasi* (*sasi laut*) prohibits the use of destructive and intensive gear (poisonous plants and chemicals, explosives, small mesh lift-nets) in specific parts of the sea. It also defines seasonal rules of entry and harvest and authorized activities in the area. Access and withdrawal rights in the marine territory are usually restricted to and shared among community residents. The regulations are enforced by an institution known as the *kewang*, which has enforcement power. Therefore, even today, *sasi* has the potential to protect the environment.

However, even though *sasi* has been in place over 400 years, in some parts of Central Maluku, it is disappearing. While in many villages on the Lease Islands, Ambon and Seram, *sasi* or remnants of it are still present, entirely functioning systems are becoming rare. *Sasi* is dynamic through time and has adapted and changed under the influence of trade (the spice wars), colonization (by respectively the Portuguese, the English and the Dutch), religion (Christianity and Islam) and the imposition of nationally defined government structures in the 1970s. Current threats to the system are commercialization, modernization and a general loss of traditional values. Interestingly, some villages have been able to maintain a strong and functional *sasi* system both on land (*sasi darat*) and water (*sasi laut* – see glossary on page 83).

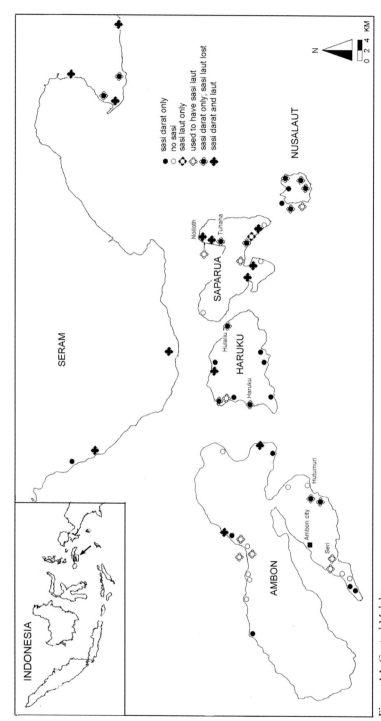

Figure 4.1: Central Malaku

People refer to *sasi* as fundamentally *adat, gereja* (church) or 'other'. In the past, the distinction of church *sasi* (*sasi gereja*) from *adat sasi* referred to the dominant governing authority in the local institution, but in modern times the partnership of local government with these authorities is implicit. In cases where respect for *adat* is very strong, *adat* leaders play a prominent role in developing and enforcing *sasi* rules (*sasi adat*). In church *sasi* it is the church that plays the most visible role. In general, a shift in authority from *adat* leaders to church leaders and to newly defined village governments (since 1979) characterizes the recent history of the *sasi* institution in Central Maluku. In several Muslim villages people did not describe their *sasi* institution as *adat sasi*; these are tabulated under the name 'other'. The role played by *adat* leaders, if any, is not clear. In these villages, where *sasi* is applied to marine resources it is a commercial agreement between local government and a harvester who pays a fee for harvesting rights (*sasi lelang*).

Various scientists have studied *sasi* (Zerner 1994; von Benda-Beckmann *et al.* 1995; Nikijuluw 1995; Thorburn 2000). Yet the existence of *sasi* and its dynamics have never been studied on an overall scale. Our research project covered most islands and villages in Central Maluku. The results are described in this chapter which tries to analyse where and when *sasi* – or aspects of *sasi* – disappeared, which factors caused it to decline but also which factors made it endure over time and/or stimulated villages to re-establish *sasi*. Understanding this process and the factors behind it will help to develop, maintain or revitalize *sasi* and other fisheries management systems.

The first part of this chapter presents the general patterns of decline of *sasi* in the region and marine *sasi* in particular. The second part goes deeper and based on case studies tries to uncover the changes and reasons for the breakdown or strengthening of *sasi*. In the conclusion the results of the two studies are synthesized and factors identified that play a role in the continued existence of *sasi*.

INSTITUTIONAL RESILIENCE DEFINED

A social institution consists of all the structural components of a society (for example patterns of behaviour) through which the main concerns and activities are organized and social needs are met (Goddijn *et al.* 1980, Marshall 1994). This general definition can be narrowed down when we look specifically at resource management systems. Berkes and Folke (1998) distinguish two major functions of a resource management institution: 1) to control access to the resource to exclude outsiders; and 2) to institute rules among users to solve conflicts between individual and collective interests in order to divide the resource benefits. The first is called the exclusion problem, the second the subtractability problem. A useful definition then is the one by North (1993), who describes an institution as the formal and informal constraints or rights and rules and their enforcement characteristics. Examples of formal constraints are rules, laws and constitutions, while informal constraints can be norms of behaviour, conventions and codes of conduct.

Resilience can be defined as the degree to which an institution or system can cope with change without collapsing, or, the ability of a system to absorb perturbations by actively adapting to an ever changing environment (Folke and Berkes 1995). Reduced resilience means that vulnerability increases, with the risk that the system crosses a threshold and collapses (Folke and Berkes 1995). Community management institutions should be understood as dynamic social interventions, shaped by local experience and influenced by external factors (Bailey and Zerner 1992). Change is inherent for such institutions. Yet if adaptability of response to changing conditions is insufficient, management institutions can break down, leaving the resource unregulated. Important attributes that relate to institutional resilience are the enforcement mechanisms for the regulations and the changes that result from internal and external influences.

METHODOLOGY

The study of institutional resilience was part of a larger study of the performance and impact of the marine *sasi* system (*sasi laut*) in Maluku using the Institutional Analysis Framework (ICLARM/IFM 1996). The overall study comprised four components: 1) identification of the extent and operation of *sasi laut* systems in 63 villages in the Lease Islands, 2) a performance and impact analysis of the *sasi laut* system in 22 villages, 3) comparative institutional analysis of six case-study villages, including biological surveys, and 4) a study of the market structure, fisheries policy and the role of the state in fisheries management. The project results are described in Novaczek *et al.* (1998).

The resilience study is based on information from both the inventory and the comparative analysis of case studies with reference also to the contextual attributes (political, economic and socio-cultural). Interviews conducted for the inventory of *sasi* included questions on whether *sasi* had ever been functional in the village, when various functions had ceased and why. In addition, key informant interviews in the case study villages covered questions on the objectives of *sasi*, the rules and regulations, the role of the village government and traditional authorities, leadership, boundaries, compliance and enforcement, and

Table 4.1: Case study villages and presence of *sasi*

Village	Sasi	Island
Nolloth	Strong	Saparua
Haruku	Strong	Haruku
Tuhaha	In the process of revitalization	Saparua
Hulaliu	In the process of revitalization	Haruku
Toisapu-Hutumuri	Disappeared	Ambon
Seri	Disappeared	Ambon

external factors having an impact on management institutions (based on Ostrom 1990; Lubis 1992; Ruddle 1993; von Benda-Beckmann *et al.* 1995). Detailed information on each of these aspects is described in the individual case studies (Novaczek *et al.* 1998). The data from the inventory shows the process of decline; the additional information was used to explain the mechanism behind this process.

PATTERNS OF LOSS OF *SASI* SINCE THE 1940S

The villages surveyed were not expected to be homogenous. Therefore to display the information the villages have been grouped by: dominant religion (Muslim and Christian), population size (class 1 = ≤1,000 people, class 2 = 1,001–2,000, class 3 = 2,001–3,000, and class 4 = >3,000) and island (to indicate the distance to the urban centre, Ambon city).

Loss of the entire sasi institution

Of the 63 villages studied, 19 had lost their entire *sasi* institution (Table 4.2). Most losses occurred in the 1990s and on Ambon and Saparua. On Haruku

Table 4.2: Attrition of *sasi* institution (for example total loss of all forms) on each island

Sasi lost	Seram	Ambon	Haruku	Saparua	Nusa Laut	Total
in 1990s	1	3	0	3	1	8 (42%)
in 1980s	0	2	0	0	0	2 (11%)
in 1970s	0	3	0	1	0	4 (21%)
earlier	0	3	0	2	0	5 (26%)
Total	1	11	0	6	0	19 (100%)

Note: One village in Ambon never had *sasi*.

Table 4.3: Attrition of *sasi* institution in villages of various sizes and religion

Sasi insti-tution lost	Size class 1 (≤1,000)	Size class 2 (1–2,000)	Size class 3 (2–3,000)	Size class 4 (>3,000)	Muslim	Christian
in 1990s	2	3	1	2	4	4
in 1980s	1	1	0	0	1	1
in 1970s	1	0	0	3	1	3
earlier	1	1	0	3	3	2
Total	5	5	1	8	9	10

Note: The village that never had *sasi* is a village of Butonese immigrants of size class 4.

Island, by contrast, some form of *sasi* has survived in every village. Losses have been steady in both Muslim and Christian villages (Table 4.3), but there is a clear difference when you consider village size. Losses have been greatest in size class 4 (>3,000 people) and much less in size class 3 (2,001–3,000). Apparently, there is an optimum size for villages with regard to *sasi*.

The erosion and loss of marine sasi

Active marine *sasi* institutions are hard to find. Out of 63 villages, only 17 had some form of marine *sasi* and a number of these were not functioning (Novaczek *et al.* 1998). Earlier, marine *sasi* was much more prevalent. We documented 18 villages that lost marine *sasi* in living memory (Table 4.4), meaning that at one time at least 35 villages (56 per cent) had this institution. In four villages (Seith,

Table 4.4: Attrition of marine *sasi* in relation to village size and religion

Marine sasi lost	Size class 1 (≤1,000)	Size class 2 (1–2,000)	Size class 3 (2–3,000)	Size class 4 (>3,000)	Muslim	Christian	Total
1990s	0	0	0	1	1	0	1
1980s	3	0	0	0	0	3	3
1970s	2	1	0	1	0	4	4
Lost earlier	2	4	1	3	3	7	10
Subtotal: lost	7	5	1	5	4	14	18
No. still existing	0	4	10	3	5	12	17
Never had marine *sasi*	6	7	6	9	11	17	28
Total	13	16	17	17	20	43	63

Institutional Resilience of Marine Sasi, a Traditional Fisheries Management System
Table 4.5: Attrition of marine *sasi* per island

Marine *sasi* lost	Seram	Ambon	Haruku	Saparua	Nusa Laut	Total
1990s	0	1	0	0	0	1 (6%)
1980s	0	2	0	0	1	3 (17%)
1970s	0	1	0	2	1	4 (22%)
Earlier	1	2	2	2	3	10 (56%)
Total	1	6	2	4	5	18 (100%)

Table 4.6: Factors related to activity of marine *sasi* in central Maluku

Village	Dominant religion	Homo-geneity	Administrative status	Size class	Activity score for marine sasi Land	Marine
Nolloth	Christian	1	*Desa*	3	12	12
Haruku	Christian	1	*Desa*	3	11	12
Pelau	Muslim	1	*Desa*	4	12	12
Siri Sori	Muslim	1	*Desa*	3	n.a.	12
Morela	Muslim	1	*Desa*	3	11	12
Itawaka	Christian	1	*Desa*	3	11	10
Amahai	Christian	1	*Desa*	3	12	10
Kabau	Muslim	1	*Desa*	3	n.a.	9
Ihamahu	Christian	1	*Desa*	2	12	9
Tengah-Tengah	Muslim	1	*Desa*	3	12	9
Hatusua	Christian	2	*Desa*	2	9	9
Porto	Christian	1	*Desa*	4	10	7
Paperu	Christian	1	*Desa*	3	9	6
Ulath	Christian	1	*Desa*	2	6*	6*
Makariki	Christian	2	*Desa*	2	12	3
Rohua	Christian	1	*Dusun* in a Muslim *desa*	3	12	3
Haria	Christian	1	Desa	4	8#	3#

Notes: Homogeneity status: 1 = 95–100% is of dominant religion, 2 = 60–80%.
(*) *Sasi* moved to church in 1992
(#) *Sasi* moved to church in 1995

69

Ouw, Seri and Rutah) information was contradictor: while the survey did not indicate the presence of marine *sasi*, one or more fishermen interviewed thought *sasi* was either in force or had been in place at one time. Nevertheless, these villages were added to the 24 villages where either marine *sasi* had never existed or had been forgotten.

In over half the cases where marine *sasi* has been lost, the loss occurred prior to 1970 (Table 4.5). Since then, marine *sasi* has been relatively stable compared to land *sasi*. Most losses in the 1970s to 1990s have been in either size class 1 (≤1,000) or size class 4 (>3,000) villages (Table 4.4), and in the 1990s the only recorded loss was on Ambon Island (Table 4.5).

FACTORS INFLUENCING ACTIVITY OF *SASI*

The level of activity of marine *sasi* was measured in every village using indicators for the presence of *sasi* (rules), closures (open and closed season), consistency of application (frequency over previous three years) and local effort (signage and enforcement). The maximum activity score is 12. Using this system we find that land *sasi* is significantly more active in villages with a population size between 2,001 and 3,000 (ANOVA, $p \leq 0.01$).

In Maluku, fishing villages are most often overwhelmingly Christian or Muslim. The seven villages where marine *sasi* was most active (score 10–12, see Table 4.6) were all homogeneously Christian or Muslim, i.e. with at least 95 per cent of the population being of the dominant religion. Out of 17 cases of marine *sasi*, three were inactive (score 3) and another three were weak (score 6–7). One of the cases of inactive marine *sasi* occurred in a relatively non-homogeneous village and a second case was in a Christian *dusun* (hamlet) of a predominantly Muslim *desa* (village). Cultural homogeneity can thus be important to the resilience of this traditional institution.

The persistence of marine *sasi* appeared to be linked to the presence of other types of *sasi*: villages with marine *sasi*, for example, usually have active land *sasi*. Resilience of marine *sasi* depends also on the interplay among governing authorities. It has been stable in the Muslim villages where the institution is governed neither by *adat* authorities nor religious leaders (Table 4.7). In a number of cases *sasi* on marine resources was abandoned (for example Akoon, Ameth, Leinitu) or weakened (for example Haria, Ulath) when *adat sasi* was taken over by the church. Compared to marine *sasi* that is of the *adat* or 'other' type, marine *sasi* in villages with church *sasi* is less active. Where *adat sasi* has survived, losses of marine *sasi* are fewer compared to villages where only church *sasi* remains (Table 4.7).

Table 4.7: Type of *sasi* in villages that have or had or never had marine *sasi*

Current status of village	Adat sasi village (n=15)	Church sasi village with no adat sasi (n=21)	Muslim sasi village (n=6)
Has marine *sasi* now	10 (67%)	4 (19%)	3 (50%)
Lost marine *sasi* in living memory	2 (13%)	7 (33%)	0 (0%)
Hist. occurrence of marine *sasi* (if ever had it)	12 (80%)	11 (52%)	3 (50%)
Never had marine *sasi*	3 (20%)	10 (48%)	3 (50%)
Percentage of loss in relation to occurrence	17%	64%	0%

REASONS FOR LOSS OF SASI BETWEEN 1940 AND 1997

During the inventory of the 63 villages, we asked whether our informants could remember when some aspect of *sasi* changed or was lost and why this had happened. Explanations were often quite explicit and included contextual information pertaining to the evolution of socio-political systems in Maluku (see Novaczek *et al.* 1998 for details). The comments were merely applicable to villages where *sasi* was actually lost or transformed.

Weak leadership and conflicts seem to be key elements in the erosion of *sasi*. Reasons that villagers gave for the partial or complete loss of the institution were: conflicts within the village government, conflicts between the village leader and *adat* authorities, conflicts between the village leader and the *kewang*, conflicts among church organizations, and conflicts over land. Conflicts between *adat* leaders and the village government leading to erosion of *sasi* were reported only in Christian villages and never on Nusa Laut.

Confusion over land and rights was in some cases due to changes in government unit boundaries. Changes in administrative boundaries and the effects of World War II were most prevalent on Ambon and Nusa Laut. In addition, pressure from worsening economic conditions has been mounting since the collapse of the price of cloves in the early 1990s. Crop failure and decline of the resource were also mentioned as causing *sasi* to collapse.

The lack of effective enforcement, in combination with economic needs, political turmoil and urbanization provided the incentives for people to non-comply. Non-compliance and subsequent problems with the *kewang* led in several cases to breakdown of *sasi*, for example in Hulaliu. Compliance and enforcement problems were most prevalent in Christian villages, particularly on Ambon Island. In eight cases, the village government delegated the authority over *sasi* to the church, in many cases causing *sasi adat* and marine *sasi* to decline.

As of 1997, 12 of the remaining *sasi* villages were affected by political or religious conflicts. In other words, in about a quarter of remaining *sasi* villages the institution is under strain.

RESULTS OF THE COMPARATIVE CASE STUDY

The findings from the in-depth interviews conducted as part of the institutional analysis in the six villages underscore the link between the different components (objectives, rules), the players and the external context of the *sasi* institution and illustrate the interactions among these through time.

Although Nolloth and Haruku villages both have a strong *sasi* institution, the types of *sasi* are distinct. Whereas that of Nolloth can be described as a system designed primarily to provide resource rent for the village government, Haruku's *sasi* has more to do with fair distribution of fish resources and conservation. Nolloth is a stable village with legitimate leadership and strong representation of traditional authorities. The *kewang* is functional and, together with the village head, serious in the prosecution of offenders. The harvest rights of *sasi* are reserved for the village co-operative (KUD) and income accrues to the village government and the harvesters. Other villagers benefit indirectly through village development. In Haruku, a more important role is ascribed to the *kewang* and relatively less to the village head, except when he is also a traditional authority. *Kewang* members feel a strong responsibility towards *sasi*. The harvest is communal and distributed among the villagers. Recently, the villagers in Haruku have become divided as a result of the installation of a new village head. This leader, elected with a slender majority, supports *sasi* but also favours mining development that threatens the resources under *sasi*. This has led to confusion and a dysfunctional village government, a situation that in turn poses a threat to *sasi*.

In Hulaliu, conflicts between the village head and *kewang*, and in particular problems with accountability for the use of resource rents in the past, lie at the root of the decline of *sasi*. The current leader is trying to revitalize *sasi*, but his position is unstable because he lacks the support of a large part of the village population. The revitalization process is thereby threatened. In Tuhaha there have been problems in the past between formal and traditional authorities. There is also a tendency to revitalize *sasi*, but the relationship between the village government and traditional authorities first needs to be restored. The village government, which is currently only partly functional, has to be reorganized before a *kewang* can be installed.

In Toisapu-Hutumuri and Seri, *sasi* is lost and fisheries management is minimal or lacking. Traditional village structures have to a large extent been replaced by formal structures at the *desa* (village) level, although less so at the *dusun* (sub-village) level. Small-scale fishing has to compete directly with large-scale fishing. Both villages lie on Ambon and close to regional markets and hence are more in contact with modernization and urban processes.

In the remainder of this section we describe the various elements of *sasi* and provide an analysis of how *sasi* functions and persists under different conditions.

Objective of sasi

The general objective of *sasi* as articulated by villagers is to protect resources from theft and destruction. Theft is prevented through active monitoring and enforcement. In Nolloth, for example, there are lengthy closed seasons and a minimum legal size for top shellfish (*Trochus niloticus*) harvested. In Haruku, destructive and overly efficient types of gear are banned. Thus in these cases *sasi* does have a conservation objective. In addition, *kewang* leaders in Haruku expressively identify equitable distribution of fish, particularly to support the village poor, to be an objective of their revitalized *sasi* institution. The use of *sasi* for economic purposes, which has a long history in Maluku (von Benda-Beckmann *et al.* 1995), is also illustrated by Nolloth. The harvest rights of top shellfish were being auctioned off by the village government when they became more commercially interesting in the 1960s. This caused dismay to some villagers who saw their personal direct benefits decrease.

A shift from communal harvests to the sale of marine harvest rights has occurred in most villages where *sasi* has been revitalized by a local government. Although in most villages the principles of *sasi* are valued and *sasi* is perceived as 'a good thing', many fishers we interviewed object to the auctioning of harvest rights, especially to outsiders. In both Tuhaha and Hulaliu, village heads plan to auction the harvest rights and use *sasi* revenues for village development. However, fishermen declared that they would respect *sasi* only if they would get direct benefits from a communal harvest.

Villagers may be kept satisfied with village development projects, but there may be problems when village income and revenues are not transparent. For example, in Nolloth in the 1980s profits appeared to be used for the personal benefits of the village head at the time, rather than for the public good. As a result, *sasi* nearly broke down.

Rules and regulations

Nolloth, Haruku and Hulaliu have written *sasi* regulations. There are various types of rules. The operational rules specify the marine species under *sasi*, gear restrictions and the timing of the harvest. These operational rules are the base on which the fishermen make their day-to-day decisions about compliance.

Collective-choice rules define the decision-making process for closures, access and enforcement. A third level, the constitutional rules, is defined through *adat*. *Adat* prescribes which persons are involved in *sasi* and what their role is, for example who or which clan is responsible for decision-making, conflict resolution, execution of ceremonies and enforcement (see also Ostrom 1990).

The process of decline involves non-compliance to operational rules, but this in turn is directly dependent on the effectiveness of the collective-choice rules. In Hulaliu a conflict between the village head and *kewang* in which the *kewang's* rights were neglected (i.e. a collective level problem), was the root cause for *sasi* to decline. Subsequent problems with compliance (or the operational level) were secondary. *Adat* as part of the village culture, however, persisted, and thus the constitutional rules remained intact.

Over the last decades operational rules have been modified. Boundaries of *sasi* areas, frequency of open and closed seasons, division of benefits, restrictions on gear use, etc. all may and do change. In practical management terms, this affects the function of *sasi* but does not threaten its continued existence. On the other hand, where the constitutional rules have been challenged, e.g. a shift of authority from the *kewang* to the church, the loss of the *kewang*, the introduction of police as enforcers or the promulgation of national fisheries legislation, then the structure or legal basis of the *sasi* institution changed and this can lead to the disappearance of part or all of a local *sasi* institution. Adaptation of constitutional rules may also, however, strengthen *sasi*. For example, in Haruku where marine *sasi* is enforced by the *kewang*, the people requested that the church become involved in land *sasi* in a period when theft was significant. Since that time, the church function is complementary to the *kewang*, who are still mainly responsible for marine resources.

Because operational and collective-choice rules seem to break down more easily, they, as particular entities, are less resilient than constitutional rules. However, the fact that operational rules, and to a lesser extent the collective-choice rules, can be changed or abandoned and then revived is an important feature contributing to the adaptiveness and resilience of the larger institution.

Role of traditional institutions
In 1979, a new government structure was introduced (Law No. 5, 1979) through which authority shifted from traditional leaders to a formally elected village head and government. Even though the implementation of this law was expected to have caused confusion in the village, in the perception of ordinary villagers it had no dramatic and immediate impact. In all villages there is some degree of overlap between formal and traditional authorities. Apparently, the requirements

of the law, i.e. replacement of the traditional government structure by a formal one, were often implemented at a pace and in a manner suited to the local situation. In most cases the local government basically incorporated the traditional structure into the formal structure, and thus change was not clearly visible.

Our study shows that the degree of overlap is decisive for the continuation and stability of *sasi*. However, some villages have been more successful in combining the formal and traditional government structures (for example Nolloth) than others where traditional authorities became marginalized (for example Tuhaha). Where newcomers entered the village government through elections, villages became politically unstable. The villages where *sasi* ceased to function had problems with village leaders who did not successfully collaborate with traditional authorities. In Nolloth, where the traditional authorities function within the new system, the *sasi* institution is strong.

The rituals and knowledge of *sasi* are traditionally passed on from father to son within certain lineages, for example, through that of the head of the *kewang*. The rituals are secret and involve an almost extinct indigenous language (*bahasa tana*). In order to preserve traditional *sasi*, it is imperative that the process of passing down of knowledge is perpetuated. Many youngsters, however, have lost interest in *sasi*. The process of 'modernization' accelerates as the younger generations leave to study in Ambon city where *adat* is regarded as a superstitious belief. There is a risk that when 'the keepers of *sasi* knowledge' die, they will take their knowledge with them. The support and participation of the younger generation, therefore, is necessary for the success of *sasi* as a viable management institution.

Leadership

Before 1979 the position of village leader was hereditary; nowadays the village head is elected by the people. Where government officials lack knowledge and are poorly informed about village issues, decision-making may rest almost exclusively with the village head. In principle, the village head is elected for four years. Yet, elections can be subject to manipulation and in other cases the people automatically 'elect' the legitimate (traditional) village head. The modern village head may therefore hold a very powerful and authoritarian position and as such he is also a key decision-maker in the *sasi* institution.

Our results support those of Riedel (1886) and Volker (1921) who maintained that compliance to *sasi* rules depended largely on strong and tactful leadership. The village head must be honest and respected or *sasi* is undermined. Local legitimacy is very important and this still stems largely from being part of the *raja* family line. In Haruku, for instance, the village head is not a long-term resident of the village and is suspected to represent the interests of the pro-mining lobby. Hence, although he is formally elected, he lacks the legitimacy to play a leading role in *sasi*. Nolloth, on the other hand, is a fine example of a situation where the village head was elected because he *is* the *raja*. This allows him to lead the formal village government and also to be fully and legitimately involved in traditional ceremonies.

External interests may influence the election of a village head, as was re-ported in Haruku and Hutumuri. Elections can be manipulated either in favour of or against traditional leaders. Under the Indonesian system, all candidates must be screened and approved by the government. At this stage, popular candidates may be disqualified, or some votes may simply be neglected during the election process. So, on one hand lingering *adat* structures may make nonsense of the concept of democratic elections, while on the other traditional leaders with broad popular support may also be vulnerable.

Boundaries

Marine *sasi* is generally applied to shallow inshore areas. Outside the *sasi* area, other parts of the village territory, including deep water beyond the fringing reef, may be rented out to outsiders. Generally, boundaries of the *sasi* and other rented areas are clearly defined, have remained largely the same over the years and are generally acknowledged. Fishers may accept areas of restricted access without complaint, but they do have reservations. For some non-*sasi* rented areas, the lack of legitimacy is compensated by a strong enforcement mechanism. Crucial in acceptance of boundaries of restricted areas are legitimacy of the leaders, direct benefits for the excluded users and the presence of a *kewang* (local enforcers).

Enforcement and compliance

Enforcement of *sasi* regulations is carried out by the *kewang*, the police, and/or the village government. In Nolloth and Haruku the *kewang* is strong and plays an important role in the enforcement of regulations. In coastal villages there is still a firm belief that ancestral spirits and God guard the *sasi* regulations and even in cases where the village government is responsible for enforcement, traditional sanctions can still play a role. 'The offender can be lucky and escape from the *kewang* or the police, but he still may get sick. Before long, he will seek the church minister or *tuan negeri* [in more traditional villages] to confess his mischief, because only a prayer or ceremony can relieve him from his burden' (Abraham Pattypelu, fisherman from Tuhaha).

The traditional *kewang* is highly legitimate and not in the least because they enforce the law without showing favouritism. The police have the formal authority to implement the rules, but they are felt to act arbitrarily and therefore are not trusted by the people. The effectiveness of the police is also hampered by the fact that they reside far from the village and when needed they take too long to arrive. In villages that have no active *kewang,* enforcement is difficult. Formally, enforcement authority has shifted from the traditional en-forcers to the village government. In some Christian villages they have sought support from the church. In Nolloth, for example, the village head and the *kewang* closely collaborate with the church minister who is present at *adat* ceremonies including those of marine *sasi*. In non-*sasi* villages the church was not seen to play a role in supporting enforcement of fisheries rules.

Where *sasi* is functional, compliance with fishing rules in general is higher than in non-*sasi* villages (Novaczek *et al.* 1998). Non-compliance by local villagers is not usually a threat to the *sasi* institution but is a sign of decline which is likely based in problems at the collective-choice or constitutional levels. Non-compliance may also be directed at an authority figure rather than at the *sasi* institution *per se*. Non-compliance by either locals or outsiders and which is not effectively controlled by the *kewang* is a threat to *sasi* because it is an incentive for people to abandon local management. Although usually intrusion in *sasi* areas is low, in times of economic and political stress the rate of non-compliance can increase.

EXTERNALITIES

In- and out-migration and (limited) tourism have no impact on village demo-graphy and appear to pose no threat to traditional institutions. Tourism in Haruku, stimulated by *sasi* ceremonies, may even help support the institution. Compared to the villages on Ambon, the communication and transportation links of the villages on Haruku and Saparua are limited. By contrast, Ambon Island villages (Seri and Hutumuri) are heavily influenced by their proximity to Ambon city. It is here that the loss of *adat* ideology and tradition is largest and appreciation of *sasi* the least. Apparently, the greater involvement of people in the process of modernization and globalization affects the appreciation that people have for *sasi* and traditional structures. This is an important aspect to take into account when reinstitutionalizing *sasi* or developing a comparable management institution that must be widely applicable.

Pollution and resource degradation resulting from modern development also pose a challenge to local resource management. The villages on Ambon see their resources declining due to pollution from fish processing and plywood factories. The environmental impacts of these operations, however, are such that they would be beyond the control and influence of a traditional village *kewang*. Revitalized local institutions require information management, networking skills and links to government departments that have jurisdiction in environmental protection.

An example of the impact of large-scale development is Haruku, a village that is influenced by mining exploration for copper, silver and gold. This enterprise seriously affects the political stability in the village and also emphasizes the limits of a village-based management institution that is not linked to higher levels of government. The *sasi* institution does not offer villagers the ability to intervene in regional development planning and licensing of mining operations. The *kewang* is powerless to prevent pollution from mining activities affecting *sasi* resources, and there is no provincial or national management body to which they can appeal.

National laws and programmes are implemented through the provincial, district and sub-district government offices, but information on fishing and environmental law rarely reaches the village level. Knowledge of fishing regulations is fragmented and generally poorly implemented. There are no government patrol boats in the area, and where it comes to protection of fishing rights, the villages are left to their own devices. This may motivate people to work together in defence of local resources. On the other hand, if *sasi* as an institution remains disconnected from governmental power centres, people may abandon local operational rules because they are ineffective against externalities.

THE REVIVAL OF *SASI* IN CENTRAL MALUKU

At this moment, fisheries management is not yet a burning issue in most villages because reduced catches are compensated for by high fish prices. Few village respondents have any clear idea of what fisheries management would entail and think that the answer to declining catches is to upgrade their boats and gear. Nevertheless, all fishermen in *sasi* villages said that *sasi* is useful and important, as did 90 per cent of fishermen in villages where *sasi* is being revived and 70 per cent of fishers in non-*sasi* villages (Novaczek *et al.* 1998). In 14 villages, respondents expressed their desire to reintroduce *sasi* (land, marine or both) or strengthen existing *sasi* practices. Plans for revitalization were found in villages of all sizes and on every island.

The tendency to revitalize *sasi* is fed by the appreciation of *sasi* by the people, not just as a management system but as a cultural phenomenon. In Nolloth and Haruku, where *sasi* is still strong, people explained: 'Sasi has a spirit, and everybody carries it because it is *adat* and part of our culture.' It is at the constitutional level that *sasi* as an institution has its strongest resilience. The constitutional rules of *sasi* are based on and part of *adat*, and because they cannot be separated from the local culture, it is at this level that *sasi* as an institution has its strongest resilience. The embeddedness in *adat* explains why *sasi* is still spiritually and ideologically significant, even where the practical execution of *sasi* has vanished.

In Hulaliu and Tuhaha the village elites are seriously attempting to revitalize *sasi*. In both cases the reason for revitalizing *sasi* has less to do with its spiritual significance than with the possibility of controlling common property resources to generate government income (see also von Benda-Beckmann *et al.* 1995).

In analysing the revitalization processes, it pays to look back to what caused the loss of operational *sasi* in the first place. The main reasons for the collapse of *sasi* in both Tuhaha and Hulaliu were political problems, lack of trust among village leaders and the subsequent withdrawal of the *kewang*. However, even though the practical execution of *sasi* was abolished, *sasi* remained part of the village ideology. The process of revitalization builds on this cultural base and re-establishment involves reinstallation of the traditional authorities and reactivation of collective-choice and operational rules. *Kewang* members have to be chosen and inaugurated, tasks delegated between the formal and traditional authorities and operational rules designed. To be successful, however, the proponents of *sasi* renewal will have to pay attention to history and be careful to avoid past practices that led to breakdown.

In recent years local NGOs, such as Yayasan Hualopu, have been working in the Lease Islands. They provided villagers with information on sustainable fisheries development and encouraged local leaders to embark on the management of village territorial waters. In 1997, for example, Yayasan Hualopu was engaged in a programme of mapping village marine territories and facilitating the development of local management plans. In this work they tried to capitalize on the basis that *sasi* provides and encouraged the reinstallation of *kewangs* and the revival of the island-level institutions (*latupati*) with an emphasis on conflict resolution and management planning. They were supported by a number of academics from Ambon-based universities, some Fisheries Agency staff, and others from the government research institute LIPI, also based in Ambon. The general plan was to promote development of a new law at the provincial level which could give legal recognition to the right of villages to enter into marine resource management and erect *kewang*-style management organizations. The aim of these supporters of *sasi* is clearly resource management and conservation.

Hence, in the process of revitalization there are three streams of thought that must be reconciled: the wish of the village fishermen to preserve *adat* culture and share in the benefits from fisheries resources while protecting their territories from outsiders; the desire of local governments to extract resource rents; and the push by academics, environmentalists and managers to develop viable local fisheries conservation and management.

CONCLUSION

Before the 1970s a large number of villages lost *sasi* due to post-World War II social, administrative and economic change, internal village conflicts and other reasons that were difficult to trace (Novaczek *et al.* 1998). The more recent breakdown of *sasi* has occurred in two distinct periods and villagers are able to articulate reasons for decline in their village.

The 1970s, at the eve of the introduction of the new formal government structure (Law No. 5, 1979), was one period of decline. A fundamental factor in the loss of *sasi* was confusion or conflict in the village or between village authorities, which undermined the legitimacy of the village leader or the institution itself. This decade was one of rapid economic growth, poverty alleviation programmes in the villages and social change. Political instability and/or a dysfunctional *kewang* invited non-compliance and led to abandonment of operational rules. *Sasi* being taken over by the church, either because of such conflicts or in an attempt to improve compliance, was a common scenario. The church, interested only in land *sasi* on coconuts, did not get involved in marine *sasi*, which in some cases then declined.

The 1980s was a period of relative stability. Villages where *sasi* was alive and functioning remained stable. In some villages there was a tendency to revitalize *sasi*. The 1990s was a period of further decline of *sasi*. The period between the 1970s and 1990s covers one generation. Modernization and commercialization as a result of improved communication infrastructure and education and the expansion of market relations, influenced the local culture and especially younger generations. The generational change, together with the rapid rate of social, economic and political change in Maluku in the 1990s is probably the reason why *sasi* is now suffering such relatively rapid losses.

The case studies underscore the inventory evidence that contemporary decline of *sasi* stems often from conflicts (see Novaczek *et al.* 1998). Conflicts can in some cases be related to the social change that resulted from the introduction of the new village structure by the national government. Also, the election system has opened up possibilities for opportunists with vested interests to take the position of village leader. On the other hand, where traditional authorities (*saniri negeri*) merged into the new government, *adat* and *sasi* have remained a significant aspect of village life. Overlap between the traditional and formal government proved to be essential in the prolongation of *sasi*.

The continuing presence of *sasi* is affected by village size and proximity to the urban centre, Ambon. Ostrom (1990) writes that the likelihood of users designing successful common property institutions will be improved if the group is relatively small, stable and homogeneous. Our research confirms this, for *sasi* is most resilient in homogeneous villages of fewer than 3,000, which are found in the outer region (Seram, Saparua, Haruku and Nusa Laut). Villages close to the capital, Ambon, where *sasi* no longer functions, have exceeded this critical size, have become heterogeneous and shifted from subsistence fishing and farming to large-scale fishing and urban employment.

Of all the forms of *sasi*, marine *sasi*, though less generally prevalent, appears to be relatively robust. Whereas *sasi* generally has suffered severe losses in recent years, marine *sasi* has been relatively stable and even showed signs of revitalization in the 1990s. This revival comes basically out of the heartfelt attachment of people to *adat* in general and *sasi* in particular but the commercial value of marine products such as *Trochus niloticus*, other shellfish and sea-cucumber for foreign markets is also an important incentive to keep or reinstitutionalize *sasi*. The process is further being facilitated and reinforced by intervening NGOs, government and academic supporters who see the potential value of *sasi* as a resource management system.

The church also has the potential to play an important role in marine *sasi*. Church *sasi* derives it strength from the strong religious beliefs of rural villagers. The church is more stable than ever-changing village governments. Church *sasi*, when applied to coconuts, provides direct individual benefits to the people and so is valued. Past shifts of authority over land *sasi* from *adat* to the church helped to shore up the effectiveness of the institution when the *kewang* lost enforcement capacity. In many cases, villagers believe that the threat of sanction by God is a more powerful deterrent than the sanctions imposed by the *kewang*. As seen from the inventory (Novaczek *et al.* 1998), where *sasi* is taken over by the church, *adat sasi* as well as marine *sasi* may be lost. However, Haruku and Nolloth provide examples where the introduction of church *sasi* actually strengthened the local institution. Therefore, in *sasi* systems that are being revitalized, the church can play an important supporting role.

In some Muslim villages, *sasi* has evolved away from *adat* and become more of a commercial transaction between the village government and whoever wins the auction for resource harvesting rights. Ceremonies and inherited positions have been abandoned, but religious leaders also have not developed a direct role in the institution. Nevertheless, this also appears to be a stable and resilient institution. The benefits and drawbacks of this form of *sasi* require further investigation, but the performance analysis (Novaczek *et al.* 1998) did show that this sort of arrangement leads to problems in compliance when local fishers see benefits accruing only to elites.

Where the people do not expect to benefit directly, they seem uninterested in the revitalization of *sasi*. A lack of transparency in distribution of benefits further hampers the process. There is a risk that in villages where *sasi* is being used as a tool to extract resource rents that *sasi* then turns into 'a government thing' controlled by local elite's. This is a disincentive for fishers to follow the new *sasi* rules.

Because the constitutional rules are part of *adat*, and 'adat is something that cannot be changed', as village officials in Nolloth stated, the process of revival concerns the reestablishment and adaptation of operational rules (harvest regulations, access rules) and collective level arrangements (re-establishment of the *kewang*). *Adat* still forms the basis of *sasi*, but a redefinition of responsibilities and involvement of non-*adat* institutions, i.e. the church, the police and higher government levels, is possible. Such adaptation of the constitutional rules carries certain risks and must be advanced with care and tact.

It was clear that *sasi* flourishes where the village leader is legitimate (*kepala adat*) and where he collaborates harmoniously and honestly with *adat* leaders and the church. Ostrom (1990) mentions reciprocity and trust as important conditions for successful common property institutions. From our study we would add legitimacy as another key factor for success. Apparently, the discrepancy between the theory of formal administrative structure and the *de facto* power structure that involves traditional authorities, makes village politics susceptible to manipulation and instability. Amendment of the law on village government (No. 5, 1979) may be required to accommodate the need for legitimate *adat* authority figures in rural villages and to increase stability of local government.

The 1990s appear to have been critical decade, for example *sasi* must adapt to modern society or it may, at the operational level, cease to function. According to Ostrom (1990) well-functioning local management systems are dependent on the enforcement, protection and legal recognition of local rights by higher levels of government. As a village organization active in enforcement, the *kewang* is more functional than the police. However, the *kewang* has never obtained formal enforcement powers. In cases where the *kewang* is being revitalized, their mandate needs to be formalized, and the *kewang* and police need to collaborate within a legal construction under provincial law. One possible model is that of Itawaka village, where, as a result of a village proclamation in 1995, the *kewang* became part of the official government. On the other hand, an arm,s length relationship with local government also has certain advantages. Various models need further investigation. Wherever the local institution is placed, it will still require legal recognition and support from higher government levels.

A shared notion of the relevance of the institution stimulates a common objective to maintain it, in spite of external influences and in a situation where the temptation to abuse the system for personal benefits is strong. The extent to which external factors affect the social structure in the village depends on the feedback mechanisms, for example the degree to which the local institution itself can mitigate the effects of external perturbations. Holling (in Berkes and Folke 1998) speaks in this context of adaptive management. *Sasi* has already outlived repeated predictions of imminent demise (Volker 1925; Cooley 1962) and is clearly both adaptive and resilient. There is therefore hope of rebuilding the institution in the form of a modern element in co-management, in which the needs and aspirations of the various proponents (fishermen, local governments, *adat* leaders, environmentalists, fisheries managers) can be successfully accommodated.

EPILOGUE

The period immediately following the completion of this research was one of intense turmoil in Central Maluku. Ambon and surrounding islands have been engulfed in worsening ethnic and religious strife. Large parts of the population have been relocated and there has been a nearly complete segregation of people according to religion. At this point it is too early to tell just what the socio-cultural, political and economic consequences will be.

GLOSSARY

Adat	Customary law and ritual practices
ANOVA	ANalysis Of VAriance between groups
Kepala adat	Chief *adat* authority
Kewang	Traditional enforcer of *sasi* rules
Raja	Village leader from the 'royal' clan

Sasi	Sets of rules which regulate resource use and social behaviour
Sasi adat	*Sasi* based on adat
Sasi darat	*Sasi* on land products
Sasi gereja	*Sasi* governed by the church
Sasi laut	*Sasi* on marine resources
Sasi lelang	The renting out of harvest rights (through an auction)
Saniri negeri	Traditional village council
Tuan negeri	Traditional *adat* leader

ACKNOWLEDGEMENTS

Institutional resilience of *sasi laut* was studied as a part of the Fisheries Co-management Project of ICLARM/IFM in collaboration with Yayasan Hualopu and Pattimura University in Ambon, Indonesia. Overall supervision was in the hands of Dr Robert Pomeroy of ICLARM. The research is funded by IDRC, DANIDA and the Netherlands' government.

REFERENCES

Bailey, C. and C. Zerner (1992) 'Local Management of Fisheries Resources in Indonesia: Opportunities and Constraints'. In R. B. Pollnac, C. Bailey and A. Poernomo (Eds), *Contribution to Fishery Development Policy in Indonesia*. Jakarta: Central Institute for Fisheries, Ministry of Agriculture, pp. 39–55.

Benda-Beckmann von, F., K. von Benda-Beckmann and A. Brouwer (1995) 'Changing "Indigenous Environmental Law" in the Central Moluccas: Communal Regulation and Privatization of Sasi'. *Ekonesia, a Journal of Indonesian Human Ecology*, no. 2.

Berkes, F. and C.S. Folke (1998) *Linking Social and Ecological Systems. Management Practices and Social Mechanisms for Building Resilience.* Cambridge: Cambridge University Press.

Cooley, F. (1962) *Ambonese Adat, a General Description.* New Heaven: Yale University Press.

Folke, C. S. and F. Berkes (1995) *Resilience and the Co-evolution of Ecosystems and Institutions.* IASCP 'Reinventing the Commons' conference, Session 23: 'Resilience in institutions and ecosystems', Bodö, Norway, 24–28 May.

Goddijn, H.P.M., P. Thoenes, M.M. de Valk, and S.P Verhoogt (1980) *Geschiedenis van de Sociologie: Achtergrond, Hoofdpersonen en Richtingen.* Meppel: Boom uitgeverij.

Holleman, F.D. (1923) *Het Adat-grondenrecht van Ambon en de Oeliasers.* Uitgave van het Molukken Instituut. Delft: Drukkerij Meinema.

ICLARM/IFM (1996) *Analysis of Fisheries Co-management Arrangements: a Research Framework.* WP No. 1, Manila: ICLARM.

Lubis, R. (1992) 'Factors Influencing the Success of Fishermen's Cooperatives in South Sulawesi'. In R.B Pollnac., C. Bailey and A. Poernomo (eds), *Contribution to Fishery*

Development Policy in Indonesia. Jakarta: Central Institute for Fisheries, Ministry of Agriculture, pp. 114–125.

Marshall, G. (1994) *The Concise Oxford Dictionary of Sociology*. New York: Oxford University Press.

Nikijuluw, V.P.H. (1995) 'Community-based Fishery Management (Sasi) in Central Maluku'. *IARD Journal*, vol. 17, no. 2.

North, D. C. (1993) *Economic Performance through Time*. Stockholm: The Nobel Foundation and the Royal Swedish Academy of Sciences.

Novaczek, I., I. H. T. Harkes, J. Sopacua, and M. D. D. Tatuhey (1998) *An Institutional Analysis of Sasi Laut in Maluku, Indonesia*. WP No. 39, Penang: ICLARM

Ostrom, E. (1990) *Governing the Commons: the Evolution of Institutions for Collective Action*. Cambridge: Cambridge University Press.

Riedel, J.G. F. (1886) *De Sluik- en Kroesharige rassen tusschen Selebes en Papua*. The Hague: M. Nijhoff.

Ruddle, K. (1993) *External Forces and Change in Traditional Community-Based Fishery Management Systems in the Asia-Pacific Region*, MAST (Maritime Anthropological Studies), vol. 6, no. 1/2, Amsterdam: Spinhuis Publishers, pp. 1–37.

Thorburn, C. G. (2000) 'Changing Customary Marine Resource Management Practice and Institutions: The Case of Sasi Lola in the Kei Islands, Indonesia'. *World Development*, vol. 28, no. 8, pp. 1461–1479.

Volker, T. (1925) *Adatrechtbundels*. Published by KITLV. Den Haag: Martinus Nijhoff.

Zerner, C. (1994) 'Through a Green Lens: The Construction of Customary Environmental Law and Community in Indonesia's Maluku Islands'. *Law and Society Review*, vol. 28, no 5.

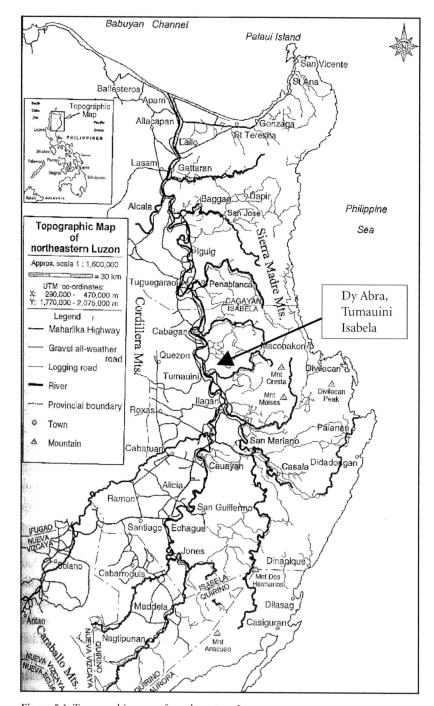

Figure 5.1: Topographic map of north-eastern Luzon

Exploring the Right Blend between Government's Facilitative Role and Farmers' Initiative in Forest Regeneration

Paulo N. Pasicolan

INTRODUCTION

C o-management of natural resources in the Philippines as a concept began in the early 1980's. The Integrated Social Forestry Program of the then Bureau of Forest Development (BFD), launched in 1982, is one of the early government attempts to collaborate with upland farmers for the protection and development of the remaining forest in the country. This was followed by other community-based forestry programmes, such as the National Forestation Program, the Community Forestry Program and the Certificate of Ancestral Domain Claim. Despite the pervading tide of the so-called participatory or bottom-up development approaches over the years, the old bureaucratic pattern of project implementation still prevails. The backlash of this persistent incongruity between concept and practice of co-management is very evident, as exemplified by the low success of a number of government or foreign-funded community-based forestry programmes.

The US$240 million contract reforestation for the Department of Environment and Natural Resources (DENR) for instance fell short of its target in 1992 due to unsustainable local participation. Although it was designed as participatory in approach and relied mainly on grassroots' participation, programme implementation however, was top-down and prescriptive. On the other hand, there exist a number of successful tree-growing projects at the farm level. Despite no direct government support, these spontaneous tree-growing activities became an integral part of the household farming system, which makes them sustainable.

This chapter reviews the strength and limitations of two tree-growing modalities in the Philippines (government contract reforestation and the farmer-initiated tree-growing). The aim is to design the ideal co-management arrangement using various tree-growing actors. The USAID-Community-Based Forestland Regeneration and Related Research Project (COMFREP) is featured in this chapter as an example of how government can collaborate with development NGO's, academics and the communities in the reforestation of public lands in Cagayan Valley Region, north-eastern Philippines. However, it is too soon to draw lessons or conclusions from the project experience, since it has just started to take off.

GOVERMENT CONTRACT REFORESTATION PROGRAMME

The programme rationale

In 1934 the Philippines still had 17 million ha of productive forest, almost half of the country's land area (DENR 1990). However, 60 years later, the figure has been reduced to about six million ha of which 5.2 million were residual forest and only less than a million ha were considered primary forest. Although reforestation activities have been carried out since 1916, the pace of forest establishment lagged far behind the rate of forest loss. From 1916 to 1987, or a span of 71 years, only about 70,000 ha had been successfully reforested under the government's regular programme (FMB 1988) compared with a yearly average rate of deforestation of 100,000 ha in the same period.

This alarming decline in forest cover coupled with the dismal performance of past reforestation programmes prompted the government to introduce the Contract Reforestation Programme. To propel this programme, US $240 million was borrowed from the Asian Development Bank (ADB) and the Overseas Economic Co-operation Fund of Japan to reforest 225,000 ha from 1988 to 1992.

Programme design

In order to hasten reforestation in the countryside, the programme was packed with attractive cash incentives for the grassroots. Participants were paid to plant trees on public lands in the first three years. Payments were spread out over a period of three years. About 60 per cent of the total contract price went to seedling establishment, the first year being the most difficult. The remaining 40 per cent was equally divided over the two following years for seedling protection and maintenance.

Field evaluation was conducted yearly as a condition for a release of the second and third instalments. Seedling survival should not be less than 80 per cent and not lower than two meters and 2.5 meters in height for long-gestation and fast-growing species, respectively, in the third year in order for the contractor to qualify for the Forest Land Management Agreement. This is a 25-year stewardship agreement that superseded the Contract Reforestation and is renewable for another 25 years. As a tenurial instrument, it provides ownership rights for the contractor over the future tree produce. As an incentive for continually maintaining and protecting the plantation without payment, the contractor can harvest the trees after 15–25 years. 30 per cent of the total tree revenue will go back to the government. The contractor can also utilize the land for inter-cropping while waiting for the trees to mature.

Impact and achievements

The programme had a good start, because for the first time the pace of tree planting exceeded the target goal for that period. This, however, was short-lived. Participation declined in the second and third year. This coincided with the decreasing cash payments that participants were to receive from the project alongside the problem of funding delays. Based on field findings, fewer seedlings survived in comparison to what was initially reported during the tree-planting phase. Overall nationally performance, the average rate of seedling survival after the third year was as low as 10 per cent of the total target (Pasicolan 1996). The programme would not have suffered so much loss if it started first as a pilot project and then gradually expanded nation-wide, as experience was gained by trial and error.

As far as the effect of project's cash payment on people's participation is concerned, the following were noted during the contracted period:

1. Paying people to plant trees on public lands was not a sufficient condition for their sustained participation.

2. When project payments were delayed, people's participation became erratic, conditional and problematic.

3. Evidence of problematic behaviour includes: a) deliberate burning down of the project by the participants, b) participants' premature abandonment of the project, c) mutilation of seedlings when payments were delayed, d) haphazard performance of project activities and e) sudden mushrooming of 'fly-by-night' contractors and NGOs.

Programme assessment

Although the programme was meant to be participatory, the bureaucratic process still prevailed. The following are the major weaknesses of the programme:

1. *'Top-down' process.* The process of programme designing was 'top down'. Field operational guidelines were all crafted by a special planning team at the DENR Central Office. Plans were based on available budget for the period rather than on participants' development options. The incentive system and tenurial instruments were pre-determined by the government without consultation at the grassroots level. Everything was from project conception to implementation was initiated by the government.

2. *'Donor-driven' goal.* Although the DENR assumed the overall management in collaboration with NGOs and POs (peoples organizations), programme implementation was donor-driven. The was also a showcase for the ADB's expanded plans for environmental lending *Contract Reforestation* besides being the flagship programme of the government. Pressured by the ADB's requirements to produce substantial outcome as a condition for the release of the second instalment of the loan, the DENR set unrealistic objectives beyond its institutional capacity (Korten 1993). The unanticipated funding delays in the end put the programme in total disarray. Target budget schedules were not followed, and sharp budget cuts were made in the succeeding years. Since most participants were motivated by cash incentives, the delays in their wages adversely affected their participation.

3. *Low institutional capacity of implementing agency.* The DENR could hardly justify the size of the huge funding. As such, it set very high field targets beyond its administrative and institutional capacity. Furthermore, these were set out on a massive scale without adequate social and technical preparations participants (ANGOC 1991). The inadequate logistics and manpower support of the DENR field offices aggravated the problem.

4. *Focus on physical targets more than social process.* Overwhelmed by the concern to meet the targeted field accomplishments in a given period as imposed by the bank, the number of haor seedlings planted was emphasized more than the dynamics of community involvement in the programme (Sajise 1993). More specifically, Umali (1989) vividly described this process as follows:
   - First, the simple order to 'plant, plant and plant' to reach the plantation establishment targets, only diverted the program's real qualitative goals/objectives (for example, social equity, provide labour, sustainable development and the necessity to maintain an established plantation).
   - Second, the choice of species was almost ad hoc. No prior and proper attention was given to site characteristics, end-uses and the marketing aspects. The choice was just based on seedling availability.
   - Third, the specific purpose of the plantation and the intended end-use of the wood and the other produce were seldom specified. Furthermore, there was no assessment of the economic, social and environmental viability of the projects.

5. *Local community counterpart support was limited.* Community social and physical assistance were not fully maximized. Community co-operation in fire fighting, local institutions and other social capital could have been

harnessed to promote sustainable collective action. Instead, the programme relied so much on the huge funding, that every activity had a tag price.

6. *Low inter-agency collaboration.* The private sector, especially the wood industry and the local banks, had not participated fully in the programme because the contract reforestation just focused on seedling establishment. Thus, at the end of the contract period in the third year, most contractors had no desire to maintain the project anymore because there was no certain market or costs for plantation maintenance.

While the programme's weaknesses were evident, it had also a breakthrough in terms of widespread public participation. For the first time in the history of reforestation in the country almost all sectors in society engaged in public tree-growing. This was much highlighted by the sudden mushrooming of NGOs and grassroots organizations. During the period of 1989–90 alone, the DENR granted contracts to 9,594 families, 2,911 community associations, 465 corporations, and 142 local government units (Metin 1991). This is in contrast to the 189 regular reforestation projects the government had maintained in 1990.

SUCCESSFUL SPONTANEOUS TREE GROWING AT THE FARM LEVEL

Over-reliance on fund-driven reforestation strategies in the past has limited the opportunity of the Philippine government to learn from the successful tree-growing experiences of small farmers. In many parts of the country today, there exists a good number of successful tree growing operations at the farm level (Garrity and Mercado 1994; Pasicolan *et al.* 1997). Unfortunately, because of the dearth of information about this tree-growing modality, it has rarely been included in designing reforestation strategies (Olofson 1980; Eder 1991; Wiersum and Veer 1983; Pasicolan 1996).

Observation sites

Four case studies of spontaneous tree growing by farmers were identified in the following localities: Quibal, Peñablanca; Maguirig, Solana; Nagtimog, Diadi; and Timmaguab, Sta. Ignacia (Figure 5.1). In each of these observation sites, the motivation for growing trees and the history of the site are different. A brief characterization of each site is given as follows:[1]

❧ *Case 1: Quibal, Peñablanca, Cagayan*

Quibal (Peñablanca municipality, Cagayan province) is a firewood-gathering community at the foothills of the Sierra Madre mountain range in north-eastern Luzon, the Philippines. Previously, it was a swidden farming community in the

1960s. Progressively declining farm productivity, however, prompted farmers to switch to firewood extraction. Logging began in the early 1970s. As a result, most households depended on fuelwood and timber sales. Over time, the community's dependence on timber and firewood sales exerted much pressure on the remaining forest in the area. In the 1980s, it became difficult for timber gatherers to maintain their previous level of wood extraction. A cutting moratorium was imposed by the then Bureau of Forestry which forced most timber gatherers to seek other livelihood options. The majority of the carabao loggers who cut down large diameter trees abandoned this livelihood and sold their chainsaws. Others shifted to firewood extraction since this does not require large timber to be extracted.

For the majority of the firewood gatherers, the scarcity of fuelwood did not threaten their livelihood. Although their production level declined, they never considered moving to a new site. Instead they started raising *Lueceana leucocephala* and *Gmelina arborea* in their backyards or farmlots in anticipation of the impending fuelwood scarcity (Pasicolan, 1996).

When asked about the feasibility of establishing a community forestry project in the area, almost all the interviewees indicated a preference for farm forestry over community forestry. They felt that it was easier to organize family labour than community labour. Second, in relation to land and tree rights, they claimed that it is easier to work out a benefit-sharing arrangement within the household than at the community level. They suggested, however, that the government should delineate an adequate planting area for each household and should also provide security of tenure.

✈ *Case 2 : Maguirig, Solana, Cagayan*

Mang Casimiro, an 80-year-old farmer from Maguirig (Solana municipality, Cagayan province) successfully established a woodlot in his 3-ha farm. In addition there were two other farmers who resisted the then Bureau of Forestry Development's attempt to include their private lots for reforestation in 1975. Today, their tree farms inside the abandoned government reforestation protect stand as a great challenge to the 'government-cash-driven' problematic tree-growing project in the community.

Most of the residents in the area were not able to develop tree farms on their own landholdings because they allowed the Bureau of Forestry Development (BFD) to take them over for reforestation. According to them, they were persuaded by the employment offered to them as labourers on the project. Also, they were told that the land still belonged to them and the BFD's concern was just to plant trees.

Originally, a large portion of the government reforestation project in the area was classified as private agricultural land as claimed by many local people. In the early 1950s, a cadastral survey was conducted by the Bureau of Lands. Many locals applied for title at that time because the area was classified as 'alienable and disposable' land. During that time, agriculture was the dominant land use.

In 1978, a government reforestation project was introduced on the same site. The locals found it expedient to work with the project because of the employment they gained while at the same time being assured of their right of ownership of the project site. Owing to the rough topography of the site, it was reclassified as forest zone after the Bureau of Lands was merged into the BFD.

Between the 1980s and the present the tenurial status of the area was transformed from one type to another depending on the kind of government project being introduced on the site at the time. For instance, it became a forest zone under the government regular reforestation project in 1978. In 1980, it was converted to a communal tree farm project by the same BFD as a result of the poor reforestation performance. Leasehold certificates were issued to participants. It was proclaimed as an integrated social forestry project in 1985 with the issuance of stewardship certificates to participants. The BFD was dissolved in the early 1980s and all forestry concerns were now subsumed under the newly overhauled agency, the Department of Environment and Natural Resources (DENR).

In 1989, the area was reverted to a regular reforestation project again by the DENR and finally became a contract reforestation in 1990. Although the DENR claimed that the area was under its jurisdiction, many community people still believed that the land belonged to them. During the years of uncertainly about the legal status of the land, there were frequent burnings on the site and thus the area remained barren and abandoned.

In the case of Mang Casimiro and the other two farmers, they grew their own trees on their small farms, while the paid labour public tree planting had been going on in the area for several years. According to the three successful tree growers, the seedlings they used in 1978 were obtained from the same government reforestation project. Although farming was their main occupation, they simultaneously planted *Gliricidia sepium*, *Leuceana leucocephala* and *Gmelina arborea* and some fruit trees such as jack fruit, mango and citrus in their lot. Today, even though the trees have grown tall, Mang Casimiro still has space to plant corn, mungbean and vegetables for home consumption. He also planted banana, papaya, pineapple, sweet potato, cassava and other root crops as subsidiary farm crops. He claims that the woodlot meets his yearly needs for household fuelwood and fencing materials. He further cited the regenerative capacity of his oldest trees in continually spreading out new wildlings in the other areas of his farm. Because of this, he does not need to do direct planting anymore. All he has to do is protect the trees from grassland fire.

Today, the almost 200-ha government contract reforestation project on the same site stands barren and abandoned. A greater portion has been turned into private pasture by a local politician. Most farmers feel betrayed by the government over what had happened to their farmlots that were occupied by the project as they note the glaring contrast with Mang Casimiro's and the two other farmers' woodlots. Others are now contemplating swidden farming in the reforestation area, while some farmers claimed they had already succeeded in making new clearings in the site.

The success story of Mang Casimiro simply suggests the importance of secured tree ownership and the farmer's enterprising attitude as conditions for spontaneous tree-growing in areas with uncertain land tenure status. Likewise, the evident failure of the government reforestation project in the area clearly indicates the insufficiency of paid labour as a condition for meaningful and sustainable public participation in tree-growing projects.

Case 3: Nagtimog, Diadi, Nueva Viscaya

Nagtimog is an upland farming community, 7 km from the main town of Diadi in Nueva Viscaya province. Bounded by a network of creeks, it is not accessible to jeepneys during the rainy season. A DENR regular reforestation project was introduced into the community in the early 1970s. Most of the local people planted trees to earn an income while simultaneously growing vegetables. However, the reforestation project did not last long because of inadequate funding for protection and maintenance. Being in a fire prone area, the project experienced yearly grassland fires, that were believed to be either deliberately or accidentally caused by outsiders and by local residents.

For some time, many local farmers wanted to squat and cultivate portions of the project site after the DENR project management abandoned the area. Most of them were restrained, however, by the DENR's constant monitoring despite the fact that no alternative government project was immediately put up in the area. For many years the site lay idle while some farmers kept on clearing new areas for swidden farming in nearby places.

The coming of the DENR contract reforestation in 1989 raised farmers' expectations of resuming the tree planting project in the area. However, adjacent communities outside the area were selected for contract reforestation. This prompted the farmers to cultivate the abandoned project site. They believed that first turning the area into cornfields could minimize the problem of grass-land fires. The continuous cultivation of the land for short-term crops would eventually weed out the grasses and other vegetative cover, thus reducing the combustible biomass load. When the area was completely cleared as a result of continuous tillage, simultaneous tree planting in-between annual crops followed.

The farmers succeeded in cultivating the area with short-term crops in the first year. They then started intercropping *Gmelina arborea*. In other clearings, they simultaneously planted short-term and tree crops in separate blocks. After five years, the *Gmelina arborea* that they planted in-between their main crops had grown to a height that disrupted intercropping underneath. This compelled them to move to other areas of the site. The good soil condition of the area encouraged them to apply informally to the DENR for more areas for farming. Also, by being confident of their rights over the trees they planted, they gained an added incentive to protect and maintain the project.

These successful reforestation activities raised the prospect of rehabilitating the long-abandoned project area. At first, only two farmers applied for usufruct access over the area on condition that they should simultaneously reforest it without corresponding payment. In return for their voluntary efforts in tree planting, the DENR assured them ownership rights over the trees they planted. Other local farmers also expressed a desire to farm on the site under the same arrangement. To date, there are around 10–15 farmers in the area occupying the abandoned reforestation site who are now growing trees simultaneously with short-term intercropping. All of them requested formal tenurial rights to legitimize their activities on the site.

The 7-ha *Gmelina arborea* plantation established by the farmers without government direct payment for tree planting now stands as another hallmark of how small tree farmholders can successfully reforest problematic government reforestation sites if they are given the right kind of institutional incentives and support system.

❧ Case 4: Tinmaguab, Sta. Ignacia, Tarlac

Timmaguab (Sta. Ignacia municipality, Tarlac province) is a rice-growing community but raising trees for household use became an integral part of the residents' farming system. Not far from the area are reforestation projects that were continually burned and abandoned by participants. However, farm-based tree-growing activities using little capital have been carried out by the farmers on the one-time Imperata-infested sites. The trees are raised to improve soil nutrients, provide household fuelwood, fodder, fruit and fences. Lately, tree growers are receiving additional income by selling the wood products to the local market. Trees were originally grown to establish peripheral boundary fencing. The increasing demand for wood products has heightened farmers' interest in planting more trees as a source of household income.

This farm-based tree-growing was a new phenomenon in the community. In 1987, a new resident of the area introduced agroforestry on his 6-ha plot of land. After three years, many of his neighbours followed his example. Today, about 8 out of 25 farmers in the community have established woodlots on their private lands. Most of the farmers established woodlots of *Leuceana leucocephala* and *Gliricidia sepium*. They also allowed naturally occuring species such as *Vitex negundo*, *Albizza procera*, *Philiostigma malabarica* and *Pithecelobium dulce* to increase in density. In addition, they planted fruit trees such as *Sandoricum koetjape*, *Anona mauricata*, *Anona squamosa* and *Mangifera indica* along with some citrus and short-term crops.

The farmers claimed that aside from benefiting economically, they also gained experience through constant experimentation on their woodlots. By observing the increase in biomass through natural regeneration processes, they realized that tree-growing can proceed even without much labour or capital. They also learned that the more plant species they introduced, the less was the damage by natural pests in their farms.

Two factors encourage the farmers to grow trees: first, they knew that they would receive the tree produce and, second, they needed a sustained supply of fuelwood and other tree farm products for home use and for the market.

Success conditions

The success conditions identified as being critical for spontaneous tree-growing were:

- assured access or secured property rights,
- interest in other tree related uses,
- practice of intercropping,
- farmers' above subsistence level situation,
- presence of a wood market, and
- farmers' enterprising attitude.

Table 5.1 shows the determinant conditions for tree-growing success for each observation site. The critical relevance of each success condition is discussed below.

- *Assured access/secured property rights*: Farmers in the four sites confidently grow trees because of the assurance that the future produce will accrue to them. In Nagtimog, the DENR's provision of usufruct and tree tenure

Table 5.1: Success conditions for spontaneous tree-growing in the four observation sites

Site	Success conditions
Quibal, Peñablanca, Cagayan	assured access/secured property rights presence of wood market
Maguirig, Solana, Cagayan	assured access/secured property rights interest in other tree related uses practice of intercropping farmers' above subsistence level situation farmers' enterprising attitude
Nagtimog, Diadi, N. Viscaya	assured access/secured property rights interest in other tree related uses practice of intercropping farmers' above subsistence level situation farmers' enterprising attitude
Timmaguab, Sta. Ignacia, Tarlac	assured access/secured property right interest in other tree related uses practice of intercropping farmers' above-subsistence-level situation presence of wood market farmers' enterprising attitude

Source: Pasicolan and Tracy, 1960.

encouraged interested farmers to plant corn in between tree seedlings in the abandoned government reforestation site. Farmers in Maguirig succeeded in managing their own woodlots following the DENR's recognition of their legal claims over the disputed reforestation site. Both Timmaguab and Quibal farmers have long-standing claims over the areas they planted with trees. In general, when farmers are assured of their ownership rights over future tree produce, the more likely they are to grow trees even on public lands, despite receiving no government direct cash payments.

- *Interest in other tree related uses*: Except for Quibal, farmers in the other three sites were not only interested in the wood product. They also grow trees for fodder, cash income, shade, aesthetics and other tree related uses. In other words, the more varied the benefits they can derive from trees to meet their household needs, the greater the likelihood farmers establish woodlots even without direct payment.

- *Practice of intercropping*: Farmers in Nagtimog had successfully raised *Gmelina arborea* voluntarily in the abandoned reforestation site after government attempts failed (Pasicolan, *et al.* 1997). The agricultural crops (for example corn, peanuts and mungbean.) interplanted with the tree seedlings compelled the farmers to always keep the site free from grassland fires. Fire lines were constructed and banana or papaya was used as firebreaks. Farmers in Maguirig and Timmaguab adopted wide spacing for fruit trees to be planted in between forest seedlings. In short, the more diverse the crop planted in the area, the greater the farmers' stake in the site; thus there is regular care and maintenance of seedlings planted.

- *Farmers' above subsistence level situation*: The financial situation of the farmers is an important success factor in spontaneous tree-growing at the farm level (Pasicolan, *et al.* 1997). Farmers in Maguirig, Nagtimog and Timmaguab have other farmholdings for their main subsistence. Cash surplus farmers, or at least those above subsistence, have considerable time and resources to invest in other economic options than others. Because there is no pressure to hack out their daily subsistence, they can even venture into risky and long-term livelihood investment, such as farm forestry.

- *Presence of wood market*: Selling of firewood to neighbouring towns and in Tuguegarao, the capital of the Cagayan Valley region, provides a big business for firewood gatherers in Quibal. With the declining supply of timber in the nearby forest, however, a number of resource users began to plant *Gmelina arborea* and *Leuceana leucocephala* in their abandoned farmlots (Pasicolan and Tracy, 1996).

  Self-sufficiency in household wood supply was the priority of farmers in Timmaguab. The growing local demand for wood products like fencing materials and fuelwood, encouraged the farmers to expand their woodlots. In both sites, the demand for wood products became commercialized even without government or private sector initiative. In short, the presence of a wood market is a powerful incentive for small farmers to voluntarily grow trees on their farmlots

- *Farmers' enterprising attitude*: Opportunism and risk-taking tendencies characterized the attitude of cash surplus farmers and those who are in search of more land to cultivate. In Nagtimog, farmers boldly risked cultivating a portion of the DENR abandoned reforestation site. Likewise, the farmers in Timmaguab, despite their sufficiency in rice production, still ventured into tree farming, a risky and laborious investment.

Strengths

The following are the positive features of the spontaneous tree-growing activities:

- *Sustainable*. Farmers' motivation to grow trees is driven by their direct household needs rather than any superficial incentive such as the cash paid for tree-planting activity. Furthermore, tree growing becomes an integral component of the household farming system. Hence, it can persist even without government direct cash incentives.

- *Strategic.* It has the potential to rehabilitate adjacent marginal public lands because it starts from where the on-site actors are, and the farmers can progressively expand their tree farms as they gain income and grow in tree husbandry experience.

- *No public funds spent.* Government funding was spared because tree growing was purely initiated by private individuals, driven by their own needs.

- *High capacity to spread out.* It can 'snowball' very easily, if given the proper institutional support from the government and the private wood industry.

- *Promotes grassroot entrepreneurship.* Small tree farmholders are challenged to be business adventurist and risk-takers.

Limitations

This tree-growing modality has also some constraints which are as follows:

- *Low capacity to expand.* Cannot fully expand into large commercial scale without full government policy support. Going big requires the private sector's financial assistance. Furthermore, the small size of land holdings, the absence of security of tenure and a certain wood market pose big limitations to the farm forestry expansion.

- *Lack of support system.* Farmers' institutional linkages to draw out technical and other logistic supports are limited, including credit assistance, crop protection insurance and other necessary assistance related to tree farming on a commercial scale.

- *Unprofitable beyond certain distance from the market.* According to a forestry practitioner in Northern Mindanao, Philippines, tree farms or forest plantations beyond a 100-km radius from the nearest market or wood-processing plant are no longer economically profitable. Transport costs from the stumpsite to the market are much higher than the cost of forest harvesting; this is not economically feasible from a private investor's standpoint.

- *Profitability is limited by economy of scale factor.* More profit can be realized in big tracts of forest plantation than in 5–10 hectares of woodlot because establishment and maintenance cost per hectare is relatively lower in the former.

- *Non-bankable.* Small tree farmholders cannot easily borrow from commercial banks. This stems from their inability to pay beyond the grace period of the loan because of cash flow problems. Likewise, they do not have the prescribed collateral for their loans as required by the lending institutions. Furthermore, small farmers cannot easily borrow from any bank because usually access to loans depends on their track records or experience in micro-enterprise development.

BLENDING GOVERNMENT EFFORTS WITH GRASSROOTS' INITIATIVES

Distilling the lessons learned from the experiences of the Contract Reforestation Programme and the spontaneous tree growers can provide valuable inputs for the development of an improved reforestation strategy in the country. This section explores the 'best fit' of complementation between the roles of government and the grassroots in a tree-growing programme. It identifies the critical contributions of the private sector in sustaining grassroots' tree-growing initiatives. The aim is to evolve an alternative co-management scheme involving the government, the local community and the private sector for the spontaneous re-generation of degraded forest lands in the Philippines.

Facilitative role of the government

The government ,as represented by the DENR, should cease from always being at the forefront of the tree-growing programme. Instead, it should take on role of facilitator, providing enabling conditions for the different stakeholders of the programme to come together in mutual partnership. The following are the key functions and activities that the government should undertake to enhance the greater participation of the grassroots:

1. Provide more enabling policies, such as attractive tenurial instruments and other forms of support services in favour of small private tree growers.
2. Simplify the process of complying with the legal requirements for taking up government institutional incentives and other support services in tree growing.
3. Release more public lands either for farm forestry or public tree growing.
4. Execute boundary delineations of released areas for communal tree growing.
5. Issue tax exemptions or rebates to private tree-growers.
6. Encourage enterprising individuals or local groups to continue to expand their clearings provided that they will develop them into tree-based systems.
7. Provide tree growers with communal funds to support livelihood projects.
8. Serve as a broker between a capital owner (government or private bank) and the tree growers who are in need of production loans.
9. Provide incentives to private industries that are interested in investing in the tree-growing programme.

10. Provide financial arrangement for small tree farm holders.
11. Initiate and strengthen tripartite agreements or institutional arrangements with local tree-growing communities and the private sector.
12. Provide infrastructure in support of the tree growers' physical and institutional needs.

Grassroots local counterpart support

Local people, often collectively represented by the community and other organized groups, are regarded as the main actors in the programme. In the past, they were treated as wage labourers of the project. The experience under the Contract Reforestation proved to be counterproductive. As the main stakeholders of the tree-growing projects, they should bear certain costs, especially in the maintenance and protection of the established plantation. Pressing them to invest their resources at a level commensurate with their capacity would strengthen their long-term stake in the project. Among their possible contributions are:

1. Family/communal labour
2. Community co-operation in fire fighting
3. Local organization
4. Social capital, such as local institutions and indigenous knowledge
5. Financial or material contributions

Enabling Role of Intermittent Actors

The private sector, and particularly the wood industry, plays a crucial role in sustaining the tree growers' motivation. Of equal importance is the financial support from lending institutions as well as development NGOs in assisting the tree growers to cope with cash flow problems during the interface between tree planting and harvesting. Among the important roles of each intermediary actor are:

ᴥ *a) Wood Industry*
- Provide market security
- Provide collateral to the bank for the tree growers
- Provide or source out production capital for the tree growers
- Extend technical assistance

ᴥ *b) Lending Institution*
- Provide production loans with low interest and long grace period
- Provide crop insurance
- Offer livelihood support fund

᠅ *c) Development NGOs*
- Create livelihood support for the community
- Provide community training programmes
- Extend other related community development services

Table 5.2 summarizes the role and the corresponding contribution of each partner institution in the proposed co-management system of forest regeneration in the Philippines.

Table 5.2: Proposed institutional arrangements among different stakeholders in tree-growing programme in the Philippines

Institution	Role	Nature of support
Government	facilitator/enabler	enabling policies provisions of more lands sourcing of funding broker between bank and tree growers arbitration/mediation legal support formulation of infrastructures technical assistance
Private Sector: • wood industry	catalyst/ reinforcer	market security production capital bank collateral for the tree growers
• NGOs		training programmes livelihood support community development services logistic support
• lending sector		production loans crop insurance livelihood fund
Tree growers/ community	main project implementor	organization local management communal co-operation subsidized labour social capital financial and material contributions

FROM CONCEPT TO GROUND TESTING

A prototype of the proposed co-management modality was first tested on the ground when PLAN International (a humanitarian child-focused organization without religious, political or organizational affiliation) and the Cagayan Valley

Program of Environment and Development (a joint-undertaking of the Isabela State University and Leiden University, The Netherlands) began to implement the Community-Based Forestland Regeneration and Related Research Project (COMFREP) in the Cagayan Valley Region, North-eastern Philippines on 1 September, 1997. Other major players included the DENR, local government units, local communities and the funding institution – USAID. The overall aim of the project was to explore a new strategy for forest regeneration through a community need-driven action plan. Using security of tenure and develop-mental assistance as incentives, the project envisaged mobilizing the grassroots in reforesting public lands without necessarily relying directly on government funds. The long-term intention is to strengthen the ongoing National Reforestation Program in the country.

Specific Objectives
The project has the following specific objectives:

1. To develop a community-based forest regeneration system that is spontaneous, farm need-driven, cost effective and sustainable;

2. To design and test sustainable community forest resource management plans that are economically gainful, ecologically sound, socially equitable and locally governed,

3. To assist the DENR in policy reformulation, particularly in the implementation of the Community-Based Forest Resource Management Programme in the country; and

4. To develop community-based intervention strategies in the areas of health, education and livelihood.

Collaborating institutions, their roles and expectations
Project implementation is under a partnership arrangement. The six partner institutions and their corresponding roles and expectations are:

• *USAID* (Philippines): Provides the initial funding for the first three years. From the donor's perspective, this joint-undertaking serves as a back-up project to its on-going policy restructuring efforts aimed at strengthening the implementation of the community-based forestry management programme of the DENR.

• *PLAN International*: Handles the project administration. It also infuses its regular funds to dovetail its community development activities with the action-research part of the project. The project serves as a social laboratory to test new paradigms in community development because it combines development activities and action research directed towards forestland rehabilitation. Although the project addresses a wide range of environ-mental concerns, human welfare remains on top of all the other develop-ment considerations at the field level.

- *Isabela State University (ISU) through the Cagayan Valley Program for Environ-ment and Development (CVPED)*: Having much experience in designing and testing field appraisal tools and methodologies over the years provides the technical expertise in carrying out the action-research component. From an 1SU standpoint, its long-term vision for the project is to establish a 'centre of excellence' in community-based forestland regeneration in Region 02.
- *DENR*: Releases and delineates public lands for communal tree-growing. Provides the legal and enabling instruments for the smooth conduct of the project in the field. It also assists in the technical work that requires its legal assistance such as the legitimization of tenure arrangements resulting from the outcome of the research later on. It regards the project as a form of a decision-support system to back up the on-going policy reforms taking place in the bureaucracy for the implementation of the community-based forestry programme.
- *Local Government Units (LGUs)*: Supra-local actors whom the project management co-ordinates most of the time in the field. They also assist In facilitating the field activities. The LGUs view the project as a training ground to practise local governance in natural resource management.
- *Communities*: Main actors of the project. They provide the organization, free labour, material support, indigenous knowledge and other social capital. For the locals or the communities, the project not only engender' the right institutional climate to harness their potentials for participating actively in the socio-economic, and political development process: the rehabilatation of the degraded communal forestland constitutes the ultimate goal of the project. After all, the most tangible indicator of the locals' social, economic and political development should be seen in the way they manage, control and develop the community resources entrusted to them.

Project characteristics
The project has the following characteristics:

- *Holistic*: It addresses the socio-economic, physical and other human welfare needs alongside of environmental rehabilitation. It combines development work and action-research. PLAN International carries out its regular com-munity development activities in the areas of health and nutrition, education and livelihood generation.

- *Community-driven research approach*: Unlike the usual scientist's prescriptive 'mode', the types of research to be undertaken are mainly dictated by the resource needs of the community. The Project Technical Team conducts the action-research in close collaboration with the locals.

- *No pre-determined tenurial instrument*: The project operates in areas without pre-determined tenure. It starts with an inventory of existing local resource needs or problems which will serve as clues for the development of a resource practice that is economically viable, ecologically sustainable and socially acceptable. More emphasis is given to the regeneration of the resource base. The specific type of tenure only comes at the end of the study as a means to further strengthen the already existing interaction between the resource-base and the local users. The locals will determine the most preferred institutional arrangements with regard to the use of community resources.

- *Build a 'cadre' of local forest regeneration specialists*: The project endeavours to raise a critical mass of local experts and technicians from the communities who will fully take over the management and technical responsibilities when it is phased out.

- *Process of continuous social negotiation*: One outstanding feature of the project is that it creates a wide space for social learning. As part of the research, coming up with the most appropriate institutional arrangement or tenurial instrument that is truly local-driven requires continuous articulation and negotiation of the local peoples' rights. The ultimate goal would be to generate a proposed policy measure for DENR and LGU consideration for the effective implementation of the community-based forest management programme in the Philippines.

Development scenarios

The project endeavours to pursue the following development scenarios:

- *Local capacity building*: The project conducts continuous training to enable local communities to manage their natural resources in a sustainable and equitable manner. A major component of this is the formal schooling of deserving youth in the community. PLAN International provides the scholarships and ISU-CFEM offers a degree programme in forestry.

- *Improved livelihood and quality of life*: The project also assists the community in coming up with viable livelihood options in terms of: 1) improving existing land use or developing current farm products and 2) expanding the economic and biological uses of the natural resources in the area through research and market networking. This is combined with the delivery of basic social and physical services in the areas of health and nutrition, education, housing and livelihood generation.

- *Environmental and resource sustainability*: While there is much concern for grassroots socio-economic and welfare development, the project simultaneously engages in forest regeneration activities. The locals through their organizations spearhead and sustain reforestation activities in understocked residual forests and grasslands areas delineated by the DENR as communal areas for forest development.

Project highlights

The project has just begun its field development activities. The first six months were devoted to community resource assessment and profiling. As far as the dynamics of co-management between the community and partner agencies is concerned, the following observations were evident from the first ten months of operation:

1. The locals voluntarily organized themselves around a common, clear agenda. Two overarching goals prompting them to unite in most of the project sites: a) to restore and protect their communal forest and b) to generate livelihood through community-based enterprises.

2. Community profiling and resource inventory were conducted with high participation by the locals.

3. Seedbed preparation was a communal activity steered by the self-evolved community organization.

4. The locals contributed free labour and even materials in the construction of temporary nursery sheds and in seedling production.

5. There is increased community vigilance against forest fires and poaching.

6. The LGU for each site endorsed the project as part of its regular projects in the village,

7. The DENR facilitated the release of public lands for the community and also initiated boundary delineation and survey activities in close collaboration with the locals and other stakeholders.

8. PLAN International started local capacity-building seminars and its health and livelihood activities.

9. CVPED completed the community profiling.

10. CVPED and PLAN International worked out the research agenda of the project in consultation with the locals.

EMERGING ISSUES IN COMMUNAL REFORESTATION

Ambiguity of the grassroots' identity as a management unit

Almost all natural resource management projects in the Philippines today are community-based in approach. The spontaneous tree growing at the farm level may not qualify for this category, because individual farmers tend to be regarded as private-interest groups. This may pose some technical difficulties when public lands are allocated for communal tree growing. Under the government's existing laws and regulations on issuance of forestland rights, the DENR cannot grant tenurial right to a private individual, unless he/she applies for the Socialized Industrial Forest Management Agreement (SIFMA). But areas targeted for SIFMA are mostly situated in understocked residual forest, usually far away from human settlements. From a strategic management standpoint, farm-based tree growing should start where the farmers are on-site. Normally, these sites are areas currently under cultivation by upland farmers. The absence of a formal binding instrument to encourage enterprising tree growers to encroach on adjacent portions of open public lands poses a big constraint to spontaneous woodlot expansion. Thus, unless the government recognizes individual rights within delineated communal lands, the prospect of having spontaneous tree-growing at the buffer zones of the forest frontiers cannot be accelerated.

Collective ownership and individual benefit

To transform degraded communal lands to farm forestry projects in a co-management system may seem unattractive from an individual's legal point of view. Because of the collective nature of ownership rights over the project, how to partition the communal lands equitably to individual families in the community requires no easy technical solution. How will the locals resolve among themselves the sharing and assigning of individual lots without any prejudice to their communal objective, that is to operate as a corporate body? Can individual resource access, still maintain a sense of communal ownership over the project? What are some institutional mechanism's to safeguard free riding or to balance individual interests with communal welfare?

'Morality' of paying farmers to do something for their future benefit

To motivate subsistence farmers to divert their productive time and efforts to something from which they can benefit sometime in the future is a difficult task. This is mainly because rural farmers are risk-averse and they do not have the luxury of time and resources for things, other than striving to earn a living on a daily basis. On the other hand, paying them to work on a project that belongs to them may ruin their intrinsic sound behaviour. In rehabilitating degraded communal lands using collective labour, how are we going to stimulate grassroots active and sustainable participation without necessarily paying them in cash? What aspects in the collaborative management can best address this dilemma?

Choice of tree species to plant
In government reforestation, the species of seedlings are prescribed by the DENR in relation to the intended use of the plantation, i.e. whether for protection, or production forestry or nature reserve. For farm forestry, usually the most preferred species are the fast growing ones because farmers are more interested in the income from the tree produce than its environmental value. If the farmer's short-term needs dictate the choice of species in reforesting communal lands that are still within the custodial domain of the government or the state, how can the long-term societal considerations be incorporated in the farming household's reforestation plan? What would be the proper proportion in terms of number of hectars or trees to be planted for production and for protection or for a watershed purpose?

Parochial bias
Implementing a project under apartnership arrangement is also a continuous process of social negotiation and a learning experience in organizational management. There is the likelihood that each member institution is locked up in its own institutional bias. Often, the 'one who holds the purse strings calls the shot'. How to be highly objective and neutral, yet flexible and open to healthy compromise is a difficult challenge, that requires special wisdom and skill in implementing collaborative undertakings.

Proper blending of local and professional knowledge
Common setbacks for local communities in coping with the legal requirements of a project are their limited technical knowledge and the government's prescribed organizational capacity as a condition for the issuance of institutional benefits or privilege. Resource inventory, community mapping exercises, preparation of management plans and implementation of the plans are normally done in partnership with NGOs or the academics. In as much as the design of most community-based projects is people-orientated, with a focus on local capacity building, we should not ignore the value of local knowledge, especially of those who have worked or have been working successfully over the years. A perfect blend between indigenous/local practice and professional knowledge should be explored to come up with culturally contextualized ways of doing things. Allowing the locals to integrate their knowledge system would

give them a sense of ownership over the project. The idea of having ownership while in the process of developing functional project approaches, strategies and methodologies creates a feeling of confidence in the locals which could in turn increase their initiatives to assume key roles in the project, even beyond its life-cycle. However the question is: what is the proper blend between local and professional knowledge that would not comprise the legal and existing standards of the DENR?

Institutional safeguards

In almost all community-based natural resource management programmes today, the local government Unit (LGU) is always included as a key actor in the management system. By law, a LGU is mandated to assume jurisdiction over the natural resources within its respective political boundary. This is a positive development towards democratizing the use of the country's natural wealth in favour of the majority poor. However, there are also some dangers ahead if the LGU is not yet technically and 'morally' prepared to take onthat new role as manager. Does devolution of powers really promote local community empower-ment or just an extension of power play over the natural resources at the local level? Are there some obvious levels of devolution of powers regarding the manage-ment of the natural resources ? What is the minimum condition to measuring LGU's resource management readiness? Have the necessary institutional mechan-isms already been put in place to guard against local executives' abusing access and control over the community resources?

The right interface

The devolution of authority in community-based natural resource management is a problematic issue that often affects the smooth transition from the highly centralized to a more localized mode of project governance. In devolution, power moves from top to bottom and, in the process, there will always be resistance. The resistance to change is one of them. This is usually provoked by the old power holders as a counter move to the emerging paradigm shift. As the power transfer process crosses many layers and boundaries of the formal structures, the more resistance is expected to surface. In the DENR, between the Central Bureau and the local community, there exist multi-layers of formal structures that have to be harmonized toward the direction of change. Failure to recognize the dynamics of power play between and among these structures or between local and supra-local actors may impinge on the smooth devolution process. In this context, there is a need to set the right interface that could pre-pare the effected actors of devolution to assume new roles. The assistance of civil society, academics and other neutral organizations is important in this aspect.

CONCLUSION

- The gigantic government Contract Reforestation Programme in the Philippines fell short of its targets in 1992, despite its huge funding, partly because it was implemented as a donor-driven programme.

- On the other hand, a number of spontaneous tree growing projects at the farm level exist without government support, but are not much highlighted. However, despite the success of these small tree growers, they can hardly expand into large commercial opperators by themselves because of certain legal and institutional constraints.

- In between these two extremes of tree-growing experience, there exists a locus of possible combinations of strength between the government's sponsored programme and the grassroots tree-growing initiatives.

- By changing the role of the government from implementor to facilitator, and by mobilizing the private sector's financial capital to support farm forestry, small farmers' tree-growing initiatives can grow into massive spontaneous and cost-effective national reforestation activities at the grassroots level.

- A successful reforestation programme depends largely on the proper blending of government institutional incentives, private sector investment and the grassroots resource capacities and development options as demonstrated by the initial findings of the Community-Based Forestland Regeneration and Related Research Project.

- To ensure long-term programme sustainability, government institutional incentives (for example tree and land tenure, provision of planting areas, tax incentives, technical assistance, infrastructure and enabling policies) and the private sector's investment (provision of production loans, crop insurance, market and price security) should match the tree growers' enterprising attitude.

- Failure to make the right blend between a government facilitative role, private sector investment and the grassroots initiative will continue to siphon off government reforestation funds.

ACKNOWLEDGEMENT

Due recognition is given to the Centre for Environmental Science, Leiden University, The Netherlands for sharing a portion of the author's dissertation. My great appreciation to PLAN International and the Cagayan Valley Programme of Environment and Development (CVPED) for allowing the USAID-Community-Based Forestland Regeneration and Related Project to be featured in this chapter.

NOTE

1   Taken from the technical paper by Pasicolan, *et al.*, 'Farm Forestry: an alternative to government-driven reforestation in the Philippines'. *Forest Ecology and Management*, Vol. 99 (1997).

REFERENCES

ANGOC (1991) *Community Participation, NGO Involvement and Land Tenure Issues in the Philippine Reforestation Program: An assessment of the ADB-Funded Contract Reforestation Program.* ANGOC.

Community-Based Forest Regeneration and Related Research Project. (1996) Approved Project Proposal to the USAID (Philippines). PLAN International and CVPED, Isabela State University, Cabagan, Isabela.

DENR (1990) *Master Plan for Forestry Development.* Diliman, QC, Philippines: DENR

Eder, J.F. (1981) 'From grains to tree crops in the Cuyanon swidden system'. In H. Olofson (Editor) *Adaptive Strategies and Changes in Philippine Swidden-Based Societies.* Laguna, Philippines: Forest Research Institute.

FMB (1988) *Philippine Forestry Statistics.* Diliman, QC, Philippines: DENR.

Garrity, D.P. and A.R. Mercado Jr (1994) 'Reforestation through agroforestry smallholder market-driven timber production on the frontier'. In J. Raintree and H. Fernandez. (eds) *Marketing Multipurpose Tree Species in Asia.* Bangkok: Winrock International.

Korten, F.F. (1993) 'Environmental Loans: More harm than good'. PURC News and Views. Manila: DLSU.

Metin, R.L (1991) 'Domestic Financial Infrastructures for Environmental Projects and Programs'. Paper presented to a symposium of the Futuristic Society 'The Philippine Environment Financing Environmental Conservation and Rehabilitation Projects/Programs', May 30–31,1991, Manila.

Olofson, H. (1980) 'An ancient social forestry. SYLVATROP'. *Philippines Forestry Journal*, vol. 5, pp. 255–262.

Pasicolan, P.N. (1996) 'Tree growing on different grounds: an analysis of local participation in contract reforestation in the Philippines'. PhD dissertation, Centre for Environmental Science, Leiden University, The Netherlands.

Pasicolan, P.N., Udo de Haes, H.A. and P. E. Sajise (1997) 'Farm forestry: an alternative to government-driven reforestation in the Philippines'. In J. A. Parrotta and J. W. Turnbull (eds), *Forest Ecology and Management Special Issue: Catalysing Native Forest Regeneration on Degraded Tropical Lands.* Amsterdam: Elsevier.

Pasicolan, P.N. and J. Tracy (1996) 'Spontaneous Tree Growing Initiatives by Farmers: An Exploratory Study of Five Cases in Luzon, Philippines'. SEARCA-ACIAR Imperata Project Paper 1996/3, ACIAR, Canberra: ACIAR.

Sajise, P.E. (1993) 'Sustainable land use systems in the Philippines: some lessons learned'. *IESAM Bulletin* vol.13 nos.(3–4).

Wiersum, K.P. and C.P. Veer (1983) 'Loan financing of smallholder tree farm in Ilocos: a commentary'. *Agroforestry Systems*, vol. 1: pp. 361–365.

Umali, R. (1989) 'Contract Reforestation: Today and tomorrow'. *Philippine Lumberman* vol., 35 no. 10: pp. 17–20.

CHAPTER SIX

Co-management of Forest Resources: The Bugkalot Experience

Dante M. Aquino

INTRODUCTION: THE BUGKALOTS THEN AND NOW

*T*he Bugkalots, more popularly known as Ilongots, are an indigenous people of the Philippines who became known because of their head-hunting activities in the past. They hugged the newspaper headlines in the 1960s because of these and so they were feared. During those days nobody dared to tread where they were likely to be encountered. That is why they were then living in a wide range of area even within the valleys now presently settled in by migrants. During those years they were generally isolated and had remained so until the early 1970s. This is also partly because the areas where they lived can only be reached through rugged terrains, which are hardly accessible even on foot.

The Bugkalots were never colonized. Spanish efforts to collect taxes and to evangelize them failed. The Americans tried to attract them to join mainstream society starting with the more accessible villages of Nueva Vizcaya but also did not succeed. The Japanese succeeded in creating fear among them, but this made them all the more isolated. They were generally left out during the Common-wealth period. These 'failures' were not only due to their punitive nature and the inaccessibility of the area but more because of the refusal of the Bugkalots to co-operate. For all these reasons they were generally isolated from the rest of the people who occupy the surrounding plains and valleys.

During a historic meeting of the Bugkalot tribe in 1967 at Madibuy (now a part of San Dionisio, Nagtipunan, Quirino Province), they agreed to abandon headhunting. At this same meeting they also decided to adopt 'Bugkalot' as a preferred term for their tribe in place of Ilongot, which was perceived to be associated with headhunting. Many things have changed since then (M. Rosaldo 1980, R. Rosaldo 1980, Salgado 1994).

There are now numerous migrant settlers who are interspersed with the Bugkalots. These migrants have greatly increased in numbers in the last 20 years and have subjugated the Bugkalots in many of the places they previously dominated. This migration was actually initiated by the government when it resettled people displaced from the Ambuklao and the Binga dam projects in the province of Benguet in the Cordilleras. Most of these, and those who followed after them, are either Igorots or Ifugaos. The Bugkalots either voluntarily moved or were driven away into the hinterlands. However, a few of them were able to assimilate into the 'invading' group (mainly because of affinity) and have remained to live with them. At present, the Bugkalots are found scattered in the confines of the mountain ranges of Sierra Madre, Caraballo and Mamparang. These are within the inaccessible areas of the provinces of Quirino, Nueva Vizcaya and Aurora (Figure 6.1).

Migration to the area was also intensified by the opening of roads during the logging boom in the late 1960. Many from the neighbouring towns and provinces took advantage of the enhanced access. Workers in the logging companies even came from as far as the Bicol region and the Visayas Islands. Many of these brought their families and some settled in some available areas or in areas opened by logging. Many opted to stay when a logging moratorium was declared in the early 1990s.

As a result of these developments, the Bugkalots of today are in many ways influenced by the migrants. They speak Filipino (the Philippine national language) and Ilocano (the unofficial regional language) with equal ease. The way they dress, the style of their houses and the manner in which they deal with people are not any different from the migrants. Futhermore, their appearance is typically Filipino and so similar in features to an Ilocano, an Ibanag or other ethnic group that they are hardly distinguishable from the invading migrants. However, there are a few relatively inaccessible *barangays* with some *sitios*[1] isolated enough to retain some semblance of Bugkalot culture, for example their houses, but none of these, is inhabited purely by Bugkalots because of intermarriages with other tribes, or migrant in-laws or their relatives.

Influences on the Bugkalots are not only from migrant neighbours or acquaintances. During the logging boom, they were exposed to new ways of resource utilization that resulted in 'easy money'. Many of them became accustomed to goods and services from outside and have become integrated into a market economy. When a logging moratorium was declared in 1992, the government introduced various forest conservation policies in various parts of the country. The Bugkalot area, because of its relatively intact forest areas (relative to other

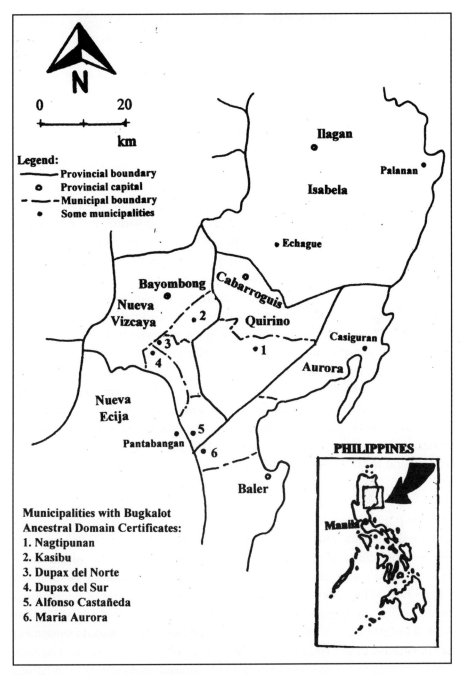

Figure 6.1: The relative location of the six municipalities in three provinces with Certificates of Ancestral Domain Claims awarded to Bugkalots

parts of the country where logging started much earlier), was always a pilot area for the government (through the Department of Environment and Natural Resources) for such programmes. Examples of these programmes range from the earlier arrangements for reforestation (individual, family and organization contracts), through the different social forestry approaches, to the various community-based forestry programmes.

Those kinds of programmes, which tried to involve them in environmental concerns influenced them in many ways. At present, even more significant policies and programmes are being implemented and 'pilot-tested' for the Bugkalots that are influencing their way of life. These include those resulting from the issuance of Certificates of Ancestral Domain Claim (CADC) to each of the municipalities with a recognized Bugkalot population and from those implemented by the Social Measure Task Force for Casecnan. Since both of these are 'development' and livelihood programmes, they are consequently changing the lifestyles of the Bugkalots.

The purpose of this chapter is to present the co-management applications and uncertainties for forest resources within the Bugkalot domain. This will be pursued by: (1) explaining how the Bugkalots came to be awarded Certificates (CADCs) for their domains; (2) presenting policy modifications that affected the operationalization of their Certificates; (3) discussing the promulgation of such policies for the domains; (4) raising relevant problems encountered during the initial implementation of government-sanctioned plans for some parts of the domains; (5) briefly introducing the newest policy shift for indigenous peoples and ancestral domains, the creation of the new National Commission on Indigenous Peoples; and (6) bringing forward some conclusions from the discussions.

ANCESTRAL DOMAINS FOR THE BUGKALOTS

After the popular People Power revolution in 1986, a new Philippine Constitution was drafted and later adopted in 1987. The Constitution of 1987 provides for the recognition and protection of the rights of the indigenous cultural communities to their ancestral lands to ensure their economic, social and cultural well being.[2] But neither the executive nor the legislative branches of government pursued efforts to enact a law for this purpose. Efforts started in the Department of Environment and Natural Resources (DENR) when it issued Department Administrative Order No. 2, series of 1993 (DAO 2, s. 1993), pursuant to such constitutional provisions. The Order (DAO 2) promulgated rules and regulations for the identification, delineation and recognition of ancestral land and domain claims.[3]

The identification, delineation and recognition of ancestral domain claims involve a tedious process.[4] For the Bugkalots, documentation began in 1994. This started in the province of Quirino and followed in the two other provinces. The Certificate of Ancestral Domain Claim (CADC) for the Bugkalots of Quirino (municipality of Nagtipunan) was awarded in late 1995. Four certificates were issued in 1996 for the Bugkalots of Nueva Vizcaya (one each for the munipalities of Kasibu, Dupax del Norte, Dupax del Sur, and Alfonso Castañeda). And in 1997, the last certificate was issued for the Bugkalots in the province of Aurora (municipality of Maria Aurora).

Domain certificates for the Bugkalots in Quirino
The CADC at Nagtipunan, Quirino, being the first Bugkalot CADC is way ahead of the others in all aspects,[5] at least in two of the ten *barangays* covered. In these two *barangays* (Landingan and Wasid), peoples organizations (POs) were organized and were used as pilot projects for community-based forest management (CBFM) by the DENR. The organizations are the Ilongot Livelihood Association, Inc. (ILAI) for *barangay* Landingan and Wasid Ilongot Tribe Association, Inc. (WITAI) for *barangay* Wasid. They have been implementing government-sanctioned forest co-management arrangements where one of the components is timber products extraction. The Natural Resources Management Program (NRMP), a foreign-funded DENR programme pampered them by way of assisting them in almost all aspects of their initial activities. Full-time project management officers were assigned to assist these organizations in the operationalization of their agreement with the DENR. The NRMP acted as the catalyst for the two organizations for the formation, training and registration of their organizations; in the bidding for an assisting organization for the initial years of implementing their Resource Management Plans;[6] by organizing and supporting the conduct of empowerment programmes (leadership training, capacity building, an information education campaign, visitation training, etc.). The NRMP also facilitated the issuance of a Community-Based Forest Management Agreement with the DENR for these two areas and the preparation of an Ancestral Domain Management Plan for the Quirino domain.

Domain certificates for the Bugkalots in Nueva Vizcaya and Aurora
While community-based programmes were being pilot-tested for the Bugkalots of Quirino, the government wanted to implement a trans-basin dam project at the Casecnan and Conwap rivers junction.[7] The project will divert water from the Casecnan River to the Pantabangan dam to augment the latter's water level for hydropower and irrigation. The project met with strong resistance because of people displacement and other undesirable impacts. The Bugkalots forwarded

20 demands before the implementation of the dam project.[8] The government in turn conducted consultations and negotiations with the concerned parties (Bugkalots, migrants, local government units and NGOs). As a result, the site was relocated and the design was modified.[9]

Then President Ramos created a Social Measure Task Force for Casecnan to address the 20-point demands of the Bugkalots. The Task Force, composed of department secretaries, is chaired by the Department of Agriculture secretary.[10] For its operation, the Task Force created Technical Working Groups (TWGs) at the regional level: for ecology and related services, for ancestral domains and for social services.

The TWG for ancestral domains became the driving force in the identification, delineation, and declaration of the domain areas for the provinces of Nueva Vizcaya and Aurora. The DENR, in co-ordination with other concerned government agencies, led the process with the logistic support provided by Task Force Casecnan.[11] Because of this, the domain certificates for the Bugkalots of these provinces were facilitated. The preparation of the domain plan, prepared by concerned Bugkalot leaders with the assistance of DENR personnel and processed for affirmation by the DENR secretary, was also facilitated by the Task Force.

POLICY CHANGES FOR THE DOMAINS

While events were unfolding in the implementation of community-based forestry programmes (CADC included) as a strategy for sustainable development of forest areas and the DENR was learning lessons in their implementation, policies were revised and rules and regulations were issued to strengthen various projects already in place. The Bugkalot domain was exposed to these fast-changing policies.

The policies issued in succession affecting ancestral domains include Administrative Orders coming from the DENR and an Executive Order from the Office of the President.[12] But for community based forest management agreements and ancestral domain areas, the specific policies issued are: DAO No. 96-34 *Guidelines on the Management of Certified Ancestral Domain Claims* and Memorandum Circular No. 97-12 *Guidelines for the Formulation of Community Resource Management Framework and Annual Work Plan for Community Based Forest Management Areas.* The Executive Order provides guiding principles for preparing domain plans, among which are:

1. The people have the right to formulate a domain plan reflective of their needs and aspirations. It should be made by the community, based on its own indi-

genous knowledge systems and practices with the option to call on external assistance;

2. The primacy of customary laws shall be recognized and respected. Ancestral domain plans shall basically affirm the people's right to self-determination (for example recognition of rights to their ancestral claims, promotion of cultural integrity, enhancement of their self-reliance and empowerment as a people, protection of the environment and the sustainable management and development of natural resources within domain claims, protection of their traditional resource rights, recognition of the right to information especially in relation to free and informed consent on all matters affecting their ancestral domains);

4. The people shall have autonomy in the preparation and implementation of their plans;

5. The role of outside institutions shall be limited to the conduct of information or education campaign activities and providing assistance in the resolution of legal and policy issues that would tend to impede, distract or prevent the people from exercising freedom in making their own plans for sustainable management of their ancestral domains.

The order also provides for the formulation and implementation of the domain plan, specifying the basic steps in its preparation including the details that should be covered by each step. It also includes some general guidelines for the formulation of work plans, supervision and monitoring of the ADMP implementation and attendant submission of reports.[13]

Management planning for the domains
Pursuant to DENR Administrative Orders No. 96-29 and 96-34, Memorandum Circular No. 97-12 *Guidelines for the Formulation of Community Resource Management Framework and Annual Work Plan for Community Based Forest Management Areas* was issued. For areas covered by community-based forest management agreements, the Memorandum requires the preparation of a Community Resource Management Framework. Such a framework is deemed equivalent to the ancestral domain management plan for ancestral domains.

The framework plan is a strategic plan of the community on how to manage and benefit from the forest resources on a sustainable basis. It describes the community's long-term vision, aspirations, commitments and strategies for the protection, rehabilitation, development and utilization of these resources. It is a document prepared by the community with the assistance of the DENR or local government staff. The framework is affirmed by the Community Environment and Natural Resources Officer of the DENR. The affirmation confirms that the document was prepared in a participatory manner (involving the community, the DENR, and other stakeholders) and that the DENR is committed to supporting the community in implementing it.

The Annual Work Plan, on the other hand, describes how the community intends to implement the goals in the framework during the year. The annual plan indicates the key activities to be undertaken in attaining such goals. It describes the community's specific objectives, strategies, activities, and targets for the year on resource protection, rehabilitation, development, utilization, and organizational strengthening, financing, marketing and enterprise development.

If extraction will be undertaken, the annual plan must include a resource use plan. In the case of indigenous people, the exercise of traditional resource uses only requires affirmation of their domain plan.[14] Otherwise (if they opt to extract and utilize forest resources along non-traditional lines), an annual plan with a resource use plan has to be prepared in accordance with the framework or domain plan.

The memorandum also sets some guiding principles that should be followed in the formulation of frameworks and annual plans:

1. *Participatory approach*: The plan preparations should be led by the organization and shall promote broad-based community participation and involvement;

2. *Multiple use forest management*: It should promote the multiple uses of forests with due consideration of attaining a balance between economic and environmental concerns. It should reflect the priority for the beneficial use of resources that entail little or no extraction especially of timber resources. Priority shall be given to the beneficial use with no extraction (for example ecotourism), followed by minimal extraction (for example of non-timber resources, water usage), with timber extraction being the last priority;

3. *Resources sustainability*: It should lead to the protection and improvement of existing forest resources, rehabilitation of degraded ones, and conservation of soil, water, wildlife and biodiversity resources and should result to higher productivity and sustainability;

4. *Integrated planning*: It should be consistent with, and forms an integral part of, the conservation and management of larger area development plans;

5. *Recognition of indigenous peoples' rights and practices*: It should promote the recognition and respect of people's rights (including intellectual property), indigenous knowledge systems and practices;

6. *Gender parity*: It should provide equal opportunities for men and women to participate and share in attendant responsibilities and benefits; and

7. *Effective resource utilization*: The plan should be based on sound ecological and economic principles. Priority shall be given to plantation timber species, non-timber forest products, and lesser-used species.

Before the department's officer affirms the annual plan of an organization for its domain or management area, he makes sure that the plan conforms with the pertinent policies and guidelines. He even prescribes a set of conditions that should be met in the implementation of the plan. These include provisions/restrictions on: the area of operation, the volume of timber by species group that may be harvested, tree marking, selective logging, implementation of labour-intensive methods and use of chainsaws, tractors, yarders, skidders, and logging road construction, log ponds, transport of logs, execution of supply contracts, provision of forest rehabilitation activities and allocation of funds from revenues and fees.

FOREST CO-MANAGEMENT: ISSUES AND INSIGHTS

For the two holders of community-based forest management agreements within the Quirino ancestral domain, some initial experiences in implementing the DENR-affirmed Annual Work Plan have been encountered. The Ilongot Livelihood Association, Inc. of Landingan was in its second year of implementing an annual work plan while the Wasid Ilongot Tribe Association, Inc. was in its initial year (as of 1998 (ILAI 1998)). It is on monitoring and observation of these initial years of operation that the issues and insights presented below have been based. Others were obtained from leaders and members of the POs and from the DENR hierarchy. Where warranted, a recommendation or two have been made. Such recommendations, similarly, were derived from interviews and from close contact with key actors, from the author's experiences in projects related to the CADCs for the Bugkalots and from his periodic stays with this indigenous people.

Co-management of forest resources: with whom?
The ancestral domain certification, the community-based forest management and other recent government programmes are all based on the concept of co-management of natural resources. Under Philippine conditions, these community-based approaches, over time, have evolved as sound and acceptable strategies for forest resources use and conservation, at least conceptually. On the implementation level, however, there is still a lot of room for improvement.

The two pioneering co-management projects in the Quirino ancestral domain are looked upon as models by the other eight organizations within the same domain as well as others in the five Bugkalot domains in the provinces of

Nueva Vizcaya and Aurora. As they are implemented in these two areas, however, the mechanics by which co-management should prosper are not in place. The concept of 'partnership' is not evident between the government and the people's organization. The latter is on the receiving end. Besides, businessmen are intruding in the partnership.

Since operations in these two areas are focused on timber extraction, there is a growing misconception at present that these co-management schemes suggest timber utilization that is far from the policy intentions. The mistakes made, either by omission or commission, by various actors in these initial implementations should be rectified so that they can be avoided in succeeding operations.

Domain plans: who prepares, who pays, who cares?
The preparation of the domain plan for the Quirino Bugkalots took some time. Primarily this was due to the fact that it was an initial effort on the part of the DENR and that there was no earlier experience of this kind. It was an advantage for the Quirino domain because an international NGO organized consultation meetings and assisted in the preparation of the domain plan. From a very thick document initially prepared by a national NGO, the plan evolved to a 15-page document 'prepared and submitted by' the Quirino Bugkalot domain federation chairman and ten sectoral representatives (the domain area is divided into sectors; a sector is composed of a *barangay* or a group of *barangays* where there are few Bugkalot households (Araño *at al.* 1997).

There are two versions of the plan, one in Tagalog and another in Ilocano (the national and the regional language respectively). Appended to it are: a five-year indicative plan (as Gantt chart); the organizational structure of the Quirino Bugkalot CADC Federation; a list of sectoral leaders (Chairman, vice-chairman and members of the Board of Directors); a brief profile on each *barangay's sitios*, total area, population by gender, and the total households; and some community maps.

The final version of the domain plan was a result of a tedious and expensive process. The output approximates the sentiments and desires of the Bugkalots because they were represented by their leaders, most of who are legitimate chieftains. The domain plan captured indigenous knowledge in many ways but also adopted non-traditional ways. Leadership line-up, for example, had been patterned after government requirements for registration. The plan is very comprehensive and contains those safeguards required of a framework plan. Most of these, however, have to be incorporated in each annual work plan.

The preparation of the annual plan, based on records, should be done by the organization's chairman of the board. In actuality, however, it is the project management officer who prepares it for the organization. This planning exercise is supposed to be organization-led with broad-based community participation and involvement. The organization leaders (at least) should be required to learn the basics of preparing their respective annual plans. This way the plan will capture the real-world situation in each area covered. Efforts should be done to develop the capability of the organizations so that they will, in the future, do this process themselves. Although DENR personnel should supervise the preparation of the plan, they should inhibit themselves from actually doing it.

Today, the annual plan is only prepared for formality's sake – only to legitimize the operation of the organization. The initial operation does not usually conform with what is planned. The organization should recognize and appreciate the need to use the annual work plan as a guide in their day-to-day operation. This necessitates the inclusion of a timetable for each activity included in the plan (ILAI 1998 and WITAI 1998).

Before it may be implemented, an annual plan needs an affirmation from the DENR community officer. This process is appropriate only if the tenets of the policies are strictly followed. In practice, what is given is an 'approval' of an annual plan with specific conditions.

On the part of the DENR, site specificity of the affirmation should be observed. Very notable is the 'standard' affirmation of annual plans, which concentrates on the resource use or timber extraction aspects despite the other priority activities listed in the annual plan. For example, the latter might include: activities and targets on plantation establishment, agro-forestry, timber stand improvement, assisted natural regeneration, and nursery establishment; resource development like forest protection, community strengthening; infrastructure development targets like enterprise development, information, education and campaign activities, and resource use. Ironically, there are no set conditions for these activities except the target areas for forest development. Even worse, there is no specific provision for monitoring and evaluation of the implementation of the plan.

The organizations are not financially independent and at present they are incapable of implementing their plans because of funding constraints. The plan does include statements on possible financial sources, but in practice private individuals provide financial assistance through memoranda of agreement or contracts with the organizations. But it is evident that all these are tied to the timber extraction aspect of the plan because those involved are wood processors, lumber dealers and furniture makers. Both organizations have existing supply contract agreements with furniture makers and other individuals who of course have vested interests.

Each organization, based on plans, will have its own processing plant (mini-sawmill). They have executed a memorandum of agreement with some individuals willing to finance their plant by paying them back in instalments or in kind from the production of the mill. The Landingan group has an operational sawmill while the Wasid group had previously constructed a shed and the mill foundation.

The annual plans lack provisions for financial management. There is no specific provision for profit sharing for example. Also very critical is the need to institutionalize accounting and the auditing of transactions entered into and performed by the organization. Enhancing the capability of the organization on financial management needs to be institutionalized.

Logging: revival of the 'good old days'
'Selective logging' is prescribed in the implementation of annual plans. The process involves specifying the cutting area for the year, set-up establishment and pre-marking sampling, tree-marking activities and an estimation of the allowable cut for the year. This process is reminiscent of the old TLA (timber license agreement) commercial logging system. The way the system is implemented in the domain area at present in some aspects is even worse.

Conducting the pre-marking sampling, the first activity, is problematic. Contrary to policy intents, this is government-led and participation by the organizations is usually limited to guiding the inventory team. No efforts are made to teach them the process so that they may do it by themselves subsequently. The situation is the same for the paperwork that follows and which shows the inventory results and how these will be reflected in the plan. The result is reflected as a stand and stock table with an estimate of the harvestable volume. No result, however, is generated for the residual trees to be left. The harvestable cut in the plan specifies the volume of trees to be cut per species grouping but not the corresponding number of trees from which this volume may be derived. There is also no indication of exactly where particular trees may be harvested.

Futhermore, the process of pre-marking sampling is not followed through to the purpose for which it was conducted – marking trees (those to be left and to be cut). Because of this there are no tree marking data that can be used as a basis for monitoring harvests and residual trees. This is aside from the fact that one of the conditions set in the affirmation of the annual plan is that 'tree marking must be completed not less than three months before felling operations and the felling directions must be specified'. Specifically, there should be a 'Tree Marking List' attached to the affirmation form. The list should specify each tree number, species, diameter and height.

It is evident that the selective logging system as implemented in the past is still the norm even if timber utilization is from domain areas which are supposed to be subject to community-based management. This system was designed for commercial big-time logging, well endowed with financial resources. Even in such a scenario, as experiences in the past showed, the system was found wanting because of problems in implementation, particularly lapses in monitoring and evaluation.

It is therefore necessary that as early as the preparation of the domain plan, or every time an annual plan is prepared, that a truly 'community-based' co-management system should be designed. Such as system should be simple enough that at least the leaders of the organization can comprehend and be able to implement it by themselves with minimal supervision from the DENR. Such a design should capture the indigenous internal mechanisms of the tribe. For example, in the Bugkalot domain areas, they have a tribal arrangement regarding areas where PO members gather (or may not gather) forest products. Such unwritten laws or arrangements should be revealed during consultations for plan preparation so that the control mechanisms for managing resource sustainability may be discussed for and adopted in plans.

Timber: where from, where to?
Only processed products are allowed to be disposed of by the organizations. The ideal set-up is for the organizations to do the milling themselves through minimally mechanized processes. As practised by the Landingan organization, milling is done via a man-driven carriage – truly a minimal mechanized processing. It would be better if the manpower came from local residents. As it is, the operators of the mini-sawmill come from outside and are non-Bugkalots. The set-up is in conformity with the agreement with the individual who provided financial arrangements for the acquisition and operation of the mill. This is tied up with the financial dependence of the organization on outside sources.

It is very necessary to monitor the arrival of round or square logs for processing at the mill site; however, accurate log scale records for logs brought to the mill are not available. These things should be monitored to evaluate whether the cut logs conform with logs marked to be cut. This is very critical for maintaining a sustained cut over time. Similarly, the outgoing processed lumber should be properly and accurately scaled and monitored. A copy of each outgoing load should be used in monitoring outgoing lumber from the Nagtipunan area, from within the DENR community area and from within the DENR provincial area.

Transporting products: receipts and documents

The transport of processed products coming from the domain area is monitored through established checkpoints along the major transport routes. The personnel at these checkpoints monitor the required documents and receipts for the transport, record them and countermark the outgoing documents. Data checked include the point sources of the products, the types and volume, charges paid, destination and other related matter.

It is important that people manning the checkpoints should be dedicated and true to their calling. It may be of help if a multi-sectoral team were to take charge of these checkpoints. Counterchecking to see if each load came from legal sources requires that the load should tally with what was released from the mills of the organizations concerned.

For documentation purposes, only 'original copies' of receipts, invoices and other documents should be used. Transporters should be made aware that nothing less will be allowed. DENR personnel are aware of the many ways and means used by transporters to cheat checkpoints. An important requirement should be that documentation is not reused. However this demands that those manning the checkpoints are not themselves involved in the fraud.

Beyond the documentation requirements is the need for physical monitoring of the processed product. This means that the load should be checked to see if the documents tally with the scales for loaded products. Under-weighing, mis-identifications and other forms of misrepresentation should be stopped. Dedication and practice are needed for this.

Labour requirements: let others do it!

The use of labour-intensive methods in the implementation of the annual plans is noble. It is to maximize the involvement and participation of the members of the organization. That is why there are limitations in the use of the chainsaw, encouragement in the use of work animals, a ban in the construction of roads, prohibition in the use of heavy machinery except in some instances, etc. However, the way the annual plans are implemented, only the leaders of the organizations are directly involved and they hire people from outside. Such labour forces come from as far as other *barangays* of Nagtipunan and from other towns in Quirino. Some Bugkalot leaders have labourers ranging who usually do timber extraction activities on a piece-wage system. These activities include felling trees, bucking and flitching or lumbering of logs, or minor transport of the sized product (*tukyod*, carrying timber on one's back with a rope support from the head) down to where major transport (by water or by truck) becomes possible. Most of these persons are involved in carrying the sized timber from the stump site to where it can be accessed through other means of transportation.

It appears that only a few Bugkalots are involved in the timber extraction activities. This may be reflective of the provisions in their domain plan that provide for additional sources of livelihood to augment household income. Another of the specified strategies to attain the plan's objectives is sustained livelihood training. More significant is the adoption of the principle that there is a need to have other sources of income to lessen dependence on timber cutting. It is evident that Bugkalots shy away from logging aspects requiring tedious manual labour. In a way, this is favourable for resource conservation. However, the involvement of well-motivated and highly skilled outsiders may hasten extraction. Besides, it is envisaged in the domain plan that benefits accruing on site should be maximized by using labour from within the organization membership or *barangay* residents.

Fee collection: who receives?
The generation of funds for different purposes is adequately provided for within the set conditions in the affirmation of the annual plans. Among the funds institutionalized in the implementation of the plan are:

1. *Community fund* – 20 per cent of the net profit, as contribution for the implementation of CADC to be deposited in a separate bank account.
2. *Community forestry development trust fund* – 30 per cent of gross revenues from sales of forest products (gross revenue less forest charges) to be deposited for reforestation or any forest rehabilitation activity to be carried out within the domain area by the ancestral domain.

These funds are aside from the regular forest charges that are collected based on the volume of trees and the category group of each tree species. DENR Administrative Order No. 22, s. 1993, section 24 provides that the trust fund shall be administered by the community for forest development purposes, but just as there is a need to institutionalize financial management for the proceeds coming from transactions related to the implementation of the annual plan, there is also a need for the systematization of trust fund management (for example collection, disbursement, accounting and auditing). The same is true for the community fund, but this is at the level of the Quirino Bugkalot Federation, the overall organization of the ten sectors within the domain.

Accomplishment reports: what for?
One of the conditions set in the affirmation of the annual plans is the submission of regular monthly and annual accomplishment reports on all programmed

timber extraction and development operations. This should follow a standard reporting format on selective logging, reforestation, timber stand improvement and enrichment planting for purposes of evaluation and field monitoring by the DENR.

In general the organizations shy away from paperwork. Data recording and filing need to be systematized within the organization. Log arrival and timber deliveries, for example , should be systematically recorded. Without such documentation and record keeping, there is no way the organization can accurately comply with the required reports. Again, the training provisions in the plans should not only be on paper.

Monitoring for improvement: for whom?
Monitoring and evaluation is ideally done for the improvement of the organization's operation, but it should be based on documented real-world data; that is, what is on paper should be verifiable on the ground. To this end, the organizations have a long way to go. Their data gathering, record keeping and documenting capabilities should be improved by appropriate training.

Monitoring and evaluation is a two-way process: the evaluators should do it thoroughly and honestly for the improvement of the organizations, and they should support it willingly and accept it openly for the improvement of their operation and performance. With well-intentioned efforts from both sides, the ancestral domains will improve in all aspects of their operation and ultimately redound to their own success.

Monitoring and evaluation is very critical for the sustainability of forest resources. Assuming that the harvestable volume (allowable cut) set forth in the annual plan is in accordance with the prescribed levels,[15] then each harvest brought out from the forest should be closely monitored. This will insure that only the allowable cut is harvested so that the sustainability of the resource is assured.

Monitoring and evaluation should not only be based on documents and the actual products brought out from the forest, it should include monitoring and evaluation on-site where the harvest came from. This will ensure that each tree cut corresponds to those that should be cut as planned. Strict implementation of monitoring and evaluation will also ensure that no illegal activities or shady deals are made. Illegal logging and timber poaching will then become a thing of the past.

It is therefore necessary that a multi-sectoral monitoring team be organized. They should be willing to do monitoring activities 24 hours a day. In addition, there is a need for the conduct of an independent evaluation team for the assessment of the overall and detailed performance of the entire ancestral domain.

It would be much better if monitoring and evaluation were to be detailed within the annual plan and be made a prominent condition in the affirmation of the plan.

THE NATIONAL COMMISSION OF INDIGENOUS PEOPLES: CHANGE FOR THE BETTER OR ...?

Republic Act 8371, otherwise known as The Indigenous Peoples' Rights Act of 1997, enacted by the Philippines Congress was signed into law by the then President Ramos. The law created a commission, the National Commission on Indigenous Peoples (NCIP), mandated to protect and promote the interest and well-being of the indigenous cultural communities/indigenous peoples (ICCs/IPs) with due regard to their beliefs, customs, traditions and institutions. The commission is an independent body under the office of the president and is composed of seven commissioners including the chairman.

Among the 17 powers and functions of the NCIP[16], many will have significant and direct bearing on existing ancestral domain areas recognized by the DENR. These are:

1. To formulate and implement policies, plans, programmes and projects for the economic, social and cultural development of the ICCs/IPs and to monitor the implementation thereof (§ c);

2. To issue certificates of ancestral land/domain title (§ e);[17]

3. To co-ordinate development programmes and projects for the advancement of the ICCs/IPs and to oversee the proper implementation thereof (§ h); and

4. To issue appropriate certification as a pre-condition to the grant of permit, lease, grant or any other similar authority for the disposition, utilization, management and appropriation by any private individual, corporate entity or any government agency, corporation or subdivision thereof on any part or portion of the ancestral domain taking into consideration the consensus approval of the ICCs/IPs concerned (§ m).

After five of the seven commissioners were appointed, 'The Rules and Regulations Implementing The Indigenous Peoples' Rights Act of 1997 (IPRA)', issued on 9 June, 1998, was promulgated to prescribe the procedures and guidelines in order to facilitate compliance therewith and achieve the objectives thereof. It is necessary that these new policies affecting indigenous peoples in general and ancestral domains in particular should be synchronized with the old policies affecting the same. It has been alleged that the rules and regulations implementing the IPRA of 1997 was fast-tracked and that the consultations held were lacking. Information dissemination efforts are presently initiated by the Task Force Casecnan which organized a regional forum for this purpose. It is hoped that through such meetings, differences will be ironed out for the attainment of the worthy purposes of the law, which will hopefully redound to the promotion of the individual and collective rights of indigenous peoples. The uphill climb for indigenous peoples' movement in the country has just began.

CONCLUSIONS

The Bugkalots have been the subject of various government programmes and projects geared towards the co-management of natural resources within their areas of jurisdiction. For almost a decade, they were exposed to the fast-evolving strategies of the government for the conservation of natural resources within their domain.

With six domain certificates issued to the Bugkalots and with only two community-based agreements issued to two of the ten sectors in the Quirino domain, a lot of potential agreements are of with the offing. The initial experiences in the two pioneer domain certificates, whether a success or a failure, will be influential in the future of the prospective co-management areas within the Bugkalot domains. There is therefore a need to do things appropriately and correctly at these sites. Mistakes, if any, should be rectified immediately. Both areas are looked upon by others as examples for the management of their respective domains. It is only in doing things the right way that these two pioneer ancestral domain management sites can be deserving models on which the other ancestral domains may base their own future. In some ways, the future of co-management of the entire Bugkalot ancestral domain in the three provinces depends on lessons to be learned from these sites.

To operationalize the worthy intentions and the sound principles of the community-based forest management strategy, there is a need for in-depth study and identification of appropriate 'community-based' knowledge systems and practices so that activities to be undertaken of the ancestral domain may be defined in accordance and with these made compatible with them. Success in the co-management of forest resources is possible only through such an approach.

NOTES

1   The *barangay* is the smallest political and administrative unit of the Philippines. It was formally used in place of *barrio* by the constitution written after martial law was declared in 1972. Within mountainous areas like the Bugkalot country, a

barangay sometimes covers a wide expanse of area with a number of isolated groups of neighbouring houses, called a *sitio*. Within these areas, such *sitios* are generally separated from the centre of the *barangay*.

2   The Constitution of 1987 contains parts specifically highlighting indigenous cultural communities: Article II, Section 22; Article XII, Section 5; and Article XIII, Section 6.

3   *Ancestral land* refers to land occupied, possessed and utilized by individuals, families or clans who are members of the indigenous cultural communities since time immemorial by themselves or through their predecessors-in-interest, continuously to the present except when interrupted by war, force majeure or displacement by force, deceit or stealth. (Sec. 3c, DENR DAO 02, s. 1993). On the other hand, *ancestral domain* refers to all lands and natural resources occupied or possessed by indigenous cultural communities, by themselves or through their ancestors, communally or individually, in accordance with their customs and tradition since time immemorial, continuously to the present except when interrupted by war, force majeure, or displacement by force, deceit or stealth. It includes all adjacent areas generally belonging to them and which are necessary to ensure their economic, social and cultural welfare. (Sec. 3.b, DENR DAO 02, s. 1993).

4   The process is spearheaded by a Provincial Special Task Force for Ancestral Domain in the Provincial Office of the DENR. In co-ordination with local government units, non-government organizations, cultural community offices, etc. and in consultation with the concerned indigenous cultural community (ICC), the boundaries of ancestral domains are identified. Information campaign is conducted and publication to this effect is made on print media and posted in prescribed places. The ICC must submit proofs of claims which may include any of the following: written accounts of their customs and traditions; written accounts of their political structure and institutions; fixture showing long-term occupation such as those of old improvements, burial grounds, sacred places and old villages; historical accounts; survey plans and sketch maps; anthropological data; genealogical surveys; pictures and descriptive histories of traditional communal forest and hunting grounds; pictures and descriptive histories of traditional landmarks such as mountains, rivers, creeks, ridges, hills, terraces and the like; or write-ups of names and places derived from the native dialect of the community.

After submission of proofs, the Task Force conducts ocular inspection of the territory, conducts consultations with people most likely to be affected by the issuance of the certificate and prepares a report. It acts favourably upon any claim that is deemed sufficiently proved, if otherwise, the contending parties meet and come up with a resolution of the conflict. After documentation process, a perimeter survey is conducted with the ICC claimants duly represented for the identification of landmarks and exact boundaries in the ground. Upon receipt of the recommendation from the provincial task force, the DENR Regional Executive Director makes a recommendation to the Secretary of DENR who issues the Certificate (CADC).

5   The documentation for the Quirino domain was initiated by the USAID-funded Natural Resources Management Program of the DENR. Initial preparations started

in 1994 during the implementation of a DENR-led project called Conservation and Development of the Residual Forests (CDRF), an NRMP-led NGO-implemented project. The project was contracted by the DENR to the Technologists for Optimal Programming Development, Inc. which collaborated with the Cagayan Valley Resources Development Foundation, Inc., both NGOs based at Cabagan, Isabela. The contract involved the preparation of a Resource Management Plan of a 3,000-hectare forest area within *barangays* Landingan and Wasid (which later became a part of the 108,000-hectare CADC area for Quirino Bugkalots). For the preparation of the plan, the contractors with representatives from the communities conducted intensive inventories on the biophysical resources (timber, non-timber, lesser-used, and other species, including wildlife) and the social resources (demographic and socio-economic surveys, key informant interviews, consultations, etc.). The project was implemented for a period of one year.

The final output of the project is a three-volume resource Management Plan for each of the two *barangays* covered. (The first volume is the plan proper, the second is the inventory results [stand and stock tables by management unit, by species group, both for timber and non-timber] and the third is the digital [geographic information system] maps.) Among the significant provisions of the plan is the establishment of a people's organization for the implementation of their respective plans and the employment of an assisting organization (AO) in the initial years of implementation. More details of the plan are presented in Araño et al. (1997).

It was after the project that the NRMP, in preparation for the implementation of the Resource Management Plan, initiated the establishment of a people's organization in each of the concerned *barangays*. And it was also during this period when documentation was prepared for the identification and delineation of an area for the issuance of a CADC for the Bugkalots of Quirino.

6   The implementation of the Resource Management Plan of the two organizations, at least for the first few years, was to be assisted by an assisting organization. The Natural Resources Management Program facilitated the bidding process. It was published in the dailies and three NGOs, one from the province and two from Metro Manila, filed their intentions to bid. However, when formal bidding was held only two bid, the other one from Manila backed out.

The discrepancies (technical and financial) in the bids were very significant. The Manila NGO has a much better offer (e.g. the organizations would be assisted in building up relevant capacities and starting at the third year the assisting organization would begin to leave the organizations to operate alone and be completely out of the picture by the fifth. The organizations were to decide which of the two should be involved. It happened that the local NGO had a powerful person who exerted pressure on the organizations. The organizations, after a closed-door overnight dialogue, decided that each wanted to have its own assisting organization. This seemed to be a nice arrangement, but the politician wanted both for the local NGO. The NRMP wanted to be apolitical and declared the bidding a failure. If only process was consum-mated then, the scenario might be different today.

7   The proposed dam site is within the jurisdiction of Nagtipunan, Quirino. This will increase the irrigable area within Region III (Central Luzon) particularly in the provinces of Nueva Ecija and Pangasinan and will augment the electrical supply for the Luzon grid. The dam infrastructure was huge (197 m high) with a large reservoir area which would cause displacement of some households. Opposition to the project came from various sectors: the Bugkalots, migrants, local government units, NGOs and religious groups. Sentiments came even from distant places: some came from Nueva Ecija (farmers' groups expressing support), while others were from the province of Cagayan more than 200 km downstream (an NGO group which was against the project). Stands varied: from 'unequivocally opposed', 'conditional yes', 'yes with reservation' to 'in favour'.

8   The 20 demands of the Bugkalots affected by the Casecnan Multipurpose Irrigation and Power Project are as follows: (1) creation of a separate Ilongot (Bugkalot) municipality, (2) declaration, identification and delineation of municipal boundaries, (3) construction of *barangay* halls and other public administrative structures, (4) provision for salaries of Bugkalot indigenous officials, (5) percentage share for the Ilongot tribe of the project's proceeds, (6) percentage share of any mining operation in the future, (7) construction of access and alternate routes to all settlements directly or indirectly affected by the project, (8) provision of free electricity while resettlement is in process, (9) construction of irrigation systems, (10) provision of employment opportunities, (11) assistance to farm production in the form of farm implements, farm animals and cattle dispersal, (12) resettlement (should there be any submersion of communities), (13) provision of food subsidy while resettlement is in process, (14) provision of free housing, (15) provision of scholarship grants for vocational and tertiary education, (16) establishment of elementary and secondary schools with the construction of school facilities, (17) provision of health services with health facilities, (18) provision of sports facilities, (19) delineation and survey of Bugkalot ancestral domains in the provinces of Aurora, Nueva Vizcaya and Quirino and (20) assistance in the management of sustainable development within the ancestral domain claims.

9   The dam site was relocated upstream from within the junction area of the Casecnan and Conwap rivers, first to Casecnan-Abaca junction and finally to the Casecnan-Taang junction. The relocation necessitated the revision of the structural plans: the dam structure was reduced (height was reduced from 197 m to 107 then to 20–25; length from 869 m to 500 then to 100–120), resulting in the reduction of the reservoir area (from 3,610 ha to 500 then to 'almost nil') and watershed area (from 115,000 ha to 59,046 then to 58,200). The expected outputs were likewise reduced: water diverted to Pantabangan dam from 1,800 million cubic meters per year to 870 then to 802; hydropower potential from 268 megawatts to 270 then to 140; and irrigation potential from 92,300 ha to 50,000 then to 50,000.

10   The Task Force was provided with a P3M budget from the president's office funds. The Technical Working Groups created at the regional level are headed by regional directors: TWG for ecology and related services, regional executive director of the

Department of Environment and Natural Resources as chairman; TWG for Ancestral Domains, regional director of the Office of Northern Cultural Communities; and TWG for Social Services, director of the Department of Social Welfare and Development.

11 The DENR (through its provincial and community special task forces [the FSTFAD and CSTFAL, respectively] spearheaded the preparation of the necessary documentation with the co-operation of other concerned government and non-government agencies and with the financial assistance from Task Force Casecnan. Likewise, the preparation of an Ancestral Domain Management Plan ADMP) was spearheaded by the DENR through the people's organizations in each of the domain areas. These and related development decisions are taken during the regular monthly meetings conducted by the TWGs, thus pressuring their earlier resolutions.

12 Since the issuance of DAO 2, s. 1993, various Department Administrative Orders (DAOs) affecting CADC areas were issued by the DENR in response to lessons learned in the implementation of the Community Forestry Program. For example in April 1993 (DAO 2 was issued in January), DAO No. 22 (Revised Guidelines for Community Forestry Program) was issued to: 'initiate community-based forest development management and utilization of natural resources within second growth upland forest to promote social equity and prevent further degradation of natural resources; to protect the remaining primary forests with the help of the community; and enhance institutional capacity of the DENR, LGUs, educational institutions and NGOs in catalyzing community-based forest management.'

In July 1995, after some time of implementation of the various community-based programmes, President Ramos issued Executive Order No. 263, series of 1995. The title of the Order is adopting Community-Based Forest Management as the National Strategy to Ensure the Sustainable Development of the Country's Forest Land Resources and Providing Mechanisms for its Implementation. In October 1996, the DENR issued DAO 96-29 known as Community Based Forest Management Program (CBFMP). The order prescribes the rules and regulations for the implementation of Executive Order 163. CBFMP became the overall umbrella programme of the DENR. It integrated and unified all people-orientated forestry programmes including the Integrated Social Forestry Program (ISFP), the Upland Development Project (UDP), the Forest Land Management Program (FLMP), the Community Forestry Program (CFP), the Low Income Upland Communities Project (LIUCP), the Regional Resources Management Project (RRMP), the Integrated Rainforest Management Project (IRMP), the Forest Sector Project (FSP), the Coastal Environment Program (CEP), and the Recognition of Ancestral Domain/Claims. Indigenous peoples with CADCs or CALCs may, at their option, participate in the CBFMP through the preparation of an Ancestral Domain Management Plan (ADMP) after which a CBFM Agreement shall be issued over portions of the CADC or CALC which are within forestlands, thus the tenurial instruments CADC-CBFMA and CALC-CBFMA. The CBFMA is an agreement between the DENR and the participating People's Organization which has a duration of 25 years renewable for another 25 years.

Also pursuant to Executive Order No. 263 series of 1995, DAO 96-30 was issued for the Integration of all the Community-Based Forest Management Strategy and People-Oriented Forestry Programs and Projects into the DENR Regular Structure. The order provided for the integration of CBFMS and POF programmes and projects to the Forest Management Bureau (FMB) until 31 December, 1997. CBFMS stands for Community-Based Forest Management Strategy while POF means People-Orientated Forestry. CBFMS and POF programmes and projects refer to: the Integrated Social Forestry Program (ISFP), the National Forestation Program (NFP-funded under ADB1); the Low-Income Upland Communities Project (LIUCP); the Community Forestry Program (CFP), the Community-Based Forestry CBF funded by RP-German); the Community Forest Management (CFM under NRMP), the Regional Resources Management Project (RRMP under ENR-SECAL), the Forestry Sector Project (FSP) funded by Forestry Sector Project Loan or ADB2) and Recognition of the Indigenous Peoples. For the implementation of these, different offices of the department have been tasked to handle each programme or project. For 'streamlining' purposes, such programmes and projects are integrated into the regular DENR structure, particularly into the FMB.

13 As provided for by DAO No. 96-34 (*Guidelines on the Management of Certified Ancestral Domain Claims*) the basic steps in preparing a domain plan include: (1) conduct of community workshops on the plan concept, (2) participatory appraisal of the domain existing natural resources and socio-economic conditions, (3) identification and indication of specific domain management units on a map, (4) formulation of indicative development activities, (5) preparation of the indicative plan in the community's own language or any they prefer, (6) presentation for final review by the community members gathered in a general assembly and (7) transmission of the adopted plan to the nearest CENRO concerned who shall forward the same to the DENR secretary and other offices through proper channels.

The order also provides that work plans (i.e. Annual Work Plans) may be formulated by the IPs to guide implementation processes indicating how each priority activity may be carried out. Specific details on Work Plans and their preparations are covered in a succeeding Memorandum Circular issued by the DENR secretary. The necessary supervision and monitoring of the ADMP implementation is under the responsibility of the DENR (through its PSTFAD) in close co-ordination with the concerned IP and other agencies. With the new National Commission on Indigenous Peoples having jurisdiction over these areas, the supplementation of functions with that of the DENR need to be ironed out as soon as possible. At least annually, the PSTFAD or any appropriate body shall submit an ancestral domain management report to the regional executive director for information and guidance.

14 Memorandum Circular No. 97-12 requires that, in case of an indigenous people exercising traditional resource uses, these indigenous systems must be validated firmly, either at the time of the preparation or during the implementation of the domain plan, through anthropological studies and other similar methods. If validated to be genuine traditional resource use practices, the IP can practice such without the need for preparing an Annual Work Plan or a Resource Use Plan.

15 Memorandum Circular No. 97-12 prescribes that the annual plan, in its Resource Use Plan (RUP), shall indicate the following: (1) the resource to be harvested/utilized, (2) the approximate area or location of the subject resource that will be harvested for that year (to be indicated in a copy of the domain or community map), (3) the expected approximate quantity to be harvested during the period, (4) the community's expected harvesting schedule and extraction methods to be employed, and (5) plans on marketing the products. The memorandum also prescribes that also to be included in the annual plan is the planned assistance of the DENR community officer staff to the people in determining the extraction/harvest levels of the resource, based on allowable cut determination prescribed by existing rules and regulations on the matter. In case of timber, the people shall be assisted by the DENR community officer staff concerned to inventory and mark those intended to be cut, and shall attach a tree marking list to the resource use plan affirmation form included in this tree marking list which indicates the tree number, species, diameter, and height which shall be the basis for the organization's allowable cut embodied in the annual plan.

16 Chapter VII, Section 44 (§ a to § q), Republic Act No. 8371, otherwise known as The Indigenous Peoples' Rights Act of 1997.

17 This documentation process from identification, delineation and certification of ancestral domains is generally adopted by the new law, *Indigenous Peoples Rights Act of 1997*, except that this function has now been taken over from the DENR by the newly created National Commission on Indigenous Peoples (NCIP) and that instead of a certificate a title is issued both for ancestral domains and ancestral lands; i.e. a CADT for a CADC and a CALT for a CALC.

REFERENCES

Araño, R.R., D.M. Aquino, J.R. Acay Jr, M.R. Romero and F.G. Talosig (1997) 'Conservation and development of the residual forest: the case of Nagtipunan, Quirino'. In R.S. Guzman and W.T. de Groot (eds), *Research for the Sierra Madre Forest*. Proceedings of the second CVPED conference, 23–26 August, 1994. Cabagan, Isabela: Cagayan Valley Program of Environment and Development pp. 101–113.

DENR Administrative Order No. 02, series of 1993. 'Rules and Regulations for the Identification, Delineation and Recognition of Ancestral Land and Domain Claims'. Manila.

—— No. 22, series of 1993. 'Revised Guidelines for Community Forestry Program'. Manila.

—— No. 95–19. 'Rates of Forest Charges pursuant to Republic Act No. 7161 (R.A. 7161) and based on the FOB Market Price of Forest Products.' Manila.

—— No. 96–29. 'Rules and Regulations for the Implementation of Executive Order 263, Otherwise Known as the Community-Based Forest Management Strategy (CBFMS)'. Manila.

—— No. 96–30. 'Integration of All the Community-Based Forest Management Strategy and People-Oriented Forest Programs and Projects into the DENR Regular Structure'. Manila.

—— No. 96–34. 'Guidelines on the Management of Certified Ancestral Domain Claims'. Manila.

DENR Memorandum Circular No. 97–12. 'Guidelines for the Formulation of Community Resource Management Framework and Annual Work Plan for Community Based Forest Management Areas'. Manila.

Executive Order No. 263, series of 1995. 'Adopting Community-Based Forest Management as the National Strategy to Ensure the Sustainable Development of the Country's Forest Land Resources and Providing Mechanisms for its Implementation'. Manila.

Ilongot Livelihood Association, Inc. (ILAI) (1998) *Annual Work Plan.*

Ilongot Livelihood Association, Inc. and Department of Environment and Natural Resources (1997) *Amended Community Based Forest Management Agreement.* April.

National Commission on Indigenous Peoples (1998) The Rules and Regulations Implementing the Indigenous Peoples' Rights Act of 1997, 9 June.

Natural Resources Management Program (1994) Framework Management Plan of the Bugkalot Ancestral Domain in Nagtipunan, Quirino, 21 November.

Quirino CADC Federation (1997) Katutubong Plano Para sa Pamamahalang Lupang Ninuno ng mga Bugkalot (Nagtipunan, Quirino), July.

Republic Act No. 8371 (1997) The Indigenous Peoples Rights Act of 1997. 29 October.

Rosaldo, Michelle Z. (1980) *Knowledge and Passion: Ilongot Notions of Self and Social Life.* Cambridge: Cambridge University Press.

Rosaldo, Renato I. (1980) *Ilongot Headhunting: 1883–1974: A Study in Society and History.* Stanford: Stanford University Press.

Salgado, Pedro V. (1994) *The Ilongots 1591–1994*. Manila: Lucky Press, Inc.

Wasid Ilongot Tribe Association, Inc. (WITAI) (1998) *Annual Work Plan*.

Wasid Ilongot Tribe Association, Inc. (WITAI) and Department of Environment and Natural Resources (1997) *Amended Community Based Forest Management Agreement.* April.

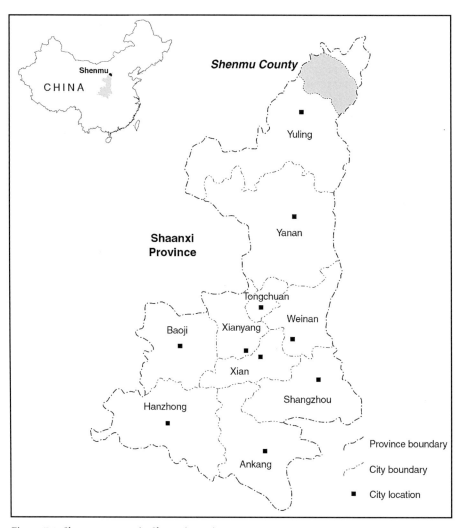

Figure 7.1: Shenmu county in Shaanxi province

CHAPTER SEVEN

Pastureland Management in Post-Reform China: Grazing on Ambiguously Owned Land

WEI HU

INTRODUCTION

A literature review of Chinese animal husbandry studies in the post-reform era suggests that a rather comprehensive series of measures is required if there is to be sustainable development of husbandry in China. The capital base of the industry should be strengthened, as should the fodder crop base; the acreage of irrigated pastureland should be increased; rotational grazing should be reintroduced; standards of animal health and care should be improved; improved species should be bred or introduced; and wider measures should be introduced to improve general pasture usage and management (Cheng and Yie 1994; HZPG 1984; Xi *et al.* 1994).

Such measures presuppose an appropriate institutional and physical framework for pastureland management. In many areas of China no such institutional arrangements are in place, however, as was reflected in a survey I conducted in Shenmu County, in the Loess Plateau district, the area examined in the present chapter. Animal husbandry, in the post-Mao reform era, is based on short-term priorities and is leading to serious overgrazing and resource degradation. Farmers now allow their animals to graze on pastureland which, although nominally still 'collective', is today characterized by ambiguous ownership and user rights. Communal management of public grassland is being seriously neglected and resource depletion is now commonplace. The husbandry resource base established in the collectivist era is being exhausted, and potentially damaging developments are occurring at an alarming pace. In post-reform China abolition of collective, state-supported grassland management has spawned a form of pastureland management and ownership that is neither private nor public. The communal pastures are consequently facing a 'tragedy of the commons' and an appropriate form of institutional and communal co-management is urgently needed (Ostrom *et al.* 1993).

Based on survey data, oral history and 20 years of historical records, this chapter examines husbandry development and the degradation of pastureland resources in the context of ownership and management systems in post-reform China. The relationship between weakened collective management and individual grazing activity is discussed against the background of damaged husbandry infrastructure and open access to public pastureland. Finally, a series of policy measures is recommended.

SHENMU COUNTY

The surveyed area, Shenmu County, lies in the north of the Chinese province of Shanxi, between 109° 42' and 110° 54' E and 38° 13' and 39° 27' N (Figure 7.1). With a total area of 7517.6 km it is the largest county of the province. The county is located in the transitional zone between the semi-arid Loess Plateau and the Mao Wusu desert and is a fragile and vulnerable ecosystem. It is characterized by three geomorphological zones, along a north–south axis. The southern zone comprises the narrow gorge of the Yellow River, surrounded by bare rock and steep cliffs, and accounts for 7 per cent of the area. The central-southern zone, 31 per cent of the area, consists of rolling loess hills with steeper outcrops of gravel and rock.

The most extensive zone, the northern, 62 per cent of the county, is mainly natural grassland on sandy soil, interspersed with moving sand dunes as well as areas of forest. The topography is gentle. In the grassland areas the water table is high, providing substantial water resources for developing forestry and husbandry. The coarse-textured soil has a poor vegetation cover. Annual rainfall, 448 mm on average, is uneven, with most (69 per cent) falling in the summer. There is frequent inclement weather such as droughts, severe frosts, hail, strong winds and torrential rainfall, often causing severe damage to arable and livestock farming.

As a transitional area between arid steppe and forest, Shenmu is suitable for animal husbandry. The land resources potentially available for forest and pastureland are substantial: 1.83 million *mu*,[1] according to the survey cited. At present 21.8 per cent, 18.8 per cent and 27.0 per cent of the land is devoted to arable farming, forestry and husbandry, respectively. The ratios between earnings are 2.6 to 1.0 to 0.7, however. Shenmu farmers are agro-pastoralists, with both arable fields and livestock. The 3.057 million *mu* of pastureland is virtually all (99.6 per cent) natural grassland, with manmade pasture accounting for a mere 11,000 *mu* (Ye *et al.* 1994), entirely inadequate for the requirements of husbandry development.

HOUSEHOLD LAND TENURE AND THE DECLINE OF COLLECTIVE MANAGEMENT

In the collectivist era, from 1952 to 1978, pastureland in China was collectively owned and managed largely by a three-tiered system of people's communes, brigades and production teams.[2] Livestock production was collectively supervised and pasture boundaries and attendant ownership and user rights were clearly assigned to local tiers of management. As common property natural grassland enjoyed protection, despite the tendency of individual farmers to work the system to their best advantage. Animal breeding and disease control programmes were set up in the communes. Quantitative restrictions (often disputed) were set on the herds of individual households, a measure introduced 'to prevent farmers going down the capitalist road'. Despite the fact that 'using more and caring less' and 'eating from a big pot' were the metaphors often employed by domestic researchers and writers to describe collective pastureland management prior to the 1980s, the 'big pot', i.e. public pastureland and husbandry facilities, was at least owned and cared for by the three-tiered collectivist management system.

Under the rural reforms implemented in China since 1978, a certain amount of arable land has been allocated to individual farming households according to family size on an initial, 15-year tenure (Hu 1997). Although land ownership is still nominally 'collective', post-reform arrangements are generally referred to as 'Household Responsibility Systems' (HRS). Initially these reforms boosted agricultural efficiency significantly (Huang *et al.* 1995). However, as household tenure came to replace the collective systems, built up in the peoples' communes over two decades, the commune system broke down. The former, three-tiered management system of communes, brigades and production teams has been replaced by township governments and village committees, and collective economic systems superseded by HRS.

This shift from collective management to HRS has broken down collective administrative systems, and the transition to a new institutional structure has been far from successful. Lacking either preparatory or supportive theory, the government's policy of rural reform has been based on 'crossing the river by touching stones' and actual implementation guided by the whims of local farmers rather than by government. The reforms echo the general observation of Ostrom *et al.* (1993) *vis-à-vis* developing countries that 'central government officials are much more interested in building new systems than in managing existing ones. The end result is that many such systems are poorly maintained.' All in all, the shift towards the family economy embodied in the household tenure regime has greatly weakened the communal functioning of townships and villages and severely disrupted rural management of natural resources.

WEAKENED PASTURELAND MANAGEMENT

Post-reform organizational changes in rural districts have led to ambiguous rights of land ownership. In theory ownership is collective, i.e. by the entire population of the village or township. Since the breakdown of the production team system, however, it is often a co-operative of village residents or the local enterprise board that acts as 'collective owner' rather than the local administration. A survey conducted in 1987 by the State Ministry of Agriculture in 1200 villages suggested that only two-thirds of the village committees had clearly delineated land ownership (Zhang 1994). Under such an indeterminate ownership regime, land use rights have been extended indefinitely. On the communal pastureland farmers let their animals graze, build their house, grow cereals, harvest fodder, dig for medicinal roots and remove topsoil, with no obligation to compensate for use, damage or degradation. Given such ambiguous property rights, there is effectively open access to common property resources (Hu and Evans 1997) without any economic accountability to users or owners.

In the villages and townships effective land ownership is also largely related to household economic power. The rapid reallocation of collective property to farmer households at the beginning of the reform era (Xu 1997) has aggravated the overall collective financial deficit, thus further weakening the functioning of the collective organizations. A survey conducted in 10,560 villages by the State Statistical Bureau indicates that at the end of 1993 the per capita budget of village committees averaged only 141.91 yuan (Jiang *et al.* 1995). Within the broader framework of the 'collective economy' of rural China, this turned thousands of people's communes into 'empty villages'.

One important consequence in the present context was that these underfunded village committees were no longer able to mobilize farmers to carry out communal projects and other village affairs. The survey I conducted in Shenmu County suggested that between 1982 and 1987 in most villages and townships these committees were not even functioning. During the survey, I noticed the living standards of individual households had apparently been improving and that many farmers had built new houses. At the same time, however, the collective organizations no longer had the financial means for mobilizing the population to manage and maintain pastureland, thus rendering them powerless as 'land owners'. Under such circumstances they were effectively unable to halt overgrazing or irresponsible use of pastureland, let alone develop irrigation systems or other indispensable services.

Prior to 1982 the collectives were responsible for the upkeep of 200,000 *mu* of manmade pasture (HZPG 1984). A sprayer system had also been installed for irrigating 250 *mu* of pasture.[3] With the adoption of HRS, arable land was contracted to individual farmers, but no public agency has taken over the collective responsibility for maintaining the communal grasslands. Equally, these grasslands were not leased to farm households. Wells, sprayer systems and other facilities associated with grassland maintenance have consequently been abandoned. There has been no new investment, no upkeep and in practice no ownership. Everyone has been herding their animals on public land, with nobody assuming responsibility for rangeland improvement. The situation is similar to that described by Hinton in Inner Mongolia, which borders on Shanxi Province:

> [A]t present, over much of the grassland, the worst possible combination holds sway - privately controlled stocking of animals on publicly owned lands. No one cares for the land because no one is responsible for it. Everyone tries to raise more animals and get as much as possible from the range, which is free to all. The result is an uncontrolled scramble for whatever forage exists and this amounts to a general attack on range vegetation. (Hinton 1990:91–93)

Moreover following the breakdown of the collectivist system of communes, brigades and production teams, original pasture boundaries were not successfully transferred to townships and villages,. As a result, neither ownership nor boundaries are clearly defined. For reasons of local geography, many villages used to participate in production teams or brigades with rights to pasture in adjacent villages. As members of their village collective, however, farmers in the latter villages are demanding equal access to public grasslands, giving rise to regular conflict. To address this problem, in the late 1980s the county government gave these 'non-pasture villages' a five-year lease on a plot of pastureland in the adjacent village, encouraging them to develop pastureland of their own during this time, with the leased plot then being returned. In practice these guidelines proved unworkable, however. Either poor grassland was leased, or non-pasture villages simply refused to return the land after the five years, as nobody was responsible for establishing alternative pastureland for other village members (pers. comm., Head of Shenmu Grassland Station 1995).

WEAKENED MANAGEMENT OF HUSBANDRY FACILITIES

The transition from collective management to HRS has been far from successful, as the traditional, collective systems for managing common property resources have been abolished without replacing them with an effective substitute. The communal rangelands have since been largely neglected or poorly maintained, as have the experimental plots, feeding sheds, veterinary stations, irrigation systems, breeding stations and other facilities. All in all, there has been an enormous weakening of the husbandry infrastructure and services established during the collectivist era. My interviews in Shenmu County reflect farmers' overwhelmingly negative appraisal of the issue (Table 7.1).

Table 7.1: Shenmu farmers' appraisal of agricultural services now compared with pre-reform*.

Choice of Answer	Response
A. improving	0 %
B. weakening	92 %
C. about the same	0 %
D. not comparable	8 %

Note: The question asked was: 'Compared with the collectivist era, do you consider current agricultural services (formerly associated with mechanization, irrigation facilities, improved seed varieties, breeding stations, farm machinery, fertilizers and pesticides, and so on) to be effective?'
Source: Wei Hu, Shenmu questionnaire.

The head of Shenmu Grassland Station reported as follows:

> In 1978, the year the station was established, we had one small truck, a large tractor, a tricycle and 55 *mu* experimental plots for grass trials and seed improvement. In 1982 these plots were reallocated, however, and all the other property sold. Now the station staff, including myself, receive only 70 per cent of their former salary, with no further station funding and no project either.

Prior to the reforms, there were 143 items of collectively owned machinery and (electronic and other) equipment on state farms and in the communes. Since the collapse of collectivist management, these have been largely abandoned or are at best poorly maintained. Formerly, there were 21 veterinary stations within the communes and an animal breeding shed in each village; adequate programmes of seed improvement and animal disease control were likewise in place (HZPG 1984). With the move to HRS this collective pastoral legacy has all but vanished. Artificial insemination, epidemic prevention and disease control, introduced in the county in 1958, played a key role in husbandry development until 1982. With the post-reform termination of these services, vets were obliged to seek a new livelihood.

Together, these developments have had two important consequences. First, the average slaughtered weight of sheep has declined, from 14 kg in 1982 to 10 kg in 1995 (pers. comm., Li Ting Chang, head of Shenmu Livestock Husbandry Bureau). It is sad to see these cat-sized sheep so easily taken to market by bicycle. Second, there has been a sharp rise in outbreaks of animal disease and, in particular, several diseases unknown prior to the 1980s. In 1994 foot and mouth disease hit nine townships in the county, leading to the slaughter of over 10,000 pigs. According to the head of the Husbandry Bureau, the disease would not have spread so widely in the collectivist era, because there was then a programme in place to ensure that every animal was given one 'dip' and two vaccinations a year. In addition, every village had a communal feeding shed and any outbreaks of disease were reported directly to the commune's livestock station by production team feeding staff. Sick animals were isolated and cases of serious disease were treated immediately before the disease could spread. Now, most of the communal feeding sheds have been abandoned and the few remaining livestock stations (now privatized) cannot carry out countywide programmes of vaccination and disease control, despite growing demand for these services as herd numbers continue to rise.

PASTURELAND DEGRADATION IN THE POST-REFORM ERA

The change of institutional arrangements has led to no positive innovations in pastureland use or management. The old collectivist motto 'use more and care less' has now become 'just use and care not'. Rural reforms have abolished systems of collective management and herd restrictions on public grassland but have not granted individual rights of tenure or ownership. Thus, collective ownership has been effectively transformed into a regime of open access. This is causing increasingly severe degradation of natural rangeland, a process aggravated further by no endeavours being made to fence off the degraded land.

According to the 1982 survey, the county has 3,009,000 *mu* of natural grassland and 180,000 *mu* of manmade pasture. Although this represents 27 per cent of the land, as a result of the former 'grain-first' policy, animal husbandry accounts for only 16.1 per cent of the county's total agricultural output.

Under HRS there has been a significant rise in herd sizes since the 1980s (Figure 7.2). Sheep and goat numbers rose by 49,265 between 1980 and 1982, only a little less than the 53,113 increase over the decade from 1965 to 1975. Overall, this has led to severe overgrazing and degradation of pastureland. Using remote sensing techniques, Xi Ze *et al.* (1994) have calculated that the county's

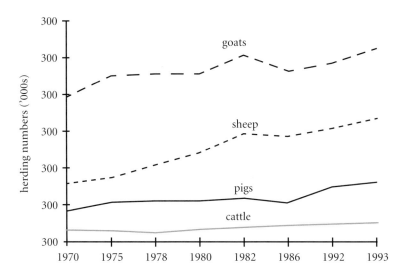

Figure 7.2: Livestock numbers in Shenmu, 1970–1993

grasslands can theoretically support 306,724 sheep, although in 1987 the actual total was 622,099. Although 126,475 goats and 80,000 sheep are fed on hay and tree leaves, respectively, the county still has an excess of 108,900 sheep. The aforementioned land resource survey reports a similar figure of 120,000 sheep over and above grassland carrying capacity (LMBS and SOS 1993).

Overgrazing has set off a process of pastureland degradation, triggering wind erosion and further deterioration of soils and, in the north of the county, even desertification. A survey of 30 grassland areas in the sandy district showed that 17 per cent are slightly degraded and 3.3 per cent moderately degraded. On the loess hills, much of the grassland that had been opened up for cereal cultivation has been abandoned because of poor yields and cannot be restored without new resource inputs. On these abandoned lands there are serious soil and water losses. In addition, goats, which make up 63.4 per cent of the county's livestock, are to be found mainly in the central, hilly region and the southern steppe. Goats can graze on slopes of 25 degrees and over, where there is little vegetation cover, and the tracks made on their frequent travels on the loess hills aggravate erosion still further. Compounding the problems of overgrazing, cultivation of maize and other fodder crops on sloping land has led to a further acceleration of soil and water losses (Hu 1998).

Since rural reform the terraces established during the collectivist era for the major crops have fallen into disrepair and construction of new terraces for fodder crops is presently inconceivable. Fodder base improvement requires a shift from low-quality grass to productive and erosion-controlled fodder crops. With the abolition of the communes in 1982 and their replacement by HRS, grassland stations and experimental plots are no longer operational, however.

In short, there is an urgent need for measures to conserve and revitalize the animal husbandry base. However, conservation requires supervision and incentives, for individual households cannot be expected to implement projects without due guidance or public funding. The new regime of unowned pastureland has merely enabled farmers to use that land free of charge, without any protective measures in place at all. The tradition of rotational grazing under communal management has been abandoned, as individual farmers allow their animals to forage at will near villages. This has caused increasing damage to pastureland and often even local desertification around residential areas. According to a survey by the Loess Plateau Survey Team of the Chinese Science Academy (1991), a single free-grazing goat can turn 0.2 *mu* of rangeland into desert in a year. For the past 16 years, farmer Qiao Chai Chai has allowed his herd of goats to forage near his home in the fixed sand dunes; over that period an area of 1,300 *mu* has been turned into desert.

Overgrazing has also led to a sharp decline in beneficial grass species and a proportionate upsurge of weeds, some of them poisonous. Among the latter is 'Horse Drunk Weed', which on one large tract of overgrazed pasture now infests one-third of the land, severely impeding husbandry development.

Manmade pasture, established during the collectivist era, accounts for only 0.4 per cent of county pastureland, too little to alleviate overgrazing. In 1982 100,000 *mu* were planted to alfalfa (*Astragalus adsurgens Pall*), 60,000 *mu* to sweet clover (*Melilotus albus, M.officinalis*) and 20,000 *mu* to other grasses. The average yield was then 600 *jin*[4] per *mu*; given that about 8 *mu* of land is therefore needed to feed a single sheep, this is unproductive. Under post-Mao rural reform even this collective resource has been left effectively unowned, however, and maintenance seriously neglected. Irrigation facilities have been abandoned and wells destroyed, and grass improvement and pasture conservation projects discontinued. Consequently, the 20,000 *mu* of manmade pasture managed collectively until the 1980s has now shrunk to a nominal 11,000 *mu*, much of it waterlogged and degraded, leading to virtual total exhaustion of a key heritage.

DISCUSSION AND RECOMMENDATIONS

In the wider Loess Plateau district, World Bank researchers have reported similar overgrazing problems in the post-reform era:

productivity of grazing land has significantly deteriorated during the past decade due to substantial build-up in livestock populations (particularly of sheep and goats) and the prevailing grazing practices under which communally owned lands are grazed by individually owned livestock. As in other countries with similar grazing systems, such practices have led to severe overgrazing, soil erosion and declines in herbage digestibility on virtually all project area pastures, as livestock owners tend to graze as many animals as possible in an attempt to maximize their share in profit from the common grazing resource without reinvesting in pasture improvement and maintenance. (Staff Appraisal Report on China, Loess Plateau Watershed Rehabilitation 1994)

Almost two decades have passed since the Household Responsibility System was introduced in 1978. In that time China's pastureland resources have seriously deteriorated under a system of merely nominal collective ownership, with no measures in place to effectively tackle the growing problems. This has undermined all other attempts to develop Chinese husbandry in a sustainable way, for it has made of the owner-collective an empty body, with no new institutional arrangements in place to protect and conserve the pastureland. In the absence of any defined system of land ownership, in practice farmers act rationally as 'miners', enjoying extra-legal grazing rights while remaining unaccountable for the resultant degradation of public pastureland. This raises an urgent question: how long can Chinese livestock production be sustained, given quasi-collective ownership of pastureland and husbandry infrastructure that is close to collapse?

This cursory review leads to a positive appraisal of the collectivist, Maoist livestock management regime, under which pastureland upkeep as well as seed improvement were successfully managed by collectivist organizations. As a form of commons management, the system was able to avoid the all too familiar tragedy. Although the herds permitted to households were restricted under the old regime, this ruling may well have been appropriate for such ecologically fragile and already overgrazed areas. Overall, it is hard to see how the current open access regime can lead to sustainable husbandry on the rangeland.

To combat overgrazing and address the other problems that have emerged under the post-reform arrangements *vis-à-vis* land ownership and use, the following remedial measures are recommended:

1. pastureland ownership should be clarified, with rights and duties duly specified;
2. to adjust herd numbers to pastureland carrying capacity, a system of rewards and fines should be introduced, to be strictly enforced by effective village governance;

3. the government should commit itself to the upkeep of husbandry infrastructure and pastureland protection (Hu 1998);
4. animal breeding stations should be re-established at rural townships and
   villages;
5. a system of pastureland co-management should be introduced: natural grassland should be brought back under collective management, with individual
   households retaining user rights to local pasture under tenure at the village
   level.

For traditional rangeland and pastures, it is thus recommended to gradually
adopt a communal management regime. The village community would then be
responsible for co-ordinating herd rotation, plant protection, irrigation, seeding,
hay harvesting and storage, thereby sharing responsibility for grassland management with households. In addressing the weaknesses of the current regime, this
kind of co-management would not only revive rational use of former husbandry
systems but would also provide village funding for grassland improvement and
other projects. In the meantime, systems based on family and co-operative
responsibility should be encouraged and implemented on degraded pastureland and sandy land, on the basis of long-term tenure or permanent user rights.
There should be effective monitoring by village or township administrations,
and households seen to generate improved grassland should be duly rewarded.

Ambiguous property rights between former collectivist agencies and farm
households in the post-reform era have led effectively to an open access regime
on public pastureland. In the absence of an identifiable public management
body, the quality of rangelands is steadily declining, with potential for vast
ecological damage. Weakened management systems at the village and township
level should therefore be strengthened, not only by means of legislation and
financial support from the state and local government but also by restoring
collective ownership of communal pastureland. Suitably strengthened, village
committees and township governments will be able to fund, supervise and manage
both medium and large scale conservation projects and reverse the spiral of overgrazing and pastureland degradation. Although supervision of rational pastureland use by the village or township may be costly, it is a *sine qua non* if the
communal pastures of Shenmu County are to be properly maintained and animal
husbandry rendered sustainable.

The government's recent programme in support of democratic village governance provides a springboard for strengthening weakened local leadership. Millions
of farmers will soon be electing their own village leaders from among candidates not nominated by the higher authorities. This should lead to strong and

dependable village leadership, which should in turn strengthen local efforts to protect the communal pastureland and, hopefully, pave the way to sustainable management of the nation's important rangeland resources.

NOTES

1 1 hectare = 15 *mu*.

2 During this era I worked as an 'educated youth' in a people's commune in a live-stock district in northern Xinjiang, China.

3 Figures cited from Table 2, Financial Expenditure Statistics, 1978, Financial Bureau of Shenmu.

4 1 *jin* = 0.5 kg.

REFERENCES

Cheng, G.W. and S.H. Yie (1994) 'Research of remote sensing applications for environment and resources survey and systematic mapping in Shenmu-Fugu Region, Shannxi Province'. In G.W. Cheng, G.W. and S.H. Yie (eds) *Remote Sensing Investigation and Mapping of Resources and Environment in Shenmu-Fugu region*. Beijing . Science Press. (in Chinese, summary in English).

Gao, X.T., K.L. Tang, P.C. Zhang and W.L. Wang (1994) 'New man-made accelerated erosion during the first and second period of construction of the Shenfu-Dongsheng Coal Mining Area'. *Research of Soil and Water Conservation Vol. 1*. Xian. (in Chinese, summary in English) pp. 23–34.

Hinton, W. (1990) *The Privatisation of China, the Great Reversal*. London: Earthscan Publications Ltd, pp. 91–93.

Hu, W. (1997) 'Household land tenure reform in China: its impact on farming land use and agro-environment'. *Land Use Policy*, vol. 14, no. 3, pp. 175–186.

—— (1998a) 'Issues for sustaining Chinese agriculture'. *Land Use Policy*, vol. 15, no. 2, pp. 167–170.

—— (1998b) 'Problems and countermeasures vis-à-vis "Household Responsibility Systems", land and agro-environment (in Chinese) *Science and Management*, Tianjin People's Press, Tianjin, Jan. and Feb., pp. 66–69; 64–67.

Hu, W. and R. Evans, R. (1997) 'The impacts of coal mining in Shenmu County, Loess Plateau, China'. *Ambio*, vol. 26, no. 6, pp. 405–406.

Huang, Y. P., W.D. Macmillan and W. Hu (1995) 'The measurement of change in agricultural efficiency in post-reform China using Landsat data'. *Proceedings of ACSM/ASPRS'95*, Charlotte, North Carolina, USA. 27 Feb.– 3 March, pp. 318–327.

Husbandry Zoning Planning Group of Shenmu County (HZPG) (1984) *Husbandry Zoning Planning of Shenmu County*. Shanxi Province (in Chinese) p. 23.

Land Management Bureau of Shenmu County (LMBS) and Land Survey Office of Shenmu County (LSOS) (1993) *Land Resource of Shenmu County* Xian: Xian Map Press, (in Chinese), p. 123.

Loess Plateau Survey Team, Chinese Science Academy (1991) *Measures to Combat Land Desertification in Northern Wind-Blown Sand Areas of the Loess Plateau* (in Chinese). Beijing : Science Press.

Jiang L. *et al.* (1995) *Analysis and Prediction of Chinese Social Development Trend* (in Chinese). Beijing : Social Academic Press of China.

Ostrom, E., L. Schroeder and S. Wynne (1993) *Institutional Incentives and Sustainable Development, Infrastructure Policies in Perspective.* Boulder: Westview Press.

Xi, Z. *et al.* (1994) 'Remote sensing investigation and mapping of grassland types in Shenmu County'. In G.W. Chen and S.H. Yie (eds), *Remote Sensing Investigation and Mapping of Resources and Environment in Shenmu-Fugu region* (in Chinese, with English summary). Beijing : Science Press, pp. 81–97.

Xu, Y. (1997) *Villagers' Governance in Rural China.* (in Chinese). Wuhan: Press of Hua Zhong Nomal University.

Ye, S.H. *et al.* (1994) 'Remote sensing investigation and mapping of current land use in Shenmu County'. In G.W. Chen and S.H. Yie (eds), *Remote Sensing Investigation and Mapping of Resources and Environment in Shenmu-Fugu Region* (in Chinese, with English summary). Beijing : Science Press, pp. 61–71.

Zhang H. Y. (1994) *Chinese Peasantry and Rural Economic Development* (in Chinese). Guizhou: Gui Zhou People's Press.

CHAPTER EIGHT

Years of Transition in Coastal Japanese Fisheries, 1868–1912

ARNE KALLAND

*A*t the time when the ideology of *mare liberum* gained popularity with expanding Western powers in the early seventeen century, Japanese lords (*daimyō*) were tightening their control over the coastal areas under a *mare closum* regime. Many domains established offices for coastal affairs (*ura-yakusho*) with ultimate authority over the domain fisheries. At the same time, however, the feudal authorities delegated much of the management of the fisheries to the village or district levels. This brought the village and district headmen as partners into what we may term 'a co-management arrangement'.

At first sight one may be struck by the continuity of the organization of Japanese fisheries from this time – if not earlier – until the present. However, after the Tokugawa period (1603–1868) the fisheries have undergone two periods of great changes: during the 40 years following the Meiji Restoration in 1868 and during the post-war years. It is the aim of this chapter to analyse the changes occurring during the first period of transition, i.e. during the Meiji era (1868–1912) through a case study of Shingū in Fukuoka Prefecture. Important changes occurred both in the resource management regime and in the ownership and control of the fishing equipment. The chapter will analyse those changes that started a trend in which the close ties that had existed between fishermen and merchants broke up and disappeared, leaving the fishermen more in control of their own future. Shingū fisheries continued to be co-managed but with a new fishing co-operative taking the place of the village as the local partner.

SHINGŪ'S FISHERIES DURING THE TOKUGAWA PERIOD

The fisheries in Fukuoka during the Tokugawa period have been extensively analysed elsewhere (Kalland 1995), and only the most important features – as they relate to Shingū – will be outlined here.

A large number of marine species could be found outside the village. While sardine, mullet, sand lance and yellowtail were caught during the winter and spring, sea bream, mackerel, horse mackerel, tuna and flying fish were taken from spring to autumn.[1] Catches fluctuated wildly for many of the species – in particular for such important migratory species as sand lance, mackerel, sardine and mullet – not least because of adverse weather conditions, particularly during the winter months when fishing activities could be interrupted for weeks. Fortunately, the poor years for one species were often compensated for by good catches of other species. The large number of species thus served as an insurance and stabilized the income of the fishermen somewhat. At the same time the situation forced the fishermen to invest in several fisheries, causing capital investments to become a heavy burden for most of them. The fishermen were, in other words, forced to become generalists, to become acquainted with a large number of species and use a number of technologies.

According to a report from Shingū the fishing seasons in the 1790s could be summarized as follows (Kawazoe 1977: 42):

Spring: Sea bream and sardine netting;

Summer: Beach netting, hook-and-line fishing for mackerel and squid;

Autumn: Sardine and sea-bream netting as well as hook-and-line fishing for mackerel;

Winter: Sardine and sea-bream netting.

One characteristic of the Tokugawa period was the co-existence of large and small fishing units, operating equipment with highly differing capital and management requirements. Part of the time most of the fishermen were engaged on nets employing 30–40 people or more. Among these nets were the large beach seines (*ōjibikiami*), which had been used to catch sardine in Shingū at least since the 1780s. A somewhat smaller beach seine called *tatsukuri-ami* was used to catch anchovy, largely used as manure. Other large nets were the sea bream nets (*tai-ami*), which had been used in Shingū at least since the late seventeenth century and the encircling net for mullet (*bora-makaseami*). At other times the fishermen operated in small units consisting of one or two boats, each with a crew of three or four people. A number of species – sand lance was of special importance – were taken by boat seines (*funabikiami*), of which the small *teguri* seine was particularly well suited to catch sand borer, small horse mackerel and saury pike. Handlining (*ippontsuri, tsuri*) and to a lesser extent longlining (*naganawa, nobenawa*) were important methods as well. Although mackerel and squid undoubtedly were the two most important species caught by handliners in Shingū, they also caught species like sea bream, horse mackerel, black porgy and grunt.

The co-existence of large and small fishing units, with partly overlapping seasons, demanded flexibility and a complex ownership structure. Most of the fishing boats were owned by the fishermen themselves, as were the simpler gear like lines, gill nets and boat seines. The more successful fishermen had also managed – partly through borrowing from public credit institutions – to organize larger nets, such as *tatsukuri* nets and sea bream nets.[2] However, the largest nets such as sardine seines and mullet nets were invariably owned by merchants, the well-known *amimoto* (absentee net owners). Many net owners were among the village leaders or ran fish wholesale businesses (Kalland 1995). It was particularly dried sardine (including anchovy) and sand lance – both were mainly used as fertilizer – that attracted these merchants. As net owners they secured a steady supply of fish for curing, and there was an extensive trade in dried fish between the net owners in order to amass volumes large enough to make shipments worthwhile. Shingû also had a marketplace for fresh fish during the Tokugawa period, but there were important limits to growth in the fresh fish trade. The system of transportation was poorly developed and large catches easily glutted the market. This market was therefore most suitable to handle species like rock cod, black porgy, grunt and other demersal fish caught in small quantities by gillnets or handlines, fisheries that usually did not attract leading merchants.

Another feature of the fisheries during the Tokugawa period was the formation of village-based fishing territories which caused an administrative (and in many cases physical) separation of farming and fishing villages.[3] The coast was seen as an extension of the feudal domain and could be allocated at the lord's discretion. Usually the lord gave communities defined as fishing villages (*ura*) exclusive fishing territories in return for corvée labour and payments of taxes.[4] The rudiments of village fishing territories were in place in Fukuoka by 1560, at which time Shingū's territory bordered Kazuru Village in the east and Nata in the west (Tone Doc. no.45A). The seventeenth century was a period of dramatic changes, however. The people of Kazuru ceased to fish, leaving its territory open for others. A quarrel between Shingū and Fukuma over the possession of a whale carcass that in 1658 drifted to Kazuru's shores (Kaneuchi Doc. no.129), prompted the authorities to formalize a new border between the two remaining fishing villages. Shingū received two-thirds of the territory (including the rights to use the beach) as well as the corvée duties (*Ura-Kiroku*).

Access to beaches was important in several ways: they were well suited for the operation of the large nets that were used, they were convenient for drying nets and fish, and the fishing boats could easily be pulled up onto the beach. Rights to beaches were complicated matters, however. The shore was a border zone between sea and land, that is between two different systems of tenure. Only the fishing villages had access to the sea, but most of the land – beaches included – fell within the borders of farming villages. To complicate the matters further, stretches of the beaches and the land beyond were held as fiefs by high-ranking samurai. The fishermen could use the beach with few restrictions for fishing activities such as hauling nets, but they needed special permits in order to dry fish and nets on beaches outside the borders of their own hamlet, and they were obliged to pay a rental to those with jurisdiction over the beach. Shingū obtained the rights to dry fish on the beaches under the juridiction of Kaminofu, Shimonofu, Shishibu and Koga (of which Kazuru was a part) and high-ranking samurai (Figure 8.1).

The Tokugawa system of sea tenure – which briefly can be defined as 'the ways in which fishermen perceive, define, delimit, "own" and defend their rights to inshore fishing grounds' (Akimichi and Ruddle 1984:1, Cordell 1984) – was based on the two principles of fishing rights and licences. Whereas the former defines access to a particular space of water, the latter gave the holders permission to operate a certain type of fishery. Small-scale technologies did usually not require any licence – with the exception of diving for abalone and turbo shell, which was the monopoly of a few villages. However, the feudal authorities took great interest in sardine seines, tuna nets, sea bream nets, whaling nets and other large nets. Permission to use these nets was given by the magistrate but only after the district headman had made sure that there were no objections to the new nets from fishing villages in the vicinity.

The sea tenure system remained far from static, however. Small, exclusive fishing territories for each village as they were defined early in the Tokugawa period were in most cases too rigid to be of much use. The fishing grounds were not of equal quality and there were great seasonal fluctuations within most territories. It was therefore desirable that the fishermen had access to a variety of fishing grounds in order to secure a year-round base for their fishing activities. The system of exclusive village territories seldom met this requirement, and 'entry' (or 'guest') fishing (*nyūgyo*) arrangements were made to remedy this situation. The process whereby fishing villages gained access to the waters of their neighbours started in the seventeenth century and accelerated towards the end of the period.

Many strategies were used in obtaining such rights, from systematic poaching to negotiations and payments of rents (Kalland 1991, 1995). At times the authorities intervened, as when one village in 1640 picked a fight with its neighbour

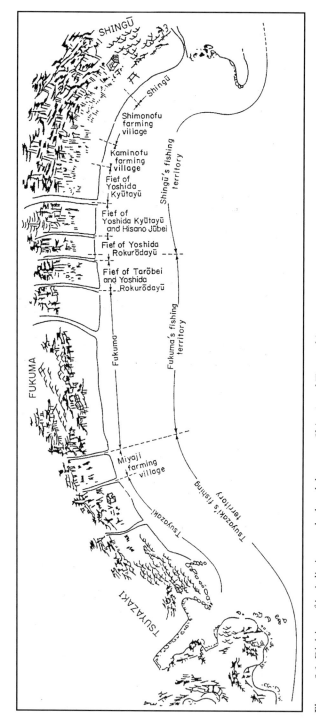

Figure 8.1: Division of jurisdiction on the beach between Shingū and Tsuyazaki, 1794
Source: Kaneuchi Document No. 286

to have the border between them moved in order to gain access to a sandy beach. The village was successful, but its headman and five elders were all beheaded for disturbing the public peace. However, in most cases solutions were found locally and in more peaceful ways. Serious disputes between villages were invariably brought to the attention of the civil district headman (several fishing villages comprised a district) who more often than not appointed a committee of village headmen to investigate the matter before a ruling was handed down. The samurai only became involved if one or both parties refused to obey the ruling, or if one of them petitioned the feudal authorities directly. Conflicts within a village were usually settled internally with the headman and elders as mediators, unless one of the parties sent a petition to the magistrate. In that case the district headman would make preliminary investigations before a ruling was made by the magistrate's office.

To summarize the situation toward the end of the Tokugawa period: the fisheries were characterized by the co-existence of small and large fishing units, with active fishermen largely in control of the former and absentee merchants of the latter. The net owners were also operating as fish wholesalers and had, through their position as village leaders, strong influence over the village fishing territory and on the allocation of fishing licences. However, their position was, as we shall see, seriously undermined in the Meiji period.

SHINGŪ'S FISHERIES DURING THE MEIJI ERA

Shingū's fisheries continued to be characterized by the two features outlined above, i.e. the co-existence of large and small fishing units and the village-based exclusive fishing territory, during the Meiji era. Most of the gear used in the Tokugawa period continued to be used (Table 8.1) and the main technological innovation, the purse seine (*aguriami*), was introduced into Shingū only in the late 1890s. But a trend discernible already in the late Tokugawa period continued, namely the growing importance of small-scale technologies, particularly boat seines (such as the nets for sand lance and sand borer), which were more flexible and cheaper than the beach seines. Catches continued to be erratic, however. Between 1897 and 1910 annual catches of sardine in Fukuoka fluctuated between 3,664 and 323 tonnes, and those of sand lance between 2,756 and 135 tonnes.[5] Moreover, many of the species frequently changed migration routes within the prefecture. Kasuya County of which Shingū is a part, landed 64 per cent of the prefectural sand lance catch in 1905, against only 15 per cent in 1910. Even for more reliable species like sea bream, catches in 1897 were more than three times those of 1901 (Kalland 1995:124). This situation had a profound influence on resource management throughout the Meiji era.

Table 8.1: Nets in Shingū during the 1870s

Net type		Tax/net in yen	No. of nets	Size of management unit	
English name	Japanese name			boats	people
Sardine nets	iwashi-ami	2.00	4	3	70
Sea-bream nets	tai-ami	1.50	3	9	37
Yellowtail nets	yazu-ami	0.20	9		
Beach seines	jibikiami	0.60		1	10–20
Sand lance nets	kanagi-ami	0.20	25	1	5–6
Tatsukuri nets	tatsukuri-ami	0.20	12	4	18
Gizzard shad nets	konoshiro-ami	0.20	22	1	4–5
Red rock cod nets	ako-ami	0.20		1	2
Dragnets	teguriami	0.20		1	2–3
Squid nets	ika-ami	0.20	22	1	3
Sea bream fry nets	kodaichi-ami		32		
	sekojikiami		10		
Net for sand borer	kisu-ami		10		
Flying fish nets	ago-ami		7		
Total no of nets			156		

Sources: The sources (Itō 1949; Fukuoka-ken 1988a, 1988b) disagree somewhat and the above figures are therefore speculative.

Increased Flexibility

Despite the apparent continuity, the collapse of the feudal regime in 1868 in-augurated important changes which affected the fishermen profoundly. Old burdens, such as corvée duties and restrictions on movement and trade were abandoned and so were old privileges. But most of all, fishermen were affected by changes in sea tenure systems.

The distinction between fishing villages (*ura*) and farming villages (*mura*) was abandoned and with the dissolution of the fiefs in the early 1870s the old fishing rights reverted to the central government. These changes signalled a period of general confusion over fishing rights with new opportunities and challenges to the fishermen. The confusion only worsened when, in 1876, the central government cancelled existing fishing privileges and opened the sea for all (Ruddle 1985). A short period with open access ensued, but as conflicts between old and new fishing villages escalated and large operators improved their position *vis-à-vis* small-scale fishermen, the old system of exclusive village territories under the local authorities (now the prefecture rather than the domain) was re-established. This was, as we will see shortly, an important modification of the Tokugawa system.

The 1870s was a period of transition whereby the fishermen in Shingū, as elsewhere, tried to exploit new opportunities while defending old rights. Shingū faced problems in obtaining new leases of beaches to dry their anchovies and sardine after the land tax system was changed and complained that 'if we are excluded from the access to the said place, there is no other way than to give up the good arrangements for fishing, and there will be exceedingly hardship' (Kaneuchi Document no. 558). Shingū succeeded to lease the beaches for five years in 1880, and probably again in 1884 (Kaneuchi Document no. 361, 365). At sea Shingū was involved in at least two disputes.

The first erupted in 1872 when people from Kazuru made an attempt to take up fishing again after a lapse of almost 250 years. Recognizing Shingū's old rights to the territory, people from Kazuru had during the summer repeatedly approached Shingū requesting permission to use a net for gizzard shad (*konoshiro-ami*) which they had jointly bought. On the 14th day of the 7th month they had again been to Shingū, only to meet deaf ears. The following day the district headman in Koga (the farming village in which Kazuru was a hamlet) wrote to his colleague in Fukuma, under whose administration Shingū at that time was placed, requesting sea space for the net. The negotiations came to a deadlock, and in the morning of the 18th the net was cast none the less. They had caught about 300 fish when 50–60 people from Shingū came and 'seized all the fish without exception', claiming that the catch was made inside Shingū's fishing territory. In his new letter to his colleague in Fukuma the district headman of Koga reported: '[They said that] if [we] ever go out with the net again, they will seize it, and with [our] apologies the net was returned [to us]. The above circumstances are extremely difficult. This is reported as people remembered today's [events]. What shall we answer to the situation?' (Imabayashi Doc. no. 173, 174). The harsh measures taken by the fishermen and the support they received from their own village leaders seem to have discouraged the Kazuru people from making more attempts to start fishing.

The second dispute was fought with Ainoshima, an island now a part of Shingū Town. Shingū fishermen wanted to fish inside the island's territory and thus continue a process which started in the Tokugawa period. Negotiations failed to bring an agreement and in the 6th month Shingū threatened to curb

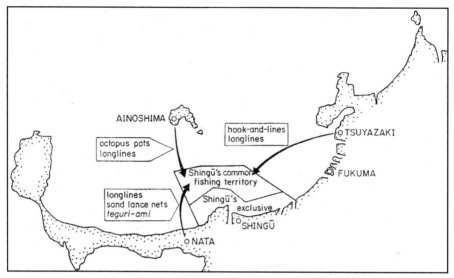

Figure 8.2: Fishing villages with *nyūgyo* rights in the common fishing territory of Shingū, 1891

all handling of fish from Ainoshima, which probably meant that the catches of Ainoshima were marketed through Shingū (Kaneuchi Doc. no. 559, 560). Ainoshima's access to the fish market, we are told in a letter from Shingū's headman to his Ainoshima colleague, 'has caused great hardship [to us]'. Another refusal and Shingū's fish market would be closed for Ainoshima, he warned. The following month eight fishermen representatives in Shingū jointly signed a document to the effect that they would not handle Ainoshima fish. Shingū apparently obtained such rights a couple of years later.

Although the open access regime was short-lived, 'guest' fishing increased in importance and became codified through several laws and regulations. To sort out the complexity of the situation, the regional fishing co-operative – Chikuhō Gyogyō Kumiai established after the government had encouraged such co-operatives in 1887 – in 1889–1891 prepared the document *Gyojō kuiki sateisho* ('An assessment of the boundaries of fishing areas') and a map defining all territorial rights in the prefecture at that time. The fishing territories in Fukuoka fell into four categories:

1. Exclusive village territories which comprised the waters closest to shore. Only occasionally did other villages have *nyūgyo* (entry) rights in such territories.

2. Beyond these there were areas administered by the same villages but where other villages had certain *nyūgyo* rights. Often such rights were recipro-cated but there were also many cases of one-sidedness.

3. Some areas, called *iriai* (commons) areas, were exploited jointly and equally by two or more villages with occasionally additional villages having *nyūgyo* rights.

4. Territories located further out at sea (*okiai*), which in principle were open to all fishermen living in the prefecture.

Shingū, bordering on Nata in the south-west, Fukuma in the north-east and Ainoshima across the sea to the north-west, provides us with one of the simpler tenure cases.[6] Only the Shingū fishermen were allowed to fish within its exclusive territory, i.e. within one kilometre off the shore. Beyond was the common fishing territory of the village in which Nata fishermen were allowed to fish with small boat seines (*teguriami*), sand lance seines and longlines. The Tsuyazaki fishermen could use handlines and longlines while those from Aino-shima could catch octopus with pots and use longlines (Figure 8.2). In return the Shingū fishermen were allowed to operate in the commons fishing ground of Nata, where they could use *teguriami*, sand lance seines and handlines. In the commons of Ainoshima they could fish for mackerel and grunt with handlines beside using *teguriami* and sea bream nets. And in the commons of Tsuyazaki they were permitted to use a bottom net called *soko-tatekakuami* (Figure 8.3).

Although the codification of 1891 undoubtedly served as a model when the first national Fishery Law of 1901 was implemented, there were several major changes introduced by the Fishery Law. The territories were now of three types (Kalland 1991):

1. exclusive territories (*jisaki senyō gyogyōken*) – sometimes jointly held with other villages,

2. territories shared by several villages (*kyōyū senyō gyogyōken*) of which one village – usually the one to which the territory originally belonged – was appointed 'in charge' (*daihyō* or *senyō gyogyō kensha*); and

3. 'offshore' (*okiai*) areas.

Most of the exclusive village territories – either held by one or several villages – survived from 1891 to 1901, although some of them changed con-siderably in shape (Kalland 1991). Only minor adjustments were made in Shingū's case, but Shingū's 'common' fishing territory of 1891 was in 1901 defined as 'shared' territories (no. 2727 in Figure 8.3). Other villages' access to this territory improved greatly. Whereas Ainoshima fishermen in 1891 were allowed to use only octopus pots and longlines in this territory, they were now allowed to use 39 types of fishing gear. Similarly, the number of technologies allowed by Nata fishermen increased from 3 to 31 and by Tsuyazaki fishermen from 2 to 15.

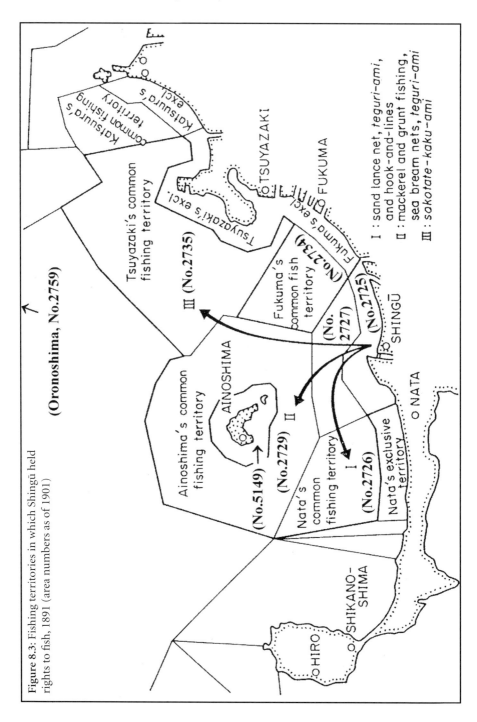

Figure 8.3: Fishing territories in which Shingū held rights to fish, 1891 (area numbers as of 1901)

I : sand lance net, *teguri-ami*, and hook-and-lines
II : mackerel and grunt fishing, sea bream nets, *teguri-ami*
III : *sokotate-kaku-ami*

(Oronoshima, No.2759)

Katsuura's common fishing territory

Katsuura's excl.

Tsuyazaki's common fishing territory

Tsuyazaki's excl.

III (No.2735)

Fukuma's excl.

Fukuma's common fish territory

(No.2734)

(No. 2727)

(No.2725)

Ainoshima's common fishing territory

AINOSHIMA

II

(No.5149)

(No.2729)

I

(No.2726)

Nata's common fishing territory

Nata's exclusive territory

SHINGŪ

NATA

SHIKANO-SHIMA

HIRO

TSUYAZAKI

FUKUMA

Fukuma fishermen, who previously had no access to this area, were now allowed to use dredges for shellfish as well as handlines. Shingū's access to the waters of other villages improved correspondingly, so that in the early 1920s Shingū fishermen reported catches from 35 different technologies in Nata's area (no.2726), from 29 in Ainoshima's (no. 2729), from 31 in Fukuma's (no. 2734) and from 32 in Tsuyazaki's (no. 2735) (Figure 8.3). Shingū's access to Ainoshima's exclusive (*jisaku*) territories was also confirmed.

Another major difference between the situation in 1891 and 1901 was the fishing area around the small uninhabited island Okinoshima (territory no. 2759).[7] Belonging administratively to Ōshima it was regarded as the exclusive (*jisaku*) territory of that village, but – probably as a consequence of the Meiji Government's efforts to increase marine catches – this area was opened to nine villages which had been given various *nyūgyo* rights. Shingū reported catches made by five different types of gear there in the 1920s. Finally, Shingū had access to several territories held jointly by all the fishing villages in Kasuya and Munakata counties, the areas held jointly by all the villages in the prefecture, and in certain areas of Saga prefecture, although Shingū did not report any catches in these areas.

In conclusion we can observe a gradual shift from a rigid system of fixed territories to a more flexible one with an extensive use of 'guest' fishing (Kalland 1991). This was brought about by two processes. On the one hand, demarcations between fishing territories were poorly made at sea – as far as Fukuoka was concerned, at least – and 'grey zones' developed particularly in bays and in the waters between small islands and the mainland. These zones which developed into territories held jointly by several villages, tended to grow in size. On the other hand, pressure to open up exclusive territories for *nyūgyo* fishing increased, so that more and more such rights had to be accepted. The result became a territorial system which was more flexible – as well as far more complex – than the original one.

It is difficult to say how important 'guest' fishing was in economic terms because statistical data is missing for this period.[8] However, between 1922 and 1926 almost half of Shingū's catches were taken outside its own territories (no. 2725 and 2727) (see Table 8.2).[9]

The increased range of operation allowed for specialization. A look at some of the territories held jointly by several villages is revealing. In territory no.2727, Shingū reported catches taken by 40 different technologies in the period 1922–26, none of which dominated in the catch statistics. The other villages that had acquired rights in this territory, however, concentrated their

Table 8.2: Catches reported by Shingū (annual average, 1922–1926)

Area no.	Area type	Village in charge	Types of gear	Catches in yen	Catches in per cent
2725	Jisaki	Shingū	45	12,457	30.8
2726	*kyōyū*	Nata	35	4,389	10.8
2727	*kyōyū*	Shingū	34	9,540	23.6
2728	Jisaku	Ainoshima	3	2,032	5.0
2729	*kyōyū*	Ainoshima	29	5,174	12.8
2730	Jisaku	Ainoshima	1	304	0.8
2734	*kyōyū*	Fukuma	31	3,018	7.5
2735	*kyōyū*	Tsuyazaki	32	3,018	7.5
2759	jisaki	Ōshima	5	548	1.4

main efforts on a few types of gear: Ainoshima had its largest catches from sea bream longlines as well as from handlines for sea bream, grunts and mackerel; Nata reported the highest catches for squid nets and sea bream longlines while Fukuma took most on mackerel handlines. These five technologies (i.e. sea bream longlines, squid nets and handlines for sea bream, grunts and mackerel) had the highest catches in value for that territory, while Shingū's own catches comprised less than one quarter of the total catches for these technologies. Similar patterns can be discerned elsewhere in the prefecture (Kalland 1991). It should also be mentioned that the gear was small scale in type, and so were most of the other technologies involved in 'guest' fishing. Typically such gear required only one boat with a crew of between three and five people. It seems, therefore, that *iriai* and *nyūgyo* rights benefited the small-scale fishermen.

Codification of rights to fishing spots
One of the most important processes in the fishing villages during the Tokugawa period was the continuous tug of war between private and communal interests regarding sea tenure. There was a marked tendency towards privatization of fishing grounds in the more capital-intensive fisheries (Habara 1954). This was particularly the case with large stationary nets (*ōshikiami, teichiami, masuami*) which monopolized tracts of sea space.

The Meiji Fishery Law implied a codification of existing rights to certain fishing spots (*ajiro*).[10] In addition to territorial rights – i.e. *jisaki senyō gyogyōken, kyōyū senyō gyogyōōken* and rights to 'guest' fishing (*nyūgyoken*) within *jisaku* territories of other villages – the law distinguished three types of rights:

1. Set-net fishery rights (*teichi gyogyōken*) gave the holders rights to certain areas for stationary equipment such as set-nets.

2. Sectional fishery rights (*kukaku gyogyōken*) gave the holders areas for cultivating fish, shellfish and seaweeds.

3. Special fishery rights (*tokubetsu gyogyōken*) allowed the holders to operate large active nets in coastal waters for species like sardines, mackerel and sea bream, as well as to construct artificial shallows in order to attract fish.

Peace and order was the motive behind many of the regulations of the Tokugawa period and this objective was certainly also very important in the Meiji Fishery Law. The fishery rights sought to separate gear that could easily come into conflict. An example is given in Figure 8.4, which shows the fishery rights in Shingū in 1906. The fishermen of Shingū were allowed to use 61 specified types of gear inside its exclusive fishing territory (no.2725) and 57 types of gear inside the joint exclusive territories (no.2727) while four other villages could use from two to 39 kinds. These were small and mobile and could be used without further licences as long as they did not interfere with the other types of fishery rights.

Eleven rights for set nets (*teichi gyogyōken*) were issued: seven for gizzard shad nets (*konoshiro-tateami*), two for flying fish nets (*ago-sashiami*), one for a yellowtail net (*yazu-tateami*) and one for a general set-net (*masuami*). Each right specified the type of net to be used, its size and exact location as well as the season for use and species to be caught. Areas were also set aside for sardine and mackerel beach seines and for sea bream nets which required special fishery rights (*tokubetsu gyogyōken*). Such rights were also needed in 1915 when Shingū wanted to construct artifical shallows in order to attract fish. No area was set aside for cultivation until after World War II, however, when an area was reserved for the seaweed *wakame* (*Undaria pinnatifida*).

Changing power relations

As these rights were based to a large extent on practices going back to the feudal past, the most important difference from the Tokugawa system was the transfer of the exclusive fishing rights from villages to local fishing co-operatives which were established throughout the country according to the 1901 Fishery Law. Although the responsibility for both fishing rights and licences ultimately rested with the national government represented by the Ministry of Agriculture, Forestry and Fisheries, one of the main features of the Japanese management regime was to delegate as much of the responsibility as possible to the local co-operatives, whereby the Japanese fishermen acquired a powerful tool to influence marine

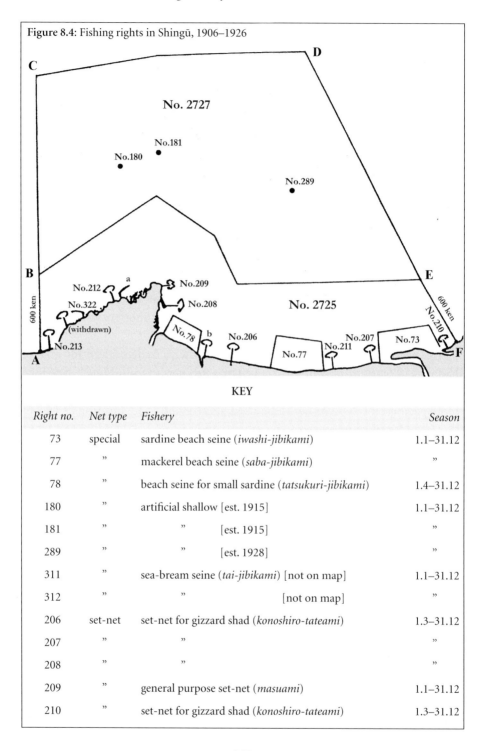

Figure 8.4: Fishing rights in Shingū, 1906–1926

KEY

Right no.	Net type	Fishery	Season
73	special	sardine beach seine (*iwashi-jibikami*)	1.1–31.12
77	”	mackerel beach seine (*saba-jibikami*)	”
78	”	beach seine for small sardine (*tatsukuri-jibikami*)	1.4–31.12
180	”	artificial shallow [est. 1915]	1.1–31.12
181	”	” [est. 1915]	”
289	”	” [est. 1928]	”
311	”	sea-bream seine (*tai-jibikami*) [not on map]	1.1–31.12
312	”	” [not on map]	”
206	set-net	set-net for gizzard shad (*konoshiro-tateami*)	1.3–31.12
207	”	”	”
208	”	”	”
209	”	general purpose set-net (*masuami*)	1.1–31.12
210	”	set-net for gizzard shad (*konoshiro-tateami*)	1.3–31.12

		KEY (*continued*)	
Right no.	*Net type*	*Fishery*	*Season*
211	set-net	set-net for gizzard shad (*konoshiro-tateami*)	1.3–31.12
212	"	set-net for yellowtail (*yazu-tateami*)	1.7–31.12
213	"	set-net for gizzard shad (*konoshiro-tateami*)	1.3–31.12
a	"	" [unknown number]	"
b	"	gill-net for flying fish (*ago-sashiami*) [unknown number]	?
332	"	"	1.4–30.6
2725	exclusive fishing right (line A-B-E-F)		1.1–31.12
2727	joint fishing right (line B-C-D-E)		1.1–31.12

resource management that better enabled the fishermen to actively defend their access to marine resources.

Shingū's fishing co-operative was established in 1902 when both exclusive and shared territories became estates of the co-operative as did allocations of set-nets, sectional and special fishery rights. This improved the fishermen's position *vis-à-vis* the merchants considerably. Merchants in their capacity as village leaders, in theory at least, lost their access to these estates and thereby their influence on questions of management. In many places the old merchants nevertheless re-tained a strong grip on the fisheries as they continued to play important roles in fish curing and marketing, as net owners and even as leaders of co-operatives.

With many Shingû merchants gradually losing their influence over the fisheries, we therefore have to look for explanations in addition to the establish-ment of the co-operative. One important factor was new administrative structures introduced in the Meiji era. The old distinction between farming and fishing villages was discontinued and fishing districts ceased to exist as administrative units. The fishing villages became incorporated into the farming districts that invariably were headed by people from farming villages. These were less know-ledgeable about the special problems relating to the fisheries than the old headmen had been. Given farmers' generally negative attitude towards fishermen at that time, they were also probably less interested. This might have made their role as negotiators and mediators in fishing disputes less effective. Moreover, in 1889 the old villages were amalgamated to form larger units. With the creation of the new Shingū Village – comprising the three farming villages Minato, Kaminofu and Shimonofu in addition to Shingū and Ainoshima – the influence of the old leadership declined further. The big landholders in the new unit emerged as the powerful leaders; the position as mayor was for decades monopolized by a family from Kaminofu.

The other important factor was changing economic opportunities. There was a general trend towards the end of the Tokugawa period that merchants in the fishing villages were losing ground to up-coming merchants in the farming villages (Kalland 1995). This process accelerated during the Meiji era with the lifting of restrictions on rural commerce. Shingū had, moreover, more specific problems to face. The village had during the Tokugawa period benefited from its proximity to Ainoshima where some of the feudal lords as well as the Korean envoys stopped on their way to and from the capital and where the feudal authorities moreover had a guard post against foreign ships. This created extra activities in Shingū and in 1692 two thirds of the households were engaged in various kinds of business but with the collapse of the feudal regime important sources of income were lost to some of the merchants. Then, at the end of the nineteenth century, railways shifted most of the traffic from sea to land, by-passing Shingū. Many of the merchants in Shingū tried their fortunes elsewhere and several of those who remained went bankrupt. The most spectacular bankruptcy was the Kaneuchi house which had dominated Shingū politics and fisheries since the early 18th century (Kalland 1983). Their *sake* brewery was lost to a merchant in a farming village.

Nets were also sold to merchants in farming villages, and in 1887 two of the four sardine beach seines and one of the three sea bream nets were owned by people from Minato village (*Kaneuchi Doc.* no.1912). As these new merchants did not have much knowledge about fishing, lived some distance from the shore and had little influence on the allocation of fishing rights, they had little choice but to hand over most of the decisions to the net leaders (*amigashira*), improving the fishermen's bargaining position considerably.

However, we should not be misled by these changes to draw the conclusion that social stratification in the fisheries ceased to be of importance. Only after the introduction of the new Fishery Law in 1949 and the end of large-scale fishing did access to influence become more equitable. The Meiji Fishery Law did not eliminate tendencies to monopolize positions and influence. Set-net, sectional and special fishery rights were issued for a fixed period of time (usually 10 or 20 years) but could easily be renewed. Individuals could acquire such rights permanently and the rights could also be inherited, leased and even sold (Ninohei 1981). Moreover, certain families continued to have a strong influence within the co-operative. This was the case also in Shingū where the Yayama family monopolized the position as chairman (*kumiaichō*) for many years. Originally a fishing family, Yayama was one of the merchant houses that rose to power towards the end of the Tokugawa period when Yayama Gonuemon became the village headman (*shōya*). His grandson brought the first purse seine to Shingū and became the first chairman of the co-operative. Several of their relatives, however, continued to be active fishermen and the Yayamas therefore maintained a closer contact with the fishermen than most of the absentee net owners had done. They represented a new breed of leader.

CONCLUSION

The exclusive village fishing territory has been the cornerstone in Japanese fisheries management since before the Tokugawa period. Apart from the upheavals of the early Meiji era when the revolutionary government made an ill-fated attempt to open up the fisheries, sea space has been closed to the general populace. Another feature is the long history of co-management in Japanese fisheries, with central and local authorities both taking active parts. The players in this game changed radically during the Meiji era, however. The feudal authorities in Fukuoka were replaced by a central bureaucracy in Tokyo, with arms extending to the prefectural and municipality levels. The village has been replaced by the fishery co-operative with representatives at the prefectural co-operative and through this to the national level. The single-most important achievement was none the less the linkage between co-operative and territory in which the latter became an estate to the former. These were the first steps towards equity, more fully achieved after the introduction of the new Fishery Law in 1949. It was also an important step towards sustainable fisheries; the near constant annual coastal catch of between 2.5 and 3 million tonnes since 1925 testifies to its success in this regard (Kalland 1996).

NOTES

1   Seaweeds and shellfish were of minor importance. The only commercial species of seaweed in Shingū in the 1820s was *kobunori* (*Gloiopeltis capillaris*). Other species were used within households. Shellfish was also of little commercial importance, but for some households seaweed and shellfish could nevertheless be of some value as they grew close to shore, often in shallow waters, and required little capital investment. Many of the collectors were women.

2   The authorities established several funds in order to provide cheap capital and thus help the fishermen to finance their boats and gear. The *ura-tamarigin* established in 1762 was the most important of these. Loans were given to finance fishing boats and nets, trading ships, breakwaters, extra taxes and corvée duties, or to give aid to

people in great poverty (Kalland 1984, 1995). A number of fishermen from Shingū borrowed money from this fund until it was dissolved in 1871. Government funds continued to be used to finance fishing boats, but credit associations (*tanomoshi-kō*) seem to have grown considerably in importance.

3 In 1685, Shingū was moved from its old location towards the beach. According to the official view this was more convenient to the fishermen. The separation of the fishermen and traders from the farmers in the old Minato Village was probably also of major concern (Kalland 1997).

4 The fishing territories were thus created for reasons of administrative convenience rather than to please the fishermen or to secure sustainable use.

5 In 1895 the value of the sand lance fishery accounted for not less than 90 per cent of the reported catches (Fukuoka-ken 1905: 169–71; Kalland 1981: 68).

6 See Kalland (1991) for an analysis of the more complicated case of Jinoshima and surrounding villages.

7 The island is an important archaeological site for the understanding of prehistoric relations between Japan and Korea. Moreover, being the location of the outer of the three Munakata shrines, the island is considered the abode of the Munakata deity and is therefore off-limits for women.

8 Catch statistics exist for some of the territories for 1907 and 1922–27, but the figures are very unreliable as the figures were probably prepared in order to evade taxes (Kalland 1981:68). There is no reason to believe that some of the figures are more distorted than others, however, so we might get an idea about the relative importance of catches in the various territories and for various gear.

9 Similar figures were found in the case of Jinoshima (Kalland 1991: 208).

10 These rights replaced several of the old licences from the Tokugawa period. Instead of issuing licences, the Meiji authorities chose to limit the number of fishing spots open to that fishery – the fishermen taking turns (decided by rotation, lottery or a first-come, first-served basis as the case might be) when there was more gear than spots. Whereas fishery rights regulated the activities within the coastal waters until 1949 (when the second national fishery law was promulgated), licences were issued for an increasing number of pelagic and offshore fisheries after 1909.

REFERENCES

Unpublished documents:
Akashi Documents. Kept at the Fukuoka Prefectural Library, Fukuoka City.
Imabayashi Documents. Copies kept at Nishi-Nihon Bunka Kyūkai, Fukuoka City.
Kaneuchi Documents. Copies kept at Nishi-Nihon Bunka Kyūkai, Fukuoka City.
Tone Documents. Copies kept at Nishi-Nihon Bunka Kyūkai, Fukuoka City.
Ura-Kiroku. Kept at the Fukuoka Prefectural Library, Fukuoka City.
The archive of Shingū's Fishing Cooperative Association.

Published Works:

Akimichi Tomoya and Kenneth Ruddle (1984) 'The historical development of territorial rights and fishery regulations in Okinawa inshore waters'. In K. Ruddle and T. Akimichi (eds), *Maritime Institutions in the Western Pacific*. Senri Ethnological Studies no.17. Osaka: National Museum of Ethnology, pp. 37–88.

Cordell John (1984) 'Defending customary inshore sea rights'. In K. Ruddle and T. Akimichi (eds), *Maritime Institutions in the Western Pacific*. Senri Ethnological Studies no.17. Osaka: National Museum of Ethnology, pp. 301–326.

Fukuoka-ken (1905) *Fukuoka-ken tōkeisho* [Fukuoka prefecture statistics].

—— (1988a) *Fukuoka-ken gyogyōshi* [Description of the fisheries of Fukuoka prefecture]. Fukuoka: Nishi-Nihon Bunka Kyōkai.

—— (1988b) *Fukuoka-ken chiri-zenshi* [Geographic description of Fukuoka prefecture], vol.1. Fukuoka: Nishi-Nihon Bunka Kyōkai.

Habara, Yūkichi (1954) *Nihon gyogyō keizaishi* [The economic history of Japanese fisheries]. Tokyo: Iwanami shoten.

Itō, Oshirō (ed.) (1949) *Fukuoka-ken shirō sōsho* [Collected documents related to Fukuoka prefecture], vol. 9. Tokyo: Shirō hensansho.

Kalland, Arne (1981) *Shingū: A Study of a Japanese Fishing Community*. London: Curzon Press.

—— (1983) 'Chikuzen Shingu-ura ōjōya sandai: Kaneuchi Shinzaemon' [Kaneuchi Shinzaemon: Three generations as district headmen from Shingū]. *Seinan chiikishi kenkyū*, vol. 5. pp. 93–136.

—— (1984) 'A credit institution in Tokugawa Japan: the *Ura-tamegin* fund of Chikuzen Province'. In G. Daniels (ed.), *Europe Interprets Japan*. Tenterden: Paul Norbury Publication.

—— (1990) 'Sea tenure and the Japanese experience: resource management in coastal fisheries'. In E. Ben-Ari, B. Moeran and J. Valentine (eds), *Unwrapping Japan*. Manchester: Manchester University Press, pp. 188–204.

—— (1991) 'Making the unworkable workable: "Guest fishing" in Japanese coastal waters'. *resource Management and Optimization,* vol. 8 nos. 3–4: pp. 197–210.

—— (1995) *Fishing Villages in Tokugawa Japan*. London: Curzon/Honolulu: University of Hawaii Press.

—— (1996) 'Marine management in coastal Japan'. In Kevin Crean and David Symes (eds), *Fisheries Management in Crisis*. Oxford: Fishing News Books, pp. 71–83.

—— (1997) 'Tokugawa-jidai no Shingū-ura' [Shingū-ura in the Tokugawa period]. In Shingū chōshi henshū i'inkai (eds), *Shingū chōshi* [The History of Shingū Town]. Shingū: Shingū-chō, pp. 378–436.

Kawazoe, Shōji (1977) '"Chikuzen-no-kuni zoku fūdoku zuroku" kaidai'. Introduction in Katō Ichijun and Takatori Shūsei, *Chikuzen-no-kuni zoku fūdoki zuroku furoku* (ed. by Fukuoka komonjo o yomukai). vol. 1, Tokyo: Bunken shuppan, pp. 9–63.

Ninohei, Tokuo (1981) *Meiji gyogyō kaitakushi* (Fisheries exploitation in the Meiji Era) Tokyo: Heibonsha.

Ruddle, Kenneth (1985) 'The continuity of traditional practices: the case of Japanese coastal fisheries'. In K. Ruddle and R.E. Johannes (eds), *The Traditional Knowledge and Management in Coastal Systems in Asia and the Pacific.* Jakarta: UNESCO, pp. 158–179.

—— (1987) 'Administration and conflict management in Japanese coastal fisheries'. FAO Fisheries Technical Paper no. 273.

CHAPTER NINE

Conflicting Bounderies: the Role of Mapping in the Co-management Discourse

MANON OSSEWEIJER

Maps present us not with the world as we can see,
but point toward a world we might know. (Wood 1992:12)

INTRODUCTION

Mapping is by and large one of the best known and popular participatory methods used in different research and fieldwork contexts as well as in projects focusing on co-management of natural resources. Maps are seen as 'versatile and powerful ways of representing information' and can be used, for instance, to gain knowledge about the location and use of natural resources, land/sea ownership, social-political issues, etc. This technique is believed to be especially appropriate for communities with a low literacy level and might 'develop the community's ability to develop, record, organize and present information'. With regard to community resource conservation, the use of maps implicates that 'everyone can take part and check that the information is accurate'. (WWF South Pacific Programme 1996: 79–82).

In addition, mapping is perceived as 'a strategy of empowerment' during the process of co-management arrangements considering natural resources: 'The transferring of mapping technology to local communities enables them to communicate their perception of land rights and resource management systems with the government and contribute to the process of resolving conflicts.' (Momberg *et al.* 1996:4). Momberg *et al.* also contend that 'community mapping should be perceived as a tool for conflict resolution to foster practical, harmonious solutions to competing interests and claims to land territories and natural resources' (1996:5; see also Poole 1995). This way, mapping can enhance local participation in land/sea use planning and conservation management.

While most sources on mapping are mainly positive, some do point at the technique's weaknesses, such as the inaccuracy of the maps drawn, the difficulty of understanding graphic representations in certain cultures and the reluctance to identify particular features related to cultural or religious significant knowledge (Borrini-Feyerabend 1997:138).

In this chapter I reflect on the method of mapping and its usefulness in the process of establishing co-management arrangements for protected areas. In doing so, I illustrate my arguments with a case study of the Aru Islands (Eastern Indonesia), where a marine reserve is the object for co-management. The case study shows that mapping as a participatory method is not always successful, which I attribute to differences between environmental NGOs and Aru islanders regarding in their views on the natural environment and on the use of maps.

THE ARU ISLANDS

The Aru archipelago (see Figure 9.1), situated in the south-eastern part of Maluku province, consists of six main islands and many small islands along the eastern coastline, inhabited by some 58,000 people. The islanders living in the coastal settlements are primarily hunter-gatherer-fishermen involved in natural resource trade with Chinese-Indonesian traders, who control the flow of resources and consumption goods in the region. The main products collected and traded are pearl oysters, sea cucumbers (*trepang*), marine turtles, shells, sharks' fins, birds' nests, copra, birds of paradise and cockatoos. Beside these money-generating activities, people are also involved in subsistence activities like gardening, hunting wild deer and pig, fishing and extracting a sago starch (Persoon *et al.* 1996; Osseweijer, 2001).

Trangan is the southernmost island of the archipelago, where fieldwork was undertaken and where the case study is taken from. Most of the people living in the villages on the east coast used to spread their resource-extracting activities over the two seasons. During the east monsoon (April–August) they would mainly focus on gardening, hunting and producing sago starch, and during the west monsoon (September–March) they would be involved in maritime resource exploitation. Ever since the 1990s, the seasons have not been taken into account that strictly anymore, and people expanded their sea-related activities. Men prolonged the diving season, not only diving for pearl oysters but also for sea cucumbers, or *trepang*, and both men and women have started to exploit sea cucumber species as a year-round activity. Sea cucumbers (mainly two species) used to be collected at night during the east monsoon, but since the prices have risen and the demand for more different species increased since 1994 people

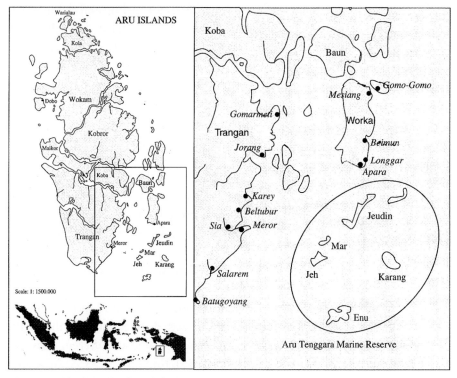

Figure 9.1: The Aru Islands and the Aru Tenggara Marine Reserve

have started to collect these invertebrates more intensively (Osseweijer 2000). In addition, many villagers are involved in turtle hunting. Either the turtles (green turtles and hawksbilturtles) are caught at the seagrass beds in front of the coast, or they are taken from the nesting sites on Enu Island.

The archipelago has a long history of trade in natural resources. Even before the VOC (Dutch East India Company) interfered with the trade, there existed extensive trade routes, whereby Aru mainly exported birds of paradise (and plumes) and pearls in exchange for sago. The nineteenth-century naturalist Wallace has written a detailed account on the trade practices in the archipelago's main town Dobo (1986 [1869]). Even today, the archipelago attracts outsiders hoping to find their luck in certain natural resource exploitation. The trade itself is still in the hands of Chinese Indonesian middlemen. Thus, nowadays turtle hunters from different Moluccan island visit Trangan's coastal area to catch turtles for the Bali market, seasonal sharkfin fishers from Sulawesi (mainly Bugis and Buton) use the waters and different kinds of large-scale, or industrial, fishing vessels (joint venture trawlers as well as Tanjung Balai Karimun ships, based in

Aru's industrial fishing town Benjina) roam the sea for shrimp and red snapper. In response to these outsiders, some local islanders have decided to sell turtles in Dobo and the men from Batugoyang villages have embraced on the new market for fins with their small-scale sharkfishing activities.

As a result of years of international lobbying, in 1991 a marine nature reserve was established in the southeastern part of the Aru Islands, southeast of Trangan Island, primarily to protect the dugong (*Dugong dugon* or sea cow) and the green turtle (*Chelonia mydas*) and their habitats. The protected area was given the status of 'strict reserve', which means that no one except researchers and rangers is allowed to enter it, not even for small-scale fishery purposes, visiting the coconut plantations or collecting sea cucumbers on the tidal flats. However, to date there is no organized protection of the reserve, there are no government conservationists in the field and local villagers as well as outsiders just enter it.

Establishment of the Aru Tenggara Marine Reserve (ATMR) was characterized by and subject to area mapping. Ever since the first recommendations based on species and habitat research by Compost (1980) and Schultz, and during the ten years before the ATMR was officially gazetted, scientists together with Indonesian government conservation officers have proposed different sizes and statuses for the protected area (see Schultz 1993). Initially, the ATMR was proposed as a 250,000-ha conservation area bordering another wildlife reserve in the north that would be open to local artisanal fishing and regulated dugong and turtle hunting (Smiet and Siallagan 1981). A later proposal argued for a strict reserve consisting of a 28,750 ha landmass (islands) and an additional 102,500 ha partly for conservation and partly for tourist purposes (BKSDA 1989). In the end the Ministry of Forestry declared an area of 114,000 ha of shallow waters, seagrass beds and coral reefs including five islands as a strict reserve where no one except scientists and conservation officers is allowed to enter (Ministry of Forestry:1991).

Thus, several maps of the region were drawn before the establishment of the marine protected area, and now that the reserve is a fact maps are still being drawn by people from environmental NGOs and by local's, often with the help of NGOs. The maps are used to gain a better insight into natural resource use, terrestrial and maritime property rights and access to and withdrawal of those natural resources. Subsequently, mapping is intended to reflect the communities' views on the marine reserve and to begin the preparing for co-management of the reserve. Management of the reserve through the collaboration of the government and the local communities is regarded by nature conservationists as the best way and the most likely method for successful protection of the green turtles. The communities approached by research teams are those living in the vicinity of the marine reserve, the villages of east and south Trangan Island as well as the villages of Barakai Island (see Figure 9.1).[1]

CO-MANAGEMENT

In the above-mentioned reserve's act of establishment as well as in a World Wide Fund for Nature (WWF) information brochure (1994), the region covered by the reserve is described as a marine region with the uninhabited, empty islands Enu, Karang, Jeh, Mar, Jeudin and Marjinjin (see Figure 9.1). In accordance with Indonesia's constitution (1945, article 33), the Department of Forestry and Nature Conservation (PHPA), the Department of Fisheries and the different levels of governmental administration consider this marine region as state property. Local customary rights with regard to these coastal areas are not recognized. The fact that islands are uninhabited and appear to be 'empty' is the reason for considering them as *terra nullius* (Pannell 1996). In this specific case, that the islands and their surroundings (reefs and tidal flats) could be in use for resource exploitation has not been taken into consideration. In fact, the islands Jeh and Mar, for example, have been planted with coconut trees by people from the villages of Longgar, Apara and Karey, and almost all other villagers have camp-sites on these islands during the east monsoon when they spend one or two weeks gathering sea cucumbers (Osseweijer 2000). Furthermore, 'empty' seems to evoke the idea that the islands are culturally meaningless to the people living in this region.

Due to a growing awareness of the existence of *de facto* marine customary property (based on social science research) and the international agreements with regard to indigenous peoples, environmental NGOs have recently been addressing this issue in relation to protected area management. The WWF's statement of principles on indigenous peoples and conservation (1996) is an example of this development. In general, development and environmental NGOs have become more and more imbued with the fact that (with respect to protected areas) 'it is unlikely that vague appeals for greater community participation or community-based management will succeed if they gloss over basic tenure issues' (Cordell 1993:65). However, as has become clear through empirical research, the fact that people have customary rights does not logically imply that they use and manage their natural resources in a sustainable manner. In the case of Aru, at the moment they certainly do not (Osseweijer 2000, 2001). Thus tenure systems should not be considered 'panaceas for halting environmental degradation', but in the end, the challenge is 'to blend a sensitivity to social justice concerns with a critical perspective on the environmental management potentials of indigenous tenure and other living customs today' (Cordell 1993:68; cf. Polunin 1984).

The best management regime, which includes these property considerations and subsequently more local participation, seems to be co-management. Co-management (also referred to as collaborative management or joint management) was first developed and applied in the North American fisheries sector in the late 1980s as a way to get fishermen more involved in management issues (Pinkerton 1989). A very general definition of co-management is 'the sharing of power and responsibility between the government and local resource users' (Notzke 1995:187).

Co-management is not only regarded as a regulation of access to and withdrawal of natural resources but also as a possible solution for problematic management or mismanagement of protected areas. In an IUCN publication Borrini-Feyerabend, for instance, defines collaborative management of protected areas as 'a situation in which some or all of the relevant stakeholders in a protected area are involved in a substantial way in management activities' (1996: 12). Ideally, management of protected areas then consists of the whole process of the identification and declaration of an area, institution building, the design and implementation of management plans, research, monitoring and evaluation. However, in many situations the process has started already and involvement of local participants is only added in a later phase.

One of the basic assumptions of co-management should be the concurrence of ideas with regard to the object to be managed, whether natural resources or a protected area (*cf.* Pet-Soede 2000). However, I believe it is safe to say that in many instances the local perceptions of the environment and the use of its natural resources differ very much from the conservationists' perceptions.[2] The very purpose of nature conservation, whether through government management or through co-management, is often not completely understood and therefore cannot be taken as a common point of departure for co-management negotiations. This different understanding of the environment, the (limitations of natural resources, and the need to protect certain species from extinction have often been taken for granted (Osseweijer 2001).

MAPPING AS A PARTICIPATORY TOOL

A first step for gaining a better insight into local perceptions with regard to the natural environment is to use a participatory method such as mapping. This method is considered to give information in a bottom-up way and, as Aberley suggests, to 'speak a map' within a community (using self-drawn maps) is often regarded as a way to community empowerment (1993:16).

Mapping can be organized in different ways, but generally it involves a group of people who are given materials for drawing or making a map on paper, in the sand or on the floor. The researcher explains the reason for drawing such a map and might start with a central feature of the landscape or village. The final map, however, is the result of local creativity and negotiations and should reflect their ideas of the important places in their environment. During the process of drawing the map, the researcher could observe internal differences within the group, which people take the lead in mapping, how others react to the map, etc. The map may turn out to be very different from official maps of the area (if at all existent), but that does not alter the fact that the participatory map shows what local people think is significant. It often reveals certain information that might be difficult to obtain when using other research methods, such as by interview (Momberg *et al.* 1996). Alcorn also shows that there are different benefits of the mapping process for local communities and sustainable natural resource management. She mentions among others: community cohesion and self-determination, strengthening resource rights, policy change, democracy and reclaiming lost lands (Alcorn 2000:4-8).

Although I agree that there is much to say for participatory mapping as a means for collecting community-based information, it is good to consider critically the general assumptions behind maps and their implications. Maps, like other forms of social discourse, are a means of conceiving, articulating and structuring the world. Often there is a bias in the reflection of social relations, since the knowledge on which the map is based is in the hands of the social elites/authorities. What we think we 'read' on a map is not just the representation of the natural environment. This is a universal phenomenon: it is true in the West and also for the non-Western areas where mapping as a participatory tool is used. Mapping has a long and politically charged history, whereby cartographic knowledge and power have been concentrated in relatively few hands, related to social elites (Harley 1990). In colonial times, land was mapped in order to strengthen the European imperialist state's position and to expand its influence (see Morphy 1993). Post-colonial, independent governments have been using maps perhaps for the same political reasons, and, today, the development-related and environmental NGOs construct maps and use participatory mapping to gain knowledge of a particular area. In all cases, knowledge is acquired, taken out of its local context and often reproduced and distributed.

A very basic assumption of Western or Western-influenced NGOs is that maps are universal items, which are produced, understood and used in the same way. To draw a map is understood as a familiar and often practised technique of communicating knowledge within a society. But not all societies are as map-immersed as Western society (Wood 1992). In addition, although field manuals for methods and techniques warn about social inequalities among participants that might come to the fore during mapping, the internal conflicts within a society and issues of power and wealth are often overlooked or underestimated. While in theory this research tool seems very participatory, in practice it may be very difficult to get a representative group of participants together without a few people dominating the drawing process. Moreover, knowledge on which maps are based, or which is visualized in maps is supposed to be general and public knowledge. It is often not realized that certain information found on maps, such as place names – which in our eyes may not seem of any special value at all – is part of a body of secret knowledge, the possession of which can generate status or power within society. Perhaps the most important problem to be faced during mapping is that co-management of natural resources or a protected area requires clearly defined and uncontested boundaries to indicate what exactly is to be managed. In the case of Aru, as in many other places, it has turned out that these assumptions do not find a uniform local response and may cause misunderstandings.

Taking all this into account, it is also necessary to acknowledge that there are different goals which can be achieved through mapping. Local people, for instance, might envisage a totally different goal from conservationists. Where the former may hope to articulate claims to customary property, the latter are more likely to prioritize biodiversity and aim to manage natural resources or to establish protected area management (Alcorn 2000:3).

ARU PERCEPTIONS OF LANDSCAPE

The landscape in Aru landscape is quite impressive. After crossing the sea, from the island Wamar (where the main town Dobo is situated) to the sea strait between the islands Maiekor and Kobroor, for hours you are surrounded by mangroves on the left and right sides of the boat. Then, reaching the east side of the islands, you enter a vast shallow water area, of mixed sandbanks and seagrass beds with coral reefs, rich in resources. People in Aru look at their landscape differently from outsiders. The latter see this vast seascape of cliffs, tidal flats and islets as a particular geographical landscape or as an environment from which natural resources can be extracted, and in this case as a part of a global conservation strategy to protect marine turtles. Aru islanders, however, perceive the landscape as places that remind them of their ancestors, or *kaijenan*, who have set their footprints there. The landscape is a collection of actions and events by the ancestors in a far away past (*ninuijejesir*) – ancestors, who are not with the people in this world anymore but reside in another dimension. The ancestral paths are not kept in written accounts but are remembered through the places in the landscape, historical narratives[3] and the linked songs.[4] Basically local history, known as *Jaltankun*, which means 'the story of the paths' is made up of all the ancestral paths together. People compare the complete local history with a tree with many branches, where every branch represents a path and is summarized, after telling the story, in a mnemonic song. The song is used as a way to remember history.

According to a few older, knowledgeable people in the village, this enormous tree of Aru history begins with the story of the island Enu-Karang. These islands are locally referred to as the origin place of all Aru people, but to outsiders are mainly known as a place visited by green turtles to lay eggs. A long time ago, when none of the ancestors had been living on the Aru Islands and only indigenous spiritual beings were living on the main islands, there were two brothers. These two brothers, who are associated with the two moiety-like groups existing in the archipelago (the group of the shark and the group of the whale), and who were also representatives of two major family groups, were constantly challenging each other. One day, when they were fighting again, one of the indigenous ancestors of Trangan Island decided to interfere and punished the brothers by causing a flood which split the island in two and forced every-one to flee the sinking island. They tried to do so in boats and other objects used as boats such as shells, and from that moment onwards each family group was led by its 'elder' travelling in search of a new place to stay. Every place they visited to rest or stay temporarily became a significant locale. Many places, such as tidal flats and islets, were created at that time. Every place – tidal flats, diving locations, islets, depths, sago/coconut plantations, wells, and rivers – received a name referring to what happened there and to the visiting family group or ancestor (*cf.* Tilley 1994, Ossweijer 2001 and Spyer 2000).

The majority of the ancestors travelled towards Aru's main islands to find a new territory to live in. Upon arrival, the elders walked and claimed land; walking and walking until they met meet other ancestors. The meeting place then often formed the boundary between both their territories. The markers of this landscape are rivers, streams, pools and other natural phenomena. For example, the river Jomon near the present-day village of Salarem is situated at the place where two ancestors met and kissed each other. During this initial period of claiming land, each family group received a territory, which thus consisted of land on the main island and all places visited at sea and on the reefs during their journey to the main islands. After all the land was divided, the elders of all families came together at the place of the indigenous ancestor who had caused the flood, and let him and each other know which territories each had claimed. This meeting place is still a sacred site, known as Jardabagul, which means as much 'to come together at the land'.

Until now, each family group has owned a territory known as '*rahuin*', which consists of land and/or sea property. However, the property seems to be formed by clusters of sites rather than bounded areas of land and sea (*cf.* Layton 1997). The *Jaltankun*, or the history of the paths, is a record of ownership, an imaginary marking of sea and land claims by the narration of ancestral tracks and songs linked to every branch. Every family group traces ownership back to this local history and is socially linked to specific topographic territories. These places are therefore important for their cultural identity. Many family names refer to significant places of historical events. For example the Kolupupin family's ancestor came from Enu and stopped near the contemporary village of Gomarmeti (North Trangan). There he filled a bailershell with sand, which he threw into the river near the present-day village of Doka in Trangan's interior. A sandbank was created where the family started to live and became known as 'Kolupupin people'. The name is deduced from *kule*, or sand, and *huhin* top. Although this family came to live in the forested interior, the place where their ancestor stopped and took the sand is still owned by Kolupupin people.

CONSEQUENCES FOR NATURAL RESOURCE ALLOCATION

Today, however, these family groups do not live separately anymore, scattered over their territories. Due to Dutch colonial interference at the beginning of the twentieth century, administrative villages (I. *desa*) were established along the coast and family groups were forced to form larger communities. For instance, the village where I have carried out most of my fieldwork, Beltubur, consists of ten family groups (or sub-groups) and therefore the village's property is built up from different families' territories. The village property consists of all land and sea territories of the families living in the village community. What makes the property issue complicated is that in the process of village formation, certain sub-groups have affiliated themselves with other villages but still hold territorial claims. Thus a family of which most members live in Beltubur, but a few others in Karey and Siya, might own a sago grove, that today officially belongs to Beltubur but which is open to all family members. Formally, to have access to another family's territory and to withdraw natural resources from it, permission should be asked from the family group's elders (cf. Meyers 1982). This way a piece of land for gardening, for example, can be given to a person of a different family.

Where the extraction of the maritime resources, such as sea cucumbers, shellfish, pearl oysters and turtles, is concerned things the procedure is slightly different. This is related to the migratory character of the resources. The reefs, islets, depths, etc. are known to be the property of certain family groups, but the natural resources cannot be claimed. According to local history, all people of Aru belong to one of the two alliances. Here is not the place to elaborate on that story, but what is important is that the villages of Trangan belong to the alliance of the whale and in principle all people belonging to the group of the ancestral whale (Urlim) are allowed to hunt, dive for and collect resources in this coastal region, known as Urlim's Sea. Thus, natural resource exploitation at sea is regulated by common property management, refered to as 'we eat together' or *tahoran tamnam*. Beside the shared membership of the social group associated to the ancestral whale, other reasons given for 'eating together' are: 1) marine resources are migratory and thus it is impossible to own these resources – they are owned by all people; and 2) many maritime resources are believed to descend from the unfortunate ancestors who could not escape Enau-Karang during the flood and became dolphins, fish, etc.

When going to the sea, people visit their family's territory or they ask permission from the rightful owners of certain reefs, for which a small ritual is carried out. However, in practice, most people just go to their own reefs, which is fairly easy since almost everyone is related through blood relations or marriage relations and seldom undertake a long journey to far away located reefs owned by other families.

ARU MAPS

The local history is not experienced, known or shared equally by all members of a family group. One or two of the elders usually knows it. They know the family's paths and linked songs. Sometimes a path is narrated at a family gathering at night while drinking palm wine and chewing tobacco or betel. The detailed story, however, with the real (secret) names of ancestors, is only given to one or two descendants who 'ask the right questions'. The historical knowledge is powerful. To know the history is not only useful for resource exploitation but for healing as well. To know the path of an ancestor means you can ask the ancestor to let sea cucumbers appear on his/her tidal flat, or wild deer in his/her part of the forest from out of another dimension. Jahari, for instance, one of the knowledgeable women in the village, belongs to the family group associated with the grouper fish (*Epinephelus spp.*), 'the fish with a big mouth with which he can eat a lot'. She can use this ancestor's real name on land as well as at sea to ask for natural resources. The ancestors use messenger spirits, always represented as animals (especially birds and other flying creatures) to bring news to the people or to keep an eye on them and protect them. To know the name and the story of such an ancestor's messenger, which is also related to specific places in the landscape, gives a person the ability to ask his/her help to heal a sick person during a ritual by bringing back the patient's lost soul.

Consequently many people only know bits and pieces of their history, but cannot not tell you, because they are not the storyteller designate, or as Layton mentions regarding the Australian Western Desert case, '[m]ost can be said about a place when at that site, *by* someone linked to it in a recognized way. If another spoke, he would be usurping an authority to which he is not entitled' (1995: 213–4). As the ancestral journeys are not written down, just passed on to younger generations by oral means, there are no artefactual maps of these journeys and subsequent customary territories. Only in the minds of the story-teller and the listeners there may be maps, which are referred to in social science literature as *cognitive* or *mental* maps (Gell 1985; Wood 1992).[5] Considering the above, it is not surprising that Aruese do not 'ordinarily separate out such image-based knowledge into legalistic objects of discourse' (Hirsch 1995:14 on Australian cases). In the past, property rights conflicts were solved within the community[6] and drawn maps were not produced for this or any other purpose. Since the 1980s, Aruese have been taking these issues to court and from then people have started drawing artefactual maps of their customary property to use as 'evidence' in lawsuits.

The maps produced in Aru are not navigational maps to find your way from A to B, but '(hi)storical' maps that show significant places and customary property of lineages. These maps are based on the accounts of ancestral paths as described above, but are not exact and complete printouts of the story. Moreover, these recent graphic representations are not always meaningful or intelligible to an outsider. There are no standard codes or symbols, only names of ancestors (their public names, not the real names), names of family groups and names of present-day villages. The story behind the map, why certain people own certain places, cannot simply be deduced from it. Tilley (1994) has described this difference between the story and the map: 'Spatial stories are about the operations and practices, which constitute places and locales. The map, by contrast, involves a stripping away of these things' (1994:32). The maps just show what is necessary but are not at all complete with regard to place and ancestral names. This practice seems related to the secretive character of the basis of the maps, i.e. the ancestral paths. Older people in the villages regard mapping a path as writing it down in a story or telling it as a story, because in all cases the ancestral walk is relived. As soon as names are put on paper, be it a story in writing or a map drawn, they turn into public knowledge, even though one still needs the explanation to really understand them.[7]

TWO EXAMPLES OF PROPERTY CONFLICTS AND MAPS

In the south of Aru, conflicts over property have recently flared up again. I deliberately use the word 'again' to avoid the assumption that such conflicts are new phenomena. Dutch colonial accounts describe such conflicts and the village head of Beltubur showed me a report written in 1921 by a Dutch district officer (*controleur* Ruyehaver) which told of property conflicts between people in the villages of Meror, Siya and Beltubur and which had been settled by this officer. The difference between today's conflicts and those in the past is that presently most conflicts are triggered off by outsiders. Whereas the majority of past property conflicts dealt with land property or who was allowed to plant trees at particular locations, the recent tensions are concerned with revenues to be received from outsiders. For example, these might be from the lease of certain islets and land locations to be occupied by pearl farms, or for the exploitation of reefs where commercial hunters will catch green turtles for the Bali market.

On the very first day in the village of Beltubur, when I introduced myself to the village head, he told me about the village's conflicts with its neighbouring village, Karey. Later that day, I was paid a visit by one of the expert-witnesses for Beltubur, who spontaneously summarized the problems, the lawsuit, the process in Tual (Kei Islands) and the finding of the court. In summary, the lawsuit Beltubur had started against its neighbouring village, a year before, was instigated by the settlement of four Chinese-Indonesian pearl oyster businesses. Through mediation by Karey, and supported by the sub-district head (*camat*) and the head of the sub-district's fisheries office, these companies had contracted four locations, three islets (Kimro, Benggori, Kumnar) and one location between Beltubur and Karey (Kolmajan). The four locations covered approximately 10 ha each, including the surrounding beaches and sea. Two of the businesses were owned by Chinese-Indonesian traders from Karey. The village head of Karey readily claimed the four locations as his village property and had received

185

the lease for five years. After finding out what was going on, Beltubur's village head, on behalf of Beltubur's infuriated inhabitants, had reacted by writing an indictment in which his village claimed the customary rights and made a charge against Karey.

In the indictments of Beltubur and Karey as well as during the process both villages unexpectedly narrated not their own '(hi)story' but each other's. Beltubur sketched the main events of the journey of the Kumnaris family, today living in Karey, to show how this family's ancestor had asked permission to live on and protect Kimro and later Kolmajan by agreement that their ancestor Failib (of Beltubur's ruling family) still owned the land. Whenever people from Karey wanted to collect natural resources or plant trees, they had to ask permission from Beltubur. This story was subscribed to by the villages of Batugoyang and Apara. Karey's representatives, with the help of witnesses from the villages of Longgar, Jorang, Gomarmeti, Salarem and Siya (for which each village head had received one million rupiah), tried to discredit this ancestral history and described how the villagers of Beltubur (no mention is made of any specific family group) under the guidance of their ancestor Failib arrived on Trangan after Enu-Karang was flooded and started to live in the interior, then moved several times. The location of present Beltubur was recognized as the fifth site that its inhabitants have occupied.

As a consequence of the lawsuit, both villages have drawn maps, which show their customary territories. Beltubur's map (Figure 9.2) was made in 1995 especially for this lawsuit and is based on ancestral paths narrated by the village elders and some lineage elders from Batugoyang and Apara. The map shows that Beltubur owns the land and sea with boundaries in the north with the village Fatlabata, in the south with Siya and Meror, in the west with the inland villages Jelia and Popjetur, in the east with the maritime property of the villages Longgar and Apara. Karey's map (Figure 9.3), drawn and signed by officials in 1996 and based on the outcome of an earlier property conflict solved by a judge in Dobo,[8] looks more official due to the signature of the district head. It claims property with boundaries in the north with the villages Jorang, Gomarmeti, Gomarsungai and Fatlabata; in the south with the villages Siya, Salarem and Dosimar; in the east with the villages Longgar and Apara and the sea gully *Gualorjin*; and in the west with the river *Meri*. Furthermore, the whole shallow water area west of *Gualorjin* is claimed.

Since Beltubur could not afford an attorney to write the indictment, the village head had written it himself. In the end, after hearing both parties' expert witnesses, the court did not accept the case as it was not conform a formal

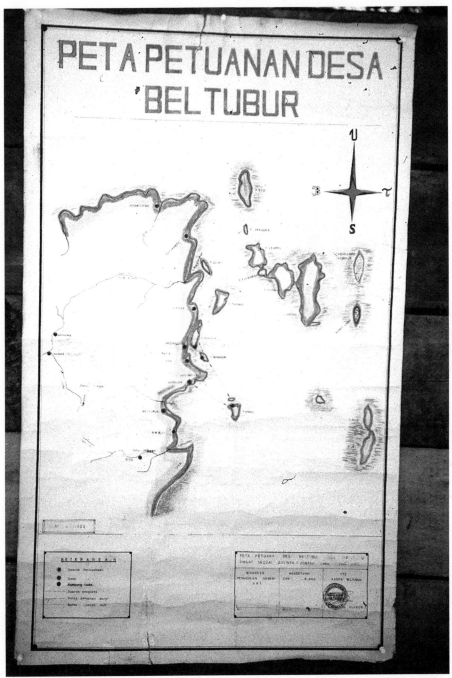

Figure 9.2: The locally produced map of the area claimed by Beltubur. Two important signatures are still missing (photo by G.A. Persoon, 1998).

Figure 9.3: The village secretary of Karey proudly shows his map of the area claimed. This map was approved by the district head as the official map (photo by G.A. Persoon, 1998).

indictment with all defendants mentioned. Karey's representatives returned home as 'winners', Beltubur's representatives returned as 'losers', who could continue the case if writing a proper indictment and suing again. Lack of money, however, has kept the village from undertaking new steps. In the meantime, tensions were still to be felt and occasionally they ended in fights, destruction of garden sheds and produce, or complete avoidance and broken contact.

Shortly after Beltubur had come to terms with the situation, the conflicts were revived again in 1998 when the village head of Karey was making deals with commercial turtle hunters working for Chinese Indonesian middlemen in Bali. He claimed the whole western part of the coastal region and, on top of that, Enu Island, and received money (though relatively little) from the turtle hunters in exchange for access to the region. Again, Beltubur (coming up for its property rights) supported by Batugoyang (a village with many local regular turtle hunters) contested this claim, this time through discussions and sometimes small incidents.

Another example of a map drawn as a result of property conflicts is the map of Batugoyang's territory. The map was drawn in 1994 to settle a property conflict with the neighbouring village of Dosimar (south Trangan), or more precisely, with the Wajin family group. The map is based on two sources: the local history of Batugoyang's dominant family group Sogalrey whose ancestral names are shown, and a 1907 sketch of a walking trail by the Dutch colonial officer Tissot van Patot.[9] Tissot van Patot's sketch, which was obtained from a tourist aboard a PELNI ship on its way to Irian Jaya, shows the trail the officer had walked from Siya through the savannah and bush landscape to Salarem and a site called Wajin. Dosimar had claimed an area within Batugoyang's territory, but thanks to the colonial sketch Batugoyang was able to show where the boundaries between Batugoyang and the Wajin family territory (now Dosimar village) run. Since 1995 Batugoyang has been in conflict again and even on a war footing with the other neighbouring village, Salarem. Salarem inhabitants claim the land on which their village is built, while Batugoyang villagers argue that it has always been their customary territory. In this case, too, Batugoyang uses the earlier described map of 1994, but so far it has not come to a court case.

CONFLICTING BOUNDARIES

Within the above described context of property conflicts, which have divided all villages in the region into the two parties led by Karey and Beltubur,[10] environmental NGOs started to visit village communities in 1997 and 1998 to find out how, in the near future, a board of representatives could be installed to deal with the government representatives in the marine reserve's management (see for instance Lakembe 1998). Mapping was thought of as one of the methods for gaining the necessary insights into the local situation.

However, the fact that local people have recently drawn maps to use in property rights conflicts does not mean that participatory mapping would not be a controversial method. From an anthropological perspective (bearing the above in mind), to map the region creates difficulties: There are the boundary conflicts between villages (more precisely: between family groups living in different villages). The village is not the unit in use where customary property is concerned. Family groups do form traditional units: although sometimes all members of a family group live together in one village, most of the time these family groups are spread over several villages. In addition, customary territories are locally defined as clusters of property and not continuous territories. Consequently, it is not possible to produce a map with clear boundaries showing 12 territories owned by the 12 villages located in the marine reserve's vicinity. Were a map to be drawn, it would show many different sites owned by many different family groups living in the area. Certain parts of the coastal sea, the reefs and the islands are also divided among family groups. However, as I have shown above, property ownership at sea has much more to do with rights to decide who has access, which can be ritually asked for, than with natural resource use (cf. Schlager and Ostrom 1993). More generally, local resistance towards mapping can be observed as caused by the NGO's different views of the natural environment and the function and purpose of mapping, i.e. the management of the marine protected area.

In the meantime, the environmental NGOs involved have not yet made a serious attempt to collect 12 different maps but have taken the map of Karey's territory as *the* map showing local customary property, i.e. Karey owning everything left of the extended vertical line dividing Penjuring Island with Apara owning everything to the right of that boundary. Karey and Apara are the only villages that have been visited by different research teams and NGO representatives to discuss customary ownership issues. As to be expected, both villages reconfirmed again and again that they indeed owned the customary rights in the coastal area. The other villages' opinions with regard to property were not taken into consideration. The contemporary property rights conflicts between the different villages are perceived as an obstacle, which should be removed so that the process of institution building for co-management can be started as soon as possible. This seems to be connected with an aim towards clarity and truth. Whereas from a phenomenological viewpoint it is only important that people experience something as true, from a legal perspective or from a NGO perspective there is a need to find out the 'truth': which map is the ultimately truthful one, who knows the real path narratives and, most important, where the boundaries run.

CONCLUDING REMARKS

Boundaries are always the outcome of historical processes and constantly subject to challenges and negotiations. So is the case in Aru. However, in Aru boundaries often seem to be rather fuzzy. This can be explained by the patchy character of customary property, and – especially in cases of outsider intrusion in marine resource exploitation – highly contested.

The boundary conflicts are mainly catalysed by the presence of external fisheries entrepreneurs and not by the scarcity of a natural resource. Thus, the coastal inhabitants of the villages seem not much concerned about the marine resource stock, which might become threatened when too much effort is put into its exploitation, but are more concerned about which village will receive the lease for the rent of islets or reefs paid by these outsiders. Consequently, boundaries have been contested and have become the reason for a long-term division of villages in the region that fight each other and do not communicate in a normal way anymore. The disruption of social life in this region has shown how social relations between the people who make and keep boundaries and the people who would like to have access across those boundaries form a basic component of the interpretation of boundaries. Power and wealth inequalities play an important role in the creation and keeping of boundaries.

In contrast, although well aware of the interpretation of boundaries and the role of power and wealth (think of the many boundary disputes within Europe and Europe's former colonies), in a Western environment and development discourse boundaries are expected to be clear, univocal and precise in indicating limits. For co-management of a protected area, these clear boundaries are necessary to determine the precise area subject to nature conservation and therefore to closure to resource exploiters. In the case of the Southeast Aru Marine Reserve, there are multiple boundary problems: after initial ideas for a reserve bordering the islands, the reserve has become a floating reserve situated at sea, with no land boundaries, and consequently faces the problem of demarcation. When starting a process to arrive at a new management regime, in this case co-management, it is of utmost importance to determine *what* is to be managed, *where* and *with whom*. The *where* part of the co-management plans is thus rather problematic. This boundary problem and the related management difficulties have been discussed by the environmental NGO's, scientists, government conservation officers and the World Bank, which has also shown interest in the environmental management of Aru's threatened ecosystems (pers. comm. K.J. Teule). However, as long as these boundaries are not clear and made clear to local people, how are the latter to know when these boundaries are crossed? And how are future conservation officers to keep intruders outside?

More important with regard to mapping as a participatory method, and related to the *with whom*-part of co-management, is the difficult situation of customary rights. Contrary to what so far had been assumed by different research teams, it would appear that there are more than just two village communities who claim the customary rights in the reserve area. Representatives of the environmental NGO active in Aru suggested of involving of the rightful owners of the region in co-management, but how does one find out who the rightful owners are? Not by visiting the same two villages time and again, I would argue, and thereby failing to take into account the other villages in the region to check the information on customary rights. A thorough consultancy would be a start, whereby mapping can be used as one of the tools to find out which claims are being made and what the main problems are.[11] However, one should not forget that the value of these maps is not absolute. As I have described, the knowledge revealed on the maps is often superficial, names and places are often deliberately left out, because people in Aru have different ideas about knowledge and its exposure on maps. Knowledge related to the natural environment is expressed in the landscape, in named places and is remembered through songs and stories, and gives people power and certain positions within society. This has everything to do with the view of landscape as held by the Arunese villagers, that differs very much from the conservationists' view. It is therefore good to realize that mapping alone will not give enough insight into customary property rights.

I hope I have explained with this contribution that participatory mapping is a valuable tool but cannot be regarded as *the* ultimate tool to bring local people and other managers together. So far in Aru, the drawing of maps has caused frictions among local people and did not lead to community empowerment or bonding whatsoever.

AUTHOR'S NOTE

This contribution is based on anthropological fieldwork carried out in the Aru Islands in the period June 1996–February 1997 and November 1997–July 1998 as a part of PhD research funded by WOTRO, The Hague. LIPI Jakarta and the

Centre for Environmental Science (PSL) of Pattimura University in Ambon sponsored the fieldwork.

I am grateful beyond bounds to the people of Beltubur who have accepted me (and my questions) and have given me a feeling of being at home during my stay in their village. Above all I thank them for sharing their knowledge and views with me. With regard to the improvements made in this chapter, I would like to thank Diny van Est and Gautam Yadama for their valuable and inspiring comments.

NOTES

1   For co-management of the marine reserve, the environmental NGO involved would like to have the rightful owners represented on a committee to deal with the representatives of the government. However, these owners do not necessarily representing all resource exploiters. In the vicinity of the reserve there are also Bugis and Buton fishermen who use the area to fish for sharks. For the sake of clarity of the argument in this chapter I do not refer to these non-local resource users.

2   There are dozens of examples where local resource users and nature conservationists are confronted with conflicting conceptions of the environment. For the situation in Aru, see Osseweijer (2001).

3   Cf. Pannell who uses the word 'topostories' for the same kind of narratives in Damer, Southeast Maluku (1996:26).

4   The most important songs are *didé* (long epic poems), *saba* (short songs about historical events), and the more recently composed *lagu* on mythical/historical events sung in modern Indonesian.

5   Ingold approaches the idea of landscape and maps in a phenomenological way. He argues that the fact that songs and stories [and locally made maps] are only intelligible to people, who possess familiarity with the landscape and its history shows that they are not like Western maps. They do not represent the world and are not consulted as Westerners would consult a map. He believes that people once familiar with the landscape do not need maps, because they get their knowledge from attending to the landscape itself. 'Far from dressing up a plain reality with layers of metaphor, or representing it, map-like, in the imagination, songs, stories and designs serve to conduct the attention of performers *into* the world, deeper and deeper, as one proceeds from outward appearances to an ever more intense poetic involvement' (1996:143).

6   Traditionally disputes over land and sea territory were solved within the village community using physical tests to show the rightful owner. In the case of sea territory, the contestants had to plant their family pole, or *sabugan*, on a particular reef and stay under water as long as possible. The stronger of the two was believed to be the rightful owner of the reef. See Osseweijer 2001 for other dispute resolution tests.

7   I have experienced this secrecy many times, for instance when drawing a sketch of the route Jahari and I had travelled to see some ancestral sites of a family group in the village of Batugoyang. She asked me to copy the sketch for her, but then to keep my sketch safely in my notebook, hidden from other people, because 'other people would not necessarily have to know'. A similar thing happened when I tried to map sago and coconut plots, hunting grounds, tidal flats and diving spots at sea. Not infrequently informants would withhold names, only describeing the places and pointing them out on a map. I was referred to the family's experts for names, which were not always given.

8   In the early 1990s, the villages of Karey and Apara quarrelled about the island of Penjuring. Both claimed rights and in the end a judge arranged a *makan bersama* agreement, which meant that the island was split up; the left part and the reefs left of the island were given to Karey, the right part and adjacent reefs were given to Apara. On the basis of this judgement, Karey has subsequently drawn the conclusion that this boundary splitting up Penjuring Island could be extended to the south, thereby dividing the whole of Urlim's sea in two parts, of which the left part was customarily claimed by Karey.

9   Ellen (1997) refers to similar usage of colonial maps and accounts.

10   All described conflicts, between Beltubur and Karey and between Batugoyang and Salarem, have divided the villages in the region in two groups: those supporting Beltubur and Batugoyang and those supporting Karey and Salarem. The reason for supporting one of these villages lies in the ritual bond between family groups, known as *pela*. *Pela* is a Moluccan phenomenon, which usually was established after warfare. Peace was made during a ritual, which consisted of drinking palm wine mixed with a few drops of blood, and an exchange of names. The parties promised to help each other and to not intermarry anymore, since both parties had become one family. The two groups of villages consist of villages and families who have *pela* relationships.

11   See Corrigan and Osseweijer (1999).

REFERENCES

Aberley, D. (ed.) (1993) *Boundaries of Home*: *Mapping for Local Empowerment*. Philadelphia: New Society Publishers.

Alcorn, J.B. (2000) *Borders, Rules and Governance: Mapping to Catalyse Changes in Policy and Management*. Gatekeeper Series no.91. London: IIED.

Bender, B. (ed.) (1993) *Landscap, Politics and Perspectives*. Oxford: Berg.

BKSDA (Balai Konservasi Sumber Daya Alam) (1989) Proposal for the Aru Tenggara Marine Reserve, Maluku. Ambon: BKSDA

Borrini-Feyerabend, G. (1996) *Collaborative Management of Protected Areas: Tailoring the Approach to the Context*. Gland: IUCN.

—— (1997) *Beyond Fences. Seeking Social Sustainability in Conservation*. Gland: IUCN.

Compost, A. (1980) *Pilot Survey of Exploitation of Dugong and Sea Turtle in the Aru Islands*. Jakarta:Yayasan Indonesia Hijau.

Cordell, J. (1993) 'Boundaries and bloodlines. tenure of indigenous homelands and protected areas'. In E. Kemf (ed.), *The Law of the Mother. Protecting Indigenous Peoples in Protected Areas*. San Francisco: Sierra Club Books, pp. 61–68.

Corrigan, B.M. and M.Osseweijer (1999) *Submission to WWF Wallacea Programme: Anthropological Consultancy in Southeast Aru*. Perth/Leiden.

Ellen, R. (1997) 'On the contemporary uses of colonial history and the legitimation of political status in Archipelagic Southeast Seram'. *Journal of Southeast Asian Studies* 28(1): pp. 78–102.

Gell, A. (1985) 'How to read a map: remarks on the practical logic of navigator', Man (NS) 20:271-286.

Harley, J.B. [assisted by Ellen Hanlon and Mark Warhus] (1990) *Maps and the Columbian Encounter : an Interpretive Guide to the Traveling Exhibition*. Milwaukee: American Geographical Society Collection / Milwaukee: Golda Meir Library, University of Wisconsin.

Hirsh, E. (1995) 'Introduction: landscape. between place and space'. In E. Hirsch and M. O'Hanlon (eds), *The Anthropology of Landscape. Perspectives on Place and Space*. Oxford: Clarendon Press, pp. 1–20.

Ingold, T. (1996) 'Hunting and gathering as ways of perceiving the environment'. In R.F. Ellen and K. Fukui (eds), *Redefining Nature. Ecology, Culture and Domestication*. Oxford/Washington, D. C: Berg, pp. 117–155.

Küchler, S. (1993) 'Landscape as memory: the mapping of process and its representation in a Melanesian Society'. In B. Bender (ed.), *Landscape. Politics and Perspectives*. Oxford: Berg, pp. 85–106.

Lakembe, S. (1998) *Laporan survei ancaman lokal pada populasi dan habitat penyu di Aru tenggara*. [Report of the survey on local threats to the turtle population and its habitat in Southeast Aru]. Ambon: WWF.

Layton, R. (1997) 'Representing and translating people's place in the landscape of northern Australia'. In A. James, J. Hockney and A. Dawson (eds), *After Writing Culture. Epistemology and Praxis in Contemporary Anthropology*. London: Routledge, pp. 122–143.

Meyers, F.R. (1982) 'Always ask: reseource use and land ownership among Pintupi aborigines of the Australian Western Desert'. In N.M.Williams and E.S. Hunn (eds), *Resource Managers: North American and Australian Hunter-Gatherers*. Canberra: Australian Institute of Aboriginal Studies, pp. 173–95.

Ministry of Forestry (1991) Keputusan Cagar Alam Laut di Aru Tenggara, Maluku. Jakarta: Ministry of Forestry.

Momberg, F., K. Atok and M. Sirait (1996) *Drawing on Local Knowledge: a Community mapping Training Manual*. Jakarta: Ford Foundation/WWF Indonesia Programme.

Morphy, H. (1993) 'Colonialism, history and the construction of place: the politics of landscape in Northern Australia'. In B. Bender (ed.), *Landscape. Politics and Perspectives*. Oxford: Berg, pp. 205–43.

Notzke, C. (1995) 'A New Perspective in Aboriginal Natural Resource Management: Co-management'. *Geoforum* vol. 26, no. 2, pp. 187–209.

Osseweijer, M. (2000) 'We wander in our ancestors' yard: sea cucumber gathering in Aru, Eastern Indonesia'. In R. Ellen, P. Parkes and A. Bicker (eds), *Indigenous Environmental Knowledge and its Transformations: Critical Anthropological Approaches.* London: Harwood Publishers, pp. 55–78.

—— (2001) 'Taken at the flood. Marine resource use and management in Aru, Eastern Indonesia'. PhD thesis. University of Leiden.

Pannell, S. (1996) '*Homo Nullius* or "Where have all the people gone"? Refiguring marine management and conservation approaches'. *The Australian Journal of Anthropology,* vol. 7 no. 1, pp. 21–42.

—— (1997) 'From the poetics of place to the politics of space: Redefining cultural landscapes on Damer, Maluku Tenggara'. In J.J. Fox (ed.), *The Poetic Power of Place. Comparative Perspectives on Austronesian Ideas of Locality.* Canberra: Department of Anthropology: Comparative Austronesian Project, Research School of Pacific and Asian Studies, The Australian National University, pp 163–173.

Persoon, G.A., H.H. de Iongh and B. Wenno (1996) 'Exploitation, management and conservation of marine resources: the context of the Aru Tenggara Marine Reserve (Moluccas, Indonesia)'. *Ocean and Coastal Management,* vol. 32, no. 2, pp. 97–122.

Pet-Soede, L. (2000) '*Options for co-management of an Indonesian coastal fishery*'. PhD Thesis. Wageningen Agrarian University.

Pinkerton, E. (1989) 'Introduction: attaining better fisheries management through co-management – prospects, problems and propositions'. In E. Pinkerton (ed.), *Cooperative Management of Local Fisheries.* Vancouver: University of British Columbia Press, pp. 3–33.

Polunin, N.V.C. (1984) 'Do traditional marine "reserves" conserve? A view of Indonesian and New Guinea evidence'. In K. Ruddle and T. Akimichi (eds), *Maritime Institutions in the Western Pacific.* Senri Ethnological Studies no.17. Osaka: National Museum of Ethnology, pp. 267–284.

Poole, P. (1995) *Indigenous People, Mapping and Biodiversity Conservation.* Biodiversity Support Program, Washington DC: WWF.

Ruyehaver, J. (1921) '*Poetoesan masalah Siya-Beltubur*'. [Resolution with regard to the conflict Siya-Beltubur]. Photocopy of unpublished hand-written document.

Schlager, E. and E. Ostrom (1993) 'Property-rights regimes and coastal fisheries: an empirical analysis'. In T.L. Anderson and R.T. Simmons (eds), *The Political Economy of Customs and Culture: Informal Solutions to the Commons Problem.* Lanham: Rowman & Littlefield Publishers, pp. 13–41.

Schultz, J.P. (1993) *Marine turtle conservation and management programme in the Aru Tenggara Marine Reserve, Maluku, Indonesia.* Final Report Project 9373/JS/Marine Turtles.

Smiet, F. and T. Siallagan (1981) *Proposal for the Aru Tenggara Marine Reserve in the Aru Archipelago, Maluku, Indonesia.* Bogor: UNDP/PAO.

Spyer, P. (2000) *The memory of trade. Modernity's Entanglements on an eastern Indonesian Island.* Durham and London: Duke University Press.

Tilley, C. (1994) *A Phenomenology of Landscape. Places, Paths and Monuments.* Oxford: Berg.

Wallace, A.R. (1986 org. 1869) The Malay Archipelago. New York, Dover Publications.

Williams, N.M. (1993) 'A boundary is to cross: observations on Yolngu boundaries and permission'. In N.M. Munn and E.S. Hunn (eds), *Resource Managers: North American and Australian Hunter-Gatherers*. Canberra: Australian Institute of Aboriginal Studies (AAAS), pp. 131–153.

Wood, D. (1992) *The Power of Maps*. London: Routledge.

WWF (1996) *Indigenous Peoples and Conservation: WWF Statement of Principles*. Gland: WWF.

WWF Ambon (1998) *Laporan survei ancaman lokal pada populasi dan habitat penyu di Aru tenggara*. [Report of the survey on local threats to the turtle population and its habitat in Southeast Aru]. Ambon: WWF.

WWF Indonesia Programme [in co-operation with the Directorate General of Forestry and Nature Conservation] (1994) *Buklet informasi Cagar Alam Laut sebagian Pulau-pulau Aru, bagian Tenggara Maluku. Program Kesadartahuan Konservasi Kelautan di Pulau-pulau Aru Bagian Tenggara Maluku* [Information brochure about the marine reserve in the Aru Islands, Southeast Moluccas. Awareness Programme for Marine Conservation in the Aru Islands, Southeast Moluccas.] Jakarta.

WWF South Pacific Programme (1996) *Community Resource Conservation and Development. A Toolkit for Community-based Conservation and Sustainable Development in the Pacific*. Fiji: WWF.

CHAPTER TEN

Imagined Models versus Historical Practices: Tana ulen and Community-based Management of Natural Resources in the Interior of Indonesian Borneo

CRISTINA EGHENTER

FROM DISFRANCHISEMENT TO PARTNERSHIP: LOCAL PEOPLE AND THE MANAGEMENT OF CONSERVATION AREAS

*T*he disfranchisement of resident people characterized the initial position on protected areas management by government and conservation organizations (Pimbert and Pretty 1994). In line with the dominant view that human activities represented a threat to the pristine state of the environment, the removal of people was seen as the best solution for preserving a protected area. However, increasing evidence showed that most wilderness areas had been modified or managed by humans at one point in time (for example, Crumley 1994; Headland 1997; Sponsel *et al.* 1996). Moreover, findings revealed that traditional activities of local communities had in certain cases prevented soil erosion and the loss of biodiversity.

The recognition that anthropogenic influence was not necessarily incompatible with the conservation of natural resources had important implications for the theory and practice of protected area management. It convinced conservation specialists of the value of the participation of resident communities in the protection, management and restoration of the environment (McNeeley and Pitt 1985; Pimbert and Pretty 1994). While it was becoming apparent that people could have an important role in the management of conservation areas, it was also clear that conservation priorities and local communities' interests were not always compatible, and could give rise to conflicts between protected areas and local people (Wells and Brandon, 1992; Wells, 1995). Local people were, for the most part, economically dependent on the natural resources of the conservation area. The regulation and limitation of their use for conservation purposes required that alternative and compensatory means of livelihood be provided outside the protected areas. Moreover, the recognition of the rightfulness of local peoples' claims to the land based on a long history of settlement in the protected area discredited initiatives of strict enforcement of protection measures such as forced resettlement or denying access to the exploitation of natural resources.

In response to these challenges, conservation specialists started to plan new initiatives designed to involve local communities and link efforts to conserve bio-diversity with the creation of economic incentives to promote a sustainable use of natural resources. Integrated Conservation and Development Projects (ICDP) and community-based management exemplify the new approach. It is assumed that local communities have a greater interest and greater accountability in the sustainable management of resources over time than does the state or other distant stakeholders. It is believed that local people, precisely because of their long-term residence in the area, possess a wealth of knowledge about the local natural environment and ecological processes and that they are more able to effectively manage those resources through local management strategies and traditional forms of tenure (Brosius *et al.*, 1998).

THE NEED FOR HISTORICIZATION OF FOREST MANAGEMENT PRACTICES

Participation of local people and adoption of local management practices became the preferred strategy of non-governmental organizations (NGOs) active in the field of biodiversity conservation. The preservation of biological diversity and natural resources was not only regarded as compatible with the rights and traditions of indigenous people but instrumental to the efforts of many forest communities to protect their forest and defend their land. (for example, WWF International 1996; WWF International-People and Conservation Unit 1998).

The view of indigenous management practices as ecologically rational and 'naturally' conservative prevailed as a sort of *a priori* justification of policy programmes of organizations like WWF. Native ecologies were seen as models for environmental conservation and sustainable development, and efforts were made to redeploy traditional practices as alternatives that are biologically, socially and economically sustainable (Eghenter and Sellato 1999).

While the idea of using local practices to advance community-based agendas might be valid, it is important first to understand the processes through which specific management practices came into existence and assess the social and economic circumstances under which they operate. The tendency to imagine indigenous management practices or use them as models, instead of historicizing them, can have serious implications for policy-making and severely limit the ability of NGOs to design viable policy options with regard to community-based management (*cf.* Eghenter 2000).

In this chapter, I will look at a study and policy case involving indigenous practices and community-based forest management in the area of the Kayan Mentarang National Park, in the interior of East Kalimantan, Indonesia (Fig 10.1). Drawing on available ethnographic data, I shall explicate the antecedents, current practices and uses of one aspect of forest tenure and management by Dayak–Kenyah people known as *tana ulen*. Subsequently I shall explore how recent practices of *tana ulen* have been reinterpreted in relation to issues of community rights and community-based management of conservation areas. This is done in order to identify the specific histories and social dynamics of *tana ulen* and assess its viability in the changing and contested circumstances of indigenous rights, access to forest resources and sustainable management of conservation areas.

According to Brosius *et al.*, the reason that many local experiments of community-based management have failed is because they have not taken into consideration the historical context nor paid attention to local perspectives. This results in what they call the 'a-historicization' and 'generaticization' of local management practices (1998: 159). But redressing this failure is not just about applying history to practice. Rather it is a matter of how we go about historicizing management practices and provide an account of practices that can disclose the factors and circumstances that might have brought about a certain management arrangement. It is important to understand how and why *tana ulen* management choices might have been made in the past, and how conditions might have changed what would be the implications if the same choices might be made again in the future (cf. Ingerson 1997).

THE SOCIAL LANDSCAPE OF THE INTERIOR OF INDONESIAN BORNEO

About 16,000 Dayak people now live in or around the Kayan Mentarang National Park. Roughly half of these people, mostly Kenyah, a small number of Kayan, Saben and Punan, are primarily shifting cultivators. The rest, mostly Lun Dayeh and Lengilu in the north, are mainly wet-rice farmers. The inhabitants of the park and surrounding areas depend on hunting, fishing and collecting wild plants for their subsistence needs. Trade in forest products, mainly gall-stones from langurs and porcupines, and aloe wood or *gaharu* (*Aquilaria* spp) and revenues from temporary employment in Malaysia are the principal ways to earn cash for buying commercial goods, cover travel expenses to the lowlands and school fees, and buy work tools and equipment.

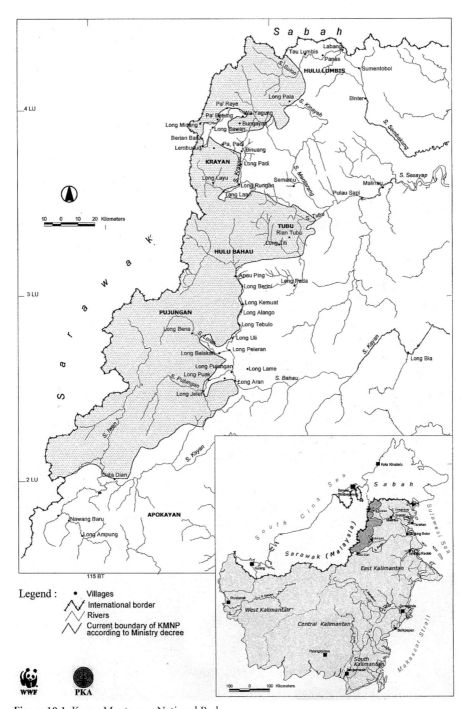

Figure 10.1: Kayan Mentarang National Park

The communities living in and around the park are still *adat* communities, largely regulated by customary law or *adat* in the conduct of their daily affairs and the management of natural resources within a customary territory or *wilayah adat* (Eghenter and Sellato 1999).

The customary chief or *kepala adat* administers the customary law with the help of the customary council or *lembaga adat*. All elected officials at village level and prominent leaders of the community sit on a customary council. The *lembaga adat* also has representatives at village level who enforce decisions made at *wilayah adat* level. The role of traditional institutions is key to understanding the communities' views of rights and the way they deliberate on issues of forest management as well as social responsibilities. *Adat*, however, is not fixed nor unchanging. As a conflict-regulating mechanism, *adat* is transformed and adapted to new conditions in a constant process.

Traditionally, Kenyah communities were stratified into three major social classes: the aristocrats, sometimes subdivided in high and low aristocrats, who claimed descent from the historical leaders of the group; the commoners, and the descendants of slaves (Rousseau 1990). Generally, all village and *adat* leaders of the communities are of aristocratic descent.

In Kenyah communities, individual claims to land are established by cutting trees or clearing forest. The right to use the land is then passed on to the successive generation. Useful trees like fruit trees, illipe nut trees, cinnamon and honey trees are owned by individuals or kin groups.

Another form of land and forest tenure is locally known as *tana ulen*. *Tana ulen*, a Kenyah term, is *tana*, or land, which is *m/ulen* or restricted, prohibited. It is an expanse of primary forest rich in natural resources such as rattan (*Calamus* spp), *sang* leaves (*Licuala* sp.), hardwood for construction (for example, *Dipterocarpus* spp, *Shorea* spp, *Quercus* sp), fish and game, all of which have high use value for the local community. In the past, *tana ulen* functioned as forest reserves managed by the aristocratic families of the community. Nowadays, responsibilities for the management of the forest reserves have been transferred to the customary councils that oversee *tana ulen* forests on behalf of the entire community and according to customary law (Eghenter 2000).

HISTORICIZING *TANA ULEN*: ITS ANTECEDENTS AND CURRENT PRACTICES

Among Kenyah people, the term *tana ulen* may be used in reference to several proprietary and management arrangements: private ownership of rice fields and fruit trees; *pulung mpa'* or forest preserved for watershed protection and valuable timber; or the land that is controlled by *adat*, or customary law, governing a community. However, the expression *tana ulen* currently and most commonly refers to a tract of forest managed by the community on the basis of a specific agreement.

In general, *tana ulen* areas are strategically located near the village where management and control are easier (there might be other areas with abundant forest resources but just too far away). As a general rule, no forest could be cleared to open rice fields in *tana ulen*. The territory varies in size from 3,000 ha to up to 12,000 ha, the size being largely dependent on the natural boundaries of the watershed of the *ulen* river basin.

Available narratives on the history of *tana ulen* show that *tana ulen* areas functioned as forest reserves managed by the aristocratic families of the community. Exploitation was highly regulated and usually limited to procuring food for specific occasions such as celebrations and ritual events of the life cycle. These could be either celebrations at village level or more private affairs. In all cases, only the aristocrats in charge could decide on when and how exploitation of forest resources could take place (Simon Devung and Rudi 1998; Eghenter 2000).

Although we can only speculate on the reasons behind the establishment of *tana ulen*, it can be argued that the main conservation factor in such practices was the desire on the part of the aristocratic families to regulate use of the forest to prevent depletion of resources needed in collective rituals and other family affairs. In the past, religious beliefs required the organization of celebrations throughout the year to mark the agricultural cycle and other social occasions like the safe return of war parties and traders. The village chief acted as prime host of collective rituals. He gave hospitality to travellers and delegations from other communities that visited the area. He also had to prepare the meals for the people of the community working in his fields as part of traditional corvees. All these responsibilities implied that he and his family needed to procure food like fish and game for the guests. The imposition of restricted access to areas with abundant resources was one way to ensure constant availability. In addition to food, construction timber was also an important resource in *tana ulen*. The existence of a forest reserve prevented the indiscriminate cutting of valuable timber which might have been used for other purposes.

Social status and stakes in the management of forest resources
Nyerges argues that it is important to look at the 'social life of resources' (1997: 10–11) and examine access to and control of specific resources in relation to the social status of the actors. This point of view is relevant when looking at *tana ulen* practices. Managed as almost aristocratic private reserves (Sellato 1998),

tana ulen areas were nevertheless opened to community members on certain occasions, but the decision on when to open a *tana ulen* rested with the aristocrats who held the privilege to manage the forest reserve. The aristocrats claimed a percentage of all products collected in the *tana ulen* and maintained the privilege to grant permission to enter the area. However, they were also responsible for monitoring its management and punishing those who violated the existing regulations approved by the council of the elders. It appears that rather than be granted full ownership, the heads of the aristocratic lineages were entrusted with the management of the reserve on behalf of the community in recognition of their multiple responsibilities. Data reveal a strong connection between the social status and power of the aristocratic family, their economic privileges and forest management, but they also suggest that other ecological and social factors were taken into consideration and, sometimes, could give rise to alternative arrangements.

A second look at areas currently classified as *tana ulen* in Kenyah communities of the Pujungan River, for example, reveals two distinct management criteria in the past. In the abandoned community of Long Saan, on a tributary of the upper Pujungan River, there were forest reserves controlled by aristocratic families and rattan forests (semi-managed wild rattan) managed by the community. Simon Devung reports from two Kenyah communities on the Bahau River that *tana ulen* areas were not exclusively held by aristocratic families. Territories or reserves were also granted by the village chief to families of commoners who had distinguished themselves in warfare or had defended the community against the enemy. In a few cases, families whose member had died in one area were given ownership privileges for that area (Simon Devung 1996; Simon Devung and Rudy 1998). However, tenure and management practices remained consistently dependent on the customary chief's policies.

Whereas all current Kenyah villages of the Bahau and Pujungan rivers areas claim, with varying degree, the existence of a *tana ulen* tradition of forest reserves, data from other Kenyah communities seem to indicate that reserves managed by aristocrats did not exist or that the term *tana ulen* was used to refer to the territory of the community governed by customary law or *wilayah adat*. Kenyah Uma Kulit and Lepo Tepu informants report that there were no forest reserves in the locations they occupied in the Apo Kayan before they migrated downriver in, respectively, the late 1950s and early 1980s. This case of apparent absence of *tana ulen* as aristocratic reserves might tell us more about the conditions that could have promoted the establishment of private reserves. For example, the Kenyah Uma Kulit people had only split from the bigger community of Jelerai and moved downstream to Nahakeramo in the late 1920s. It is possible that the relatively short time spent in the area might have prevented the migrants from developing more permanent claims to forest resources in the form of 'private' *tana ulen*. The abundance of resources and low competition in the new area might have made measures to ensure tighter control of resources superfluous. Moreover, the leadership of the group might have been weakened in number and prestige by the split from the older community and, subsequently, might have lacked the authority to claim a forest reserve and impose a system by which they could levy duties on collection of forest products.

Past practices of access and management of forest products in *tana ulen* areas may be correctly linked to the social position and power of the aristocratic families. Moreover, the evidence available also suggests that the existence and control over forest reserves might have been more prominent in communities where the rigidity of the class division was more pronounced and the authority of the chief stronger.

Current management practices in tana ulen
After the end of the Dutch colonial rule in 1945, the new Indonesian state imposed increasing bureaucratization and substituted its centralized administration and national law for *adat*. The incorporation into the new state meant the delegitimization of the main bases of traditional aristocratic authority: *adat* law, ownership of slaves and right to levy duties. The conversion to Christianity in the 1950s and 1960s, as well as several moves of people from the interior to areas of the lowlands, further undermined the exclusive control of village affairs by the aristocratic class. Growing outside influences, and new economic and educational opportunities, eroded the support for traditional hierarchy and the role of the elders. Increasingly, in the villages of the interior, younger generations felt they did not have to comply with *adat* regulations, including those managing the access and use of *tana ulen* areas.

In this situation, the 'de-aristocratization' of *tana ulen* forest reserves was inevitable (Eghenter 2000). The proprietary status of what previously were areas managed by members of the aristocratic lineage on behalf of the community changed to *tana ulen leppo,* or community forest reserve (Blajan 1999). While the balance of power has shifted from private reserves to village reserves, other aspects of the social and political context have stayed the same. Regulations with regard to access to and control of *tana ulen* areas might now rest with the customary assembly or *lembaga adat,* but the head of the customary assembly is still an aristocrat, often the descendant of previous managers of *tana ulen*. Moreover, members of the aristocratic class may in some cases still enjoy free access to the resources and receive a fixed percentage of the amount of the forest products harvested in the *tana ulen*.

Nowadays, *tana ulen* areas are protected and managed by the communities by means of customary councils. They grant permission to individuals to collect forest products in the *tana ulen* area and decide on when to open *tana ulen* for collective exploitation. *Tana ulen* is, in principle, off limits to outsiders including people from nearby villages. Collection of specific products is restricted by customary regulations with regard to times of collection, tools and methods employed, usually only traditional ones, and quantity and kind of products harvested. Collection of forest resources on a collective basis, for either direct consumption or sale, is contingent upon the need to procure money for village celebrations at Christmas and New Year or special projects like the building of a community centre. The market value of certain forest products also affects decisions regarding collection.

Within the general framework outlined above, regulations governing the management of *tana ulen* areas may vary from community to community. In some cases, they are very detailed, written norms concerning the conditions and techniques for collecting all valuable forest products. In other cases, only certain resources are explicitly regulated. Sometimes, regulations contain only a general clause that customary fines would be incurred by all individuals who do not comply. Sometimes details about the amount of the fines, in money or heirloom items like *parang* or *gongs*, are provided with regard to specific violations.

CONTESTED RESOURCES AND CHANGING AGENDAS FOR *TANA ULEN*

The increasing commercial exploitation of forest products in the 1980s and 1990s has resulted in heightened competition over resources that have challenged traditional management practices by local communities. With several forest concessions expanding or starting their activities in the Bulungan regency, in the northern part of the province of East Kalimantan, Dayak communities found themselves with few legal means to maintain privileged access to their customary lands that were inside a logging concession. New government strategies for forest conservation have also contributed to the exacerbation of the issue of long-term rights of local communities to use and exploit forest resources, both in the interior and the lowlands.

Under conditions of increased competition, the people in some Kenyah communities reinterpreted the concept and practices of *tana ulen* in the service of their efforts to reassert exclusive control, or *m(ulen)*, over contested resources.

They asked for the recognition of a *tana ulen* area and exclusive management by the community as a way to fight back the encroachment by timber companies.

For example, in early 1998, the logging company STB, which had been operating along the Bahau River, conducted a survey in the *tana ulen* areas of four communities upstream. The *tana ulen* areas happened to be included, wholly or partially, in the concession of the company as indicated on the company's map. The members of the survey, however, did not clarify their purpose to the communities nor gave them the opportunity to negotiate an agreement. The event triggered an immediate reaction on the part of the chiefs and the customary assemblies of the concerned communities that feared that their *tana ulen* would be logged, and they would lose valuable resources like hardwood, *gaharu*, and rattan. Shortly after, they organized a meeting and solicited help from the local government and NGOs on how to defend the *tana ulen* areas and secure ownership claims for *tana ulen* against the logging company.

In 1996, in Long Tungu, on the lower course of the Kayan River, the local village council declared a large forest area along the Tungu and Bekiau rivers as *tana ulen*. Another *tana ulen* area had already been established in the 1980s in a core area of forest not far from the village. The forest was rich in hardwood (*Eusideroxylon* sp or Borneo ironwood, and *kompassia excelsia*) and other forest products that people used and traded. The timing of the initiative coincided with the decision of the management of the timber company PT. ITCI to prohibit the people of Long Tungu from opening rice fields in the forest concession. Moreover, the community demanded that the company pay compensation and contribute to community development projects in the village.

Another example of increasingly contested resources is the control and trade of non timber forest products. Starting in the early 1990s, large numbers of outsiders from places as far away as Java and Sulawesi started coming in large numbers to the interior to harvest forest products. The activities sponsored by Chinese and Arab traders based in the towns of the lowlands reached their peak in 1993–95, and again in 1998–2000.

While exploitation was not limited to *tana ulen* areas, these areas also came under pressure by outsiders collecting products with high market value, particularly *gaharu*. Being outsiders and belonging to different ethnic groups, they do not acknowledge nor respect local *adat* regulations and rights. They tend to cut indiscriminately both infected and non-infected trees, and use chemicals and other means to poison salt springs where langurs come to drink.

The realization that local people might be excluded or only get a small share of the forest wealth encouraged more local people to undertake longer expeditions in search for forest products. It also prompted communities to take initiatives to strengthen their exclusive access of forest resources in their *tana ulen*. A policy commonly adopted has been the strict enforcement of the principle that *tana ulen* resources are for the use of the community only, to the exclusion of all outsiders. In a weaker version of this policy, outsiders may be allowed to access *tana ulen* as long as they ask for permission and pay an entry fee to the treasury of the village council.

However, the increased competition of forest products exposed the limits of the local *adat* authority. Already deprived of its legitimacy and with its prestige eroded by competitive normative systems, the local enforcement and management practices were inevitably weakened and their effectiveness compromised. For example, the customary councils often deliberated on the need to stop outside collectors from accessing their land or otherwise confiscate their supplies and belongings. They denounced the situation, but sometimes lacked the necessary legal authority and internal consensus to impose their will. Often they were willing to accept payments and gifts in return for letting outsiders in, or simply imposed a minimal fee to be paid by each person collecting forest products in their territory.

TANA ULEN AS A MODEL FOR COMMUNITY-BASED MANAGEMENT OF PROTECTED AREAS

In this complex picture of revived community claims, the activities of the WWF project in the Kayan Mentarang National Park brought the issue of the congeniality of traditional forest management for community-based management of protected areas to the fore.

Stretched along the mountainous interior of East Kalimantan, Indonesian Borneo, the Kayan Mentarang National Park lies at the border with Sarawak to the west and Sabah to the north. With 1.4 million ha, it is the largest protected area of rainforest in Borneo and one of the largest in Southeast Asia. A strict nature reserve since 1980, the area was declared a National Park by the Minister of Forestry in October 1996 (figure 10.1).

In 1991, WWF Indonesia started a project in collaboration with the Directorate of Nature Protection and Conservation (PKA) of the Indonesian Ministry of Forestry and LIPI, the National Institute of Research (Eghenter and Sellato 1999). The project aimed at securing the communities' support and participation in the sustainable management and protection of forest resources inside the conservation area. The WWF employed various approaches and techniques in order to set the conditions for collaboration and openness necessary for the establishment of a joint management of the conservation area. These included: social science research, community mapping, biological surveys and participatory planning.

The results of field activities, and in particular the community maps, provided invaluable data on local forms of land tenure and strategies for exploitation of forest products. They showed the legitimacy of local claims to land and natural resources and highlighted the central role of traditional institutions with regard to forest management. These factors appear to justify WWF expectations that local communities would support community-based management of the national park.

The staff involved in the mapping activities and other researchers had also documented the existence of *tana ulen* (for example, Blajan 1999; Simon Devung 1996). They stressed the village ownership. They also pointed out the importance of *tana ulen* as a common property arrangement regulated by customary law to the advantage of the entire community and some of its weakest members like orphans and widows (Sirait *et al.* 1994). It is precisely in connection with these results that WWF staff first proposed *tana ulen* as a model for the community-based management of the entire Kayan Mentarang conservation area. *Tana ulen* was interpreted as a cogent example of *a* conservation ethic among local communities and a good case for promoting the use of indigenous forest management practices in the management of the National Park. In the language and rhetoric of WWF reports, *tana ulen* became a forest communally owned and a refuge for wildlife and plant species (for example, Sorensen and Morris, 1998).

The historical antecedents and variations of current *tana ulen* practices, and related circumstances that gave rise to them, were neglected. The features of *tana ulen* management that were more deeply linked to stratified Kenyah communities and the role of aristocrats were downplayed. This 'curtailed' example of *tana ulen* served well the socio-environmental agenda of WWF well and the effort to legitimize the participation of local people in the sustainable management of the conservation area: how indigenous communities had traditionally cared for the forest by instituting communal management to protect and conserve forest resources.

It has been convincingly argued that whether *tana ulen* conserve for the benefit of the communities or conserve for the privilege of the ruling class of their former managers might not have any relevance with regard to the conservation goals of the WWF project (Dove and Nugroho 1994). In other words, the social and historical circumstances of *tana ulen* would not matter much as long as the main objective of protection of biodiversity pursued by the National Park was secured. However, precisely the environmental impact of *tana ulen* practises had not been investigated by the WWF project. Were forest habitat and biodiversity better protected under *tana ulen*? Did regulations regarding the exploitation of *tana ulen* guarantee a sustainable use of forest resources by local communities over a long term? Could other factors such as low population density in the area and inconsistent demand for forest products alternatively explain the continuous availability of resources in the forest? These key questions were not raised nor addressed as the project prepared to set the objectives of the management plan and research programme. The mere existence of *tana ulen* practices, however sketchily documented, was deemed sufficient evidence that a sustainable community-based management of the forest was already in place.

Other important considerations on social aspects of *tana ulen* and their possible impact on local communities were also neglected. The data had revealed that past *tana ulen* management practices could not be disengaged from a social hierarchy of access to and control of resources where the aristocrats enjoyed most of the benefits and privileges. The changes in current practices indicated that a shift of power had occurred towards a village-based form of management, but the history of customary council-led management is relatively short and uneven, and the status of *tana ulen* in some Kenyah communities is premised on a weak management system where criteria are minimal, somewhat unclear or not fully developed. For example, the most active communities in defending *tana ulen* were the ones where the role of the descendants of the former managers was stronger and social authority in the community less contested. Consequently there was a risk that the application and strengthening of *tana ulen* as a model of community-based management could result in the legitimization of the power status quo and sustain social discrimination.

In other respects, the close association of traditional *adat* leadership with the management of *tana ulen* could give rise to additional problems. The delegitimization of the former had probably weakened control and undermined effective enforcement of regulations. Moreover, if traditional leaders were once the stewards of the forest and entrusted with its management for their own benefit and that of the community, their power is often now wielded on behalf of personal economic and political interests. Examples of permits to enter *tana ulen* areas granted by the customary chief or other leaders to outsiders upon the payment of a fee indicate that often the members of the customary councils and appointed managers of *tana ulen* may prove to be the principal catalysts for accelerated resource exploitation instead of resource conservation.

PAST PRACTICES FOR THE FUTURE

The evidence on *tana ulen* indicates that without an understanding of the patterns of social relations within which management choices are made and enforced, and how interventions by conservation planners might affect that process, efforts to apply past practices of traditional forest management to create community-based management of conservation areas might not have much chance of success. Inadequate understanding and historicization can result in misformulation of policy.

Since 1997, a new approach has been slowly emerging at the WWF project. Besides recognizing that *tana ulen* might have not been at any time the perfect model of community-based management of forest resources, there is the acknowledgement that the idea of *tana ulen* still serves important social and political goals with regard to the recognition of customary rights and access to forest resources (cf. Zerner 1994).

The agenda of the WWF project is slowly evolving to reflect a new emphasis on working with the communities to evaluate and revise current *tana ulen* regulations and elaborate new ones if needed for the management of the traditional use zones of the National Park area.

The project staff analysed local customary regulations to gain a sense of the local view and ethic of conservation. For example, it became clear that regulations include both old restrictions as well as more recent ones that were adopted by the communities following changes in environmental conditions and the availability of certain resources. The principle of sustainability, for example, is expressed in the importance of not wasting animals or forest products by collecting more than needed or harvesting them in ways that would hamper their future reproduction or growth. In recent deliberations, some customary councils have imposed temporary bans on the hunting of animal species that are perceived as threatened or vulnerable. These and other elements reveal local concerns with renewable supplies and the need to guarantee future availability of natural resources. The regulations clearly seem in agreement with conservation management concerns. As such, they can be effectively integrated to form a strong and legitimate basis for community-based management of the national park.

The development of a community-based management for the national park requires that management solutions be adapted to local conditions and integrate local management strategies. The following represent some of the main recommendations on community-based management policy made by the WWF Kayan Mentarang project to the government:

1. Preserve locally developed regulations on use of forest products that guar-antee sustainability, including suggestions and criteria for animal population management; this strategy is likely to increase the chances of compliance among local people.

2. Create an inter-*adat* institution or forum which co-ordinates management activities and addresses environmental concerns that often transgress local boundaries of customary lands.

3. Secure official recognition of local tenure rights and management arrange-ments like *tana ulen* and build the capacity of customary councils in their role as managers of their forest and the conservation area.

CONCLUDING REMARKS

The idea that the management of a conservation area can be built using local models of resource management practices remains an essential consideration and starting point. However, the experience with *tana ulen* seems to challenge the strategy of conservation organizations simply to transpose and apply existing indigenous forest management models in unqualified ways to secure community-based management of protected areas.

The experience at the Kayan Mentarang National Park confirms that historic-izing local practices can help make the right management decisions. This might imply harder work than just assuming unlikely alliances between local residents of a conservation area and conservation planners, or imagining traditional practices as ideal models of community-based management. Instead, by high-lighting the linkages between *tana ulen* practices and their variable circum-stances over time, conservation planners and communities can start 'applying history to policy' (Ingerson 1997:616) and develop alternatives for community-based management of resources that conjugate biodiversity conservation with the empowerment of local people.

REFERENCES

Blajan, K. (1999) 'Jaringan Pemasaran Hasil Hutan di Kawasan Sungai Bahau Kecamatan Long Pujungan' [The forest products market network along the Bahau River, district of Long Pujungan]. In C. Eghenter and B. Sellato (eds), *Kebudayaan dan Pelestarian Alam. Penelitian Interdisipliner di Pedalaman Borneo*. Jakarta: Ford Foundation and WWF, Indonesia, pp. 181–200.

Brosius, P., A. Lowenhaupt Tsing and C. Zerner (1998) 'Representing communities: histories and politics of community-based natural resource management'. *Society and Natural Resources*, vol. 1, pp. 157–168.

Crumley, C. (ed.) (1994) *Historical Ecology: Cultural Knowledge and Changing Land-scapes.* Santa Fe: School of American Research Press.

Dove, M. and T. Nugroho (1994) *Review of 'Culture and Conservation' 1991–1994.* A Sub project funded by the Ford Foundation, World Wide Fund for Nature, Kayan Mentarang Nature Reserve Project in Kalimantan, Indonesia.

Eghenter, C. (2000) 'What is *tana ulen* good for? Considerations on indigenous forest management, conservation, and research in the interior of Indonesian Borneo'. *Human Ecology: An Interdisciplinary Journal,* vol. 28, no. 3, pp. 331–357.

Eghenter, C. and B. Sellato (eds) (1999) *Kebudayaan dan Pelestarian Alam. Penelitian Interdisipliner di Pedalaman Borneo* [Culture and conservation. Interdisciplinary research in the interior of Borneo]. Jakarta: Ford Foundation and WWF Indonesia.

Headland, T. (1997) 'Revisionism in Ecological Anthropology'. *Current Anthropology,* vol. 38, no. 4, Aug–Oct: pp. 605–630.

Ingerson, A.E. (1997) 'Comment on T. Headland's "Revisionism in ecological anthro-pology"', *Current Anthropology,* vol. 38, no. 4, pp. 615–616.

McNeely, J. and D. Pitt (eds) (1985) *Culture and Conservation: The Human Dimension in Environmental Planning.* London: Croom Helm.

Nyerges, A.E. (1997) 'Introduction. The Ecology of Practice'. In A.E. Nyerges (ed.), *The ecology of practice. Studies of Food Crop Production in Sub-Saharan West Africa.* Netherlands: Gordon and Breach Publishers pp: 1–38.

Pimbert, M. and J. Pretty (1994) *Participation, People and the Management of National Parks and Protected Areas: Past Failures and Future Promise.* United Nations Research Institute, Social Development and International Institute for Environ-ment and Development, and World Wide Fund for Nature.

Rousseau, J. (1990) *Central Borneo. Ethnic Identity and Social Life in a Stratified Society.* Oxford: Clarendon Press.

Sellato, B. (1998) 'Les peuples traditionnels, les ONG, la manipulation de l'image des interactions entre societe et milieu naturel, et le role du chercheur' [Traditional peoples, NGOs, the manipulation of the image of the interactions of people with their environment, and the role of the researcher]. Dixieme Colloque de la Societe d'Ecologie Humaine, Marseille, November.

Simon Devung, G. (1996) *Sistem Tradisional Pengelolaan Hutan Oleh Dan Untuk Masyarakat, Contoh Kasus Dari Daerah Sungai Bahau.* Jakarta: Culture and Conservation,WWF/IP Kayan Mentarang.

Simon Devung, G. and A.K. Rudy (1998) *Sistem Pemilikan Tanah Tradisional Pada Masyarakat Adat. Di kawasan Taman Nasional Kayan Mentarang.* Samarinda: Pusat Kebudayaan dan Alam Kalimantan dan WWF-I Kayan Mentarang.

Sirait, M. *et al.* (1994). 'Mapping customary land in East Kalimantan, Indonesia: A tool for forest management'. *Ambio,* vol. 23, no. 7, pp. 411–417.

Sorensen, W.K. and B. Morris (eds) (1998) *The Peoples and Plants of Kayan Mentarang.* Jakarta: Unesco.

Sponsel, L., T. Headland and R. Bailey (1996) *Tropical Deforestation: The Human Dimension.* New York: Columbia University Press.

Wells, M.(1995) 'Biodiversity conservation and local development aspirations: new priorities for the 1990s'. In C.A. Peerings *et al.* (eds), *Biodiversity Conservation*. Kluwer Academic Publishers, pp. 319–333

Wells, M. and K. Brandon (1992) *People and Parks. Linking Protected Area Management with Local Communities*. World Bank, WWF, and USAID.

WWF International (1996) *Indigenous Peoples and Conservation: WWF Statement of Principles*. Gland.

WWF International-People and Conservation Unit (1998) *Principles and Guidelines on People and Forests*. Proposed to the WWF/WB Forest Alliance, May.

Zerner, C. (1994) 'Through a green lens: the construction of customary environmental law and community in Indonesia's Maluku Islands'. *Law and Society Review*, vol. 28, no. 5, pp. 1079–1121.

CHAPTER ELEVEN

Co-Production of Forests in Andhra Pradesh, India: Theoretical and Practical Considerations

GAUTAM N. YADAMA

INTRODUCTION

Community and state partnerships are at the centre of current development approaches in much of Asia, Africa and Latin America. Sharper focus on community and collaborative arrangements between state and community is motivated by two factors. First, there is a greater recognition of civil society in the social and economic development of the poor and second there is a realization that the state confronts limitations as the primary engine of development. Nowhere is the importance of civil society and the local and the limitations of the state more evident than in the approach to management of natural resources. Nowhere is the public policy thrust in natural resource management more focused on local community involvement and the civil sector of society than in South Asia. The public policy shift towards community and devolution from the centre to the periphery is most pronounced in the forestry sector of South Asian countries. For instance, Nepal has undergone a radical and rapid shift devolving control of forests from the centre to local communities. India is in the midst of an extensive experiment crafting state–community partnerships in the management of forests. There is an ongoing debate in Bhutan on the role of local communities in the management and conservation of Bhutan's prospering forests.

Forging and implementing collaborative community forest management systems is a complex undertaking. The complexities are enormous and are both endogenous and exogenous to the state–community collaboration. The challenges of co-managing forest resources are historical as well as contemporaneous. This chapter addresses the pressing issues involving joint or collaborative management of forests in India. Specifically, this chapter focuses on the implications of emerging theoretical work on collective action and the production of public goods for management and conservation of community forests in the tribal regions of Andhra Pradesh, India. In addition, this chapter draws on the experiences of several tribal communities and a non-governmental organization to illustrate how the state and tribal communities engage in the co-production of community forests. Foremost, this chapter addresses theoretical ideas and then applies theory to the case of joint forest management in the tribal region of Vishakapatnam district in Andhra Pradesh, India.

JOINT FOREST MANAGEMENT PROGRAMME

Historically, Indian tribal perspectives on forests and the government policies affecting forests have followed different trajectories. State policies driven by industrial demands were in direct conflict with the customary use of forests by forest dwelling tribal populations. Colonial state policies since 1878 and post-independence forest policies characterize tribals as indiscriminate users of forests and sought to protect forests from the tribals. Over the period 1988 to 1997, under the Joint Forest Management (JFM) Policy of the Indian government, various state governments have been engaged in an experiment to devolve authority for forest management to local communities. This new approach to control, protection and management of forests has profound implications for forest dwelling tribals.

Historically, Indian forest policies have alienated people from the forests. Consequently the rate of deforestation increased. Specifically, post-independence forest policies contributed to an expansion in agricultural production, met industrial demand for raw materials and tightened control of forestlands through restricted access to forests and forest products (Haeuber 1993: 485–514). Forest protection policies increased the hardships of vulnerable social groups by denying them access to forests resources (Barraclough and Ghimire 1995: 204). While the state took responsibility for managing forest resources, it did not have the commensurate resources to effectively manage and police the forests from traditional forest users. Before state intervention, forests were managed as communal property; the crucial role of forests in the economic subsistence of individuals, families and the community was the basis for managing them as communal resources (Chopra *et al.* 1990). A failure to recognize community control of forests led to a collapse in institutional norms that as instrumental in protecting and managing forest resources for local use. A shift in property rights to the state steadily undermined the rights of tribals to use and extract forest resources and impoverished the tribal household, whose survival is linked to the availability and access to forest resources.

Beginning with the National Forest Policy, 1988 to the current JFM policy, the thrust of Indian forest policy has been forging management partnerships with local communities. In rediscovering a legitimate role for local communities in self-governance of forests, the state has begun to devolve the control of forests. The limited success of social forestry in providing forest resources for local communities, the continued rate of deforestation and the perpetual conflict between people and forest departments prompted the Indian government to consider a set of policy proposals that radically departed from existing forest policies.

Moreover, the success of state and community forest co-management experiments in Arabari, West Bengal and Sukhomajri in Haryana, provided a framework for decentralizing forest management. Those experiments were sufficient evidence that local populations and communities be given a stake in their forests to regenerate, protect and manage forest resources for the benefit of both the people and the state. Largely the 1988 National Forest Policy was the beginning of this new initiative: delegating the responsibility for managing forests to the local communities. National Forest Policy in tandem with a 1990 circular issued by the government of India serves to: legitimize local communities' access to forests; encourage community formation of forest management committees; and guarantee a portion of the produce from the forests (Singh and Khare 1993: 34–48). This new policy proposal – JFM – promotes a partnership between the state and local communities as an effort to manage forests that benefit both the people and the state. This co-management links forest protection and the concerns of communities dependent on forests.

The Indian government and the governments of 17 Indian states, between 1988 and 1997, have sought to increase the participation of people in forests through the JFM programme. JFM seeks to create partnerships between local communities and the state through of the forest department. The goal of these partnerships is to enhance forest conservation and improve the economic outlook of tribal communities. 'participating villagers free access to most Non-timber Forest Products (NTFPs) and a 25 to 50 per cent share of poles and timber at final harvesting. In return, the villagers are expected to protect the forests after forming an organization conforming to the membership and structure specified by the forest department' (Sarin 1995: 30–36).

JFM attempts to change the state of existing forest resources and the nature of community and individual activities as they relate to resource extraction from local forests. The objective of JFM is to affect forest use patterns, improve forest conditions at the local level, bolster governance of forest resources by local communities and thereby improve the management of forest resources for the social and economic development of local populations.

According to some estimates, 15,000 Forest Protection Committees (FPCs) are operating in India. The range of these FPCs extends across southern Bihar, West Bengal, Orissa, and the northern tribal regions of Andhra Pradesh (Poffenberger 1995). Non-governmental organizations (NGOs) have been playing an important role in facilitating this new partnership between forest departments and local communities. For example, NGOs have been instrumental in articulating the needs of forest-dependent communities to the state. Under JFM, households in a village or a cluster of villages have the right to become members of a forest protection group. A management committee composed of 10 to 15 elected representatives from members of the forest protection committee is constituted to implement a JFM plan. JFM policy stipulates that women should make up 30 per cent of the committee. The committee also consists of a forest guard, representatives from NGOs, village officials, a representative of the tribal development authority in the case of a tribal area and a deputy forest range officer. This managing committee serves a two-year term.

Responsibilities of a FPC include protection against grazing, fires and thefts of forest produce, development of forests in accordance with the management plan and assistance to forest officers in the development of forests (Society for Promotion of Wastelands Development 1993: 27–36). A Vana Samrakshana Samithi (VSS), or forest protection committee, has usufruct rights to non-reserved items. Non-reserved items are leaf and grass fodder, thatch grass, broom grass, thorny fencing material from specified species, fallen lops, tops and twigs used for fuel. A VSS does not have automatic rights to products classified as reserved items, such as tendu leaves, that have been previously leased. Yet, three years after its formation, a forest protection committee is entitled to 25 per cent of timber and poles harvested. Furthermore, the forest department will sell the unused portion of the 25 per cent, with all revenues given to the forest protection committee. A forest protection committee is also entitled to one-third of the revenue from the 75 per cent share of the forest department.

To be relevant, joint forest management should properly recognize the role of forests in shaping current tribal household economies. Moreover, forest co-management in tribal communities must recognize the long history of conflicts over forests between tribals and those who lay claim to these forests (including the government, non-tribals, industrial houses and radical insurgent groups). Present-day co-management strategies are bound to fail if they ignore the historical significance of conflict and mistrust within tribal communities and between state and tribal villages. Fortunately, JFM represents a paradigmatic shift from previous models of forestry development. The emphasis of co-management strategies must be to develop trust and reciprocity within forest communities and between the forest department and the community. The goal is to induce co-operative behaviour and collective action among representatives of a community and the forest department. Ideally this is done through a set of carefully crafted institutional arrangements for the governance and sharing of forest resources. Such institutional arrangements must simultaneously hold the community and the forest department responsible for and accountable to each other. A fundamental aim of such arrangements is to surmount mistrust between the local state entities and forest users so that local knowledge of forests and extant social structures can be leveraged for effective resource management (Vira 1997).

Trust, reciprocity and building trustworthy reputations are essential for fostering collaboration and collective action. Then, how do representatives of community and state foster trust in each other and reciprocate that trust? Outlining the broad theoretical underpinnings of resource co-management arrangements is helpful in understanding the complexities of social capital, collective action and ensuing benefits to state and community. Co-management of forests obligates an understanding of what constitutes a community, its history with the state, including possibilities and prospects for a partnership based on trust and reciprocity, and other exogenous factors that strengthen or strain such state–community partnerships.

CO-MANAGEMENT AS CO-PRODUCTION WITHIN A COMMUNITY CONTEXT

Co-management, with an emphasis on partnership between community and the state invites careful consideration of: 1) the social and economic traits endogenous to a community; 2) the capacity of the state and community to forge effective partnerships in management; and 3) the context – within which these state–community partnerships are forged – that might positively or adversely affect co-management of forests. Three separate but interrelated discussions on community, co-production of public goods and behavioural approaches to collective action reveal the complexities of co-managing natural resources and the conditions under which it is most likely to emerge. A summary of this discussion is largely based on the work of Agrawal (1997), Ostrom (1996), and Evans (1996a and b).

Community
Communities are fraught with conflict. To assume that communities are homogenous and harmonious is to risk any chance of successful collective manage-

ment of forests emerging. Discussion of community is ubiquitous in writings on conservation. However, few unpack the black box of community and address what resides within their definition of community. A given community's association with the forest is engulfed in historical and socio-political processes. Therefore, a consensus or common understanding of community is problematic. Sharpe spells out how a forest community might be shaped by the wider political economy:

> Settlements in the forest are not, as it were, remnants of some 'traditional' past but the focus of all the historical and politico-economic processes that have affected the region: migration, forest exploitation, the exploitation of people, primitive accumulation by external agencies and institutions ... Local debates around forests are full of cogent discussions of the issues raised by external intervention in local affairs. But these debates do not exist merely as discourse. They also reflect, and are reflected in, the everyday life of forest villages: the 'communities' on which conservation and forestry projects build their attempts to develop sustainable use of forest ... The inhabitants of contemporary forest settlements have highly differentiated relations with the wider world. These patterns in turn promote differentiation in wealth and status within settlements. Such differentiation in turn allows complex cross-cutting alliances amongst settlement members and between settlements, as well as the emergence of patron–client networks ... All these members of ethnic groups range from mobile migrant labourers with relatively little commitment to constructing 'community' to long-settled households which own land and houses. (Sharpe 1998: 25–45)

Agrawal (1997) tackles all of the salient issues raised by Sharpe in his analysis of the role of 'community' in conservation. Conservation programmes in constructing mythic communities can do harm to those disenfranchised in a community. If the poor in a community are to benefit, it is critical that joint forest management or other similar decentralized interventions carefully assess the social, economic and political cleavages in a community. According to Agrawal (1997: 25), 'the more challenging and critical task, therefore, lies in understanding how devolved decision making would actually work so that marginalized actors could be represented in decision making, and how their representation would influence the character of conservation-related outcomes. Questioning community aids this critical task.' Then, Agrawal constructs a case for why community-based conservation must recognize the presence of multiple actors and interests in a community; local processes and nature of collective decision making; and institutional arrangements – rules and rule systems – that shape

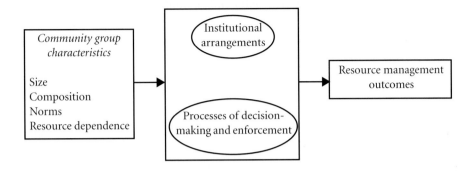

Figure 11.1: Arun Agrawal's framework of community in conservation
Source: Agrawal, 1997.

the interaction of community members vis-à-vis each other and the forest. Disaggregating a community and its interaction with outside actors is critical for forging realistic and workable forest co-management arrangements.

Broadly, Agrawal (1997: 34–35) frames community in conservation as follows (see Figure 11.1). Community size, composition, prevailing norms, and resource dependence – all attributes of community – shape the way different members of a community interact. Interactions among unequal actors with varying control over personal and community resources in turn determine the types of institutions or rules and rule systems that emerge for governing natural resources. 'Institutions should be understood, therefore, as provisional agreements among unequally placed actors on how to accomplish tasks. They are formed and contested in multiple processes marked by an array of forces' (Agrawal 1997: 27). The processes of decision making and enforcement in a community and attendant institutional arrangements, in turn, shape resource management outcomes.[1] This framework of community places greater emphasis on the internal processes in a community and the interactions with players outside the community and the wider political economy in shaping institutional arrangements for governing natural resources. The capacity of state and community to work collaboratively and produce joint forest management arrangements is a function of the internal political, social, and economic dynamics of a tribal community and its relations with the state both historically and contemporaneously. Successful co-management of forest resources rests on the ability of government and citizens jointly to produce public goods and services. Ostrom (1996), and Evans (1996b) elaborate on the conditions under which state and community are able to forge effective partnerships to co-produce public goods.

State–community partnerships: co-production of public goods
Ostrom (1996: 1073) defines co-production 'as a process through which inputs used to produce a good or service are contributed by individuals who are not "in" the same organization'. Co-production is rooted in the idea that citizens can be active participants in the production of public goods that are consequential to them and that state bureaucracy, wherever possible, should actively seek citizen involvement in the production of public goods. Such partnerships between state and civil society are sometimes necessary in the production of public goods because 'not all of the inputs that could potentially be used to produce an output are under full control of a single, public-sector principal' (Ostrom 1996: 1079). When inputs of a state and community are redundant, then co-production is not possible, as there is no potential for synergy. On the other hand, when the necessary resources to produce a public good are distributed between the public sector and a community, and these resources are not substitutable, then a public good is best produced using a combination of government and local community resources (Ostrom 1996: 1079–1080). According to Ostrom (1996: 1083), 'co-production of many goods and services normally considered to be public goods by government agencies and citizens organized into polycentric systems is crucial for achieving higher levels of welfare in developing countries, particularly for those who are poor'. Co-management of forests is such a public good, contingent on inputs from both citizens and the forest department.

Ostrom (1996: 1082) identifies four conditions that increase the probability of joint production of public goods by the state and citizens:

1. There must be a complementary production possibility where each party has co-productive units that are complementary and not substitutive.

2. Legal options must be available for all parties involved in co-production, thereby increasing the array of decision options available to principals without central or higher-level authorization.

3. Clear and enforceable contracts between citizens and government agencies must be present to ensure credible commitment to one another. Such contracts reassure communities and government that any increases in resource commitment towards the production of public good by one is met by commensurate levels of commitment by the other.

4. There must be incentives to encourage inputs from government officials and citizens toward the production of public good.

While co-production is predicated on synergy between state and community, Evans extends the discussion to the nature and structure of that synergy. The two forms of synergy, one based on complementarity and the other on em-beddedness, imply very different state–community relations (Evans 1996b: 1130). This distinction is important for understanding the extent to which the state and communities are enmeshed in the production of public goods. Comple-mentarity is the minimum condition required for the production of a public good, where the public sector and community realize that the necessary inputs do not reside exclusively in one or the other domain and are therefore likely to collaborate. Synergy, due to embeddedness, is built on networks that bind citizens and government officials, where 'social capital is formed by making some who are part of the state apparatus more thoroughly part of the communities in which they work. The networks of trust and collaboration that are created span the public/private boundary and bind state and civil society together' (Evans 1996: 1120). Complementarity is evident when the private and public sectors realize that they each need the other's input to produce the necessary public goods.

Complementarity is only the potential for co-production. Successful cases of synergy involve 'concrete ties connecting the state and society which make it possible to exploit complementarities. Norms of trust built up from intimate interaction are not restricted to relations within civil society. People working in public agencies are closely embedded in the communities they work with, creating social capital that spans the public–private divide' (Evans 1996: 1130). Synergy through embeddedness is predicated on stocks of social capital. Those communities with pre-existing endowments of social capital are more likely to supply public goods in collaboration with government, but social capital is also constructable and not merely a given.

Context for co-management: structural antecedents to state–community collaboration
In her recent work on behavioural approaches to rational choice theory, Ostrom (1998) identifies structural factors that facilitate or impede collective action. Ostrom's framework is useful in placing the co-management of resources within the context of community, and in the context of the wider political economy. The proposed framework by Ostrom (1998) is helpful in understanding the complexity of co-management of resources. It is useful in understanding how structural elements of community and government bureaucracy impinge on the emergence of trust, norms of reciprocity and reputation among actors within community, and between state and community, and the eventual generation of co-operation leading to varying levels of benefit. In this empirically grounded collective action theory, Ostrom disaggregates the various processes into the core relationship between trust, reciprocity and reputation, two levels of structural

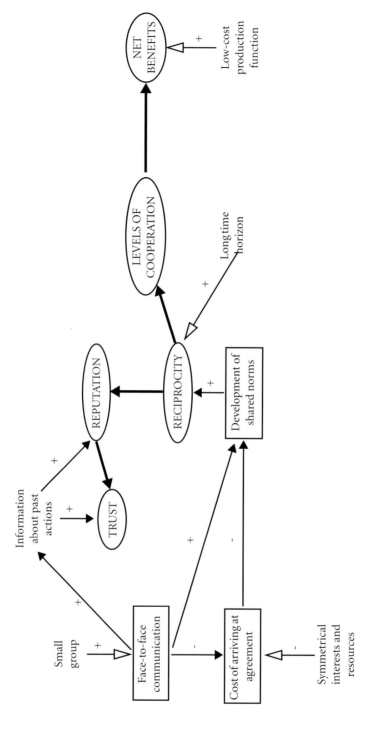

Figure 11.2: Behavioural theory of collective action
Source: Ostrom, 1998

antecedents that have a bearing on this core (see Figure 11.2). The utility of this framework is in its ability to link the behaviour of actors steeped in social dilemmas with exogenous structural determinants. Co-management of resources, especially forests, must be examined from this behavioural perspective with clear recognition of the ways in which structural factors shape, temper and moderate individual and collective decisions of actors.

At the core of a behavioural model of collective action is trust, norms of reciprocity, and investments in reputation. These three endogenous factors are mutually reinforcing. An increase in one should lead to a concomitant rise in the other two. A rise in levels of trust should lead to greater reciprocity and increased investments in maintaining a trustworthy reputation, leading to a further consolidation of trust among the actors engaged in collective action. The degree of collaboration in the production of collective goods is a function of the level of reciprocity among boundedly rational actors. Net benefits accrued by a group is in turn a function of the degree of co-operation among the actors. 'Thus at the core of a behavioural explanation are the links between the trust that individuals have in others, the investment others make in trust-worthy reputations, and the probability that participants will use reciprocity norms ... This mutually reinforcing core is affected by structural variables as well as the past experiences of participants' (Ostrom 1998: 12).

Ostrom (1998: 13–15) identifies four broad structural factors that are exo-genous to the core relationship between trust, reciprocity and reputation (see Figure 11.2). These are information about past actions, face-to-face communica-tion, the cost of arriving at agreements, and development of shared norms. When there is greater face to face communication, it is easier to arrive at agree-ments and develop shared norms. Face-to-face communication also increases the probability of preserving information about past actions. Shared norms and information about past actions determine the level of trust, reciprocity and investments in a trustworthy reputation. The behavioural framework of collective action also incorporates four other structural factors that are exogenous to the structural factors identified above. These are group size, symmetry in interests and resources, time horizons of actors and cost of production function. Smaller groups increase face-to-face communication. Symmetrical interests and resources drive down the cost of arriving at reasonable agreements. When the time horizon of actors is long or discount rates are low, levels of reciprocity are high among those engaged in co-production of public goods. When the production costs are low, the net benefits accrued are high. Figure 11.2 represents all of the above propositions. Collaboration and co-management are a complex undertaking evident from the theoretical discussion about community, state–community relationships and the context for co-production of forests.

The next section considers some of the problems and prospects for co-managing forests in the tribal communities of Andhra Pradesh, India. First there shall be a discussion of the context in which forest co-management is deployed followed a critique of joint forest management experience in the tribal hill tracts of Vishakapatnam district in Andhra Pradesh, India.

TERRAIN OF CONFLICT: FORESTS AND TRIBALS

Conflict is ubiquitous in the tribal villages of Andhra Pradesh, and especially in the Eastern Ghats. Land alienation and control of forests account for much of the conflict among tribals, the government and non-tribals. Land alienation among tribals is from land grabbing by non-tribals and money lenders due to large development projects that displace tribals, and because of illicit land transfers – often by the state – for mining resource rich forests. The state and tribal communities in India have had a contentious relationship *vis-à-vis* the use and access to forests. In the Eastern Ghats (Vishakapatnam, Srikakulam and East Godavari districts), tribal perspectives on forests have never converged with those of the state. Tribal rebellions in this region – in colonial and post-independent India – have been in resistance to state intrusion and domination of forests and forest-based resources.[2] The hill tracts of Rampa and Gudem in Andhra Pradesh, where joint forest management is now being implemented, witnessed a series of rebellions or *fituris* against colonial authority and intrusion into forests.[3] These rebellions were, in large part, a response to restrictions on forest use, production of traditional liquor, and the practice of shifting cultivation (*podu*) in the forests.[4] Further fuelling this conflict between tribals and the colonial government was the active promotion of non-tribal traders in developing a marketable trade in forest products, including palm liquor. This remains a source of conflict between tribals and a powerful group of non-tribal traders and money-lenders.

Non-wood forest products (NWFP) and tribal household economy
The fight for forests and forest resources by tribals is merely a struggle in defence of their livelihood. Such a conclusion is inevitable upon examination of data revealing the inextricable link between extraction of forest resources and tribal household economy. Studies conducted in the tribal regions of Bihar, West Bengal and Karnataka, India offer clear evidence for the extent of dependence of tribal households on non-wood forest product collection. For example, in two southern districts of Bihar, 41 per cent of the families collect Mahuwa

flowers (*Madhuca indica*); 31 per cent collect Tendu leaves (*Diospyros melanoxylon*) used in the making of indigenous cigarettes; 23 per cent of the families collect mushrooms and Mahuwa seeds; 55 per cent of the families collect tamarind (*Tamarindus indica*); and 31 per cent of the families depend on the collection of wild broom (Rao and Singh 1996: 337–341). Even higher rates of dependence on NWFPs, ranging between 56 and 73 per cent, have been recorded by the same study in Midnapore district of West Bengal (Rao and Singh 1996: 338). In a study of Soliga tribal households, Hegde *et al.* (1996: 243–251) found that the income contribution from the collection of NWFPs is disproportionately greater than the time spent in collecting the products. Their study indicated that households living on the periphery of the forest spent 39.25 per cent of their time in collection and realized 47.63 per cent of their income from NWFPs. For tribals living closer to the forest the figures are 54.46 per cent 60.44 per cent, respectively. Moreover, '[v]ariance in income from the extraction of NTFPs is much less than that of income from other vocations, indicating that the collection of NTFPs constitutes the most reliable source of income' (Hegde *et al.* 1996: 249–250). The critical role NWFPs play in the livelihood strategies of tribal households is highlighted by the favourable income returns to the time spent in collection and the stability of income from NWFPs.

In Andhra Pradesh, tribals collect a large variety of NWFPs. These products include tamarind (*Tamarindus indica*), adda leaf (*Bauhinia vahlii*), gum karaya (*Sterculia urens*), marking nut (*Myrobalanus chebula*), Mahuwa flowers and seeds (*Madhuca indica*), wild broom (*Thysanoloena maxima*) and soap nuts (*Sapindus emarginatus*). One study estimated that income from the sale of NWFPs in Andhra Pradesh constitutes anywhere from ten to 55 per cent of total household income (Burman 1990: 649–658). In comparison to Orissa, Bihar, and Madhya Pradesh, India (all with large tribal populations), tribal households from Andhra Pradesh accrue a very high proportion of their income from the sale of NWFPs (Burman 1990: 651). Tewari (1998: 101) estimated that in Andhra Pradesh, 10 to 55 per cent of tribal household income is directly from the sale of NWFPs and this dependence increases markedly as a tribal household becomes marginalized. As a household becomes poorer, non-wood forest products become more central to household subsistence. Thus, from an economic standpoint, NWFPs play a pivotal role in the livelihood strategies of tribal households in Vishakapatnam district as well as in the entire Eastern Ghats region. Household studies conducted in different hill tract tribal villages of Vishakapatnam district further illustrate the high degree of tribal dependence on forests. Data indicate that income from forests comprises more than 50 per cent of the household income. Even in areas where forests are virtually absent, approximately 13 per cent of the tribal household income is from forests (Yadama *et al.* 1997).

State intervention and pressures on forests

In the hill tracts of Andhra Pradesh, long held resource conflicts with origins in colonial times have been exacerbated by large-scale development projects. With the building of hydroelectric projects, irrigation dams and mining operations, many thousands of tribals have been displaced from their lands.[5] Consequently there has been an influx of landless tribals from the neighbouring state Orissa into the tribal hill tracts of Andhra Pradesh. Many were not only displaced and forced to migrate but were faced with a severe shortage in revenue lands, cleared of forests, and therefore suitable for cultivation. Left with few choices, migrating tribals settled in reserved forests. They cleared the forests for agriculture and further exacerbated existing conflicts with the forest department. Madhav Gadgil and Ramachandra Guha characterize the conflicts between state and citizens as follows:

> Not surprisingly, the conflicts between the state and its citizens have persisted, and the Forest Department continues to be a largely unwelcome presence in the countryside. However, forest conflicts in independent India have differed in one important respect from conflicts in the colonial period. Earlier, these conflicts emerged out of the contending claims of state and people over a relatively abundant resource; now these conflicts are played out against the backdrop of a rapidly dwindling forest resource base. In other words, a newer *ecological* dimension has been added to the moral, political, and economic dimensions of social conflicts over forests and wildlife. Cumulatively, these processes have worked to further marginalize poor peasants and tribals, the social groups most heavily dependent on forest resources for their subsistence and survival. (Gadgil and Guha 1995: 86)

In the tribal hill tracts of Vishakapatnam, existing conflicts have not been helped by ambiguities in the demarcation of revenue and forest boundaries. Such ambiguities are a source of contention as the state refuses to grant title deeds to many tribal families. At the same time, there has been a steady transfer of title deeds from tribals to non-tribals in contravention of the Land Transfer Regulation Act of 1970. Absentee landlords abound, and eviction of tribals by middlemen and contractors holding false title deeds is commonplace. Data – albeit from 1988 – indicates that in Andhra Pradesh there were 45,865 tribal land alienation cases filed in the courts involving 172,538 acres of tribal land. Of this disputed land, only 81,845 acres were eventually restored into tribal hands (Mahapatra 1994: 16).[6] This snapshot provides a glimpse of the competing claims on tribal lands and the fractured landscape in general. Tribal communities in this part of Andhra Pradesh have been contesting the forest department on the one hand and revenue authorities on the other. Pressures on tribal life and resources mount with the steady influx of petty traders, contractors and middle-men, all having contempt for the tribal way of life. Joining this list of competing claims on forests and revenue lands in the tribal hill tracts are the mining interests of large Indian industrial houses. Along with powerful mining interests, the state in the guise of the forest department and encroaching non-tribals, the Eastern Ghats region has had a strong presence of leftist movements ready to exploit discontent among tribals.

The presence of strong mining concerns, leftist movements, and non-governmental organizations mobilizing tribal communities makes planned development a challenge in the hill tract tribal villages of *Eastern Ghats*. Even more challenging is the planning and implementation of a joint forest management programme in this charged environment.

Has JFM fostered true co-management between the state and local tribal communities? How do the newly introduced co-management arrangements address deep-seated mistrust between tribals and the forest department? The next section turns to field observations on joint forest management in Vishakapatnam and makes some generalizations. All of the observations come from field visits to Malevalasa, Panasavalasa, Karakavalasa, Dingriput, Vanakachinta, Nandigaruvu and Nimmalapadu villages in the tribal hill tracts of Vishakapatnam, Andhra Pradesh.[7] Generalizations about joint forest management are discussed in the light of theoretical issues raised previously on the community, co-management and collective action.

COMMUNITY, SOCIAL CAPITAL AND CO-PRODUCTION: NEGLECTED FACTORS IN THE CO-MANAGEMENT OF FORESTS IN HILL TRACT TRIBAL AREAS OF ANDHRA PRADESH

The JFM programme in the tribal areas has been plagued by many problems. Chief among these is a blatant lack of attention to political, social and economic cleavages in tribal communities. The approach to forging co-management has been very simplistic. The typical process has been for the forest department to approach a village, often with the help of an intermediary NGO, offering a range of incentives in return for entering forest co-management arrangements with the state. Incentives range from funds to build a community school, a village meeting place or a better approach road into the village. It is usual for forest department officials to offer a range of incentives to a village or a group of villages in order to constitute and register a forest protection committee. A joint forest management programme in the tribal hill tracts of Andhra Pradesh is built on an exchange of incentives for co-management agreements. A micro plan is prepared once a village or a federated group of villages agrees to the formation of a forest protection committee. A forest protection committee consists of representatives from village households and the local forest guard representing the forest department. This committee is largely responsible for collectively co-managing a community forest. An intermediary NGO is responsible for mediating disputes that may occur among members of a forest protection committee. The probability of disputes is greatly increased in forest protection committees that are formed across several communities. The above is a uniform and standardized procedure for establishing joint forest protection committees between communities and the forest department. It is also common to involve an NGO as an intermediary between the state and the community. At the outset, this process of establishing forest co-management seems viable and effective. While numerous forest protection committees have been established, this model, however, has not been particularly effective in the tribal hill tracts of Eastern Ghats.

There are several reasons for being sceptical about the longer-term viability of these state–village entities.

1. The current approach to forming village forest protection committees ignores the wider political economy of a tribal community. The process is ignorant of history and contemporary social, political and economic forces in the way they influence the dynamic between state and tribal communities.

2. Co-management strategies have focused disproportionately on frivolous incentives, which in the end have little bearing on fostering and sustaining co-production of community forests by the people and the state.

3. While the use of NGOs is a very effective strategy to gain access to the people, eventually the state and citizens must cross the divide and work together. An over reliance on external agents impedes any chance of sustained trust and reciprocity between local state functionaries and tribal communities.

4. There is an absence of forward-looking policies and legislation to create an enabling environment for co-production of community forests in the tribal areas.

In the next section, the above factors are addressed from the perspective of community, social capital and co-production literature as well as from recent theoretical work on behavioural approaches to collective action.[8]

Community out of context

The more fundamental work of building community-based institutions and forging long-term collaborative arrangements is rarely addressed in JFM programmes in Andhra Pradesh (Yadama and DeWeese-Boyd in press). The forest department had been approaching joint forest management as another project to follow a long succession of forest management models. Joint forest management is not seen as a paradigmatic shift in the way the forest department relates to community and conservation.[9] For those entering the Indian Forest Service, a study of perceptions of joint forest management indicated that they perceived JFM to be a project (Pandey 1997: 527–535). The same study indicates that many of the professionals in training expressed confusion over the goals of JFM and even doubted if JFM is an end to well stocked forests. The divide in the perceptions of the state and others in what constitutes joint forest management is powerfully conveyed in a discussion of the process leading to the funding of the Andhra Pradesh Forestry Project by the World Bank (World Bank 1996: 53–59). The Andhra Pradesh forest department has been a reluctant convert to co-management and does not see joint forest management as a way to radically alter the way tribals and the state interact *vis-à-vis* forests. The preoccupation is with meeting the goal of rapidly registering as many forest protection committees as possible, without any care given to structuring new institutional arrangements between the state and tribals. There is not enough attention to nurturing and strengthening governing arrangements when forest protection committees show promise and initiative. Pressure to meet set targets for establishing more forest protection committees is largely responsible for a callous approach toward establishing co-management arrangements. The focus is directly on registering forest protection committees, then on nurturing and developing strong co-management regimes built on norms of trust and reciprocity within a community and between state and community. Under these circumstances, it is impossible to envisage these newly formed forest protection committees functioning for long periods. These observations are further justified in the face of empirical evidence suggesting the conditions required to undertake successful and sustained public–private collaborations in development (Ostrom 1996; Lam 1996; Evans 1996b).

Synergy between state and community, based on complementarity of inputs is an initial condition for co-management of forests. Complementarity, according to Evans, creates a potential for synergy but not the organizational basis for realizing the potential. Embeddedness, in the form of state officials being directly involved in organizing and sustaining citizen participation, facilitating community meetings, and mediating conflicts, is essential for co-management to be sustained. Synergy, based on embeddedness that connects citizens and public officials across the public–private divide, relies on social capital – norms of trust, reciprocity, and maintenance of reputations (Evans 1996b: 1120–1124). Clearly, a case can be made for the complementarity of inputs between the state and citizens in joint forest management. It is in the interest of the tribal house-holds to partner with the state so that tribal communities may gain control of the forests near their villages and manage them in the long-term interests of communities. On the other hand the forest department in co-managing the forests is in a better position to hold tribal communities accountable for better protection and management of forests. Moreover in partnering with tribal households, the forest department in the end meets the forest needs of tribal communities but more importantly realizes increased forest revenue. The forests now protected and managed by communities will likely yield more bamboo and generate greater revenues – for the forest department – from commercial demand for bamboo. Therefore, a potential for synergy based on complement-arity does exist in the case of joint forest management (Evans 1996b).

As Evans emphasizes, however, synergy based on complementrarity has to transcend into synergy that is from embeddedness. Embeddeddness is predicated on stocks of social capital, that is trust, reciprocity and investments in reputation. The core relationship between trust, reciprocity and reputation is also at the centre of Ostrom's behavioural framework of collective action. This mutually reinforcing core determines the level of collaboration and eventually, the net benefits from co-management. Trust and reciprocity in tribal communities are severely strained for many reasons. Historically many of the tribal villages have suffered deep divisions as some tribal households have been co-opted or have aligned themselves with outside interests in the forest department, non-tribal traders or other political or commercial entities outside of their community. In addition to the divisions within a community, tribal communities and the govern-ment (as discussed previously) mistrust one another. To say the least, the political and social landscape in which these forest co-management arrangements are being deployed is severely fractured and hostile to fostering forest co-management built on trust and reciprocity. Even under such conditions, the forest depart-ment when presented with the opportunity to foster trust, has squandered the chance. Tribal communities have been steadfast in demanding that when jointly managed forests yield commercially lucrative bamboo, it is proper for the govern-ment to share the revenues with the forest protection committee. The forest department has refused to reconsider its JFM policy of not sharing revenues from bamboo contracts with villages that helped protect that bamboo. The forest department would have positively affected the trust of tribal villages by including a policy provision to share those revenues. Again Evans makes an interesting observation about the relative capacity of communities and governments to engage in the construction of synergy. He conjectures that,

> If synergy fails to occur, it is probably not because the relevant neighbourhoods and communities were too fissiparous and mistrustful but because some other crucial ingredient was lacking. The most obvious candidate for the missing ingredient is a competent, engaged set of public institutions. If synergy can regularly emerge out of communities that seem quite ordinary in terms of their stock of social capital, but governments vary dramatically in terms of their ability to act as counterparts in the creation of developmentally effective civic organizations, then perhaps the limits to synergy are located in government rather than in civil society. (Evans 1996b: 1125)

Indeed, what sort of incentives has the forest department offered to foster trust and reciprocity and to enable credible commitments from tribal communities?

Institutional incentives and co-management

Forest protection committees are voluntary co-management arrangements. They are not strict contractual arrangements between tribals and the government. The forest department routinely offers incentives in an effort to enlist the collaboration of communities in forest protection. These incentives typically have been promises to build community-meeting places, a village school, an approach road into the village or sign posts at the entrance of a village. Seldom are these incentives related to joint protection and management of the village forest and associated forest products. Communities respond with greater enthusiasm when the forest department offers greater control and authority over forests as an incentive to co-manage. For example, in Andhra Pradesh, all non-wood forest products collected by tribal households are sold to a government forest co-operative. The prices offered by the state co-operative do not compare favourably with prices in the open market. Tribal households are legally obliged to sell all non-wood forest products that they collect to this co-operative. The co-operative, in turn, sells this produce in the open market. A state monopoly of non-wood forest products is a great disincentive to tribals. The forest department in dismantling this archaic co-operative system will surely provide an impetus for tribal villages to engage in co-management of forests. In dismantling the co-operative, the forest department will have leveraged more trust from citizens and demonstrated a genuine concern for the welfare of forest dependent tribal households. Moreover in removing structural barriers to markets, the state acts to promote low-cost production functions and increase net benefits to communities from co-management of forests (see Figure 10.2) (Ostrom 1998: 15). Other by-products of dismantling the state monopoly of non-wood forest products is the effect on lowering the discount rate of appropriators and increasing preferences for long-term benefits over short-term gains. Ostrom (1998: 15), in her behavioural framework of collective action, identifies a long time horizon as having a positive effect on the core factors of reciprocity, reputation and trust. Incentives could also come in the form of statutory rights.

Joint forest management is voluntary and forest protection committees are formed on good faith agreements between a community and the state. These arrangements must sustain themselves purely on trust and reciprocity between the forest department and the tribals. Legal recourse for either party does not exist. In the tribal regions of India, and in many other parts of the world, the two commodities even more scarce than forests are trust and reciprocity between the state and citizens. History looms large as an impediment to developing trust and reciprocity. A sure way to instill trust is not to rely solely on informal mechanisms and good faith but to give both parties – tribal communities and the forest department – the means to exact commitment from the other through statutory rights. This will surely repair and bridge the credibility gap that exists between the state and tribal communities. In providing legal rights to a forest, tribal communities are assured that they need not depend on the good graces of a forest guard to be assured of the benefits from protection. Besides, 'without the advantage of being considered legitimate, a small group of local appropriators can face high costs in trying to exclude well-financed, government-supported users who do not have local property rights' (Ostrom 1990: 205). Evans (1996b: 1124) makes useful suggestions in this regard: either synergy between the public and private is due to social capital endowments or is constructed slowly but surely through imaginative organizational and institutional arrangements. Synergy that is a result of endowments requires existing stocks of social capital. In the case of JFM in Andhra Pradesh, synergy has to be created by deploying forest protection committees in a legal and public policy milieu that instills confidence in both the tribal communities and the forest department to make credible commitments. In conditions of high distrust and suspicion, establishing statutory rights might be the only way to reduce the 'cost of arriving at agreements' and to ensure commitments to agreements. As the costs of arriving at agreements decrease, the likelihood of developing shared norms increases and eventually fosters reciprocity, investments in reputation and trust: the three elements critical for successful co-management of forests.

Role of NGOs and state in creating an enabling environment

Reliance on NGOs as intermediaries is effective in increasing the capacity of a community to negotiate co-managerial agreements with the state. NGOs play a vital role when the divide between the state and communities is large. Over reliance, however, on NGOs to resolve every dispute and conflict within a community and between the state and the community can be detrimental. In the end, a community and the state must reach across and work collaboratively. Eventually trust, reciprocity, and reputations, have to be fostered directly between the forest department and a community. The presence of an NGO can hamper synergy due to embeddedness. It is more difficult for the state and community – in the presence of an NGO that is firmly entrenched between the state and community – to cross the public–private divide and establish strong ties.

Successful co-management arrangements also require that the state creates an enabling environment at the local level through a set of policy strategies in related areas. Mining is a big threat to forests in Andhra Pradesh and elsewhere in India. If a government is serious about devolving authority to promote forest co-management, then they must also pursue a set of related policy measures that police illicit mining in forests. Pursuing a bundle of inter-related policies has the effect of leveraging forest co-management. Especially when forests are highly contested, it helps to pursue in tandem a broad set of policies that not only strengthen state–community collaborations but also undercut potentially destructive activities such as mining. What is required is a polycentric approach to policy-making, where the state reinforces its co-management policies at one level with a set of supra policies that anticipate and effectively address factors that threaten to undermine the co-management of forests.

CONCLUDING NOTE

Natural resource co-management is not easily undertaken. It is complex and implicates a range of problems that require serious consideration. It is not enough just to focus on a community's ability to come together. It is equally important to address how a community and state negotiate with each other. To understand the complexities of co-management, we need cogent theoretical frameworks that allow us to model endogenous factors that are critical for enabling collective action. In addition we need to consider exogenous factors that have a direct bearing on the micro-institutional arrangements. Institutional arrangements to manage community forests must focus on endogenous cleavages within communities as well as on the external pressures on various actors in-volved in co-management. Co-management arrangements cannot be uniformly replicated without consideration of the historical and prevailing social, political, cultural, and economic conditions. Some of the important considerations should be trust, reciprocity and the premium local actors put on maintaining reputations. It is difficult to foster collaboration within a community and between the state and the community in the absence of these mutually reinforcing factors. Another important element in building sustainable co-management arrangements is also the policy environment external to these arrangements. It is essential that a state through progressive and forward-looking policies, fosters an enabling environment where newly established forest co-management is not undermined. The experience of JFM in Andhra Pradesh offers a window into these complexities. Historically the state and tribal communities have mistrusted each other. Forest use and management have been at the core of contention between tribals and the state. Moreover, commercial pressures and pressures from mining interests on the forests have further exacerbated the mistrust between tribal communities and the state. Undertaking co-management of forests is difficult given these historical and contemporary conditions shaping state–tribal relationships. Co-management of forests requires some degree of sophistication on the part of the state, unlike the current approach of mass-producing community forest user groups. Successful co-management of forests dictates attention not only to fostering micro-institutional arrangements at the community level, but also to shaping the larger legal and policy environment that enables community-based forest management to be sustained and flourish.

NOTES

1 Agrawal is careful to point out that he is not presenting a theory of community-based conservation, rather he is presenting an alternative way of thinking about the role of communities in conservation.

2 Conflict between tribals and the state in East Godavari, Vishakapatnam, and Srikakulam districts has historically been exacerbated by the '*Muttadari*' system introduced by the British. *Muttadars* were responsible for collecting land revenue. Any surplus over the designated revenue due (*Kattubadi*) to the government was then retained by the *Muttadar*. The pervasive power of the *Muttadars* led to unrestrained exploitation of the tribals.

3 The first rebellion known as Rampa Fituri, was in 1803. The second revolt was in 1879 against the *Muttadars* and the British, and this rebellion was widespread. Then from 1922 to 1924 there was a third rebellion of Koya tribals instigated by Alluri Seetharama Raju. The fourth rebellion by the Naxalites was between 1968 and 1972.

4 See Rangarajan (1996) for a nice historical elaboration on the legal and policy controversies surrounding swidden cultivation and forest management in tribal regions.

5   See Jaganath Pathy (1992) *Tribal Transformation in India: Economy and Agrarian Issues,* for a detailed account of the number of displaced tribals under various projects and planning periods.

6   The situation of land alienation, the same study reveals, is even more grave in other states with sizeable tribal populations. In Madhya Pradesh, 99,864 tribal cases were filed and in Orissa it was 76,527 cases.

7   Field visits were conducted in December 1995 and January 1996. Additional data were gathered by staff members of Samata, an NGO, involved in implementing the joint forest management programme.

8   See Ostrom (1996: 1073–1087); Evans (1996a: 1033–1037, and 1996b: 1119–1132); Lam (1996: 1039–1054); and Ostrom (1998: 1–22).

9   A quick review of articles on Joint Forest Management in the journal *The Indian Forester* will substantiate this claim. A large number of the publications on JFM in this journal are written by members ofthe Indian Forest Service. Therefore it is a reliable and valid barometer for gauging how state functionaries view co-management of forests. There is considerable confusion in some of the writing about what constitutes joint forest management. Others in their writings on JFM indicate how the forest department has changed the 'wrong ways' of the people and turned people away from illicit forest activities.

REFERENCES

Agrawal, Arun (1997) *Community in Conservation: Beyond Enchantment and Disenchant-ment.* Gainesville, Florida: Conservation and Development Forum.

Barraclough, Solon L. and B. Krishna Ghimire (1995) *Forests and Livelihoods: The soical Dynamics of Deforestation in Developing Countries.* New York: Macmillan Press.

Burman, J.J. Roy (1990) 'A need for reappraisal of minor forest produce policies'. *The Indian Journal of Social Work,* vol. 51, pp. 649–658.

Chopra, K., G. Kadekodi, K. Kadekodi and M.N. Murty (1990) *Participatory Develop-ment: People and Common Property Resources.* New Delhi: Sage Publications.

Evans, Peter (1996a) 'Introduction: development strategies across the public–private divide'. *World Development,* vol. 24, pp. 1033–1037.

—— (1996b) 'Government action, social capital and development: reviewing the evidence on synergy'. *World Development,* vol. 24, pp. 1119–1132.

Gadgil, M. and R. Guha (1995) *Evology and Equity: The Use and Abuse of Nature in Contemporary India.* London: Routledge.

Haeuber, Richard (1993) 'Development and deforestation: Indian forestry in perspective'. *The Journal of Developing Areas,* vol. 27, pp. 485–514.

Hedge, R., S. Suryaprakash, L. Achoth and K.S. Bawa (1996) 'Extraction of non-timber forest products in the forests of Biligiri Rangan Hills, India: contribution to rural Income'. *Economic Botany,* vol. 50, pp. 243-251.

Lam, Wai Fung (1996) 'Institutional design of public agencies and coproduction: a study of irrigation associations in Taiwan'. *World Development,* vol. 24, pp. 1039–1054.

Mahapatra, L.K. (1994) *Tribal Development in India: Myth and Reality.* Delhi: Vikas Publishing House.

Ostrom, Elinor (1990) *Governing the Commons: the Evolution of Institutions for Collective Action.* Cambridge: Cambridge University Press.

—— (1996) 'Crossing the great divide: coproduction, synergy, and development'. *World Development*, vol. 24, pp. 1073–1087.

—— (1998) 'A behavioral approach to the rational choice theory of collective action'. *American Political Science Review*, vol. 92, pp. 1–22.

Pandy, Gopa (1997) 'Joint forest management: perceptions of new incumbents in Indian forest service'. *The Indian Forester*, vol. 123, pp. 527–535.

Pathy, Jaganath (1992) 'The agrarian situation in tribal areas'. In Buddhadeb Chaudhurri (ed.), *Tribal Transformation in India: Economy and Agrarian Issues*, vol. I, pp. 208–226.

Poffenberger, Mark (1995) Public lands reform: India's experience with joint forest management Unpublished Mimeo. Berkeley: Asia Forest Network, Center for Southeast Asia Studies.

Rangarajan, Mahesh (1996) *Fencing the Forest: Conservation and Ecological Change in India's Central Provinces 1860–1914.* Delhi: Oxford University Press.

Rao, A. Ratna and B.P. Singh (1996) 'Non-wood forest products contribution in tribal economy'. *Indian Forester*, vol. 122, pp. 337–341.

Sarin, Madhu (1995) 'Joint forest management in India: achievements and unaddressed challenges'. *Unasylva*, vol. 46, pp. 30–36.

Sharpe, Barrie (1998) "First the forest": conservation, "community" and "participation" in South-West Cameroon'. *Africa*, vol. 68, pp. 25–45.

Singh, Samar and Arvind Khare (1993) "Peoples" participation in forest management'. *Wastelands News*, vol. 3, pp. 34–38.

Society for Promotion of Wastelands Development (1993) *Joint Forest Management Update: 1993.* New Delhi: SPWD.

Tewari, D.D. (1998) *Economics and management of non-timber forest products.* New Dehli/Oxford, Oxford University Press.

Vira, Bhaskar (1997) 'Deconstruction of participatory forest management: toward a tenable typology'. OCEES Research Paper No. 14. Oxford Centre for the Environment, Ethics and Society, Mansfield College, University of Oxford.

World Bank (1996) 'Sharing Experiences'. *The World Bank Participation Source Book.* Washington: The World Bank.

Yadama, Gautam. N., Bhanu R. Pragada and Ravi R. Pragada (1997) *Forest Dependent Survival Strategies of Tribal Women: Implications for Joint Forest Management in Andhra Pradesh, India.* Bangkok: Food and Agriculture Organization of the United Nations.

Yadama, Gautam and De-Weese-Boyd (in press). 'Co-Management of Forests in the Tribal Regions of Andhra Pradesh, India: a study in the making and unmaking of social capital'. in Bhaskar Vira and Roger Jeffery (eds), *Participatory Natural Resource Management: Analytical Perspectives.* London: Macmillan.

CHAPTER TWELVE

The Road to Community-Based Resource Management in the Philippines: Entries, Bends, Tolls and Dead Ends

PERCY E. SAJISE, FRANCISCO P. FELLIZAR, JR AND GIL C. SAGUIGUIT

INTRODUCTION

*I*t took some time for human society to realize that the issues of environment and development are linked together. This is especially true for countries in Asia and the South Pacific where, this realization is often overwhelmed by issues of poverty, political instability, short-term economic gains and inequity of access to resources. This is however, also true for developed countries, where this realization has been constrained by the 'technological fix syndrome' and the dominance of conventional, less environmentally orientated economic and policy analysis for decision making. The later has also frequently provided, a negative environmental link between the so called developed/industrialized and developing/less industrialized countries of the world. A common factor that has served as a barrier to the internalization of the relationships between environment and development for both groups of nations is a lack of understanding and appreciation of the complex nature of environmental problems and the recognition that environmental problem analysis and the generation of options for solutions will require new approaches and methodologies.

Today, the environmental problems of deforestation, pollution, improper land use, deterioration of aquatic resources, soil erosion, declining agricultural production and biodiversity, and an undermining of local institutions and knowledge in support of environmental integrity generally prevails in Asia and the South Pacific. The grim aspect of nuclear pollution and prospects of rising sea levels in the future also haunts some places in the South Pacific and island countries in Asia. It became a common realization – except perhaps for those who are the victims of poverty and hunger whose concerns are immediate and who are confronted with limited options – that sustainable development cannot be realized with continuing environmental deterioration and that something must be done to reverse the process. It is in this context that we believe our work on community-based resource management will be a key factor in reversing this process within the context of a burgeoning human population exerting more pressure on the dwindling resources in our regions.

COMMUNITY-BASED RESOURCE MANAGEMENT (CBRM)

The development paradigm which supports the top-down approach has been left by the wayside in the course of time. CBRM will be broadly defined in this chapter as a process by which the people themselves are given the opportunity and/or responsibility to manage their own resources, define their needs, goals and aspirations, and to make decisions affecting their well-being. CBRM as an approach emphasizes a community's capability, responsibility and accountability with regard to managing resources. CBRM also implies that people have access to and control over resources and that they too have knowledge, expertise and technology to manage the resources productively. It is inherently evolutionary, participatory and locale-specific and considers the technical, socio-cultural, economic, political and environmental factors impinging upon a given community. CBRM is basically seen as community empowerment for resource productivity, sustainability and equity. Co-management, defined as the sharing of responsibilities for decision-making on resource management by various stakeholders, is an element of CBRM. CBRM, however may be considered as an empowering process, where other stakeholders (NGOs, LGUs, government agencies, the private sector) assist in developing the capacity of local communities to assume greater responsibilities for their decision-making, access to benefits and accountability for the use of their resources.

WHY CBRM?

For centuries, resource management in the Philippines has been strongly centrally determined, top down and non-participatory, but during the *barangay* period, control became more locally based (Figure 12.1). The Philippine Constitution and various Pds including PD 705, or the Revised Forestry Code, generally defines control, management, and goals in the utilization of the country's natural resources. Major features of these provisions are the following:

- the state generally is the steward and therefore allocates and manages our natural resources through existing bureaus and departments;
- natural resources' utilization should benefit both present and future generations of citizens of the country and

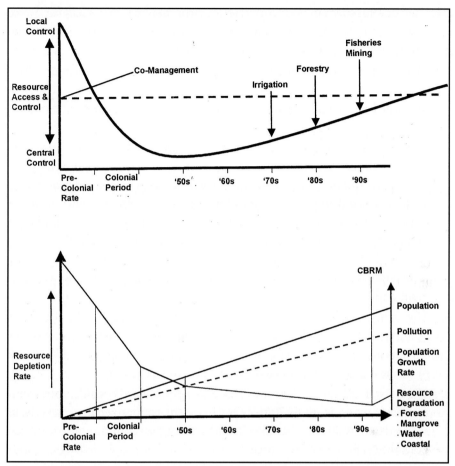

Figure 12.1: Conceptual representation of CBRM historical trends and resource use in the Philippines

- ecological, cultural, and developmental considerations should be taken into account in the utilization of our natural resources.

Various provisions in our Constitution build in the concern for generating inter- and intra-generational and continuing benefits from our natural resources. The right of every Filipino to enjoy a productive and wholesome environment is also guaranteed by our Constitution as stipulated in Article 11, Section 16. However, the present state of our environment and various life support systems has given rise to grave concern and alarm. At the global level, the Earth Summit of 1992 in Rio de Janeiro sent a message to the world that without better environmental stewardship, development will be undermined; and without accelerated development in poor countries, environmental policies will fail. Sajise *et al.* (1992), in a report covered by the U. P. 'Assessments on the State of the Nation' described the state of our environment as follows:

1. The forest cover the country is only 20.5 per cent today compared to 57.3 per cent 90 years ago. To regenerate enough forest cover to bring it back to the same level would require 177 years at the present rate and efficiency of reforestation.

2. Agricultural production efficiency for important grain crops (rice and corn) has been declining since 1985. This is because of expansion into marginal lands as a result of land conversion and lack of access to lowland production areas by upland migrants. The decline in agricultural efficiency is also a result of degradation of the agricultural resource base due to degradation of the soil resource base, pest incidence and chemical pollution. This is very profound as 58.2 per cent of our total population and 65 per cent of the rural population is directly or indirectly dependent on agriculture for employment and livelihood.

3. The rich freshwater endowment of the country is fast deteriorating. For example, 40 rivers (including all rivers feeding Metro Manila) out of 384 river systems are now considered biologically dead due to pollution; 480,802 ha of freshwater areas are affected by saltwater intrusion.

4. The coastal habitat and resources have also diminished considerably. Coral reef destruction is up to 70 per cent in extent, mangrove areas have been reduced to only 30 per cent (139,725 ha) and seagrass communities have been destroyed. This coastal resource destruction and improper fishing methods have resulted in the overall decline of fisheries production. Sustainable yield limits for fisheries *may have been exceeded already.*

5. In urban and settlement areas, the growth of human population in areas of comparatively small size and the lack of a planning framework upon which to base development have led to incompatible and inappropriate land uses which in turn have become the main cause of environmental deterioration such as water pollution, problems of waste disposal and deteriorating health and nutrition.

The deterioration of our life support systems is expected to be exacerbated in the following decades by the following actors:

*   high foreign debt burden;
*   poverty;
*   rapid population growth;

- inequity;
- weak institutional capacity;
- lethargy of local communities;
- stagnant economy; and
- non-responsive political system.

In accordance with the definition of sustainable development, present trends regarding the capacity of life support systems in the Philippines will not allow the country to pursue a path of sustainable development. Exacerbation of this condition is also predictable if present trends continue. Zosa-Feranil (1992) predicts a low population estimate of 91 million and a high estimate of 110 million Filipinos by the year 2010. If poverty, inequity, weak institutional capacity to protect the environment together with a high foreign debt burden will continue to prevail in the next decade, the Philippines will be following a course of unsustainable development accompanied by the prospects of low levels of quality of life for our people.

It has been recognized, therefore, that current trends in the use of resources to achieve sustainable development are untenable and that alternative methods offer opportunities to reverse this trend. Consequently, there has been a shift to forward-looking policies and strategies that advocate community-based initiatives to rehabilitate, conserve and protect the resources, based on enhancement of local knowledge and skills and accountability.

CBRM PROGRAMMES

The number of programmes and projects which have been implemented or are currently being undertaken in the Philippines that employ CBRM indicate its viability as a strategy for sustainable development. This approach is being used in the sectors of forestry, fisheries, mining, irrigation and fresh water (Fellizar 1993).

Forestry
Prior to 1987, provisions in the Philippine Constitution gave full responsibility for the management of natural resources to of the State. With the ratification of the 1987 Constitution, some changes in state policies with regard to the use and disposition of natural and forest resources came into effect. Some of the important changes relate to people's rights to a healthy environment, the equitable distribution of opportunities and benefits from natural resources and the rights of indigenous cultural communities. Another basic policy relating to CBRM is Presidential Decree No. 705 or the Revised Forestry Code of the Philippines,

243

which provides for and requires the proper management of occupancy within forest lands.

People-orientated forestry programmes only started in the early 1970s (Serna, 1993). These were effected in recognition of the failure of earlier punitive measures to arrest shifting cultivation and the realization that shifting cultivators can instead be partners in development.

Programmes in CBRM from 1974 to 1981 include the following: Forest Occupancy Management, Citizen Tree Planting, Communal Tree Farming, Family Approach to Reforestation and Industrial Tree Plantation. In 1982, all these programmes were consolidated into an Integrated Social Forestry programme (ISF) which provided security of land tenure in the form of a Certificate of Stewardship Contract for 25 years renewable for another 25 years for forest occupants residing in these areas prior to 31 December, 1981.

Encouraged by some positive indications of reversal in the destructive attitudes of forest occupants towards the forest with the implementation of the ISF, the National Forestation programme (NPF) which contracts out reforestation projects to individual farmers and communities and the Communal Forest Management Programme (CFMP) with tenurial security instruments were additionally implemented. These forestry CBRM include: (1) community organization and training, (2) contract reforestation, (3) upland development, (4) sustainable forest utilization, (5) timber stand improvement, (6) assisted natural regeneration, (7) forest protection and conservation; and (8) development of livelihood systems.

Some major problems presently encountered in the implementation of forestry CBRM are:

- Low levels of skills, capabilities and inappropriate attitudes of ISF personnel, as well as NGO contractors;
- Unrealistic targets and inadequate funding;
- Lack of co-ordination among involved government agencies;
- The sale of Certificate of Stewardship Contracts;
- Poor organization of communities.

In 1995, CBRM for the forestry sector was strengthened by the issuance of Presidential Executive Order No. 263, adopting the Community-Based Forestry Programme for sustainable forest management.

Fisheries

The evolution of CBRM and co-management in the fisheries sector is well described by Muñoz (1993) and Pomeroy (1995). Community authority over fishing rights was strong during the pre-colonial years but was replaced by strong municipal government control during the Spanish and American periods of occupancy. This was reinforced by Presidential Decree 704, or the Fishery Act of 1975.

The impetus which brought about the need for greater involvement of local communities in the management of fishery resources was the enactment of the Local Government Code (LGC) of 1991 which devolved to local governments the responsibility for the delivery of certain basic services that formerly belonged to the sectorally orientated national agencies. Earlier, however, the Department of Agriculture have launched the Fishery Sector Programme (FSP) in 1987 which was funded by the ADB and the OECF. The FSP focused on coastal fisheries, aquaculture and offshore and EEZ waters. Among others, support policies for FSP included decentralizing the management of near shore fishery resources to municipalities and local fishing communities as well as promoting community-based initiatives to rehabilitate, conserve and protect the coastal resources and to diversity the incomes source of small-scale fisherfolk toward other income opportunities. NGOs will be engaged to assist and undertake community organizing. Fishery co-management was also embodied in the Medium-Term Development Plan (1993–1998). Community-based management of fishery resources will be further bolstered by the impending Fisheries Code proposed by the legislative branch of the government.

Irrigation

The National Irrigation Administration the (NIA) is mandated as the national agency to promote the development of projects to supply irrigation water to farms by virtue of Republic Act No. 3601 enacted on 22 June, 1963. During the next ten years after its establishment, NIA focused on physical construction and yet it was the maintenance and operation (0 & M) which were the principal problems encountered. In an attempt to solve them, in 1968 the NIA evolved an institutional development scheme for mobilizing the active participation of irrigation water users. The users were involved in project identification, planning, construction, operation and maintenance. The success of this approach was largely because of the promulgation of supportive policies: an amendment to Presidential Decree No. 552 which empowered the NIA to carry out the 'delegation of the partial or full management of national irrigation systems to duly organized co-operatives or associations' (Galvez 1993).

The participatory approach was very successful for the communal irrigation system and this experience was transferred to the National Irrigation System. The implementation of this approach has shown that the following could be achieved (Bagadion 1990):

- more responsible irrigation associations,
- increased contribution by farmers,
- acceptance of completed facilities and financial obligations,
- better canal maintenance,
- more collections of fees,
- fewer water conflicts, and
- greater acceptance of 0 & M responsibilities.

At present, more and more Irrigators Associations are engaged in undertaking co-operative projects beyond 0 & M responsibilities.

Mining sector

The inclusion of a small-scale mining (SSM) approach developing the mining industry in the Philippines is well described by Wyco *et al.* (1993). Recognition of the importance of SSM first caught the attention of government when, during early 1980s, SSM were proliferating throughout the country while large-scale mining was finding it hard to survive. SSM has a shorter development. It is estimated that capital invested in SSM nation-wide is smaller than in equivalent large-scale mining at the time that most large mines were failing. It is also less sensitive to international economic pressures. Problems on operation, sanitary and environmental pollution must, however, be addressed appropriately.

Policy support for SSM was provided by Presidential Decree No. 1899 promulgated in 1984 which simplified procedures for obtaining SSM permits and Republic Act No. 71076 promulgated in 1991 which created the People's Small-Scale Mining Programme.

CBRM LESSONS

The implementation of CBRM projects in the Philippines has provided various perspectives and lessons (Fellizar 1993). For example, the key elements essential to the CBRM approach are the following:

1. The role of community organizing involves putting up the necessary organizational structure, as well as in improving the communities' capacity to manage their affairs;

2. It focuses on opportunities for improvement while paying attention to community tradition;

3. Change agents are viewed as enabler-facilitators;

4. A major goal should be to improve the decision-making capacity of the community; this involves increasing options while reducing risks.

There are at least five principles associated with CBRM strategies such as:

- as a process;
- as a participatory approach;
- concerned with conservation and sustainable use of resources;
- linking local and national policy levels;
- providing necessary incentives.

CBRM, to be effective, must be necessarily be anchored on peoples' needs, capacity and that financial, technical and educational inputs must be compatible with the needs and capacities of communities. A landmark piece of legislation, the Local Government Code (LGC), passed by the Philippine Congress on 10 October, 1991 provides the legislative backing for the full implementation of CBRM by Local Government Units (LGUs). However, the capacities of LGUs must be increased to make fully use of the legislative powers provided to them to implement CBRM (Brillantes 1993).

In all cases, CBRM strategies can only be implemented and sustained if the needed policy support is also provided.

THE MAIN ROAD TO CBRM

The collective experiences of CBRM implementation in the Philippines indicate that it is characterized by a series of four steps or processes that have continuous feedback loops. Each process is also performed using a set of tools or methodologies as well as activities. A common set of guiding principles, however, applies to the tools or methodologies used as well as the activities performed for all the steps involved in CBRM.

Guiding principles

The common guiding principles for CBRM tools/methodologies and activities are the following:

- *Needs based*: the perceived needs of the community and the stakeholders should serve as the basis for actions in the implementation of CBRM
- *Participatory*: in the conduct of all the steps and procedures in CBRM the community and all the other stakeholders should be involved and must actively participate.
- *Incorporate cultural practices and indigenous knowledge*: CBRM must start where the people are: their prevailing beliefs, practices and knowledge systems.
- *Holistic and interdisciplinary*: this refers to the methodologies used, the mode of scientific investigation which should be used as well as the analysis in the formulation of plans, programmes and possible impacts of CBRM interventions.

- *Incorporate gender concern*: CBRM must consider the 'gender lens' for generating the needs and resource pattern analysis so that appropriate groups can participate in the development process.
- *Rapid and timely*: this calls for holistic but rapid and appropriate methods for resource and social analysis such as participatory rapid rural appraisal and agro-ecosystem analysis.

Steps and procedures in CBRM

The steps and procedures in CBRM actually follow the regular project development cycle of assessment, planning, implementation and monitoring and evaluation (Figure 12.2). The major difference is the community organizing intervention that must be present in all the steps or procedures of CBRM. Another is that the tools/methodologies applied as well as the activities involved are participatory and characterized by the guiding principles in CBRM.

Methodologies and activities

❧ *Participatory assessment*

Participatory assessment is primarily involved not only in the assessment of the resource base but the interactions between the community and its natural resource bases. It should assess what, where, how much, who controls and other patterns of resource use by the community. The methods used here can be a sequence of application of participatory methodologies starting with Participatory Rapid Appraisal, Agro-Ecosystem Analysis (PRA/AE) followed by a more focused resource inventory (GIS), a socio-economic survey, gender analysis, extended cost benefit analysis and ecological profiling, depending on the results of PRA/AE as well as time and resource constraints. Using PRA/AE, action programmes as well as research areas can be identified that will serve as inputs for the planning phase.

❧ *Participatory planning*

The participatory planning process must necessarily involve the community and all other identified stakeholders of the resources in the area. It will revolve around five major areas: technology, institutional design, policy support, economic incentives and political legitimization. The plans should be assessed for its social acceptability, ecological appropriateness and economic viability.

❧ *Community-based project implementation*

Project implementation by the community will be related to livelihood, resource conservation and protection, boundary delineation, training and organizational arrangements. Community organizing will be an important component of this process. Support activities for providing tenurial security, institutional linkages,

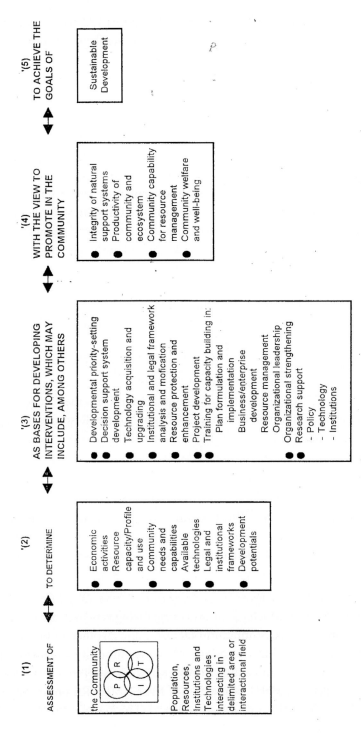

Figure 12.2: Conceptual framework for community-based resource management

credit facilities (when appropriate) and research support will also form part of this process including the needed policy support. Political legitimization is also needed for this phase of CBRM implementation.

ᔭ *Participatory monitoring and evaluation*
The community should be involved in the monitoring and evaluation process. A set of sustainability indicators which combine social, economic and ecological parameters should be generated by all parties involved the various hierarchical levels; farm/household, landscape/community, regional and national. The major indicator at the higher levels will be related to policy support to promote local level sustainability. The monitoring and evaluation process for CBRM projects will feed back into the various steps involved in CBRM implementation. In an input–output form, the CBRM inputs are comprised of inputs from various actors at various hierarchical levels: CO, NGOs, business sector, technical (management, communication, technology, research etc.), policy and financial. The process will consist of the steps involved in CBRM, and the outputs will be comprised of community capacity building, increased productivity, conservation of resources, co-operative action and CBRM supportive policies.

THE ROAD TO CBRM: OF ENTRIES, TOLLS, BENDS AND DEAD-ENDS

Based on several CBRM projects in the Philippines and from the conclusion of the International Workshop on Community-Based Natural Resource Management in Washington 10–14 DC May 1998, sponsored by the World Bank, the road to CBRM is influenced by several variables which need to be well defined.

What will constitute the community?
The community should consider social, geographical and resource aspects. The bottom line, however, is that CBRM requires the participation of all stakeholders in the development of policy and the empowerment of communities to act as collective managers of their natural resources for sustainable development.

What is the most appropriate way of organizing communities for CBRM?
There are several ways by which community organizing is being conducted for CBRM. One is conflict-based community organizing and an other is opportunity-based community organizing (Bagadion 1995). Community organizing for CBRM in Mount Makiling in Laguna Province in the Philippines was issue or conflict-based (Bagadion 1993), while that of the CAMPFIRE programme in Zimbabwe (Maveneke 1998) was incentive-based. The key questions involved

in community organizing are: what are effective community-based groups? Why organize them and how do you organize them? The road to CBRM is rough and rugged. Developing a community's capability for development is fraught with difficulties and uncertainties. Reaching the desired end is a daunting journey, one having multiple and varied entry points, tolls, bends and possibly dead-ends.Multiple entries are the different approaches, strategies and interventions involved in empowering people and communities. Different resources, capabilities and situations require particular entry points. Tolls are the costs in terms of time, money, human resources and, in some cases, the risks on the part of the individual community worker. Costs are usually borne by the community, the change agent or organizations involved in the project implementation.

Bends involve the unpredicted/unanticipated consequences of certain actions, which, although well-meaning, may lead to disruptions and/or readjustment of strategies and activities. Necessarily, these circumstances and events have inherent costs, that could be detrimental to the overall CBRM goals, but such bends could lead to a better way of doing things, better perspectives and faster and more effective means of implementation.

Dead-ends occur when the original goals of CBRM projects are not achieved owing to reasons involving lack of money and personnel, continuing indifference and incapacity of the community, and other political and social factors that may trigger the discontinuance of projects. They may also occur when the community remains chronically passive and dependent upon external assistance and leadership.

The CBRM projects employ varied interventions depending on the conditions and needs of particular sites. In a study of CBRM project implementation in coastal areas for instance, projects can be categorized according to the different activities and the sequence of activities. Such differences could be due to the orientation and experience of the implementing organizations and those of the grant donors.

The choice of entry point activities is crucial in providing a confidence mechanism for the project implementers. Depending on the immediate needs of the community at the time of project initiation, the most appropriate project intervention must be undertaken. In coastal areas where the resources are subjected to exploitation by big commercial fishing operators, intervention may take the form of empowering the community to deter further destruction of resources through organizing and legal means. In other areas, the initial entry point activities may take the form of; research, resource assessment and monitoring, education and training, community organizing or resource manage-

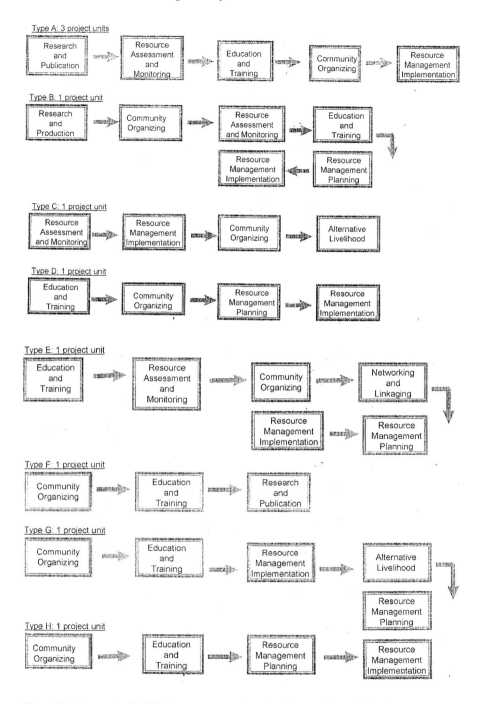

Figure 12.3: Sequence of CBRM programme and project interventions, Philippines, 1984–1994

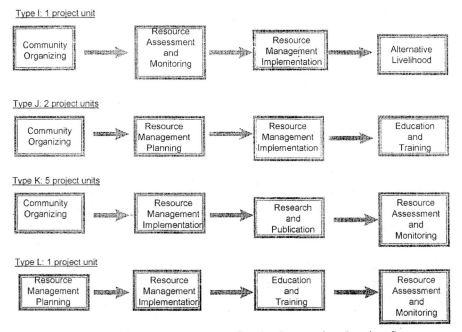

Figure 12.3: Sequence of CBRM programme and project interventions (*continued*)

ment planning. In most cases, however, coastal projects employ community organizing as the most prevalent initial activity. Livelihood development becomes a common element in the entire sequence of activities in most projects in coastal areas (Figure 12.3).

No matter what form and approach entry may take, there is no substitute for genuine community participation. Partnership must be established between the community and the implementers right at the initial stages of the project. In most coastal CBRM projects, it has been observed that:

- early involvement of community members facilitates the development of partnership;

- communities will take responsibility for resource management only if it is clear that they can benefit from management and that they can be effective in their roles as managers;

- social preparation should always precede technical intervention;

- establishment of a formal community or a fisher folk organization is a requirement for effective CBRM programmes and projects;

- in some, organizations evolved only after people themselves recognize the need for the organization;

- continuous education and organization support is critical throughout the project life;
- to be successful, the community members must also invest their own resources in project activities; and
- a need for constant and concerted effort to strengthen institutions and build indigenous capacity to sustain resource management and development actions beyond project life.

Problems arising

'There is no free ride' as the saying goes, as far as CBRM implementation is concerned. Costs vary depending on the demands and needs of the communities. Initial planning for instance already exacts a toll on the community in terms of man hours, that would have been spent in earning a living. In a coastal village, where fishermen go out fishing at night, attending meetings for dialogue and consultations requires a lot of sacrifice. This is the reason why in most consultations, housewives usually are the ones present. For of the project implementers, whether governmental or otherwise, costs are likewise involved. Money, human resources and materials are needed for the continuance of projects.

One issue to be raised here is the willingness of the community and its leadership to bear the costs of the project alongside external project organizations and agencies. There is a tendency for communities to depend on external resources and initiatives for project implementation. This is precisely the reason why education and skills training become an important intervention in the process of community empowerment.

Community is a complex social organization whose needs must be met, capacity enhanced, and there must be opportunities for self-expression and creativity. In some cases, project implementers are more obsessed with project targets and physical accomplishments, thereby losing sight of the very objectives of CBRM. This propensity is usually pronounced in projects with external funding, whose continuance depends greatly on progress reports. Such reports however, more often than not rely heavily on quantitative indicators of progress but they are quite oblivious to the qualitative aspects of community life.

Another counter-productive aspect of CBRM implementation, for which vigilance is needs caution, is the tendency to overload the community with activities and resources way beyond their capacity to manage more responsibly. This is because project implementation is more concerned about meeting schedules than adequately addressing community concerns. A manifestation of this is the usual inclination to prescribe the setting up of co-operatives as a mechanism for self-help and project implementation. Many failures have resulted from such a move. This is not to say, however, that co-operatives are bad *per se*. The point being raised is the need to be more sensitive to the desires and capabilities of the community instead of prescribing options that may have worked in some areas previously. In a recent planning exercise for CBRM in Calancan Bay, Marinduque, it was revealed that the community heartily disliked co-operatives as the organizational mechanism. Instead, they prefer family-based enterprises but supported by a common facilitating mechanism such as market assistance.

There are cases, too, in some projects where the implementers are too enamoured of organizing work as a panacea, subsequently discovering that the community was actually more organized than they had imagined. At times organizing becomes more detrimental to the existing informal institutions, even to the extent of losing cultural integrity. Indeed, there are bends that caution implementers to slow down, to adjust strategies, to recalibrate them so that they are attuned to the current realities and capabilities of the community being assisted.

Sustainable CBRM projects are desired. There is, therefore, an imperative to ensure that projects being planned and implemented are certain to achieve their avowed objectives. There are warning signs that need proper consideration. These include among others: the growing and persistent indifference of the community to the project despite efforts and resources being plowed into it; the presence of antagonistic community leaders due to past negative experiences; inappropriate planning and implementation strategies; the lack of a supportive policy environment for the project; and total dependence on external resources for project implementation.

Avoiding dead ends necessarily requires sensitivity to and adequate knowledge of the community realities and the capacity to determine, together with the community, the most appropriate package of intervention and strategies with the end view of sustaining such efforts. Confidence-building mechanisms are indeed of great value. These may take the form of pump-priming activities, organizing and managing community funds, having a dedicated and respectable change agent and/or reputable support group, and a clear, realistic and shared vision.

CONCLUDING REMARKS

The application of CBRM strategies to sustainable development requires entirely new approaches and perspectives aimed at integrating people's concerns and capacities in the planning and implementation of projects. To those who are used to top-down approaches, CBRM involves a paradigm shift and a radical shift in methodologies and orientation.

Gaining entry to and building trust in the community is very crucial at the initial stages of the project. Also critical is the process of strengthening or establishing organizations which the local people will regard as their own – as structures and channels which can be made to work for their net benefit. The majority of costs (tolls) for maintaining these organizations have to be borne by the communities, households and individuals. External assistance should be provided only in positive-sum ways that must not substitute for local contributions. The concepts of pump-priming and catalytic influence should help in building confidence in the community rather than creating dependency on external organizations and agencies.

Initially, CBRM may require outside assistance to create and strengthen local capabilities for self-managed development. Care must be taken not to superimpose external ideas and preferences over those of the community's. Rather, more serious and systematic efforts should be undertaken to recognize the 'bends' and undertake measures to continually upgrade local institutional frameworks and strategies for mobilizing and managing resources and opportunities to meet the community's economic, social, political and cultural needs. All these efforts require sensitivity and continuing readjustment of activities and approaches, combining alternatives in a 'both-and' manner instead of a narrowly conceived 'either-or' stance.

Ensuring the sustainability of CBRM projects may require early recognition of danger signs of possible dead ends. Actions must be taken to install the appropriate monitoring and feedback mechanisms to immediately remedy any dysfunction in the project implementation. It has to be noted, however, that the real avoidance of dead ends depends to a greater extent on the capability of the community to manage their own development and to a certain extent on the facilitating and supportive roles of partner agencies and organizations.

Much has yet to be learned in so far as CBRM design and implementation in the Philippines is concerned. As earlier indicated, the road to CBRM is bumpy and cluttered with a host of uncertainties and tests. The learning goes on, as there are more entries to check, tolls to care, bends to negotiate and dead-ends to avoid.

Traversing the road to CBRM, demands collective wisdom, strength and commitment from everyone - the implementers, policymakers, researchers and academics, and the peoples in the community. Together, CBRM can be made more effective and, yes, sustainable.

REFERENCES

Bagadion, B.U. Jr (1990) *The NIA Experience in the Participatory Approach.* NIA–Ford Foundation Program. Quezon City, Philippines: NIA.

—— (1993) 'Notes and observations on community-based resource management'. In F.P. Fellizar Jr (ed.), *CBRM: Perspective, Experiences and Policy Issues.* ERMP Report # 6. College, Laguna and Halifax, Nova Scotia.

—— (1995) 'Environmental management and public participation: reinventing collective action'. Paper presented at the First Pacific Environment Conference. Beijing, PROC, September, 1995.

Brillantes, A.B. Jr (1993) *The Philippines Local Government Code of 1991: Issues and Concerns in the Environment Sector.* ERMP, College, Laguna, Philippines.

Fellizar, F. Jr (1993) *Community-Based Research Management: Perspective, Experiences and Policy Issues.* ERMP, College, Laguna, Phillipines.

Galvez, J.B. (1993) 'Community-based resource management perspectives experiences and policy issues related to irrigation'. In F.P. Fellizar Jr (ed.) *Community-Based Resource Management: Perspectives, Experiences and Policy Issues.* College, Laguna, Philippines, pp. 103–108.

Maveneke, T.N. (1998) 'Local participation as an instrument for natural resource management under the communal areas management program for indigenous resources, (CAMPFIRE) in Zimbabwe'. Paper presented at International Workshop on C13NRIVI. Washington DC, 10–14 May, 1998.

Muñoz, J.C. (1993) 'Community-based resource management as an approach for implementing coastal resources management component of the fishery sector program'. In F.P. Fellizar, Jr (ed.), *Community-Based Resource Management: Perspectives, Experience and Policy Issues.* College, Laguna, Philippines, pp. 82–89.

Pomeroy, R.S. (1995) 'Co-management institutions for sustainable fisheries management in southeast asia. Paper prepared under the Auspices of the ICLARM North Sea Centre Collaborative research project on Fisheries Co-management projected funded by Danida.

Pomeroy, R.S. and M.B. Carlos (1996) *Review and Evaluation of Community-Based Coastal Resources Management Projects in the Philippines, 1984–1994.* International Center for Living Aquatic Resources Management (ICLARM).

Sajise P.E. *et al.* (1990) *U.P. National Assessment Project.* State of the Philippine Environment. UP Press.

Serna, C.B. (1993) 'Community-based resource management: perspectives, experiences and policy issues related to forestry and upland development'. In F.P. Fellizar, Jr (ed.), *Community Based Resource Management: Perspectives, Experiences and Policy Issues.* College, Laguna, Philippines, pp. 64–81.

CHAPTER THIRTEEN

Fisheries Co-management: Key Conditions and Principles Drawn from Asian Experiences

ROBERT S. POMEROY, BRENDA M. KATON AND INGVILD HARKES

INTRODUCTION

*I*n 1994, the International Center for Living Aquatic Resources Management (ICLARM) in Manila, Philippines and the Institute for Fisheries Management (IFM) at the North Sea Centre, Hirtshals, Denmark initiated the Fisheries Co-management Research Project in collaboration with national research partners (NARS) in several Asian and African countries. The collaboration between ICLARM, IFM and NARS was based on a mutual interest in gaining practical experience in research in fisheries co-management; to demonstrate its applicability as a sustainable, equitable and efficient management strategy; and to develop models for use and adoption by governments, fisheries communities, NGOs and others. The first phase of the project ended in 1998 and a second phase is planned.

The project strategy is to conduct research in a variety of aquatic resource systems and countries around the world. The selection of several different aquatic resource systems and countries of the to implement the project is to determine whether fisheries co-management can be a viable management strategy under varying conditions (political, social, cultural, economic, biophysical, technological). The overall purpose of the project is to determine the prospects for successful implementation of fisheries co-management strategies. The project will not advocate or promote fisheries co-management but systematically and comparatively document and assess models and processes of co-management at national government and community levels and their results and impacts. General principles and conditions which facilitate successful implementation of fisheries co-management will be identified.

It is this last sentence which is the subject of this chapter. The purpose of this chapter is to present results of the research: specifically, key principles and conditions which facilitate the successful implementation of co-management, as identified through the project's research activities in Asia. These research results represent just one set of results from the various activities of the project. The chapter will begin with a discussion of the strategy and data sources used in the research. Conditions and principles identified through the research will be discussed in the next section. The chapter will conclude with policy implications for fisheries co-management in Asia and world-wide.

RESEARCH STRATEGY AND DATA SOURCES

Data for this paper comes from research undertaken by ICLARM staff and NARS partners in the Philippines, Vietnam, Thailand, Malaysia, Indonesia, and Bangladesh between 1994 and 1999. Over 25 individual research projects and activities were undertaken during the life of the project. These research projects include: (1) reviews of community-based coastal resource management and co-management experiences in Vietnam (Thong et al. 1996) and Thong and Thieu 1998); Philippines (Carlos and Pomeroy 1996), Indonesia (Nikijuluw 1996), and Thailand (Tokrisna et al. 1997); (2) case study analysis in Bangladesh (Khan and Apu 1998 and Thompson *et al.* 1998), Thailand (Masae 1998), Indonesia (Nikijuluw 1996 and Novaczek and Harkes 1998), Vietnam (Van and Hai 1998), and Philippines (Pomeroy and Pido 1995, Katon *et al.* 1997, Katon *et al.* 1998, Baticados and Agbayani 1998, and van Mulekom and Tria 1999); (3) impact evaluation of co-management arrangements (Pomeroy *et al.* 1996); (4) hypothesis testing of advantages or benefits of co-management (Kuperan *et al.* 1997, Kuperan *et al.* 1998, Harkes 1998); (5) government legal, institutional and policy analysis (University of the Philippines 1996, Fellizar *et al.* 1997, and Torell 1998); and (6) meetings and workshops (Foltz *et al.* 1996 and Pido et al. 1996). This chapter is a synthesis of some of the findings from this body of research. In addition to the above research projects, selected secondary publications were used as references.

CONDITIONS AND PRINCIPLES FOR SUCCESSFUL CO-MANAGEMENT

Some of the conditions and principles presented here are already known, while others are new. It should be noted that this is not a definitive list of conditions and principles but is hopefully another step forward in identifying those conditions and principles that can lead to successful implementation of fisheries co-management. If these conditions are met, the chances of achieving viable co-management arrangements are enhanced. If not, an alternative management strategy may be more appropriate.

The importance of each condition to the successful implementation of fisheries co-management will be rated based on a scale of high, medium and low. (Note that the score for each condition will be presented in parentheses after the condition title.) A score of 'high' indicates that the condition was identified as being critically important for success in more than 15 of the research reports and workshop or meeting papers of the project. A score of 'medium' indicates that the condition was found to be important for success in eight to 15 of the research reports and workshop or meeting papers. A score of 'low' indicates that the condition was identified as being of low importance for success in less than eight research reports and workshop or meeting papers of the project.

The conditions that came out of the Asian experience are largely changeable conditions. They are capable of being shaped by policy, project interventions and other appropriate measures. Only a few of these conditions may be classified as existing at the time co-management was introduced but are not strictly unchangeable. These include: existence of an individual incentive structure, availability of a conflict management mechanism, overlap of interests among the partners, adequate financial resources and species to be managed.

Individual incentive structure (high)

The success of co-management hinges directly on an incentive structure (economic, social, political) that induces various individuals to participate in the process. Such individuals may include a resource user, a resource stakeholder or a politician. The co-management process often involves giving up individual short-term benefits for real and perceived long-term benefits. Often, the short-term costs are high in terms of lost income or voluntary labour. For a poor fisher with a family to feed, the incentive structure to support and participate in co-management must be clear and large. Risk is involved for the individual in changing management strategy. The fisher must understand and agree to the co-management arrangements. Fishers must recognize an incentive for co-management before the process begins and/or need information to further develop their understanding and recognition of the incentive. The recognition of resource management problems may take the form of a progressive decrease in fish catch, disappearance of valuable species, declining mangrove stands and existence of resource use conflicts. An impetus is needed to propel co-management forward (Pomeroy and Berkes 1997). In successful cases of co-management in the Philippines, awareness of resource-related problems prompted stakeholders to enter into collective action, particularly in communities that are heavily dependent on coastal resources and are vulnerable to non-sustainable resource uses (Katon *et al.* 1997; Katon *et al.* 1998; Baticados and Agbayani 1998). This is largely due to the threats to survival, economic livelihood and food security that deteriorating resource conditions bring about.

The incentive may start simply as a hope for a better tomorrow but usually 'matures' as the individual gains more information and as the process develops over time. It is often easier and faster to implement co-management arrangements where the resource user recognizes an incentive for participation on their own and undertakes action rather than when an incentive is presented to a resource user by an external agent. One method to measure that an incentive structure for participation and action does exist in a community is when the community members invest their own resources (labour, money) in the project.

Different incentive structures appeal to different individuals. For an individual resource user, the incentive may be economic, primarily in terms of higher income, food availability or protection of livelihoods (Thompson *et al.* 1998; Khan and Apu 1998). It may also be social, in the form of higher prestige among peers or legitimate access to coastal resources (Segura-Ybanez 1996; Katon *et al.* 1997; Baticados and Agbayani 1998). Economic incentives are also important to resource stakeholders, such as fish traders and processors, who are directly dependent on a steady supply of fish products for their livelihood. For resort owners, dive tour operators and managers of tourist-related businesses, the preservation of coastal ecosystems and the maintenance of clean coastal waters are vital because these have a direct bearing on the earnings they derive from those who patronize their businesses.

Other resource stakeholders may be motivated by different incentives. The concern for stable ecosystems, food security for present and future generations, improved living conditions and equitable property rights often underlie the motivation of development advocates, external agents and members of resource management councils. The reduction of conflicts and the streamlining of plans and policies through co-management arrangements may motivate government administrators, planners and policy-makers to support co-management.

For politicians, the incentive to support co-management may be rooted in the desire to be recognized for their achievements in governance and resource management. Such achievements strengthen their capacity to win more votes from a broader base of constituents and improve their chances of being re-elected to positions of power and influence.

Leadership (high)
Local leadership is a critical and necessary condition for the success of co-management. Local leaders set an example for others to follow, set out courses of action and provide energy and direction for the co-management process.

261

While a community may have leaders, they may not be the correct or appropriate leaders for co-management. Local elites may be the traditional leaders in a community, but they may not be the appropriate leaders for a resource conservation and management effort. Leaders may need to be drawn or developed from the ranks of resource users. These individuals may be more acceptable and respected by their peers. In Bangladesh, the local leaders of the *baors* (lakes) were identified and elected by the fishers. The leader's term of office was limited so as to give others the chance to gain leadership skills and to reduce the possibility of corruption (Khan and Apu 1998). Reliance on one individual as a leader can be a problem. In certain Philippine cases, projects failed when the leader died, left political office or left the area because there was no one to take the leader's place (Katon *et al.* 1998). The external change agents must not act as leaders because the community will become dependent upon them. The community must look inward to develop local leadership itself. Training and education efforts must strive to build and develop leadership skills among a variety of individuals in the community so that the co-management activity does not become dependent on any one person.

Core group formation is strategic in identifying and developing leaders (Buhat 1994). The members of the core group may be drawn from committed individuals who consistently participate in co-management activities and who share a concern for sustainable resource management. Core groups normally take responsibility for the initial implementation of co-management strategies. From their ranks, capable leaders often emerge to guide present and future undertakings. Documented experiences affirm that locally recruited and trained leaders, both formal and informal, are a potent force in mobilizing residents for collective endeavours, spearheading awareness campaigns and outreach efforts and motivating stakeholders to take action (Pomeroy *et al.* 1996; Katon *et al.* 1997).

Empowerment (high)
The marginalization of coastal communities has led to the problems of poverty and resource degradation. Addressing marginalization would require empowerment or the actual transfer of economic and political power from a few to the impoverished majority. By transferring the access and control of resources from a few to the community at large, the community is gradually empowered in the economic realm. Simultaneously, political empowerment ensues as community management and control over the resource are effectively operationalized (Addun and Muzones 1997).

Individual and community empowerment is a central element of co-management. Empowerment is concerned with the capability-building of individuals and community in order for them to have greater social awareness, to gain greater autonomy over decision-making, to gain greater self-reliance and to establish a balance in community power relations. Empowerment covers a range of actions including enhancing community access to information and services, ensuring community participation, developing critical consciousness or consciousness-raising of the people and gaining control over the utilization and management of natural resources. Empowerment can be considered as an individual and a community desire to change something. Empowerment is undertaken at individual and community levels. Individual empowerment leads to community empowerment. The empowerment process must be balanced since it may have differential impacts on the community, leading to a mere redistribution of power elites instead of a balance of power. There is a tendency for rural power structures to gain control over resources. Co-management can be easily hijacked by the shifting power holders. Empowerment reduces social stratification and allows groups in the community to work on a more equal level with the local elite (Thompson *et al.* 1998; Khan and Apu 1998).

Empowerment is only functional if it is based on the socio-cultural and political context of the community. The co-management process needs to adopt a gender-balanced perspective and must acknowledge the position of women. Women should be given the opportunity to develop themselves and actively participate in the co-management process (Foltz *et al.* 1996).

Individual and collective empowerment are enhanced by capability building through education and training efforts that raise the level of knowledge and information of those involved in the co-management process. Co-management often requires a conscious effort to develop and strengthen the capability of the partners for collective action, co-operation, power sharing, dialogue, leadership and sustainable resource management. Coastal villagers may not always have a tradition of collective action. Functioning organizations of resource users may not be in place. Moreover, the range of skills and knowledge required to address the complex dimensions of resource management may not be adequate. In these cases, capability building is a must.

To reverse the effects of destructive fishing practices, change non-sustainable practices or provide viable alternatives, people must learn new management skills and new technologies. Appropriate knowledge, skills and attitudes are vital in preparing them to carry out new tasks and meet future challenges (Pomeroy *et al.* 1996). Capability building must address not only technical and managerial dimensions but also attitudes and behavioural patterns. Training and education may include leadership, situation analysis and problem-solving, consensus building, value reorientation, technology application, livelihood and enterprise management, conflict management, advocacy, facilitation, networking, ecological and socio-economic monitoring and evaluation, and legal/para-legal, among others. In the Philippines and other Asian countries, the experience affirms that capability building strengthens the confidence and sense of empowerment of resource users and partners. Providing opportunities to visit communities with successful resource management projects also helps create the enthusiasm and the motivation to embark on similar activities in their own village (Katon *et al.* 1997). Capability building, moreover, enables local residents to sustain resource management interventions and pursue new initiatives.

Social preparation and value formation (high)
Linked to empowerment is social preparation and value formation. The inability to sustain co-management may be partly attributed to the insufficient time allocated to the social preparation phase of the process and to rapport building and value formation in the community. Social preparation should always precede technical and material interventions. Cutting corners during the social preparation phase to yield to pressures to produce material accomplishments is likely to weaken the foundation for self-reliance in the community. Good social preparation is manifested in positive attitudes towards collective action and in the readiness of community members to take on responsibility for resource management and decision-making (Pomeroy *et al.* 1996).

Trust between partners (high)
No co-management arrangement can survive unless a relationship of trust and mutual respect is developed and maintained between the partners. The establishment of trust between partners usually takes a long time to develop and takes concerted effort by the partners. There is some risk involved by the partners in participating in co-management. Fishers usually have a low level of trust of government, for example. Trust will require the development of good communication channels and open and ongoing dialogue. Meeting objectives and mutually agreed targets enhances trust. These actions reduce risk and stimulate partner cohesion which will have a positive effect on building trust. This can be started in the early stages of the co-management process and strengthened over time. In the Oxbow Lakes of Bangladesh, trust was developed among the fishers by upholding the rules. Those individuals who consistently disobeyed the rules were dismissed from the fisher organization (Khan and Apu 1998).

Providing forums for discussion are fundamental to developing trust among partners. A process must be developed to understand needs and expectations of all partners. In some cases, needs and expectations may not be straight-

forward. Values held by different groups, including cultural, religious and traditional beliefs, must be respected. Public discussions that encourage a free and
non-threatening exchange of information foster effective communication. Dialogue clarifies an understanding of needs, expected roles, extent of responsibility
sharing among partners and expected benefits and costs in the short term and
long term, among others (Baticados and Agbayani 1998).

Property rights over the resource (high)
Property rights, either individual or collective, should address the legal ownership of the resource and define the mechanisms (economic, administrative, collective) and the structures required for allocating use rights to optimize use and
ensure conservation of resources, and the means and procedures for enforcement.
The case studies in the Philippines show that when user rights are specified and
secure (such as with a mangrove certificate of stewardship contract), there is a
change in the behaviour and attitude of the resource user toward conservation
and a much greater chance that the intervention will be maintained. Without
legally supported property rights, resource users have no standing to enforce
their claim over the resource against outsiders. In most cases, local initiatives
require active collaboration with government to protect and enforce user rights
(Pomeroy *et al.* 1996). Local interventions were sustained where property rights
existed, were clear and were enforced (Pomeroy *et al.* 1996).

Organizations (high)
Co-management requires the existence of legitimate organizations that have a
clearly defined membership. These organizations should have the legal right to
exist and to make arrangements related to their needs. The organizations must
be allowed to be autonomous from government and political pressure. They are
vital channels for representing resource users and stakeholders, asserting property
rights and rules and influencing the direction of policies and decision-making.
The organization will need to be recognized as legitimate by the community
members, resource users and stakeholders to be able to carry out its mandate.
The organization should also represent the majority of resource users in the
community.

   In the Philippines, the formal recognition by the government of the role of
resource users as valuable partners in development confers legitimacy to the
establishment of co-management organizations and favours the pursuit of co-
management arrangements. People's organizations are formally allowed to enter
into partnerships with local government units on a broad range of concerns
such as promotion of ecological balance, local enterprise development, delivery
of basic services, capability building and enhancement of the economic and social

well-being of the people (Katon *et al.* 1997). The more successful community-based co-management projects in the Philippines were those where organizing is not a prerequisite but rather the community organization evolves after the people recognize the need for it (Sandalo 1994).

Conflict management mechanism (high)
Arbitration and resolution of disputes are imperative when conflicts arise over co-management and institutional arrangements. If resource users are to follow rules, a mechanism for discussing and resolving conflicts and infractions is a must. There is a need for a forum for resource users to debate and resolve conflicts and to appeal decisions. Conflict management should be conducted at the local level where solutions can be found quickly. It is often useful to have a mediator who can objectively assess and propose solutions to the conflict. While the government can act as an outside mediator for local conflicts and as an appeal body, heavy reliance on the government to resolve conflicts is not good. Co-management thrives in a situation where forums and appeal bodies are available for deliberation and conflict resolution. The Philippine and Bangladesh experiences show that conflict management tends to be less problematic when the resource users are involved in rule formulation and enforcement and when sanctions are imposed on the rule violators (Katon *et al.* 1997; Katon *et al.* 1998; Khan and Apu 1998).

Partnerships and partner sense of ownership of the co-management process (high)
Active participation of partners in the planning and implementation process is directly related to their sense of ownership and commitment to the co-management arrangements. Partners involved in co-management need to feel that the process not only benefits them, but that they have a strong sense of participation in, commitment to and ownership of the process. External agents working to plan and implement the co-management arrangements must allow the partners to recognize themselves as the owners and directors of the process. Early and continuous participation of partners in planning and implementation of co-management is related to success (Pomeroy *et al.* 1996). This allows partners to demonstrate their commitment to the process. Not only does this type of involvement serve to adapt activities to local needs but partners also gain a better understanding of the problems involved in implementation and a greater sense of empowerment and confidence. Objectives need to be developed jointly by the partners and external change agents.

Partnerships in co-management must grow out of a mutual sense of commitment (Segura-Ybanez 1996). Adequate co-ordination, communication and consultation are necessary. It is important to have clarification about each other's role, goals, purpose, operation, style and limitations (Carlos and Pomeroy 1996). The process of clarification must take place through equitable dialogue and partnerships. When the actions of collaborating partners are not synchronized and consistent, resource users see too many role 'players', and this may lead to misconceptions and wrong expectations, and eventually hamper success. Thus an appropriate operational structure and agreement should always be developed based on the needs of co-management arrangement so that co-ordination between partners will be effective without being too costly to the structure.

Effective enforcement (high)

Vigorous, fair and sustained law enforcement requires the participation of all partners. Enforcement can be carried out separately by an enforcement unit, or in collaboration between local informal or traditional enforcers (church, senior fishers, local leaders) and formal enforcers (police, coast guard). Local enforcement efforts may need to be backed up by government enforcement bodies to ensure objectivity. It may be necessary to have government law enforcement agencies involved in dealing with outsiders in order to have better co-operation.

The motivation to comply with regulations depends upon rational decisions where the expected benefits of violating the rules are measured against the risk of getting apprehended and penalized. It is also linked to socio-cultural mechanisms that regulate behaviour (fear of ancestral spirits, social exclusion, moral obligation). A key variable for determining compliance is the individual's perspective of the fairness and appropriateness of the law and its institutions (Kuperan et al. 1996). The willingness to comply is linked to the perceived legitimacy of the authorities charged with implementing the regulations. Local enforcers (*Bantay Dagat* in the Philippines, *kewang* in Indonesia) can be very effective provided they are formally legitimized. Rules should be simple so those affected by them can easily understand and comply. There needs to be good communication between the enforcement unit and the resource user group.

Adequate financial resources/budget (high)

Co-management requires financial resources to support the process. Funds need to be available to support various operations and facilities related to planning, implementation, co-ordination, monitoring, and enforcement, among others. Funding, especially sufficient, timely and sustained funding, is critical to the sustainability of co-management efforts (Segura-Ybanez 1996). In many instances, resource user organizations are unable to continue existing programmes or start new ones due to limited financial resources that members can raise on their own. Often co-management projects which are initiated and funded from outside sources fail when the project finishes due to the inability of the partners to fund the activities. Funds also need to be made available on a timely basis to sustain and maintain interventions. The co-management arrangements must be supported and accepted so that partners will be confident enough in the process to invest their own funds and time. Co-management must be designed from the start with a secure internal budget source. Community members will need to invest their own financial resources in the process. Too much dependence on external sources will have an impact upon sustainability of the arrangements (Carlos and Pomeroy 1996).

Appropriate scale (high)
Scale is fundamental in most co-management initiatives. The scale for co-management arrangements should be appropriate to the area's ecology, people and level of management. This includes the size of the physical area to be managed and how many members should be included in an organization so that it is representative but not so large as to be unworkable. Decisions on physical scale include not only the boundaries of the area to be managed but also the species or ecosystem level to be managed. The scale of the management unit should be appropriate for the human resources and the ecology of the area. The boundaries should be based on an ecosystem that the resource users can easily observe and understand. In terms of members, it is observed that small groups are more manageable than larger groups. In co-management where a great number of people are involved, it is wise to divide them into smaller groups to facilitate and enhance supervision, control and management. In general, a limited scale (both in terms of membership and jurisdiction) will support participatory democracy and therefore enhance co-management provided that the management structure has appropriate stature and power to initiate the process. Expansion of scale is easier once initial activities succeed and are sustained, that is, start small and simple and show results early (Buhat 1994).

Stakeholder involvement (medium)
Partners in co-management need to recognize that the stakeholder community is broader than the local resource user community. Stakeholders are defined as organizations, social groups and individuals that possess a specific, direct and significant stake or interest in the resource and area (IUCN 1996). They are motivated to take action on the basis of their interests and values. Stakeholders include, but are not limited to, part-time resource users, resource users from other communities who are dependent on the same resource, traders and business people, boat owners, tourist resort operators and advocates of resource manage-

ment. In a number of cases across Asia, the identification of stakeholders has been made by non-governmental organizations that spearheaded resource management efforts.

A well-balanced representation of stakeholders tends to facilitate a politically neutral process. The process of involving stakeholders is time consuming but may be expected to lead to more acceptable and sustainable arrangements. There should be clearly identified benefits and costs to all stakeholders, both short and long term, for participating as a partner in co-management. It should be recognized that coastal communities are not homogeneous and that there are different viewpoints among the stakeholders. Reaching a consensus on issues can be difficult even in small communities. Issues may need to be addressed on both a community-wide and a resource or species or gear specific basis (Baticados and Agbayani 1998).

Many costal co-management projects have failed because the target audience of the project was only the fishers. The projects failed to consider and/or include the other resource stakeholders in the process. In the Philippines, for example, early community-based management projects focused their activities only on fishers. While this proved useful for the fishers, it often alienated other stakeholders such as fish traders with whom the fishers had a credit-marketing relationship. Through this relationship the fish traders could often control the actions of the fishers. The alienation of the fish traders led them to coerce the fishers to give less active support to the project. This led to eventual breakdown of the organizational and institutional arrangements made under the community-based management project (Carlos and Pomeroy 1996).

For a co-management arrangement to work, it is essential for stakeholders to have a good understanding of each other's positions, needs and apprehensions. The conduct of informal consultations at the outset helps create interest in common issues and allows stakeholders to express their views on alternative management options. Establishing rapport with stakeholders from an early stage is important. This is facilitated by: meeting with leaders of stakeholder groups; showing a genuine interest in local issues; explaining the reasons for touching base with a wide group of people and groups; ensuring that the host community understands the reasons for talking to other stakeholders; and clarifying unrealistic assumptions expressed by community members.

Local political support (medium)
The co-operation of the local government and the local political 'power structure' is necessary to support and participate in the co-management arrangements. As discussed above, there must be an incentive for the local politicians to support

co-management. There must be political willingness to share the benefits, costs, responsibility and authority for co-management. Co-management will not flourish if the local 'power structure' is opposed in any way to the arrangements. The case-studies in the Philippines show this quite clearly. In those communities where the local political 'power structure' was not included in the process or was opposed to the project for some reason, the community-based management interventions failed to be sustained after the project ended (Pomeroy *et al.* 1996). Resource users may lack the confidence and political skills to interact effectively with political officials. It will take time to break down these barriers to allow for partnership. In the Philippines, some fisher organizations take a 'no political alliance' policy and build informal ties with all political parties in a community to 'spread the bet' and protect themselves from political change (van Mulekom and Tria 1999).

External agents (medium)

Co-management often needs external change agents to expedite the process. These external agents assist in defining the problem; provide independent advice, ideas and expertise; guide joint problem-solving and decision-making; initiate management plans; and advocate appropriate policies. The external agent should be objective and serve a catalytic role in the development process. The external agent should not directly interfere in the process but may guide or provide information on how to proceed in the process or with a policy. Documented experiences underscore the role of external agents in setting in place a process of discovery and social learning. These catalysts open the eyes of resource users, stakeholders and partner organizations to pressing issues, urge them to search for appropriate solutions and challenge them to take collective action (Katon *et al.* 1997; Katon *et al.* 1998; Baticados and Agbayani 1998). Change agents may come from NGOs, academic or research institutions, project teams and other groups. External agents should have a temporary relationship with the co-management process, serving their particular function and then phasing out.

In the Philippines and other Asian countries, it is not unusual for coastal communities to be aware of deteriorating resource conditions. However, these communities normally need assistance from external agents in carrying out a thorough situation analysis and digging deeper into the root causes of problems. External agents fill a special role in terms of drawing out insights with a participatory style of facilitation, processing the insights and guiding the community in reaching its goals. Their willingness to spend long hours in the community to work with local people, an ability to focus on community objectives and their linkages with donors and other supportive organizations are among the factors which favour their catalytic role.

However, the recruitment of external agents, such as NGOs, may not always be ideal in establishing co-management. The staff may be young and may not readily be accepted by traditional societies (Claridge and O'Callaghan 1997). Some of them may have ideological views on development that may not be acceptable to the community or the government. Others may be reluctant to involve the government and the business community even though they are stake-holders in resource management. They may also lack funds to finance continuing operations.

Clear objectives from a well-defined set of issues (medium)
The clarity and simplicity of objectives helps steer the direction of co-management. Partners need to understand and agree on the issues to be addressed, know what must be achieved, where the activities are headed, and why. Clear objectives developed from a well-defined set of issues are essential to success. Those involved in the co-management process must see and agree that the issues are important to their daily existence. The co-management process may involve multiple objectives and multiple implementation strategies. These should be prioritized and linked where possible.

Fundamental to co-management is a common understanding of the situation, comprehension of the root causes of the problems and the issues and an agreement on appropriate solutions to the identified problems. A fishery tends to be better managed when resource users, stakeholders and partner organizations have a good grasp of why they are managing the resource and what results are envisaged (Katon *et al.* 1997).

One of the major reasons for failure of certain community-based management projects in the Philippines is lack of problem recognition by resource users. This may sound like a simple issue but due to the top-down approach of many co-management projects, the resource users are really not active but passive recipients of project interventions. The project objectives are conceptualized outside the community and without true community participation. As such, the resource users may not fully recognize the problem in the same way as the external change agent. The resource users may also work with the project only for what they can get out of it, not fully participating for long term success. Of course this is not always the situation. In some cases, the resource users recognize that there is a problem and take the initiative for action themselves.

Networking and advocacy (medium)
Networking is bringing together information and expertise in support of co-management. The development of a network of community organizations is a powerful tool for implementing co-management. Networking of communities

involved in similar resource management issues provides opportunities to learn from others, deepen insights into actual experiences and inspire new initiatives at other sites (Katon *et al.* 1997; Baticados and Agbayani 1998).

Networks may take many forms: alliances of support groups, organizations of stakeholders and federations of resource users. They may be formal or informal. Networking is closely associated with the establishment of four types of linkages: 1) with other communities and projects involved in similar co-management initiatives; 2) with sources of power and influence; 3) with NGOs and business groups; and 4) with donors and government agencies.

Networking is closely associated with advocacy. Advocacy argues the case for a particular course of action or situation. It is the political struggle for the recognition of people's rights at various levels (Addun and Muzones 1997). At the local level, it involves a campaign directed at resource users and stake-holders, formal and informal organizations and local seats of decision-making. At the national level, it involves working towards a federation of fishers through networking, as well as pushing for relevant policy and legislative reforms. If the co-management arrangement is to withstand competing demands that have negative repercussions on fisheries, advocacy is imperative. Advocacy, however, must be consistent with the culture and political context in which it is used.

Enabling policies and legislation (medium)

Co-management cannot work effectively in a vacuum where there are no supportive policies and legislation. If co-management initiatives are to be success-ful, basic issues of government policy to establish supportive legislation, rights and authority structures must be addressed. Policies and legislation need to spell out jurisdiction and control, provide legitimacy to property rights and decision-making arrangements and clarify the rights and responsibilities of partners. The legal process formalizes rights and rules and legitimizes local participation in co-management arrangements.

If supportive legislation and policies are in place, partners tend to have less difficulty in asserting their rights and roles, particularly if the judicial system is fair and objective. The legal basis for the resource user's participation in resource management is vital and must address fundamental concerns, which include: 1) who has the right to use the resource; 2) who owns the resource; and 3) what is the legal framework for implementing co-management arrangements. The arrangements may be undermined in the absence of a legal basis. The role of the government in establishing conditions for co-management is crucial, particularly in the creation of legitimacy and accountability for institutional arrangements and the delineation of power-sharing and decision-making.

In the Philippines, the enactment of the Local Government Code of 1991 (LGC) ushered in the formal devolution of powers and responsibilities from the central government to local government units and people's organizations. The changed administrative arrangements resulting from the LGC have created a supportive environment for co-management to prosper (Katon *et al.* 1997). An administrative power shift placed coastal local governments at the forefront of resource management (Katon *et al.* 1998). At the local level, the passage of complementary ordinances and the integration of sustainable resource management in local policies and plans have further enhanced co-management efforts.

Government agency support (medium)
Effective links between government agencies like fisheries departments, local fisheries service, research institutions, extension service and environmental agencies enhance co-management arrangements. Government agencies need to be capable and willing to partner, support and interact with other stakeholders in the co-management process.

The government agencies provide assistance and services (administrative, technical and financial) to support the local organizations and co-management arrangements. The co-operation of the government must always be stimulated, solicited and nurtured by the partners, as without this support the co-management arrangements may have difficulty being implemented (Calumpong 1996).

Government agencies can serve to oversee local arrangements and deal with abuses of local authority, conflict management, appeal mechanism and applying regulatory standards. Government fisheries administrators may be reluctant to share power with fishers. They may fear infringement by local resource users and their representatives upon what they consider their professional and scientific turf. The authority, responsibility and functions of government agencies should be specified in the co-management contractual agreement.

Fit with existing and traditional social and cultural institutions and structures of the community (medium)
New co-management plans and strategies should be based on (sometimes diverse) local social and cultural institutions and structures and contribute to strengthening or revitalizing these institutions and structures. The needs and expectations of the community may not always be straightforward due to the social and cultural value system.

In many coastal communities, there exist traditional or informal systems of resource management. These systems have often worked well at meeting management objectives of the community and at achieving ecological sustainability, social equity and economic efficiency. Co-management can be based on strong family or community relationships such as in Thailand (Masae 1998) or on traditional or informal systems such as in Indonesia (Nikijuluw 1996). *Sasi*, a local resource management structure in Indonesia, is imbedded in the local culture and based on traditional law. Local enforcers (*kewang*) and traditional leaders play a vital role in the functioning and resilience of this resource management system over time. Local indigenous knowledge of ecological processes is an important cultural resource that can guide and sustain co-management. Reluctance to acknowledge and utilize local knowledge can act as a severe constraint in the development of viable resource management strategies.

Overlap of interests (medium)

Co-management is most likely to be successful where there are significant over-lapping interests among the partners, where the partners are affected in similar ways by the arrangements and where there will be no big winners or losers (Mitchell 1995b). It is a prerequisite to have a clear sharing system, and a mechanism for recirculating back into the communities some of the wealth generated by co-management arrangements (Thompson et al..1998).

Flexibility (medium)

Co-management arrangements should be flexible enough so that partners have the ability to change plans in response to new issues, needs, problems and opportunities (Yap 1996; Calumpong 1996). A flexible approach towards the development and formalization of the rules and regulations should be adopted recognizing the cultural and traditional patterns of utilization of resources in the community. There should be flexibility to cope with the unexpected, for example failure of communication and co-ordination, unplanned decisions. Unexpected reactions to rules can develop as they are implemented. If the rules and rules-making system are too rigid and incapable of adapting to change, resource users will not comply with the rules.

Species (medium)

Co-management tends to be more successful for managing sedentary aquatic species such as reef fish, crustaceans and molluscs in nearshore waters than for migratory and pelagic species and in inland waterbodies such as lakes. The sedentary species tend to be targeted by small-scale fishers and have easily identifiable users and boundaries. Similar gear and fishing operations are used, and a small number of species are targeted (Thompson *et al.* 1998; Khan and Apu 1998; Katon *et al.* 1997; Katon *et al.* 1998).

Co-ordinating body and agreements (medium)

Adequate co-ordination is particularly important when several partners are involved or when more than one intervention is taking place in a single area

(Foltz *et al.* 1996). An independent body with representatives from the different partners can function to systematize the co-management arrangements (Baticados and Agbayani 1998). The aim is to facilitate quick and efficient decision-making, conflict resolution, planning and co-operation. The co-ordinating body can serve to manage 'turf' issues between partners or government agencies.

Poor co-ordination can lead to confusion, unnecessary duplication of efforts or even activities at cross-purposes or in conflict (Foltz *et al.* 1996). An appropriate operational structure should always be developed based on the needs of the co-management arrangements so that co-ordination between partners will be effective. The co-ordinator of the process must be experienced in interest-based planning. It is very important to establish at the very beginning the actual mode of co-ordination. The co-ordinating body can act as an appeal body for those who question decisions made by local management and enforcement bodies. In the Philippines, the creation of fisheries and aquatic resources management councils at the village level act to co-ordinate, give guidance and bring consensus in planning, implementation and enforcement. The members of the management councils include resource users, NGOs, the private sector and local government (Fellizar *et al.* 1997).

To develop mutual understanding between the partners and to strengthen compliance with the co-management arrangements, it is useful to have a written contract of the co-management agreement. This contractual agreement, developed jointly by the partners, would specify the aims, role, function, authority, responsibility, financial, conflict management mechanisms, and rights, among other requirements, between the partners in the co-management arrangement. Partners may initially enter into an informal working agreement as they develop the co-management arrangements and find out about each other, but this agreement must be supported later by a formal contract to be used during the implementation process. A clear understanding of the long-term goals of power-sharing is established in which the differing interests and needs of the partners are reconciled. There should be flexibility in the agreement so that changing arrangements and relationships over time can be accommodated.

Technology (medium)
Co-management tends to be more successful in small-scale fisheries than commercial fisheries. The small-scale fishers operate closer to the shore in coral reefs, sea grass and mangrove resource systems, use simpler fishing technology, and may target sedentary species (Baticados and Agbayani 1998; Katon *et al.* 1997; Thompson *et al.* 1998; Khan and Apu 1998).

POLICY IMPLICATIONS FOR FISHERIES CO-MANAGEMENT

The conditions discussed in the section above are those which have been identified from Asian experience for the successful implementation of community-based co-management. These conditions are meant to serve as a guide in the planning and implementation of co-management. The conditions must be viewed in the distinct political, biological, cultural, technological, social and economic context of the Asian region and the individual countries. We need to bear in mind the role these unique characteristics play in shaping the process and implementation of co-management in Asia. They are different from Western societies and reflect the so-called Asian values. Resource management systems must be viewed in the context of the complex interactions of these characteristics that have shaped past and present situations and that have a capacity for influencing the future. These characteristics include the small-scale, subsistence based fisheries, the local community traditions, the social and political structures, the political and economic restructuring that is occurring in the region and the need for food security.

Some of the conditions can be met by means internal to the community, while others require external assistance. The number and variety of conditions illustrates that the planning and implementation of co-management must be conducted at several levels. These levels include the individual (i.e. individual incentive structure); the stakeholder (i.e. stakeholder involvement, local political support); the community (i.e. fit with existing and traditional social and cultural institutions and structures of the community); the partners (i.e. partnerships, co-ordinating body and agreements); the government (i.e. government agency support, enabling policies and legislation); the external agent; and the overall process (i.e. trust, networking and advocacy, leadership, organization, financial resources).

None of the conditions exist in isolation but each supports and links to another to make the complex process and arrangements for co-management to work. In addition, all of the parties (resource users, stakeholders, external agents, government) have different but mutually supportive roles to play in co-management. The role of government in co-management is often associated with the passage of enabling policies and legislation, vigilant and effective enforcement, arbitration of disputes among partners when these cannot be resolved by the parties themselves, provision of financial and technical assistance to sustain co-management activities and promotion of a stable political and social environment. The role of the external agent involves initiating a process of discovery and social learning, guiding problem-solving, building local capabilities and advocating appropriate policies. Resource users and stakeholders are largely responsible for the day-to-day management of resources, participation in consultations, design of appropriate resource management measures and assistance in monitoring and law enforcement. The fulfilment of these complementary roles is crucial to the operation and sustainability of co-management.

Implementation is often a balancing act to meet these conditions as timing and linkages in the co-management process and arrangements are important. For example, developing trust between partners is associated with effective communication and comes before the development of contractual agreements between partners. The recognition of resource management problems is associated with the development of clear objectives from a set of well-defined issues.

REFERENCES

Addun, R. and D. Muzones (1997) 'Community-based coastal resource management: Tambuyog's experience in the Philippines'. In G. Claridge and B. O'Callaghan (eds), *Proceedings of the International Conference on Wetlands and Development at Kuala Lumpur.* Wetlands International, pp. 219–230.

Ahmed, M., A.D. Capistrano and M. Hossain (1997) 'Experience of partnership models for the co-management of Bangladesh fisheries'. *Fisheries Management and Ecology,* vol. 4, pp. 233–248.

Baticados, D. and R. Agbayani (1998) *Case Study of Institutional Arrangements in the Fisheries Co-management of Malalison, Island, Central Philippines.* Iloilo: Southeast Asian Fisheries Development Center.

Bissdorf, H.G. (1996) 'The Banica River Watershed Development Project: NGO–PO–GO Partnership'. In C. Foltz, R.S. Pomeroy and C. Barber (eds), *Proceedings of the Visayas-wide Conference on Community-based Coastal Resources Management and Co-management.* Fisheries Co-management Research Project Working Paper No. 4. Manila: International Center for Living Aquatic Resources Management (ICLARM), pp. 76–77.

Buhat, D. (1994) 'Community-based coral reef and fisheries management, San Salvador Island, Philippines'. In A. White, L. Hale, Y. Renard, and L. Cortesi (eds) *Collaborative and Community-based Management of Coral Reefs.* Connecticut: Kumarian Press, pp. 33–49.

Calumpong, H. (1996) 'Landscape approach to coastal management in Bais Bay, Negros Oriental'. In C. Foltz, R.S. Pomeroy and C. Barber (eds), *Proceedings of the Visayas-wide Conference on Community-based Coastal Resources Management and Co-management.* Fisheries Co-management Research Project Working Paper No. 4. Manila: ICLARM, pp. 50–57.

Carlos, M. and R.S. Pomeroy (1996) *A Review and Evaluation of CBCRM Projects in the Philippines: 1984–1994.* Fisheries Co-management Research Project Research Report No. 6. Manila: ICLARM.

Claridge, G. and B. O'Callaghan (eds) (1997) *Proceedings of the International Conference on Wetlands and Development at Kuala Lumpur.* Wetlands International.

Fellizar, F.P., R.G. Bernardo and A.P.H. Stuart (1997) *Analysis of Policies and Policy Instruments Relevant to the Management of Fisheries/aquatic Resources with Emphasis on Local Level Issues and Concerns.* Los Banos: Southeast Asian Regional Center for Graduate Study and Research in Agriculture (SEARCA).

Foltz, C., R.S. Pomeroy and C. Barber (eds) (1996) *Proceedings of the Visayas-wide Conference on Community-based Coastal Resources Management and Co-management.* Fisheries Co-management Research Project Working Paper No. 4. Manila: ICLARM.

International Center for Living Aquatic Resources Management (ICLARM) and Institute of Fisheries Management (IFM) (1996) *Analysis of Fisheries Co-management Arrangements: a Research Framework.* Fisheries Co-management Research Project Working Paper No. 1. Manila: ICLARM.

Harkes, I. (1998) *Institutional Analysis of Sasi in Central Maluku, Indonesia. 1998.* Fisheries Co-management Research Project Working Paper. Manila: ICLARM.

IUCN (1996) *Collaborative Management of Protected Areas: Tailoring the Approach to the Context.* Gland, Switzerland: Social Policy Group of the IUCN.

Katon, B., R. Pomeroy, and A. Salamanca (1997) *The Marine Conservation Project for San Salvador: a Case Study of Fisheries Co-management in the Philippines.* Fisheries Co-management Research Project Working Paper No. 23. Manila: ICLARM.

Katon, B., R. Pomeroy, M. Ring and L. Garces (1998) *Mangrove Rehabilitation and Coastal Resource Management of Mabini-Candijay: a Case Study of Fisheries Co-management Arrangements in Cogtong Bay, Philippines.* Fisheries Co-management Research Project Working Paper No. 33. Manila: ICLARM.

Khan, M.S. and N.A. Apu (1998) *Fisheries Co-management in the Oxbow Lakes of Bangladesh.* Chittagong: Chittagong University.

Kuperan K., Mustapha N, Pomeroy, R.S. (1996) *Transaction costs and fisheries co-management.* Fisheries Co-management Research Project Working Paper no.15, Manila: ICLARM.

Kuperan, K., N.M. Abdullah, I. Susilowathi, and C. Ticao (1997) *Enforcement and Compliance with Fisheries Regulations in Malaysia, Indonesia and the Philippines.* Fisheries Co-management Research Project Research Report No. 5. Manila: ICLARM.

Kuperan, K., N. M. Abdullah and R.S. Pomeroy (1998) *Transactions Cost and Fisheries Co-management.* Fisheries Co-management Research Project Working Paper No. 15. Manila: ICLARM.

Masae A. (1998) *An analysis of fisheries co-managements arrangements: The case of Ban Laem Makham, Sikao District, Trang Province, South Thailand.* Prince of Songkla University. Fisheries Co-management Research Project Working Paper no.37, Manila: ICLARM.

Mitchell, D.A. (1995a) *Management of the Intertidal Clam Resource. A British Columbia Experiment in Limited Entry and Local Participation.* School of Public Administration University of Victoria.

Mitchell, D.A. (1995b) 'Co-operative management: can we get the incentives right?' Presentation to the Maritime Awards Society of Canada. University of Victoria.

Mulekom, van L., and E. Tria (1999) *Community-based coastal resource management in Orion, Bataan, Philippines: a case study on the development of a municipal-wide community-based fisheries co-management system.* Fisheries Co-management Research Project Working Paper no.36, Manila: ICLARM.

Nikijiluw, V. (1996) *Co-management of Coastal Resources in Bali Island, Indonesia.* Fisheries Co-management Research Project Working Paper No. 7. Research Institute for Marine Fisheries and ICLARM.

Novaczek I., and I. Harkes (1998) *Institutional analysis of sasi laut in Maluku, Indonesia.* Fisheries Co-management Research Project Working Paper no.39, Manila: ICLARM.

Novaczek, I., I.H.T. Harkes, J. Sopacua and M.D.D. Tatuhey (2001) *An institutional analysis of sasi laut in Maluku.* ICLARM Technical Report 59. Penang, Malaysia: ICLARM

Ostrom, E. (1990) *Governing the Commons: the Evolution of Institutions for Collective Action.* Cambridge: Cambridge University Press.

—— (1992) *Crafting Institutions for Self-governing Irrigation Systems.* San Francisco: Institute for Contemporary Studies Press.

Pido, M. (1996) *The management system of marine fisheries and other coastal resources in Palawan, Philippines: concepts, experiences and lessons.* Fisheries Co-management Research Project Working Paper no. 4, Manila: ICLARM.

Pido, M.D., R.S. Pomeroy, M.B. Carlos, and L.R. Garces (1996) *A handbook forrapid appraisal of fisheries management systems* (version 1). Manila: ICLARM.

Pinkerton, E. (ed.) (1989) *Co-operative Management of Local Fisheries: New Directions for Improved Management and Community Development.* Vancouver: University of British Columbia.

Pomeroy, R.S. and M. Carlos (1997) 'CBCRM projects in the Philippines: a review and evaluation of programs and projects, 1984–1994'. *Marine Policy,* vol. 21 no. 2, pp. 1–19.

Pomeroy, R.S. and F. Berkes (1997) 'Two to tango: the role of government in fisheries co-management'. *Marine Policy* vol. 21 no. 5, pp. 465–480.

Pomeroy, R.S. and M. Williams (1994) *Fisheries Co-management and Small-scale Fisheries: a Policy Brief.* Manila: ICLARM.

Pomeroy, R.S. and M. Pido (1995) 'Initiatives towards fisheries co-management in the Philippines: the case of San Miguel Bay'. *Marine Policy,* vol. 19 no.3, pp. 199–211.

Pomeroy, R., R. Pollnac, C. Predo and B. Katon (1996) *Impact Evaluation of Community-based Coastal Resource Management Projects in the Philippines.* Fisheries Co-management Research Project Research Report No. 3. Manila: ICLARM.

Sandalo, R.M (1994) 'Community-based coastal resources management: the Palawan experience'. In R.S. Pomeroy (ed.), *Community Management and Common Property of Coastal Fisheries in Asia and the Pacific: Concepts, Methods and Experiences.* Manila: ICLARM, pp. 165–181.

Segura-Ybanez, M (1996) 'Sustainability of community-based resource management in the Central Visayas Regional Project – Phase I'. In C. Foltz, R.S. Pomeroy and C. Barber (eds), *Proceedings of the Visayas-wide Conference on Community-based Coastal Resources Management and Fisheries Co-management*. Fisheries Co-management Research Project Working Paper No. 4. Manila: ICLARM, pp. 84–92.

Thompson, P.M., S.M.N. Alam, M. Hossain and A.B. Shelly (1998) *Community-based Management of Hamil Beel: a Case Study of Fisheries Co-management in Bangladesh*. Dhaka, ICLARM.

Thompson P.M., S.M.N. Alam, M. Hossain and A.B. Shelley (1998) *Community-based management of Hamil Beel: a case study of fisheries co-management in Bangladesh*. Fisheries Co-management Research Project Working Paper no.36, Manila: ICLARM.

Thong H.X., P.T.H. Van, P.G. Hai and R.S. Pomeroy (1996) *A review of coastal fisheries management strategies and a baseline socio-economic survey of small-scale fishing household communities in Vietnam*. Fisheries Co-management Research Project Working Paper no.21. Manila: ICLARM.

Thong H.X, Thieu (1998) *Traditional organisations in fishing communities of small-scale fisheries in Vietnam*. Institute of Fisheries Economics and Planning, Hanoi, Vietnam. Fisheries Co-management Research Project Research Paper no.8. Manila: ICLARM.

Tokrisna, R., P. Boonchuwong and P. Janekarnkij (1997) *A Review of Fisheries and Coastal Community-based Management Regime in Thailand*.

Torrell M. (1998) *Institutional, legal, and policy perspectives on the management of aquatic resources and the aquatic environment in wetlands, floodplains, lakes and rivers in the Mekong River Basin*. Paper presented at the 7th Conference of the International Association for the Study of Common Property, Vancouver, British Columbia, Canada, June 10-14.

University of the Philippines (1996) *Study on the Management of Fisheries/aquatic Resources at the Local Level*. Fisheries Co-management Research Project Research Report No. 7. Manila: ICLARM.

Van, P.T.H. and P.G. Hai (1998) *Case Study of Community-based Coastal Resources Management in Vietnam*. Vietnam: Ministry of Fisheries.

White, A., L. Hale, Y. Renard and L. Cortesi (eds) (1994) *Collaborative and Community-Based Management of Coral Reefs*. Connecticut: Kumarian Press, Inc.

Yap, N. (1996) 'Community organizing in Leyte: the Labrador experience'. In C. Foltz, R.S. Pomeroy and C. Barber (eds), *Proceedings of the Visayas-wide Conference on Community-based Coastal Resources Management and Fisheries Co-management*. Fisheries Co-management Research Project Working Paper No. 4. Manila: ICLARM, pp. 70–74.

CHAPTER FOURTEEN

A Synoptic View of the Co-management
of Natural Resources

ROY ELLEN

INTRODUCTION

*I*n these concluding remarks, I shall attempt to make a few connections between some issues raised in the previous chapters and broader questions found in the development, environmental conservation and anthropological literature. In particular, I shall seek to address comparative and conceptual issues and to challenge widespread assumptions regarding how schemes designed to co-manage natural resources really work. I write not as someone with any direct experience of designing, implementing or monitoring co-management schemes but as an outsider with some knowledge of traditional forms of natural resource management and what happens to them under pressure of social and ecological change.

IN COMPARISON

Four chapters in this book are devoted to the Philippines and three to Indonesia, and one each to Vietnam, Japan, India and China. One chapter is more generally concerned with coastal Southeast Asia. With such an asymmetric geographic spread the contributions are not in any obvious statistical sense representative of what is going on in the various Asian countries covered, but they are all indicative and raise some interesting common problems. The authors approach the issues from different disciplinary perspectives and with different agendas: as conservation biologists, human rights lawyers, government consultants, policy-makers or even as studiedly aloof academic deconstructionists. Some are unashamed enthusiasts and advocates for co-management solutions, others more cautious and reflective, even sceptical. Many of the contributions are case studies, some in fair depth, others are historical and a couple synthesizing and general. Seven of the chapters concern forest resources, four marine resources and one chapter pastureland. One chapter looks at several ecological zones reflecting a complex regional environmental history.

Certain kinds of resources are therefore privileged over others – in this book most obviously forest – and it is arguable that developments in the area of forestry are now setting the intellectual agenda for discussions of co-management more generally. As Yadama indicates for South Asia, the policy switch from top-down towards community-level organization is most pronounced for forestry. Much the same might be said for the Philippines, except that historically the earliest experience (and success) in co-management there has been with respect to irriga-tion (Sajise, Fellizar and Saguiguit). Indeed, the comparative evidence seems to suggest that people widely and immediately recognize the necessity of co-operation in relation to sharing water resources for agriculture, and it is here that we often find the strongest, most resilient and effective indigenous institutions such as the Balinese irrigation association, or *subak* (Lansing 1991). In Indonesia generally, however, explicit co-management strategies have until recently been most pronounced with respect to marine resources, though the set of economic and political changes which accompanied the southeast Asian economic crisis and the end of the New Order regime, collectively described as *Reformasi*, have now led to considerable local activity in the forestry sector.

The point I think that needs to be made here is the importance of dis-tinguishing the special circumstances of different resources, which may require different co-management arrangements (reflecting, for example, different kinds of traditional rights), while at the same time acknowledging that no single resource is ultimately independent of any other. As Persoon and van Est stress, manage-ment of timber and fish extraction differ fundamentally from community conservation of biodiversity, and indeed the management of marine resources raises different issues from forest resources. On the other hand, 'wild' resources cannot be understood separately from cultivated ones, though these latter are sometimes completely omitted from biodiversity projects. Similarly, it has long been accepted that conservation and general ecological sustainability are not the same thing, that the sustainability conditions for specific resources will vary and that sustainability of resource extraction is different again from other desir-able meanings of sustainability (Ellen 2000: 172–174, McNeill 2000). This all suggests that policy and project objectives always need to be clear with respect to the resources concerned and levels of sustainability envisaged.

THE HISTORY OF MODERN COMMUNITY-BASED MANAGEMENT

As several contributors (Persoon and Van Est, Sajise, Fellizar and Saguiguit) point out, co-management rhetoric and practice has been fostered in Asia through the failure of top-down development strategies, the same failure which has encouraged participatory approaches more widely, and led to recognition of the relevance of local knowledge (Ellen and Harris 2000). The trend has been accelerated by processes of democratization, the work of environmental NGOs (which have often had the support of dissident politicians and scientists), and donor agencies under pressure from the first three – particularly in relation to issues which have a high profile in Western political agendas, such as the rights of indigenous peoples (as an extension of human rights), poverty alleviation and food and environmental security in relation to sustainability. Co-management has been additionally recognized as an appropriate way forward where the landscapes which conservationists seek to preserve are fundamentally anthropic. Such landscapes bear testimony to the fact that extraction is not necessarily incompatible with conservation, that local 'tribal' people are not inevitably indiscriminate users of resources and that involvement of local people in decision-making is often essential for their effective maintenance (for example McNeeley and Pitt 1985). This point is often made by way of contrast with the observation of indiscriminate non-sustainable practices of in-coming migrants and extractivists (Yadama, Eghenter), though we should avoid unexamined claims regarding the ecological insensitivity of immigrants (c.f. Atran 1999).

These developments, and the revitalization of tradition which sometimes accompanies them (Harkes and Novaczek) have, it is true, occasionally been undermined by overenthusiastic romanticization and the misleading implication that nature conservation and the lives of tribal people are virtually synonymous (Persoon and Van Est). The contemporary resonances of such a view (which we must extend to the pronouncements of some traditional peoples themselves) have deep roots in a Western history of scientific discovery beyond Europe. This history links biological and indigenous ethnic difference together, and is evident, for example, in the juxtaposed zoological and anthropological categories and displays of numerous 'Natural history museums' (Ellen 1996: 109–10; c.f. Stocking 1985) and in the naive curatorial convention of treating 'cultures' as species-like units. If such a view is potentially pernicious, the grounds for confusion are further increased by recent discussions of the impressive world-wide correlations between biological and cultural diversity (Maffi 2001).

Co-management, in the sense in which it is usually conceived today in development and natural resource discourse, is not new. The WWF/IUCN World Conservation Strategy of 1980 marks a particular milestone in this respect. Co-management ideas had already appeared in the Philippines by the early 1980s as part of a programme of Integrated Social Forestry, in relation to the north American fisheries by the late 1980s (McCay and Acheson 1987, Pinkerton 1987), while the 1980s and early 1990s saw Joint Forest Management (JFM) legislation in place in several Indian states (Sundar 2000). Academics operating in the development field were promulgating versions of co-management in the early 1980s (Chambers 1983), followed shortly after by NGOs such as IUCN. These early experiments spawned mutants and clones, trading under under several guises and with as many acronyms and abbreviations: integrated conservation and development projects (ICDP), joint management, community-based management (CBM), community-based resource management (CBRM), community-based wildlife management (CMW), community level conservation, adaptive management, local management and indigenous management. We now have case studies of a wide variety of co-management arrangements, some of which report success but many also report failure. Some, like Zimbabwean CAMPFIRE and Moluccan *sasi* (Harkes and Novaczek), have become iconic, taking on virtual existences which resonate uncomfortably with the empirical realities. In much of this, during the last decade, a body of work by Elinor Ostrom (especially 1990) has been influential in promoting and evaluating such schemes, projects and programmes. Ostromian design principles, with their checklists of numerous 'key issues for successful co-management', have been followed by the work of others and are reflected in several chapters in this book.

Constructive as much of this work is, its sheer bulk, the occasionally impenetrable jargon, and its evangelical spirit, is sometimes wont to give the impression that co-management is an entirely new and revolutionary addition to the repertoire of techniques available to regulate natural resource production. In the short history of modern development consultancy and biodiversity conservation this may be so, but in the long term it is palpably not. In this volume, Kalland describes fisheries co-management as between fishermen controlling small production units and merchants controlling larger ones up until the Meiji era in Japan (1868–1912), and thereafter a shift from rigid fixed territories to more a flexible system which left the fishermen more in control. In this context, the co-managing partners of local fishermen shifted from feudal authorities in Fukuoka to a bureaucracy in Tokyo, while the village was replaced by a village co-operative, providing important steps towards a sustainable fishery. My own unpublished field data (c.f. Zerner 1994) show how some *sasi* arrangements in Maluku have historically been deliberate means by which politically dominant groups have regulated production and marketing (for example, cloves and copra) in order to maintain some kind of distributive justice among rulers and dependent groups, quite independent of any outside partner or central government agent. Similarly, Sajise, Fellizar and Saguiguit remind us that local control of resources was typical of pre-colonial *barangay* in the Philippines and that it was the colonial bureaucracy which instituted top-down management of all kinds through absolutist forms which have steadily eroded since the 1960s, first in relation to irrigation then forestry and most recently, fisheries.

Conceptualising management

Although wide in its application, both literally and generically, the concept of *management* became established in the vocabulary of governance with the rise of the modern business enterprise in the West during the second half of the nineteenth century (George 1972). In this context it rapidly came to refer to a set of bureaucratic practices related to planning, organizing, directing and controlling both human and non-human resources, all of which were designed to raise the efficiency of the industrial firm, and which were increasingly performed by a specialised group of operatives. By the second half of the twentieth century, management had become reified, an esoteric 'science', institutionalized through schools of management and with a professional structure. Such usages are reflected in the common meanings of the words 'manager', 'managerial', 'managerialism' – with their implication that management is somehow *opposed* to labour. There is, therefore, a class and power dimension to the concept of management, generally linking it to a supervisory – and therefore superior – status. However, in a number of applied technical practices, most notably forestry, the term management independently acquired rather different meanings, perhaps best reflected in the notion of husbandry. Thus, when the concept of management derived from the theory of effective business organization was, secondarily, applied to more technical, mundane, husbandry practices, and to the lower status groups involved in such, it had the rhetorical effect of elevating the practices referred to, making them more valuable, important and sophisticated than we might have thought. Thus, through the conflation of different senses of the term 'management', 'biodiversity management' and 'common property management' for example are transformed from a technological repertoire into an organisational culture validated by modern business practice. We manage risks, and cleverly avoid the pitfalls of sharp conceptual divides between farming and extraction, by speaking of the 'management of natural resources'. We turn the practical skills of Penan hunter-gatherers into, by turns, esoteric art and scientific mastery, by describing them as 'management'. Moreover, in the context of the kinds of issue discussed in this volume there is a tendency for the concept of management and sustainability to elide.

It is not, of course, unreasonable to stress the importance and effectiveness of particular cultural practices by using management in this more encompassing way, as long as we understand that we are referring broadly to the same quality and range of practices. Unfortunately, governments and other official and intrusive parastatal and non-state organizations often have different ideas as to what constitutes management from those of local communities. The co-management model is itself a government or outsider model, and although there may be sufficient shared meaning for the various parties involved to agree on the appropriateness of the term, and perhaps on a modicum of common purpose, they may otherwise speak quite different organizational languages with different agendas. For many functionaries in government, management is likely to be about, say, administration of licences to extract resources, or mechanisms for controlling the movement of people. By aggregating phenomena as diverse as land tenure, legal procedures, form-filling, soil revitalization, report-writing, weeding, supervision of staff, seed selection and selective felling, under the term management, we somehow not only make the more menial legitimate but are also inclined to blur the differences between what might best be treated as separate kinds of social behaviour.

Deconstructing the hyphen in co-management
Co-management, by definition, involves two or more parties. When prefixed to a noun in English 'co-' implies joint, togetherness or mutuality. The parties involved may vary in their formal definition and social composition, but one will always constitute a local (insider) entity and the other some non-local (outsider) entity. In their paper, Sajise, Fellizar and Saguiguit present different versions of the model.

The most common party to any co-management arrangement, and on the local side of the equation, is what is described as 'the community'. As Persoon and van Est point out, this term is used no less loosely than 'management', and as several studies in this collection make clear, there remains an unfortunate tendency to treat community as a black box, as a 'warmly persuasive word' (Williams, quoted by Persoon and van Est), conveying an often illusory image of solidarity and concealing a multitude of problems. Community, in the sense of Tönnies' (1887) *Gemeinschaft* is often taken to imply a small, integrated and identifiable collectivity of moral equals engaged in mutually beneficial social exchange. The difficulty in many situations where co-management is envisaged is that this description hardly applies. Indeed, there is frighteningly little agreement in the literature as to what communities really are, making generalizations and their comparative study hazardous (Hillery 1955). Villages, for example, are often assumed to be communities but are sometimes units of bureaucratic convenience (as with the Indonesian *desa*), often with roots in colonial administrative reform, and hiding profound social divisions, along ethnic, caste, class, kinship or factional lines (Breman 1988, Kemp 1988). Yadama indicates problems of this kind in relation to the Indian cases which he discusses, and in the Philippines, Certificates of Ancestral Domain Claim (CADCs) artificially divide ethnic groups into smaller units which are unable to reflect local social realities which people regard as important. There are sometimes closer, and organizationally more significant, ties between members of different settlements and villages than within them. Thus, among migrant Balinese, irrigation associations (*subak*), which in Bali itself divide villages but unite farmers relying on a common source of water, have proved a more effective basis for production-level organization in the context of Indonesian transmigration schemes than the more diffuse *banjar*. Communities, then, are not necessarily communities of equals, and the boundaries of socially effective groupings may not match those recognized by the state or other outsider co-managing units. Moreover, the implications of co-management will vary as between cognatic loosely based traditional societies of the kind found in much of the Philippines and Borneo, and areas where there are persisting strong traditional corporate groups based on kinship or other primordial ties such as in Sumatra, parts of eastern Indonesia, much of India and China. Such varying kinds of 'social glue' are linked to different cultures of sharing, ownership, land tenure and decision-making – all of which have an impact on the effectiveness of particular co-management schemes. Where the community side of the equation involves different ethnic groups, or combines indigenous peoples and incomers, then these problems will only be compounded. Communities, therefore, need to be carefully defined and located, not arbitrarily assumed. And whatever form they might take, they are not always the most appropriate basis for co-management schemes anyway (Persoon and van Est). Less morally charged descriptions of the local unit, such as 'local resource users', at least avoid some of the dangerous pitfalls which accompany the notion of community.

Co-management models also tend to have simple premises about the channels for arriving at collective agreement, though local management decisions are often made by individuals rather than through idealized democratic fora.

This tendency privileges ascribed leaders in societies where inherited position is still important, individuals who have achieved legitimate authority in customary ways elsewhere, while in some cases decision-making is the outcome of *de facto* power relations which may not command general legitimacy. Inevitably, some individuals are disproportionately involved, while others are excluded or under-represented (women and lower status groups, smaller rather than larger sub-groups, incomers rather than indigents). In Yadama's chapter it is, for example, forest guards who are likely to participate most actively. Consensus and representativeness cannot be taken for granted, though where decision-making is shared it is often consensus which influences outcomes rather than the will of the majority. Even where local decision-makers have been inducted in the objectives of a co-management project and tutored in appropriate evaluative procedures, it is fallacious to think in terms of bloodless disembodied 'managers' instilling business virtues and constructing new moral economies and audit cultures.

A sub-set of problems relating to the definition of community arises in projects which rely on, or advocate, community mapping. For co-management to work, such logic predicts, it is best that there should be clear and uncontested boundaries on the ground. But although community mapping is often presented as a strategy for community empowerment and conflict resolution, as Eghenter describes for the Kenyah and as Yayasan HUALOPU hoped for Maluku in 1997 (Harkes and Novaczek), it can easily become a means of disempowerment and conflict generation. Community mapping is particularly hazardous where traditional land rights are what Max Gluckman (1972) called 'serial' (meaning nested, overlapping and fluid), as amongst many upland swiddening, nomadic and pastoralist groups (Campbell 2002). Thus, Osseweijer describes attempts by an NGO to 'empower' two Aruese villages by drawing maps to better define local resource and land rights which had led to conflict. The key political and methodological question in such situations is always 'who draws the map?' In the Aru case the question had to be answered through court arbitration. Maps, more generally, therefore, concretize and freeze social relations of resource use which were previously fluid and ambiguous, but no less effective for that. Of course, it is in situations where local resource owner rights are threatened by outsiders that the greatest justification for mapping can be found, and it is in such moments that 'communities' can come into existence. Elsewhere, certitude with respect to ownership is important not because local people wish to retain resources but because they wish to alienate them. Thus, where the same Nuaulu clan has split over several generations, members in different villages on the island of Seram may feel they have the authority to grant access to loggers, or there may be conflict between clan and village level, reinforced by historic cleavages over legitimate representational authority (Ellen 1993, 1999).

Unpacking and identifying the other (external group) side of the co-management hyphen is hardly less problematic. Some definitions of co-management assume that the outside partner will always be 'the government', in some form or another. But this need not be so. Where the non-local group is governmental, responsibility is often devolved to a government department, most commonly (for the historical reasons already referred to) forestry departments. However, problems may arise where, in practice, different government departments claim authority over overlapping aspects and areas of the same jurisdiction, resulting in inter-departmental conflict. In Indonesia, this has frequently been the case between the forestry department, the transmigration directorate and local government. Other problems may arise where there is no contact between government departments which clearly share an interest in the management of the same resources. In Vietnam (Polet) those responsible for national parks and those responsible for land classification (agriculture) do not appear to interact. While co-management is in theory shared between Can Tien National Park and commune and district authorities, in practice this does not happen. Also, while we tend to treat the state and village as separate entities in co-partnerships, in practice the state reaches right into the village, in the sense that members of the community may be state employees, even employees in the departments or agencies represented in the co-management arrangement (von Benda-Beckmann, F. and K. 1998); and although we can reasonably claim to have evidence for deconstructing the local community and understanding its dynamics, comparable research is not really available on the government partners in co-management schemes. In the absence of a significant body of comparative research, however, we might reasonably assume that different administrative and political cultures give rise to different kinds of dynamic in implementing co-management schemes. Thus, we might expect to find differences between the more centralized regimes of China and Vietnam and the more devolved regimes of the Philippines, Malaysia and (under *Reformasi*) Indonesia.

Less frequently, co-management contracts are with NGOs. There are no direct examples of such arrangements in the present volume, though the role of Yayasan HUAPOLU in Maluku *sasi* management (Harkes and Novaczek) comes close. In some cases the NGO may stand as a proxy for the government, and having NGOs as intermediaries can be effective. Local peoples may sometimes treat powerful NGOs as if they were an arm of government, and sometimes NGOs behave in ways which encourage such misunderstandings, as has been described is for the Crater Mountain Conservation area in Papua New Guinea (Pearl 1994, Ellis 2001). Sometimes there may be a three-way split: between community, government and NGO. This may be the best way of describing the successful Ikalahan Educational Centre in Nueva Vizcaya (Dakila-Bergonia 1996). Elsewhere, the superordinate partner may be a commercial firm, as described by Kalland for Japan, as is the case with many modern logging concessions. Sometimes businessmen, while not part of the original co-management plan, may nevertheless intrude on a partnership (Aquino).

Linkage, power and participation

Where due recognition is given to the difficulty of constituting the units involved in a co-management partnership, and to the different kinds of entity on either side of the hyphen, it is still often assumed that all co-management schemes work in much the same way. In fact, even in terms of formally recognized types, it is clear that power and responsibility may be shared in various ways, depending on whether the role of a non-local partner is 'facilitative', 'instructive', 'consultative', 'cooperative', 'advisory', or merely 'informative' (Persoon and van Est, following others); or whether arrangements are 'contractual, consultative, collaborative' or 'collegial' (Biggs 1989). The problem with such typologies is that while they indicate that not all co-management regimes need be the same, they are at the same time fundamentally innocent of social dynamics, especially power relations existing between individuals. They also suggest qualitative taxonomic differences in theory that may in practice be continuously variable and difficult to locate, ranging from complete control by external agencies to (almost) complete control by local stakeholders. At this latter extremity are situations where the role of government is single-stranded, where, for example, it seeks merely to prevent outsiders intruding upon the land of local peoples. Hobbes claims that such an arrangement has achieved benefits for Pala'wan people in the southern Philippines. A similar permissive regime that some point to as a success story is that of the Baduy homeland in upland West Java (Iskandar and Ellen 2000).

Despite the egalitarian ethos of the model, in practice co-management relationships are seldom balanced and generally display external partner bias from the start. They are bureaucracy-led rather than community- and problem-orientated. Officially they may speak of equality, but the very legalistic culture of discrete rights and obligations which suits governments and NGOs is often alien to local communities. It is usual for external partners to define the terms of reciprocity, to rule certain local customary rights irrelevant or to ignore them, and to retain responsibility for administrative processes. It is almost always governments and NGOs who take initiatives and who control the means by which initiatives can be taken, while local communities always seem to be on the receiving end (Aquino). Even 'indigenous knowledge' is routinely codified, its relevance legitimated and its uses controlled by external partners (Ellen and Harris: 2000). Legislation, such as the Philippines Indigenous Peoples' Rights Act of 1997, is by definition enacted by governments, not local communities; and Certificates of Ancestral Domain Claim (CADC) and Certificates of Ancestral Domain Title (CADT) are neither designed nor started in consultation with local people. On Luzon, Agta are 'awarded' land as their domain, though territorially it is often less than they recognize as really theirs. Moreover such domains are often challenged by other stakeholders who have greater means to pursue counter-claims up to the level of the supreme court. Often local participants are only brought in at a later phase in a plan (Osseweijer) when key decisions have already been made. In situations such as these it begins to look as though co-management is no more than an external partner ruse to convey an *appearance* of equal and fair treatment for local populations but otherwise to continue as before. More deviously, such arrangements may serve to divide-and-rule, and to more effectively administer local user groups. Even where external partners start with good intentions, such arrangements may still become instruments of control. And when failure occurs, because it is governments and other external bodies who generally monitor performance and write documents, it is more likely to be attributed to local communities than to anyone else.

Thus, a political movement which started out as a deliberate strategy to avoid 'top-down' management appears to have ended up as just another example of the same, dressed up in the language of participation. Even rapid rural appraisal (RRA) inputs of a few days are increasingly becoming acceptable in the consultancy and NGO world when redesignated 'participatory' rural appraisal (PRA). Indeed, nobody would dream of doing anything now unless it was so labelled. Consequently the term has lost much of its force, and despite the rhetoric, old bureaucratic patterns of implementation prevail, while measures of evaluation and monitoring can become cosmetic paper exercises which have little relation to real success or failure.

It would seem, therefore, that another shift in the community-based management paradigm is due to ensure that change really does take place at the grassroots (Pasicolan), to move beyond official verbiage and external appearances and in each case to work out from first principles what is needed and most suitable. It is no good simply defining this in terms of government or official values and practices; there must be a genuine meeting of minds that binds parties together into an effective relationship. This means grounding each arrangement in an understanding of and respect for those local values, world-views and behaviours that interface the relationship, especially concepts and perceptions of reciprocity, trust, law, synergy and benefit. We need to know if local notions of sharing and exchange are the same as those that underpin the assumptions of the external partner and how these will influence interpretation of a contract. David Ellis (2001) in his recent account of the Crater Mountain Conservation Project in Papua New Guinea has demonstrated the radical disjunction which may often exist between official, external and ideological notions of partnership based on Western notions of reciprocity and local notions of appropriate exchange into which these ideas are (mis)translated. Moreover where external partners take it for granted that complex ideas can be simplified by representing them in terms of flow-diagrams and paper trails, we may be mystifying our local partners as much as ourselves.

Seeing the picture from diverse angles is essential. An appreciation of the rights and duties associated with various property regimes is obviously crucial (Persoon and van Est), because upholding these rights determines a particular outcome. Co-management will not succeed if basic tenure issues and sensitivity to social justice concerns are glossed over (Cordell 1993: 65, 69), and it may well be that the spontaneous co-management which emerges as a practical and equitable response to a particular resource-management problem is better than any 'off-the-shelf' model, simply because the parties are encouraged to work things out for themselves. At this end of the spectrum, the arrangement may not be recognizable as 'co-management' at all, and such terminology is hardly essential in order for good schemes to work (see Pala'wan and Baduy examples referred to above). Thus, the New Order (Suharto) Indonesian government did not deliberately recognize Nuaulu land rights as part of a community-based scheme, but recognized them for pragmatic political reasons, because they were widely accepted by other local non-Nuaulu (Ellen 1993, 1999). Similarly, in some cases acceptable and workable compromises take the form of what we might crudely call 'a deal', as when Nuaulu received free houses in a trans-migration zone as part payment for loss of forest rights in a local resettlement zone, or where Bugkalot received a community-based programme in exchange for conceding territory for a dam (Aquino). Such bargaining may seem tacky, but it is no more so than comparable compromises arrived at between the government and local farmers in the setting up of, say, British national parks.

The bottom-line condition, though, is that local partners make their own decisions with equal access to relevant information.

Time perspectives and political change

There is a kind of presentism implicit in many off-the-shelf co-management solutions. It is, therefore, significant that a central feature of this volume is a repeated insistence that co-management must be seen less as a timeless technical fix from the development tool-kit, than as a bespoke arrangement to be understood locally, historically and dynamically. The reason so many co-management projects have failed is precisely because this has not been taken into account (Brosius *et al.* 1998). Custom is not fixed and unchanging. Nuaulu conceptions of the natural world and notions of appropriate forest tenure have progressively altered and diversified over the last 30 years, as their geographic and cultural horizons have widened, and as their forest has been subject to new external pressures (Ellen 1993, 1999). Eghenter shows clearly in her discussion how Kenyah *tana ulen* forest reserves moved from aristocratic control to control by a customary council, and how in that new context they became a means of reasserting rights in the face of encroachment by timber companies. In yet other parts of Indonesia (such as Manado), and in the Philippines, land has been taken out of the customary domain altogether. The temptation to reinvent the past when invoking the benefits of 'traditional' practices or communities has to be resisted for it may not work at all, or may even have the effect of preserving old inequalities and identities which local people may, otherwise, over time, ignore or actively seek to reject. The Bugkalot domain plan (Aquino) captured indigenous knowledge in many ways but also adopted non-traditional strategies. Traditional institutions (such as *sasi*) can become moribund in the context of inflexible co-management schemes (Harkes and Novaczek), or the introduction of institutions of 'co-management' may themselves lead to the reformulation of values, rules and social relations (Li 1999). Local group practices must be understood as fluid, even if hitherto there is local evidence for their stability, and even if local populations themselves seem comfortable with the notion of unchanging tradition.

Flexibility must, therefore, be built into the solutions on offer. What is appropriate behaviour in normal times might not be so in an El Niño year or under other kinds of extreme, economic, environmental and social stress. And measurements of success may well vary depending on the unit of time employed and on which parties are consulted. Bureaucracies are inevitably obsessed with 'project cycles' and the phasing of inputs and outcomes. But 'projects' always come to an end, and some attention must be paid to the consequences of withdrawing inputs available only during the life of the project. When this happens there must be realistic statutory rights to fill the structural vacuum, some framework to ensure security, and power and responsibility must be devolved to effective continuing institutions. We normally look to the state to provide these, though this need not always be the case. This is the context in which some authorities have been recommending the establishment of a supra-regional body for the Sierra Madre in north-eastern Luzon. We must similarly unpack time perspectives when it comes to evaluating success. External partners typically rely on narrow measures, again determined by initial objectives and project lifetimes, often derived from questionable economic models (including nowadays inappropriate attempts to price environmental functions for natural resources). For example, as Persoon and van Est point out, evaluation projects may be seen as resources in their own right by local people, successful if they offer employment for even a short time. Moluccan *sasi* may be acceptably seen as serving different purposes in different places: providing resource rent to sub-sidize a co-operative in one village or to regulate the distribution of harvestable fish in another.

The consequences of major changes in the political climate may make a significant difference to how co-management schemes work and may confound original plans and objectives. Thus *Reformasi* in Indonesia has led to a dissolving of state responsibilities without new effective institutions being put in their place (Persoon and van Est), a new decentralized forestry policy from 1999 on-wards has legitimated the involvement of large numbers of small firms, co-operatives and regional and national NGOs, the latter sometimes acting as mouthpieces for particular factional and ethnic interests. The liberal political regime has allowed local cultural minorities to organize themselves as 'indigenous' groups, and there is now co-ordination at the national level. The kind of political instability which Indonesia has experienced since 1999 has become a real test for the resilience of co-management arrangements and, for the time being, the future is quite frankly uncertain. It is instructive to compare this situation with that described by Wei Hu for Chinese public pastureland on the Loess Plateau. Here, the permissive open-access regime adopted after the end of the collectivist era has resulted in serious overgrazing, and a shift towards household tenure has severely disrupted rural management of natural resources. With hindsight, Wei suggests, the Maoist livestock management regime had positive features, most obviously preventing the familiar 'tragedy of the commons'. He therefore recommends the introduction of a system of pastureland co-management, involving both households and pasture tenure at village level. It may well be that similar hybrid solutions may represent one way forward in other parts of Asia.

Possible and preferred futures

'Co-management' has, therefore, become part of a global environmental discourse but still remains something of a chimera and is least useful where it becomes a mere shibboleth in the pronouncements of governments and NGOs. But even where motives are pragmatic and serious, and sound arrangements for community-based schemes exist conceptually, there may still be a lot of room for improvement at the level of implementation (Aquino). Mechanistic approaches, with their checklists and flow diagrams, may meet the demands of audit culture, tight management models and be bureaucratically neat and convenient, but they are frequently a major obstacle to effective implementation, administratively burdensome, short on flexibility and misleading in their simplifications and assumptions regarding cause-and-effect. We should, quite rightly, be suspicious of complex conceptual frameworks presented in two-dimensional diagrams of social process. In real life, decisions seldom 'flow', or if they apparently do so then often in directions and ways quite other than those indicated by arrows in diagrams. 'Key' conditions have the unnerving habit of shifting, and what we put in diagram boxes are usually of different dimensions and magnitudes of complexity and, anyway, all too often leak.

The alternative is a more experimental, organic, processual approach, working best practice out from first principles given the particular parameters of the situation, finding practical, simple and local solutions to managing natural resources in the interests of both local populations and the wider political entity. Co-management must be based on legitimate organizations of a suitable scale with a clearly defined membership, autonomous from government and political pressure but able to manage conflict and with a sense of ownership of the process. Of the cases referred to in the present collection, the spontaneous farmer tree-growing schemes described by Pasicolan seem to exemplify this approach. Governments are best placed to be facilitators not implementers, making it easy for things to happen, ensuring that the bureaucratic burden is minimal while providing a clear regulative and supportive infrastructure. The support should, where appropriate and when requested, involve the provision of technical assistance, effective information (both in terms of local knowledge of resources, scientific knowledge and knowledge of government regulations) and even, in carefully prescribed circumstances, incentives. Co-management will not always work, nor is it always appropriate, and where the common good demands overriding the rights of local communities to traditional resources, then compensation must be a consideration. People need to know where they stand.

Despite their different emphases, all contributors to this book are committed to co-managerial strategies simply because the alternatives often seem worse, and because (presumably) co-management is better than no management at all. While failures are legion, and natural resources and biodiversity values continue to erode at alarming rates, even where co-management regimes are in place, fortress conservation and top-down organization have not worked either, and are often socially, morally and politically unacceptable. Because, by definition, co-management methodologies seek to tap the needs and values of present and future stakeholders (whether they be local, regional or national), they may additionally provide a counterweight to diminishing the impact of professional codes of ethics which some commentators see in those interdisciplinary programmes generally favoured in the field of development. To expand the productive extended metaphor based on the hazards of road driving employed by Percy Sajise, not only are there no free rides or short cuts, but the articulated priorities of local peoples must always be both our point of departure and our final destination.

REFERENCES

Atran, Scott (1999) 'Managing the Maya commons: the value of local knowledge'. In Virginia D. Nazarea (ed.), *Ethnoecology: Situated Knowledge/local Lives*. Tucson: University of Arizona Press, pp. 190–214.

Biggs, S.D. (1989) *Resource-poor Farmer Participation in Research: a Synthesis of Experiences from Nine National Agricultural Research Systems*. OFCOR Comparative Study Paper. 3. The Hague: International Service for National Agricultural Research (ISNAR).

Benda-Beckmann von, F. and K. (1998) 'Where structures merge: state and off-state involvement in rural social security on Ambon, eastern Indonesia'. In S. Pannell and F. von Benda-Beckmann (eds), *Old world places, new world problems: exploring resource management issues in eastern Indonesia*. Canberra: Australian National University, Centre for Resource and Environmental Studies, pp. 143–180.

Breman, Jan (1988) *The Shattered Image: Construction and Deconstruction of the Village in Colonial Asia*. Comparative Asian studies 2. Dordrecht: Foris for the Centre for Asian Studies, Amsterdam.

Brosius, P. A. Lowenhaupt Tsing and C. Zerner (1998) 'Representing communities: histories and politics of community-based natural resource management'. *Society and Natural Resources* vol. 11, pp. 157–168.

Campbell. J.R. (2002) Interdisciplinary research and GIS: why local and indigenous knowledge is discounted. In Paul Sillitoe, Alan Bicker and Johan Pottier (eds), *Participating in development: approaches to indigenous knowledge*, London: Routledge, pp. 189–205.

Chambers, R. (1983) *Rural Development, Putting the Last First.* London: Longman.

Cordell, J. (1993) Boundaries and bloodlines: tenure of indigenous homelands and protected areas. In E. Kemf (ed.), *The law of the Mother: protecting indigenous peoples ion protected areas,* San Francisco: Sierra Book Club, pp. 61–68.

Dakila-Bergonia, A. (1996) 'Community-based resource management: a case of the Ikalahan education foundation (KEF)'. In Sajise, P and Briones, N. D. with Dakila-Bergonia, A., Butardo, M. Z., J. Duma, and J. Orno (eds), *Environmentally Sustainable Rural and Agricultural Development Strategies in the Philippines (Lessons from Six Case Studies].* Los Baños, Laguna, Philippines: SEAMEO SEARCA, College.

Ellen, R. (1993) 'Rhetoric, practice and incentive in the face of the changing times: a case study in Nuaulu attitudes to conservation and deforestation'. In Kay Milton (ed.), *Environmentalism: the View from Anthropology.* London: Routledge. pp. 126–143.

—— (1996) 'The cognitive geometry of nature: a contextual approach'. In Philippe Descola and Gisli Palsson (eds), *Nature and Society: Anthropological Perspectives.* London: Routledge, pp. 103–123.

—— (1999) 'Forest knowledge, forest transformation: political contingency, historical ecology and the renegotiation of nature in central Seram'. In Tania Li (ed.), *Transforming the Indonesian Uplands: Marginality, Power and Production.* Amsterdam: Harwood, pp. 131–157.

—— (2000) 'Local knowledge and sustainable development in developing countries'. In Keekok Lee, Alan Holland and Desmond McNeill (eds), *Global Sustainable Development in the Twenty-first Century.* Edinburgh: Edinburgh University Press, pp. 163–186.

Ellen, R. and Holly Harris (2000) 'Introduction'. In R.F. Ellen, P. Parkes and A. Bicker (ed.) *Indigenous Environmental Knowledge and its Transformations: Critical Anthropological Perspectives.* Amsterdam: Harwood, pp. 1–33.

Ellis, D. (2001) 'Between custom and biodiversity: local histories and market-based conservation in the Pio-Tura region of Papua New Guinea'. PhD thesis, University of Kent at Canterbury.

Gluckman, M. (1972) *The Ideas in Barotse Jurisprudence.* Manchester: Manchester University Press.

George, Claude S. (1972) *The History of Management Thought.* Englewood Cliffs, NJ: Prentice-Hall.

Hillery, G. (1955) 'Definitions of community: areas of agreement'. *Rural Sociology,* vol. 20, pp. 116–131.

Iskandar, J. and R. Ellen (2000) 'The contribution of Paraserianthes (Albizia) falcataria to sustainable swidden management practices among the Baduy of West Java'. *Human Ecology,* vol. 28 no. 1, pp. 1–17.

Kemp, J. (1988) *Seductive Mirage: the Search for the Village Community in Southeast Asia.* Comparative Asian Studies 3 Dordrecht: Foris.

Lansing, John Stephen (1991) *Priests and Programmers, Technologies of Power in the Engineered Landscape of Bali.* Princeton, NJ and Oxford: Princeton University Press.

Li, Tania Murray (1999) 'Marginality, power and production'. In Tania Murray Li (ed.), *Transforming the Indonesian Uplands: Marginality, Power and Production*. Studies in Environmental Anthropology 4. Amsterdam: Harwood, pp. 1–44.

McCay, Bonnie J. and James M. Acheson (1987) 'Human ecology of the commons'. In Bonnie M. McCay and James M. Acheson (eds), *The Question of the Commons: the Culture and Ecology of Communal Resources*. Tucson: University of Arizona Press, pp. 1–34.

McNeeley, J. and D. Pitt (eds) (1985) *Culture and Conservation: the Human Dimension in Environmental Planning*. London: Croom Helm.

McNeill, Desmond (2000) 'The concept of sustainable development'. In Keekok Lee, Alan Holland and Desmond McNeill (eds), *Global Sustainable Development in the Twenty-first Century*. Edinburgh: Edinburgh University Press, pp. 10–29.

Maffi, L. (ed.) (2001) *On Biocultural Diversity: Linking Language, Knowledge and the Environment*. Washington DC and London: Smithsonian Institution Press.

Ostrom, E. (1990) *Governing the Commons: the Evolution of Institutions for Collective Action*. Cambridge: Cambridge University Press.

Pearl, M.C. (1994) 'Local initiatives and the rewards for biodiversity conservation: Crater Mountain Wildlife Management Area, Papua New Guinea'. In D. Western and R.M. Wright (eds), *Natural Connections: Perspectives in Community-based Conservation*. Washington DC: Island Press, pp. 193–214.

Pinkerton, Evelyn (1987) 'Intercepting the state: dramatic processes in the assertion of local co-management rights'. In Bonnie M. McCay and James M. Acheson (eds), *The Question of the Commons: the Culture and Ecology of Communal Resources*. Tucson: University of Arizona Press, pp. 344–369.

Stocking, G.W. (1985) 'Essays on museums and material culture', In G.W. Stocking (ed.), *Objects and Others: Essays on Museums and Material Culture*, History of Anthropology vol. 3. University of Wisconsin Press, pp. 3–14.

Sundar, Nandini (2000) 'The construction and destruction of "Indigenous knowledge" in India's Joint Forest Management Programme'. In R.F. Ellen, P. Parkes and A. Bicker (ed.), *Indigenous Environmental Knowledge and its Transformations: Critical Anthropological Perspectives*. Amsterdam: Harwood, pp. 79–100.

Tönnies, F. 1957 [1887] *Community and society*. New York: Harper.

Zerner, C. (1994) 'Through a green lens: the construction of customary environmental law and community in Indonesia's Maluku islands'. *Law and Society Review* vol. 28 no. 5, pp. 1079–1122.

Index

The Nordic Institute of Asian Studies (NIAS) is funded by the governments of Denmark, Finland, Iceland, Norway and Sweden via the Nordic Council of Ministers, and works to encourage and support Asian Studies in the Nordic countries. In so doing, NIAS has been publishing books since 1969, with more than one hundred titles produced in the last ten years.

Nordic Council of Ministers